## Advanc
## *Sun of Sunnyville…*

"Tender yet satiric, empathetic yet frank about human failings… it's got a sharp eye and a big heart."

— *BookLife/Publishers Weekly*

## Praise for *Sunnyville…*

"In this fantastic debut, Donovan fills a Florida retirement community with a full range of eclectic, unforgettable characters, lifting the veil of the American psyche; the story reveals the breezy—and oftentimes chaotic—world of retirement with some fictional people you may or may not recognize without their filters on or hearing aids turned up. This one's a delightful, engaging read that allows you to fully appreciate everything good in your life, body, and soul."

— *Nashville Lifestyles Magazine*

"Donovan has a poetic flare for storytelling and artistic descriptions of life."

— *Swift Reviews*

"Literate, observational and very entertaining…"

— *The Muse's Muse*

This book is a work of fiction. The characters, incidents, and dialogue are drawn from the author's imagination and are not to be construed as real. Any resemblance to actual events or persons, living or dead, is entirely coincidental.

Printed in the United States of America

ISBN: 978-0-9911882-4-6

## ALSO BY RICKO DONOVAN

The Broken Promised Land

Sunnyville

# ACKNOWLEDGMENTS

I would like to express my profoundest gratitude to Gulfport Writers Group and Inkhearts for all the valuable critique and encouragement, to Wildacres Writers Workshop for providing a foundation for learning the elements of crafting a good story, and to anyone who lent an encouraging word or two on the initial drafts.

# Sun of Sunnyville

RICKO DONOVAN

# 1

Every summer the snowbirds would cram belongings into minivans, SUVs or airport shuttles to fly north, cutting the population of Sunnyville nearly in half. Some of those residents who remained couldn't stay cooped up inside and chose to suffer an oppressive heat that covered them like a parka. Others hunkered down in temperature-controlled environments on the advice of doctors. A good portion of the comings and goings through the gates at Sunny Glen Palms were for doctor visits. One of the busiest hurricane seasons on record would plague the Sunshine State that summer of 2004. Sunnyville had up until then lay outside the path of the wind monsters, unscarred and free of any debris left in their wake. That summer they'd arrive like one unwelcome guest after another. One of these guests was named Charley, full of hot air and nothing but trouble.

It was just before nine o'clock on an August morning. The bright sun shone down on a landscape of neatly trimmed grass, palms, bougainvillea, azalea, and hawthorn around freshly paved streets and villa homes. Sunny Glen Palmers commenced to draw their curtains, pull the blinds up and go about their business. For some, business meant switching on the coffeepot and fetching the newspaper to attack the crossword. For others, gathering golf clubs and attaching the bag to the cart. Some prepared for a half-day of volunteering. A few devout Catholics readied themselves for daily Mass at Our Lady of Lourdes nearby. There were the rare birds who woke with an eagerness to throw themselves into a passion previously untapped and now begging much of their time. Learning an instrument. Teaching yoga. Cultivating a garden. Writing the great American novel. Others had given up almost entirely on life and remained hidden under the covers. Whatever the attitude, nearly all Sunny Glen Palmers had resigned themselves to the likelihood that a privately managed over-fifty-five retirement community would prove to be the final destination on the route of their life.

Sunny Glen Palms was sprung from the clearcutting of an immense acreage of swampy forest and this carried both the drawback of stripping away any cover from high winds and the benefit of guaranteeing there were no trees to bring devastation to nearby homes. Those palms that remained in Sunny Glen Palms bowed in the breeze at a careful distance from these dwellings. When Wyndam Properties purchased the land and planned the community, they intentionally avoided planting any trees near to houses and this had a favorable effect on insurance premium rates.

A young lady in an older model Honda turned off Sunset Boulevard and drove slowly towards a facade with tall imposing arches and flanked by tall palm trees—a guardhouse separating the general public from the domain of Sunny Glen Palms. Steering over to the right and the visitors' lane as her mother had instructed her to do. Given a turbulent familial past, she readied herself to pass through the gates of hell. Driving since the crack of dawn—heavy-eyed, heavy-headed. Rifling through her purse to produce an ID while a portly man in blue shorts and a short-sleeve gray collar shirt waddled out of the booth to flag her down. She opened her window and he greeted her in the impersonal manner guards do, while thick heat invaded the air-conditioned car. She produced her license although he hadn't requested it. In the mugshot photo she was smiling, a Caucasian, aged forty-five. The guard checked her name against a manifest while another guard marched to the rear of the car to scrawl her plate number on a clipboard. How fitting, she thought—that her mother, emotionally unavailable as she was all these years, would choose to live in a place with admission checkpoints and other security measures in the final stages of her life.

The guard obliged her and sketched a map to her mother's address on a piece of notepad with the visitors pass, handing them to her and wishing her a good day. She smiled at him, guessing he did this job part-time to fend off boredom and savor a morsel of authority.

A morning mist hovered over the shuffleboard court to her right. Just beyond that, a volleyball court with a sagging net. An emergency paramedic vehicle approached her on its way out the gate.

She shot along Sunset Boulevard into unfamiliar territory, on the main drag that snaked around Sunny Glen Palms and gave access to virtually all of the neighborhoods, missing the twenty-five mile-per-hour speed limit sign *and* a speed bump. The car bounced over the sudden rise in the road. An elderly couple turning onto the main thoroughfare shot her chastening glances and inaudible remarks as she passed them. She slowed and turned her head this way and that to take in a neatly arranged series of villa style houses with freshly-cut grass, sprinkler systems and flowerbeds. Empty sidewalks. She waved to an elderly man fetching a newspaper and he either didn't notice or didn't bother to respond.

She gleaned the map with a mix of urgency and apprehension to reach the destination. A sign for South Club and a community pool caught her attention and she veered left instead of right, drawing the car onto the grass between the road and sidewalk. She clutched the steering wheel and drew a heavy sigh, attempting to gather herself. Deciding at last to forestall the inevitable by killing some time at the pool.

*

Kenny Fitzroy was sleeping in later and later, an early round of golf no longer in the cards. He shoved his way out of musty covers and perched himself at the side of the bed, rubbing at sleepy eyes. A nostril blocked, pressure in his head. Sinuses had plagued him from a young age, leaving him prone to illness, disrupting his sleep, robbing him of the get-up-and-go of childhood. The sun was up, its rays spilling through the blinds. The curtains his Aunt Eustice had troubled herself to fashion for him during a holiday visit three years ago lay crumpled on the floor with accompanying curtain rods tucked away in the storage closet. When Mom had passed, his aunt drove up from her winter home in Punta Gorda, just an hour or so to the south, to help Kenny get settled into his mother's retirement house, the greater portion of a single surviving child's inheritance.

No round of golf this morning because at one of last January's Pub Nights at the South Club he'd got into a heated political debate with his then golf partner Frank Alsatian. His ideological adversary had baited him and he fell for it hook line and sinker. Kenny really wasn't much of a golfer anyway, he mostly missed tooling around on the golf cart in the fresh air.

He stood upright and negotiated his way around the clothes scattered about the faux wood floor. In the hall he staggered like a drunk to the bathroom and switched the light on. His receding hairline left a tuft of hair along the path to baldness. His spindly legs supported a belly and waistline with a slight bulge sprung from middle age. He coughed and spat into the sink. That no-golf thing was starting to eat at him a little. He didn't know many people at Sunny Glen Palms and usually turned up at events a lone onlooker. Maybe Gerry Hagoden would hit the links with him once in a while as a pair, he thought. Or maybe practice alone on the putting green. Or maybe he'd just give up golfing altogether.

Waking up alone to silence had been the manner Kenny Fitzroy had greeted each day from the age of nineteen when he'd left the nest. After receiving his diploma, he moved into a spare room of an old house in Austin for a spell. The spell lasted over twenty years and he never moved out of that room. Mom funding him during the times he came up short meeting his meager financial obligations. Film projects didn't get off the ground. Submissions and proposals ended up in dead letter offices. Freelance journalism for those free weeklies he read to kill time. In between jobs for which he considered himself overqualified. Then, with Mom's encouragement, he entered the nursing program at University of Texas and at last he had a career to speak of. Changing bedpans, lifting overweight patients, fielding complaints and conveying them to doctors. Kenny Fitzroy was already burned out before a career's flame even caught. Already at philosophical odds with health insurance companies and the pharmaceutical industry, subject to enormous amounts of paperwork, he begrudgingly aided and abetted in the overmedicating of patients. His coworkers' motivations, by his standards, lacked even a hint of altruism, they competed for higher paid shifts while he obliged the schedulers.

He put a pot of coffee on and sat down to his laptop and the New York Times. He was only fifty-seven years old and he was already waking up to coffee, the news, and the crosswords. Where he imagined he should be content in his leisure, he was instead very restless in it.

He shoved a videotape of the Grateful Dead into the old VCR and settled himself back on the sofa with the coffee. The phone rang. He was startled at the shrill sound coming from the cordless base in the kitchen. It was a rare thing altogether and it caused him a surge of anxiety. Four rings while he vacillated between answering it or letting it go to the answering machine. At last, he lifted it from its base. An unrecognizable girl-like voice chirped. "Kenny?"

"Yes."

"This is Kathy. Kathy from Connecticut? Remember me?"

"Connecticut," he said.

"Yes. Your family reunion, remember?"

"Oh yeah! Of course."

The voice belonged to an adult. He was tickled. He sure remembered that alright. Memorial Day weekend, up north at Aunt Charlotte's. His late mother's sister had invited him to escape the sweltering summer heat to join them for a week in their cooler environs up north. An all-in-one town bicentennial, Memorial Day, and family reunion. Kathy from Connecticut. The sole one-night-stand in Kenny Fitzroy's modern history.

That was the last he'd seen of her, and he hadn't sent her so much as a postcard. He'd thought from time to time of getting her number from cousin Betsy but he didn't. Perhaps it was the lull of summer's end and the onset of autumn's tendency to nostalgia and melancholy that had triggered her phone call out of the blue. Anway, he was tickled.

"How are you?" she asked.

"I'm okay."

"Not out golfing today?"

She remembered! He had told her he golfed regularly—he told himself that too, that he was just on hiatus. He hadn't been asked back to the links since the fallout with Frank Alsatian, he didn't expect to be and he couldn't think of any other golfers to approach and that's just how things went sometimes at Sunny Glen Palms.

"Not too hot out, is it?" she asked.

"Um, no, not really. It's just—I just, well…"

Truth was, he missed golfing. The leather bag of clubs was now part of a permanent museum collection, gathering dust against the walls of both the living room and dining area, boxes that remained unpacked after three years. The television sat on a swivel rattan table with a shelf underneath for the VCR player, and he'd been through a couple of those because he tended to put them to pretty good use. A stereo system fit snugly among a bookcase with shelves of vinyl LPs, CDs and cassettes in what would be the living room. Kenny was an audiophile of the first order. It began at a young age, this business of collection. Five dollars from his mom and he'd be pedaling his Schwinn downtown Palo Alto, his father likely sleeping off a hangover in the deep dark confines of the master bedroom at their ranch house. The collection blossomed into a full-blown habit when Kenny went off to UCLA to study film. His tastes broadened in scope from what would now be termed classic rock to all that groundbreaking stuff coming out of New York and the CBGBs scene—Patty Smith, Television, Lou Reed and right into the counter-cultural burst of punk rock and the whole indie rock thing. He subscribed to music magazines like NME and saved every back issue. When these items began to fill up a shared dorm room, roommate turf battles arose in the modest 20 x 16 space. Eventually he had to move off campus and into an old house divided into rooms for college students. He hunted and gathered every item of interest for an era of popular music and culture up until the late eighties and then only the product of artists whose careers had been sprung before that time-period. At that point, he'd run out of room in his musical tummy and his palette couldn't be wetted with any new kinds of cuisine. And popular music had changed—what sold now was utter horseshit to Kenny Fitzroy's sensibilities. He was admiring his music collection while they made small talk when her voice went quiet, her tone serious.

"Kenny," she said, "I have some news."

*Oh God*, he thought, *oh no.*

Kenny Fitzroy always imagined the worst and it was no different now, awaiting elaboration. His mind went to the first thing a fellow thinks when a woman he's slept with states that she *has some news.*

She wasted no time delivering the news.

"Are you *sure?"*

He switched off the VCR reflexively, bringing a hand to his head and watching the screen fade to black.

"Yes."

That one word carried enough gravity to make him collapse onto the couch with the phone nestled in his lap. Now her voice came small to him cradled in the palm of his hand. He remembered her saying how the soft and high-pitched tone marked indelibly in her genes always caused major challenges in asserting herself, be it expressing anger or debating a point.

"I started feeling queasy in the morning," she was now speaking just above a whisper, "so I took the supermarket test. Then I went to see my OB GYN. I had to wait a few days. It's been nerve-wracking."

"Uh huh."

Kenny wiped at his brow and brought the wireless phone back to his ear with trembling hand. "Do you… I mean, does, does it look like…"

"I haven't been with anybody else, if that's what you mean."

"No, I – I just meant. Um."

He fell silent. The king of verbosity, the absolute authority on running monologues sure to cause eyes to glaze over, the champion long-distance mouth-runner, the conversational pharmacist who could dispense words in overwhelming doses, he of a presumptive higher intelligence whose oratory could rankle even the most patient of ears—suddenly struck dumb, incapable of conjuring up a single word.

*

From her perch on one of the chaise lounges over at the South Club pool-deck, Peggy Beamish dropped a brochure for recreational vehicles to her lap and drew a hand over her eyes like a visor, squinting at the young woman she spied across the pool opposite from the hot tub and the public restrooms. Clearly not a regular, clad in jeans and a T-shirt, pale white arms clutching a knapsack. She dropped it onto one of the chaise lounges, sat down and turned her face to the sun. An elderly man hoisted himself out of the pool on the ladder just in front of the stranger and Peggy chuckled to herself. It was Boris, and he was clad in his usual pool attire—cotton underwear, stretch boxer briefs. A perfectly good swimsuit to him, and no one bothered themselves to correct him, including the staff—he was after all too gentle a creature to make a fuss over the fact that his male anatomy presented like an onyx sculpture inside the clinging black boxers. Peggy knew the stranger with the knapsack was afforded an unavoidable view of the sculpture.

The security guard was making his rounds. He did so more frequently in the winter months with the heavy onslaught of holiday and school break visitors, making inquiries around the pool deck, making sure they had their guest badges. Five dollars at the business office bought one week.

At the other end of the pool, a little kid made a running start and then cannonballed into the water, causing a giant splash. A good bit of it landed square in the lap of an old lady in a one-piece suit sitting on a chaise lounge nearby. She dropped the book in her hands, a spy thriller from the library, to her lap and glared at the boy's head when it broke the water's surface. "No running!" she hollered, causing the pool crowd, including Peggy Beamish, to turn their attention full on her. "Nathan!" she hissed over at the security guard, waving her paperback at the pool, "Don't you people enforce the rules here? I mean, I don't know where my HOA dues go to anymore! If it's not one thing it's another! Do something why don't you?!"

Nathan, in a clean white-collar polo shirt and the blue shorts to which he hitched his thumbs while bouncing on his heels and talking casually to one of the guests, was taken off guard by the commanding tone, one presumably ascribed to him and him alone in these environs. He was also embarrassed to have been addressed so in front of those who were both his benefactors and in his charge. He was hard-headed and he didn't appreciate it, not one bit of it.

"Janet, please." Her friend alongside her on the next chaise lounge, who had been laying on her stomach, had by now turned over and sat up straight. But her tone was bereft of any authority and the glare she received from Janet in response made it clear to Nathan that he'd have no arbiter, no calm voice of reason to assist him in maintaining his dignity and his job at the same time.

"Look Mrs. Simpson," he said and his nemesis immediately blanched, face going from red to white in an instant at having been, in two remarks from two people, exposed at full identity—the anonymity she preferred in her meanness torn asunder like a curtain, "we can't control everything," he said evenly, "we do what we can." He turned his attention on the boy, whose mother had by now met him at the steps of the pool and began quietly scolding him in a kind of pantomime, as if to appease the crowd without humiliating him in public.

Nathan navigated his way around chaise lounges and tables to check for their guest badges and offer consolation. This wasn't quite what Janet Simpson had in mind for retribution and she aired her concerns across the water to them at the end of the pool. Nathan turned and cut his hand at the air to signal her to tone it down a bit, she was attracting a crowd. "What's this world coming to?" she said to her friend loud enough so as to be sure everyone heard, "No respect for elders, then you got this old man doddering around in his underwear and nobody says anything." She flapped her book in front of her and harrumphed down at it. "Those wet underpants leave nothing to the imagination, and he just parades around here like nobody's business. Between him and that young fella who I just happen to know isn't fifty-five if he's a day, prancing around in that bikini."

She was saying what a lot of them would have liked to say, the trouble for them being that you just didn't come out and *say* such things. But there were plenty of opinions shared privately regarding Boris's underwear, its potential hygienic risk in a public pool, not to mention the morality angle. Betty Molnar was one of these—now she averted her eyes and turned her head away so as not to be drawn in.

*That's enough*, was what Nathan the part-time security guy, a retiree himself, would have liked to have barked in response to Janet Simpson, sat upright with her legs folded like royalty, Queen Janet as it were, master of all she surveyed. *That's enough*, he would say in a world that suited him, because that's what you would say to a four-year-old child and that, in his estimation, was what Janet Simpson, twenty-odd years his senior, was behaving like. He decided his single neutral retort would suffice in asserting his authority without seeming unreasonable after the surprise attack. But Janet had more ammunition and soon rained down a flurry of words away from the more mannered friend and directly over to Nathan.

"I'd like to see you check their badges and verify who exactly it is she's a guest of," she declared.

"*I'll* take care of this."

"Oh you will, will you? Tough guy." She fetched her book from beside the chaise lounge and returned her gaze to it, muttering incoherently. But even so, all eyes danced between her and Nathan. Nathan shepherded the boy and his mom to their seats, glaring at Janet Simpson so long as she had her nose in a book. Soon things returned to normal and Betty Molnar could return her attention safely to the pool deck—and Peggy Beamish to her book, deprived of live entertainment that just didn't normally present in what she regarded as the doldrums. The voice of Shirley Hagoden sounded nearby chattering over a game of cards. Peggy knew Shirley only in passing. Shirley and her husband Gerry had been the subject of gossip for weeks, over a kiss he'd bestowed upon a visitor, the French woman. But like all news it had a shelf life. The next scandal came and quenched it like a giant wave at the seashore. Peggy thought she might like Shirley if she got to know her. For the moment she was disinclined to associate with the woman, loath to join the spurned wives club. She preferred such things, as they pertained to her, to remain ancient history.

She glanced over at Shirley and her girls fanning themselves with their cards and talking animatedly, sipping at soft drinks augmented with gin or rum or vodka or whiskey. The secret that was no secret. The security guys who patrolled the pool in white polos and blue shorts knew the game and they all looked the other way. After all, what harm could possibly come of it? Inside the gates of Sunny Glen Palms, golf carts hadn't up until now posed any serious threat to pedestrians.

"Excuse me," a voice near her head startled her and she turned on her stomach to see a bulky figure silhouetted against the blazing sun. "Hi," it said, "Winifred Grainger." The figure thrust out a hand and Peggy took and briefly shook it. "Sorry to startle you," the voice dropped to nearly a whisper.

"That's alright," said Peggy, pushing herself to a seated position on the chaise lounge.

"It's just, well…"

"Quit playing awkward," said Peggy while the woman shuffled her feet and averted Peggy's incredulous stare. "Go on, spit it out."

By now she could discern more clearly the big-boned woman in a dark blue one-piece swimsuit looming over her. She had the wrinkles of one too long in the sun, a rather affected smile on a dried prune face.

"Well," the woman said in a confidential tone. "It's just that I see you here often. By yourself, and I wanted to invite you to a group I'm starting."

"What sort of group?" Peggy asked at a more conversational level.

"A bereavement group. For women. For widows."

"Oh I see," said Peggy. "Well I guess you can count *me* out. Unless you include those with marriages long dead."

Peggy looked on impassively while the woman gave a polite laugh.

"I'm sorry."

"Uh-uh, don't be," Peggy said. "It's my headache. Good luck with your group honey. Just remember, there are plenty of single men around here. Begun to notice a few myself lately."

"Well," the woman said, returning her voice to a conversational level. "Grief is a process. Some shorter than others, but it can take some time."

"Trust me, a little hanky-panky can speed that process right along," Peggy said with a dismissive wave. Winifred Grainger gave a half-smile and shuffled off.

On the other side of the pool, the young woman had taken the bag with her to the restroom and emerged soon after in a bikini not as skimpy, Peggy noted, as what a lot of young women were starting to sport in public. And she bore none of the confidence these young things displayed while trotting out the attire in public. She walked rather as if she were stepping around broken glass to an unlit bathroom in the middle of night. Peggy reached for her straw beach bag and groped around inside it for the bottle of Hawaiian Tropic. She spread some on her arms and was about to walk it over to the stranger on the other side of the pool, but Shirley Hagoden was already shuffling over in her flowery one piece waving her own bottle around. The girl took the tube from Shirley, rubbing lotion at her stomach and tattooed arms, then allowing Shirley to dab it on her back and shoulder blades. She could hear Shirley's gravelly voice issuing from across the water but she couldn't catch the girl's name in the flurry of words. She was sure Shirley Hagoden had begun to pry the basic information from the young visitor, laughing and coughing while she applied the suntan lotion to pasty white skin. But in fact, to Shirley Hagoden, each casual question posed to the young lady seemed an interrogation, her acquiescence to the generous lathering of lotion upon her back obliged only begrudgingly.

Peggy sighed, letting her eyes pan a pool deck sprinkled from end to end with the furniture of leisure time. Tables under giant handle-wound umbrellas. Metal-framed chaise lounges and chairs woven with white plastic strips. Upon them a slew of the aged, hats of one kind or another upon their balding heads, bodies bronzed by the Florida sun. On the sunny march to the funeral home, thought Peggy, like cows put out to pasture. She gathered her things into a straw-woven beach bag and downed the rest of her vodka cranberry. Catching wind in the golf cart, on her way back to air conditioning and the soothing effect it always had on the heels of extreme heat and sun exposure. Shuffling about in the kitchen, opening and closing cabinets, scrawling the shopping list onto a notepad in a tiny neat cursive. Her husband Mike flipping through the pages of the Tampa Tribune on one of the cushioned chairs in the living room area of a house with an open floor plan. The kitchen was one area Mike didn't spend much time in, neither in Florida nor back in Michigan. It was quite a downsizing when they flew south. They'd been forced to sort through a lifetime of acquisitions in a frenzy amid bare walls and cardboard boxes. Peggy sifting through domestic items thoughtfully acquired at yard sales or store sales or inheritance—neatly-folded linens, place mats and dining sets. Sorting items into piles, battling nostalgia to determine what would remain cargo on the ship of life and what could be thrown overboard. They unpacked the keepers and situated them in the Sunnyville house—family heirloom flatware, candleholders, a pewter sugar bowl, a wedding present wall clock. The remnants of a fifty-year marriage. She called over her shoulder to her husband. "Ready to go grocery shopping?"

"In a minute," he said evenly.

*In a minute*, she thought to herself, leaning against the counter, toying with a coffee cup dating back to the seventies, a cup she had drunk from many a time while poring over drafts of a presentation to newlyweds for an organization called Marriage Encounter. Peggy poured the last cup of the day into a lime green porcelain cup with a simple silhouette map of the Great Lakes. A cup that survived unscathed while she raised three kids, worked mostly part-time to help make ends meet, abided the man she slept beside most every night of her life. *Amazing*, she thought, *how it's sometimes the simplest things we cannot dispense with, we have to hold on to, like a security blanket.* A white cup with the Marriage Encounter logo had the slightest chip in it and she'd chucked it. Her gaze fell upon another holdover, a plaque on the wall above the cabinets. *Bless This Home With Love & Laughter.* It had followed them around for decades and she couldn't recall where and when she'd acquired it. It hung first in the hallway of their first modest two-bedroom one-bath home, then beside the basement door in their larger home in the suburbs, and now there it hung above the cabinets in Peggy's kitchen. It could go unnoticed, a quiet sentry, but every so often Peggy would pause in front of it—an invocation intended to soothe and praise that now only served to mock and ridicule.

*

The young woman didn't linger long at the pool. It was just before ten o'clock when she summoned enough courage to head to her mother's house. At the side of the house was a screen door, beyond that a wooden door with a brass knocker and faux flower basket was ajar. She rapped on the door, tentatively at first and then with increasing urgency, pressing her face up against the glass, peering in with both dread and hopefulness. Waiting for a figure to appear. The kitchen was lit but there was no sound anywhere within.

She cracked the door open and called out, *Mom*? It sounded funny to her ears. It felt oddly inappropriate to enter her mother's house unbidden. The same mother whose house she routinely ran in and out of as a girl.

She stepped inside, calling out again. *Mom*? She hadn't told her mother exactly when she'd arrive—maybe Alice was on the back porch she glanced at the back of the house? She stepped on neatly trimmed grass at the side of the house to have a look. The sliding glass doors were shut on a modest back porch. Perhaps, she thought, her mother was on an errand, shopping in anticipation of company. No, her mother would never leave a house unlocked.

She returned to the side door and let herself into the kitchen. From the adjoining den she could hear the television—faintly at first and then an uptick in volume with a commercial. She entered the den and there, curled up on the floor, lay her mother. From that moment it seemed she'd been catapulted to another world altogether, everything suspended as if time itself had frozen and she'd entered a space where it was truly an abstract. She started towards the body and stopped. Then she tore herself from the house as if it were a sort of darkness itself, as if there may be more horrors to encounter if she lingered any longer.

At the same time Lily Westfall was shuffling across Fairway Drive in the Meadowbrook subdivision to fetch what she knew most likely was a clump of junk mail and advertising flyers from her compartment in the shared box. Out of habit she looked both ways, although the speed limit was ten-miles-per-hour, traffic scarce. She'd just turned to look both ways when the young woman came running down the road haphazardly at her, mouth agape and arms flailing. Lily knew instinctively this young lady did not belong on Fairway Drive. The scene made no sense to her bewildered eyes, failing eyes that made everything blurry. She shot a glance across the road and saw with no small measure of relief that her neighbor Ed, beset with what she deemed to be early onset Alzheimer's and prone to odd and aberrant behavior, was nowhere to be seen.

"I'm sorry!" the woman's shrill cry stabbed the humdrum of a sleepy neighborhood and Lily squinted at a pasty white face stretched in fear.

"It's my mother! Up there." She kept pointing up the street behind her, lowering her voice when she came up so close that Lily could feel the warm breath on her own cheeks. "She's on the floor. Out cold," she panted, "I don't know what to do."

"Did you call nine-one-one?" Lily gaped as the stranger clutched her elbow, brushing at strands of auburn hair and nodding with such force as to shake beads of sweat from her face.

"Yes, yes! Can you come with me, please! I-I don't know what to do."

"Well *ho*ney…" Lily stuffed the mail back into the tiny compartment and speed-walked in her blue polyester pants and floral-print blouse, hand on hip, trailing the woman all the way up to the driveway and through the garage into a single-level house exactly like that of her own. She'd never had occasion to enter anyone else's house on the street. There were days when this saddened her, days when she reflected wistfully on a childhood spent running with playmates through familiar houses, over thresholds that parents crossed regularly to gather the way adults did. Nowadays everyone seemed more and more to just keep to themselves.

"In *here*."

The woman pointed to what Lily knew would be the den. She squinted and froze at the sight of a woman curled up on the floor. The television was on when whatever happened, happened—a commercial for Medicare part B insurance blared while she knelt over an elderly woman. No pulse. Long ago she'd had staff-training in CPR in a pediatrician's office, but had never been taken to task. Her memory had been razor-sharp until recently and she worried that she may have forgotten the procedure. She pulled the woman onto her back. But when she attempted resuscitation, the nose she pinched was stone cold, the open mouth frozen in place. She nonetheless pressed the side of her head to the woman's chest and it was as lifeless and still as the floor itself.

The young woman collapsed to the floor and knelt beside her inert mother, running her fingers over the face as if to summon a mask to animation. Lily knelt at the other side of the body, as the young lady took a purpled hand in hers only to watch it thump lifelessly to the floor when she released it. Lily wrung her hands, frozen in place beside an elderly woman she'd only glimpsed occasionally from her driveway, thumbing the cold wrist once again for a pulse. She pushed herself to her feet and glanced around to every corner of the den—which oddly took on high definition, as if someone had dialed up the brightness and contrast, along with a menacing silence and stillness. "I'm sorry," she said, wringing her hands, frozen in place standing beside an elderly woman she'd only glimpsed occasionally from her driveway, the imploring stare of a complete stranger fixed on her. She shrugged, shook her head once again. "I'm so sorry."

"No," the woman rasped. "Please God no."

The television continued, a commercial for floor wax. Lily fetched the remote and switched it off, out of reverence to the dead. The young lady rose to her feet. Lily directed her to a futon across from the television, sat down beside her and placed a hand on her shoulder. Beyond the open doorway lay the untroubled rooms of the rest of the house and she thought she might go on the prowl for a church bulletin, a do not resuscitate order, an address book with the numbers of family and friends. That role would have been more to her liking than this—providing comfort and emotional support to a complete stranger. How much lighter the load if there were more than just the two of them in that den become a death tomb.

She got her wish with the sound of the emergency paramedic vehicle pulling up in the driveway just outside, doors opening and slamming shut and not long after the sound of scuffling feet across the kitchen tile. Into their reverential stillness spilled a young man in police uniform. Hot on his heels a pair of older gray-haired men wheeled a stretcher into the room. The EMTs began checking for pulse, pulling on the pinky finger, shining a pencil light at eyes with a vacant stare. Lily rose from the couch and sang out, her voice imbued with a sort of despair odd to her own ears, that she'd already tried to resuscitate the woman she referred to as *her* because she didn't get the name. Now the young officer stood before the young woman still sat on the couch, who answered for herself as Barbara Thunderclap and the lifeless body as her mother, Alice Thunderclap, a name Lily recognized from the list on the community mailbox. She shuffled to the guest bathroom for a Kleenex as if sleepwalking, seeing herself steal about a stranger's house even if it had an identical floor plan to her own. Only a few minutes ago she'd gone out to fetch the mail at her usual time in her usual way and now this.

The scene in the den was busy but absent the urgency of life-saving—the officer gently querying Barbara, having established her relation to the deceased, now inquiring as to her arrival time and approximately what time she discovered the corpse. One of the EMTs, Roy, engaged Lily briefly and she surmised that he was a volunteer in a mostly volunteer emergency squad. His partner announced to the policeman that lividity and then rigor mortis had set in and he'd place the time of death at least three hours previous, probably more like six. The policeman went to the kitchen to place a call to the coroner. In the meantime, Roy told Lily that most people engaged Sunnyville Funeral Home not far outside the gate, and Lily told him that was indeed where her sister Dorothy's viewing and funeral service were held a few years ago. Roy suggested Lily check with her friend whether her mother had any stated preference. In the den the EMT had begun packing up his gear and Roy jumped in to help. Coaxed by Lily's perfunctory massage of her shoulder, Barbara pulled her face from her hands and pushed at hair strewn about it. To Lily's question about any idea of her mother's wishes she merely stared blankly—Lily knew full well the young lady was in a state of shock. Her sister Dorothy died at home a few years ago with a do-not-resuscitate order, a mutual understanding between them. Arrangements were made no less from a state of shock, but at least she'd been in familiar territory. The woman beside her, she thought, had no such compass to navigate out of her shock—having just arrived, a fish out of water.

Lily offered to probe likely places for important papers, for more than just a box of Kleenex. To this Barbara vacantly nodded her assent. And so Lily sprung into action and a utilitarian role she was most comfortable in. She shuffled to the master bedroom and the most likely place to unearth important papers, the place she kept her own important papers.

She began at the top drawer—all socks and underwear. Then down through drawers filled with blouses and shorts, at last the bottom drawer where, mixed in among a few one-piece bathing suits, lay important papers bound in thick rubber bands. They were arranged in two neat stacks of manila envelopes and folders. She rifled through them, squinting at each one until her fingers met a two-pocket laminate folder with End-of-Life Instructions emblazoned on the front. She opened the folder to pore over its contents. Without her reading glasses, she had to lift the folder right up to her nose. The first thing to hit her eyes was a Sunnyville Funeral Home logo. She cursed her failing eyes trying to glean the essential information from the papers stuffed in both pockets. At last she gave up, stuffing the Will back under the bathing suits. She brought the other folder to the den and handed it to the policeman, who was finishing his report. He told the EMTs that absent any fresh calls, he would wait with the ladies for the coroner's arrival.

The young woman had been relocated to the living room and sat on the sofa staring vacantly in front of her while the EMTs lingered in the kitchen with the officer. Lily took this as an opportunity to take her leave, back to the more predictable and comfortable environs of her home. She had a dog to let out, she said. She nodded at the men and started for the door to let herself out. Just as she touched the handle, the young woman came up beside her and touched her elbow. "Sorry," she spoke just above a whisper in close proximity, the men's loud voices rendered a privacy to the women's exchange.

"Nothing to be sorry about honey," said Lily. "I'm so very sorry for your loss."

"I-I don't mean to impose. But would you mind staying… riding with me to… to wherever it is they're taking my mom?"

"Well alright. Let me take care of the dog and I'll come right back," said Lily and, just like that, entered a covenant with a complete stranger.

*

Kenny Fitzroy lay on one of the chaise lounges on the pool deck of the North Club. He may well have been spotted were he to have opted for the South Club, and today he didn't want to be spotted and summoned for anything from small talk to the long-winded monologues he was known for. He'd left his modest condo in Andover and walked along the grass by the man-made pond behind the North Club. The bright sun under a clear blue sky and dips in the pool could neither cheer him up nor take his mind off of Kathy from Connecticut. That phone call. The fateful visit.

Almost three months ago. It was after a dinner of picnic leftovers with Aunt Charlotte and his cousins. Cousin Janet was just visiting—had left for California and college, married and raised the family. Cousin Betsy had married her high school sweetheart and never left town—now she was staying with her mother indefinitely on the heels of a messy divorce. It was Sunday and Betsy had the day off tomorrow and they were anxious to leave the house after a solid day of being homebound. They wanted to meet up with friends at their favorite local dive bar. They wanted their reluctant cousin Kenny to bestow some of his trademark verbosity on introverted friend Kathy, one of Betsy's co-workers. He'd have preferred to stay in, perhaps fix himself another slice of apple pie with a tall glass of milk and call it a night. But his cousins had plans percolating. They persisted, at last he gave in and found himself huddled somewhat begrudgingly in Betsy's Ford Escort with the others. He didn't care to be bound to their discretion as to when to leave. When they arrived to that stuffy low-ceilinged drinking establishment adorned with red-white-and-blue streamers and crossed the threshold into the din of conversation and the jukebox, he felt the stirrings of a panic attack. The family reunion and picnic in the open air was one thing—he didn't go much for crowds in close quarters. Upon introduction he found something in her inexpressive manner and lack of gestures that put him at ease, just when he was beginning to settle into his usual restless and uneasy self. Kathy was just slightly on the heavy side and had auburn hair and freckles and blue twinkling eyes. She probably could have used braces he thought, but falling short of runway model looks didn't stop her being assertive with him. It wasn't until later that evening he encountered, in a more prescient moment, an endearing shyness. She asked him to dance and he thought he made an absolute fool of himself out on the dance floor clowning around amidst the revelers displaying their moves. He had the sense dancing was not typically a part of this dive—it was more of a talk shop than a dance hall. But the town's bicentennial put everybody in a celebratory mood. When she asked what he did he said he was retired and it appeared to have sounded impressive to her. He didn't mention his lethargic nature, the time alone on the couch watching movies. He told her he played golf regularly and this also rang nice on her ears. She said she worked a boring corporate job and didn't elaborate. They were getting along, warming in each other's company, when cousin Janet tugged at his elbow and said they were tired and her sister was in the toilet getting sick, too much beer at once. They were leaving early after all. Only now he didn't want to—he was in the middle of a conversation with a charming younger lady, enjoying himself. To his own astonishment he heard himself saying he wished to stay just a little bit longer and Kathy chuckled at this unintended song lyric reference. She said she was more than happy to give him a lift back—she lived nearby to them and it wasn't putting her out any. So he helped cousin Janet walk cousin Betsy to the car, asking repeatedly did they mind him remaining behind. They reassured him that it was fine, enjoy the evening, we'll leave a spare key under the mat at the back door. He never did end up lifting the mat to retrieve the key. He ended up at Kathy's one bedroom condo for a nightcap. They had a few more nightcaps and then she was too drunk to drive and he wasn't going anywhere before daybreak.

The not-too-far walk to her condo took them through a historic neighborhood of run-down homes begging gentrification. Large oak trees cast shadows on craftsman-style homes with unlit windows, some of them broken. Empty driveways, save for a few in which sat old beat-up seventies model cars from the era of the Dodge Dart he'd inherited from his mother. Sidewalks were cracked, many of them upended by tree roots. He could smell danger in the air, glanced anxiously in front, to the sides, and behind him—he was in unfamiliar territory where danger and instability lurked in every corner, very much opposite the safety and orderliness that he'd been lulled into down in Sunnyville. The houses that lined these streets weren't peopled with middle-class retirees poring over investment portfolios with CNN business news blaring from a large-screen TV, but rather with working-class folks embroiled in their working-class lives—overdue credit card bills, child support, alimony, paychecks that forever came up short. He sensed it along that walk, the reminder that beyond the gates of Sunny Glen Palms and beyond the town limits of Sunnyville lay what so many had come to term *the real world*. It was as if there were no sunny side of the street here, lit up with show tunes like that world of nostalgia in which his Florida neighbors were ensconced. There was only the brutal reality of work life here and if these homes were ever to be improved upon it would have to be with the solid equity of those for whom the corporate world had ensnared. This was how Kenny Fitzroy saw it anyway, trundling along the broken sidewalks, Kathy having linked an arm in his so as to steady herself. An obscure crack caused her to lose her footing—he drew her in to him and she folded into his side, glancing up at him, their eyes meeting. The moment of knowing, an unspoken complicity in the potential that it was not long before their lips might join in a first kiss.

In her top floor condo, on the heels of a large bout of his words and her accompanying laugh, she took his hand and in her carpeted bedroom they undressed in an awkward silence and collapsed into a four-poster bed. He couldn't guess at the significance of the tryst for her but for him it was a momentous break in a long stretch of celibacy, his first sexual encounter in more than a decade.

In the morning they had coffee. She heated up cinnamon rolls in the microwave amid paltry exchanges—he not a morning person, she a little self-conscious about her weight. She had herself wrapped in a terrycloth robe, hair wrapped up in a towel, her facial features appearing somewhat hard and chiseled to him in the light of day without makeup. He left after breakfast. He took her phone number and he said he'd call. He never did.

*

It is strange to observe that aspect of ourselves which allows a marked difference in the manner we treat those nearest and dearest to us from the way we do mere acquaintances. The congeniality, the degree of decorum we afford strangers, yet withhold from those we would consider the closest to us. Familiarity casts a wide net to allow inconsideration, indifference, or even rudeness. It is perhaps human nature's grandest irony.

Peggy Beamish brooded upon this paradox, standing in the snack aisle of the Winn Dixie observing husband Mike speaking animatedly to Isabel Amador, his face brightening at every response from her. This on the heels of an economy of words from the moment they backed the car out of their driveway in Sunny Glen Palms. His obligatory grunts, yeses and nos trailing along the aisles of the supermarket, a marked annoyance at some of his wife's purchase decisions. She squeezed absent-mindedly at a package of Cheese Doodles while observing her husband's exchange of pleasantries with a woman she guessed to be almost half her age, glancing from one face to the other. This morning over breakfast he'd made reference to his wife's weight in an unflattering manner. She reflected on this, watching Isabel Amador—whom she imagined her husband might describe as lithe, waiflike, perhaps even skinny—rock her shopping cart back and forth as if there were not food items in the basket but an infant she was lulling to sleep. Peggy approached and Isabel gave a brief nod of recognition.

"Hello there young lady." Isabel's tanned face brightened, creases around her smile. Disarming and hard to read. Peggy half-smiled and ran her fingers through dyed blond hair with natural curls and wondered if it were an innocent remark or a backhanded compliment. She was slightly overweight. She had more than a few years on Isabel and it clearly showed. She winked conspiratorially. "Is my husband bothering you?"

"Why not in the least," said Isabel. "Your husband's got the most delightful sense of humor. You are one lucky lady."

Mike's sunny disposition had by now begun to cloud over—he rolled his eyes and shook his head.

"Oh yeah," Peggy looked her husband up and down. "He's a funny one alright."

Isabel was one of a minority of the unattached in Sunny Glen Palms. She was not yet fully retired—she did some freelance editorial work to help make ends meet. It seemed Sunny Glen Palms was now seeing more over-55s turn up at its gates not yet prepared to completely throw in the towel from the workforce.

"Did he happen to mention his fiftieth wedding anniversary party," Peggy wanted to know.

"Oh my," said Isabel, bringing a hand to thin delicate lips. "How can *that* be? Did you marry at the tender age of ten or something?"

While the ladies bantered back and forth in this playful manner, Mike resignedly took a backseat. He fidgeted with a box of Corn Flakes and then excused himself to the deli counter. The ladies were now running the show, his wife had come in and stolen his thunder.

"Don't forget we need provolone for the lasagna," Peggy called to her husband's back.

When he returned from the counter with an armful of cold cuts, he found the ladies still chatting away, Isabel still rocking her cart back and forth and Peggy toying with the flap in the top basket of hers.

Their extended conversation irked Mike, in some sense his wife had hijacked any inroads he was making with a charming young lady, if nothing other than to flirt. Flirting was in fact one of Mike Beamish's favorite skill sets. Besides, he didn't want to idle away the better part of an afternoon in the supermarket. Better to idle at home in front of the PC, a machine he'd become better acquainted with, thanks to the computer club at the North Club. He got most of his news from his new desktop computer. News of Israeli Prime Minister Sharon announcing a plan to unilaterally withdraw from the Gaza Strip, news of Apple's iPod conquering the world, news of American forces trying to win the hearts and minds of the people of Iraq, news of a likely second term for the Bush administration. It was August of 2004 and he was finally catching up with technological advances. He had to get back to the news.

He looked imploringly to his wife before turning to smile politely at Isabel, who whisked her cart around and said see you at the pool or the club, whichever comes first.

Mike waved and tugged at the cart, anxious to finish the shopping, get on with killing time, in whatever manner presented itself.

On the way out, while his wife visited the restroom, he and the pretty young lady leisurely returned their empty carts to the stall. He scrawled his cell phone number onto a scrap of paper and folded it, then stuffed it into Isabel Amador's delicate sun-bronzed hand.

*

They trailed behind the minivan along Sunset Boulevard in Lily's car. When they reached the gate, Barbara recognized the same guard she met upon entry, who leaned out the window and waved at the funeral director. They followed the minivan to the county road a few blocks to a shopping center and after a few turns they pulled up to a building distinct from those in the strip mall beyond it—sandstone walls with tall pillars at the front, distinctive faux-oil lamp fixtures on either side of tall doors with fancy brass handles. Sunnyville Funeral Home.

Whatever the grave misfortune of Barbara's having arrived at her mother's doorstep on the wrong side of timing—a hair too late rather than just in the nick of time—it was fortuitous nonetheless that her mother was by nature an exacting and methodical creature. The laminate double-pocket portfolio that Barbara clutched to her side and ferried through the doors of the funeral home left nothing to speculation regarding Alice Thunderclap's burial instructions. They'd confirmed the mute-point of a do-not-resuscitate order. They followed the funeral director, a tall middle-aged man who walked with the stiff and mannered comportment befitting the job. Mr. Sorenson claimed to have remembered Lily, but she wasn't convinced. She and Barbara settled themselves in cushioned chairs before an expansive mahogany desk in his dimly lit office. Barbara handed Mr. Sorenson the portfolio across the immense distance of the desk and he thumbed through the documents, glancing up with the sad smile Barbara guessed came with the job. "Your mother's instructions are very explicit. As Mrs…."

"Westfall," Lily drew her reading glasses from her pocketbook.

"As Mrs. Westfall noticed, your mother's wishes are for a cremation and a memorial Mass. Which differs from a funeral service in that it occurs after cremation. So there is no viewing, just a memorial service."

Barbara glanced over at Lily, buried in the folds of an immense chair that had a diminutive effect, rendered her either a feeble old lady or a small child, her feet barely touching the floor. "Well," she said, "Alice must've gone to mass at Our Lady of Lourdes. It's only a few blocks from the gate, on the other side of Sunset Boulevard. It's where all the Catholics go."

"Now," Mr. Sorenson scratched lightly at sideburns gone to gray, "It appears a certain Roger Thunderclap is listed as executor of the estate."

"That's my brother," Barbara said vacantly.

"Right. Is he contactable?"

Barbara shrugged. "I guess so."

Mr. Sorenson cleared his throat. "Now, as to the matter of settling funeral expenses."

Mr. Sorenson told them very tactfully that, absent an insurance policy, funeral expenses would need to be covered up front by the family. In the meantime, it wouldn't hurt to obtain banking information from Alice Thunderclap's effects. He suspected there might be a joint account with Roger as executor, as was typical. Lily took this as an opportunity for a break from familiar old surroundings that only served to resuscitate memories of her sister Dorothy. Leaving Barbara to Mr. Sorenson and the paperwork, Lily took Alice Thunderclap's house key and left the room.

Back at her neighbor's house she stood before a modest desk in the guest room. Shaking her head, she rummaged around Alice Thunderclap's drawers to ferret out a checkbook. She was famished. It was nearly seven o'clock and she hadn't had dinner like usual at five-thirtyish and she felt a blood sugar crash coming on. She usually took the heart pills with dinner. She considered foraging inside the dead woman's refrigerator for a light snack and dismissed the thought.

At the back of the top drawer, snuggled in its fine leather jacket lay the checkbook. She opened it and there was a check register with a running balance. 12,277.07. Checks with both her and her son's name inscribed on them. Merrill Lynch paper statements indicating significant investments. She definitely wasn't living on social security alone. There would not be enough to cover the funeral without family contributing up front. Lily drummed her fingers on the checkbook and stuffed it into her purse. She had the good sense to thumb through Alice's address book for son Roger Thunderclap's phone number and scribbled it on a sticky note. She turned the key to lock the front door and double checked.

The street was quiet on the walk back to her house. Her little terrier Rex greeted her at the door, followed her into the kitchen wagging his tail, his nails clicking and clacking against the linoleum floor. She let him out on a small patch of grass beyond sliding glass doors at the back porch and filled his little metal food bowl, almost succumbing the call of her own hunger, once again deciding against it. She gathered her pocketbook and flung it inside the car while engaging the automatic garage door. Darkness wasn't far away. She couldn't remember the last time she'd had to drive at night. The ophthalmologist had strictly forbidden it. Things were blurry and she had to strain her eyes to keep up with the road.

At the guard gate, she realized that in her haste she'd forgotten to lock the house up behind her. She considered turning back, but this was Sunny Glen Palms after all, a built-in immunity inside the gates against the sort of people who went around breaking and entering. Those who chose to live here had a commendable moral code, disinclined to commit even the most minor of offenses. A gated community that kept the riff-raff outside of its gates. Hadn't she herself felt odd entering a stranger's house to retrieve a checkbook just moment ago, even with the express permission of a family member?

She returned to the funeral home and the quiet confines of an office where it appeared the blinds were always drawn against the sunlight in reverence to the dead. They were wrapping up. Barbara had managed to get through the initial arrangements. She glanced over her shoulder at Lily's entrance, checkbook in hand, much to the relief of the proprietor. He flipped through the checkbook as if it were his own. Then he announced they'd have to phone Roger to obtain payment before they could proceed any further. He slid the desk phone over to Barbara. Lily handed her the sticky note bearing his name and number. With great trepidation she dialed her brother. To her great relief, his wife answered and she conveyed the news. Mr. Sorenson leaned forward, elbows on the desk and hands folded under his chin. Roger, said her sister-in-law Natalie, was away on business and she'd call him immediately. How are you doing anyway, she asked.

"Oh, hanging in there Natalie," said Barbara somewhat impassively. "Thanks for asking. Yes, yes… It's been too long. Thanks so much, dear Natalie." She hung up and pushed the phone back across to Mr. Sorenson and said her brother would be in touch. He nodded with a wan smile. Their business was finished, it was almost six o'clock and they could go home.

At Alice Thunderclap's house, the answering machine blinked fresh messages. Lily pressed play. She met Barbara's gaze and the two readied themselves for some form of guidance—a message from the coroner, the family, the authorities, the funeral home perhaps? The booming voice of God Almighty Himself assuring her that He understood her pain, that she could take comfort in the knowledge that her mother was now in his hands and would recline in a divan to drink martinis amidst ethereal harp music for all eternity? Instead they heard a less authoritative male voice—hesitant, anxious and diminutive enough in fact that Lily had to turn the volume up full and restart the message.

*H-hullo Alice? Um, Kenny here. Listen, I… sorry I, we missed you at the last um, last um Tuesday at Bridge night. Hey, are you planning on g-going to Pub Night tonight? At the South Club? I hear they're having it special catered tonight. N-not the usual hamburger-hotdog routine. I'm gonna go I think. Probably around seven, or like maybe earlier, we'll see. I hope you can make it cause… well, they're something I wanted to ask you about… well, maybe see ya there.*

Barbara cocked her head. "You know this guy? Sounds kinda young for my mother."

Lily shrugged. "Uh-uh."

"What's this Pub Night?"

"Oh, I don't know much about it. A Thursday night something-or-other at the South Club."

"Have you been to it?"

"No," Lily said, shaking her head. "It's kind of a younger crowd."

"Would you come along with me?"

"Now?"

"I'm very hungry," Barbara said, "and I don't feel up to cooking or going outside the gate. And I couldn't stand being alone in this house. Not right now."

Lily shrugged, bandying her head from side to side. It was almost eight o'clock. She knew a barbeque grille was usually part of Pub Night and the added catering was enticing. She'd denied the call of hunger two times now and damned if she'd do so a third time. The heart pill could wait. "Okay," she said. "Let's go."

*

Pub Night was well underway over at the South Club. One of the staff acted as deejay, offering a selection of mostly fifties and sixties era rock n roll. Chairs and tables were moved to the walls to make way for a dance floor. A good many danced to music played at a decibel level just loud enough to cause participants to shout and those poor souls with hearing aids to be constantly leaning in and adjusting them.

Betty Molnar was a few cocktails in and she had Peggy Beamish's ear. Mike Beamish had foregone his wife for another pair of ears, and she badly wished to find a more pleasant and less politically-charged conversation. Really, said Peggy when Betty Molnar came up for air, she'd heard enough about Iraq and the terrorists. Who knew what was really happening over there, Betty Molnar and the likes of her certainly didn't. Peggy was of two minds—on the one hand she was upset to learn over the course of her life that wars were not waged to usher in democracy but to advance the money interests of the corporations that ran America, at the expense of programs that might benefit the ever-expanding lower class. On the other hand, she felt with a kind of world-wise weariness that she had no hand in it nor any control over it—hadn't they retired to seek out the golf greens, swimming pool, the Minnesota Club, the Order of Hibernians? Not so she could get herself all worked up, argue and lose sleep over ideologies that had no bearing on everyday life.

"I mean," Betty Molnar tugged at Peggy's elbow, "what's to be done with these women wanting equal this and equal that, the kids are being abandoned in the process, know what I mean? There's nobody left to raise these kids. Broken families. What we need to do is make it mandatory for one parent to stay at home. I don't care if it's the husband or the wife, just one parent!"

"Oh Jesus," said Peggy, aware at the same time of the futility of any contradictory response, "not everyone has the resources you and I may have had. A shit ton of poor people can't afford to, you know, what with having to work two jobs and all."

This line of thinking sent Betty Molnar off into a tirade and Peggy rolled her eyes and shook her head mutely. The conversation was not and would never be any part hers. She excused herself to the rest room, turning briefly to raise a middle finger at Betty Molnar's back.

Winding her way through the human obstacle course wondering why can't we find better company, a better quality of friends than this? Slowing her pace upon spying her husband engaged once more in a conversation she deemed of inappropriate duration with that infernal Isabel Amador. In her distraction, she slowed her step just enough to cause a collision with a woman striding along with an alacrity way over the social speed limit.

"Oh God, I'm so sorry!" her collider exclaimed, a determined face gone apologetically soft, while Peggy dusted herself off.

Peggy was now wearing her vodka cranberry on a yellow blouse with floral designs. She glanced down to survey the damage, then returned her gaze to a woman she did not recognize. A round face on full display, what with her graying medium-length hair pulled back in a bun, freckled skin bronzed by the sun.

"I'm a clumsy one, forgive me." Her voice emanated from a grim and determined mouth but at the same time Peggy met a pair of twinkling blue eyes flanked by crow's feet. "Wait a sec," the woman said, raising a finger.

Peggy looked on while her collider scurried to the bar, eager to make reparations. She returned clutching a stack of napkins, trailing Peggy to the Ladies room like a makeup artist in the wake of a starlet.

The door closed on the cacophony and they found themselves in the stillness of a windowless vault. Peggy leaned over the sink and ran the cold-water tap, beside her the stranger doused the napkins and dabbed at the dark stain on her blouse. She stuck her hand out and the woman handed over the napkin.

"I'm so sorry," she repeated. "I wasn't watching where I was going."

"That's alright. I guess I wasn't paying much attention either."

"What can I do? Can I go and fetch you another shirt while you wait here?"

Peggy laughed. "I don't think you'd be able to find my house. I mean, we do leave our door open. Anyway, that's way too much trouble to go to. I guess I'll just have to call it an early night," she sighed. "I wasn't gonna stay much longer anyway."

"Well, perhaps you can let me buy you a drink. Next time."

"Tell you what," said Peggy. "I just might take you up on that. But let *me* do the pouring."

The woman blinked impassively, then brought a hand to her mouth and started laughing. "I'm Marge," she said when she'd collected herself. "Marge Cumberbatch."

Peggy tugged at her shirt, shook her head. "Peggy Beamish," she said. "Guess I'll say I'm *sorta* pleased to meet you." She took Marge's hand. *"Cumber*batch. What ethnicity is that?"

Marge shook her head. "I don't know. *I'm* Irish, but my husband is some mix of German and I don't know what else."

They appeared together in the full-length mirror, making eye contact somewhat awkward. *Am I to address the mirror image*, thought Marge, *or turn to address the real lady beside me?* Peggy glanced over at the woman beside her. Marge Cumberbatch had tightly wound hair and the kind of cheeks you wanted to pinch. Big-boned. She stood on short sturdy legs, had a slight belly under substantial breasts and a somewhat thick neck.

Peggy returned her gaze to the mirror and Marge. They began to speak to their respective images. In stark contrast to the noise just outside the door it was quiet in there.

"You seemed to be in an awful hurry," Peggy was re-applying her lipstick, thinking *this is just like the old sock-hops, everything's come full circle and we're just a bunch of old kids.*

"I don't know what gets into me sometimes," said Marge. "I just rush about like a crazy person."

"You nervous about something?"

Marge sighed, glancing down at the sink and then back up to Peggy's reflection. "Husbands," she said.

Peggy rolled her eyes. "I know. Tell me about it."

But the remark was not an invitation to elaborate and Marge knew it. They stood silently, Peggy studying her face and Marge fussing with her hair and then the door opened and broke their spell.

They re-entered the lobby. Peggy turned right towards the security desk and the double doors beyond that which led to the parking lot. Marge tagged along to bid her goodnight, once again apologizing.

"That's alright," Peggy smiled and winked. "Just give me a heads-up next time so I can wear one of my B-grade shirts."

Marge returned to the din of conversation and spied her husband ensconced in a conversation with a skinny guy in a loose-hanging golf shirt, scruffy jeans and scuffed-up tennis shoes. Her husband Ted was waving his hands and tapping the bar emphatically with his usual animation. His audience of one looked a little young to be a resident of Sunny Glen Palms.

Although his boyish looks made him appear to be under the age-limit, Kenny Fitzroy was in fact just a hair on the right side of the rules.

Appearing as he did on the heels of his mother's inheritance was a fact he did his best to conceal, although his former golf partner Frank Alsatian managed to draw him out on the matter, something he'd come to regret because Frank Alsatian could run his mouth with the best of them. Kenny got singled out by Ted Cumberbatch while scanning the room somewhat frantically for Alice Thunderclap. Ted thought the guy looked a little lonely, just had that forlorn look—skulking about in his golf shirt, baggy jeans and worn tennis shoes. At first sight, Ted had taken him for one of the staff. Maintenance or something. Ted Cumberbatch guessed his wife was still smarting from his public outburst over her poor parking skills with the golf cart and so he'd have to canvas the room for other company. It appeared Betty Molnar had exhausted herself and had left the premises. So it was Kenny Fitzroy—the only participant of Pub Night not engaged in any way with anyone else. It sure looked to Ted as if he were trying to find somebody, but some guys always had that look about them. Forever in search of something. So now Cumberbatch had Kenny Fitzroy's ear, an odd thing indeed, because Kenny Fitzroy could talk up a storm and he seldom came up for air. The truth was he didn't get out much and so when he did there was a lot to spill, a lot of words to be rid of. He always had words for himself, puttering around that condo-like residence over in the old section of Sunny Glen Palms, where exterior paint peeled and things often went unrepaired. He sat at the bar, listening to Ted ramble on about his investment portfolio over the classic rock of baby boomers.

Kenny sat and listened. Another Beach Boys song came on and he thought to himself that he didn't mind the Beach Boys if you singled out the talent of Brian Wilson and the genius of the album Pet Sounds. But early stuff like "Little Deuce Coupe", "Barbara Ann"—was mere comfort food for baby boomers, the generation of over-consumers, gluttonously gobbling up plastic products that ended up in landfills. A generation of smokers, golfers, overeaters, auto enthusiasts. He found himself amidst them prematurely—this wasn't his music and these certainly weren't his people, these plain-speakers with investment portfolios and a vast array of prescription medications.

Cumberbatch took a big gulp of beer and Kenny soon found himself the receptacle for a litany of anxieties Ted regularly shared with his wife Marge—the rental house in Michigan they'd wanted to unload but was now being appraised at a value far lower than what they had been carrying it at, the market up there having absolutely *tanked*. He switched gears from that to their troubled son who'd been laid off from GM, now sullen and uncommunicative, doing legal battle with an ex-wife, having got out from under his own house, now settling all too comfortably with a batshit crazy girlfriend, cohabitating rent-free in what should be the rental house. Cumberbatch batted his hand at the air. "I mean," he said, "kid's gotta move on sooner or later, don't ya think?"

Kenny shrugged his shoulders, only half paying attention, drumming his fingers on the edge of the bar while he scanned the room for Alice Thunderclap. They'd met through Bridge Club. On a few occasions when her car was in the shop he'd given her a lift to the North Club community room where Bridge was held. In her he found a confidante. Alice had tried to draw him out on why it was he'd never married. Not in an offensive or judgmental manner, but rather in a sort of mothering way. She had taken him under her wing a few times at Pub Night and he felt an unusual calm come over him in her presence. She would teasingly nudge his elbow and point at one visiting relative or another close to him in age, jiggling her plastic cup of zinfandel, *what about cute little blondie over there? How about that saucy brunette? Whyn't you ask her to dance Kenny?* She was the closest thing he had to a friend after the falling out with his golf buddies last winter.

He badly needed to spill his guts about Kathy and the phone call. The big news. In a rare role reversal, his conversational partner was beginning to get on *his* nerves, and he grew more and more anxious with every word uttered by Ted Cumberbatch.

"Kid went through a difficult time, I realize that y' know? But really, she's gone and she's not coming back and Jesus, just move on and get on with life."

"Yeah," Kenny nodded absently.

"I mean me and Marge, of course we've had our share of problems, disagreements, but some-how we never called it kaput. What about you? You got any kids?"

On any other night that question might have served to induce a mere smidgeon of discomfort. Kenny'd have answered in some flippant manner, something like I was just too good a catch for all of the fish in the sea, I never let them get the shackles on me, or some such remark to get himself off the hook. But this was not any other night—*that phone call* rendered him absolutely tongue-tied. He looked Ted Cumberbatch right in the eye and shook his head. Then he hefted his beer and walked away.

Outside on the patio, at one of the cast-iron tables, sat Lily Westfall, Across from her Barbara Thunderclap toyed distractedly at the food on her plate with a plastic fork. Lily could think of nothing to say, what was there to say after all? She was ravenous by the time they'd loaded their plates at the buffet table out on the patio. She cleaned her plate and glanced around at the busy thoroughfare of people. Out of a sea of strangers she spotted Shirley Hagoden. She only knew Shirley to say hello to from time to time in the winter months at the pool, on the rare occasions she went over for a dip. Shirley spotted her and sauntered over, a cup of beer in one hand, a cigarette in the other, jiggling to the music. "Hey there stranger," she beamed to Lily. "Real nice to see you gracing us with your presence at this shebang."

After Lily introduced Barbara and they all exchanged pleasantries, she asked if Shirley knew anyone from Bridge named Kenny.

Shirley set her beer cup on their table, her eyes lit up and she snapped her fingers. "Kenny Fitzroy!" Then she scrunched her eyebrows. "Kind of a strange bird, that one." She rolled her wrist in elaboration. "A big kid, if you know what I mean."

Lily nodded and then Shirley turned her attention to Barbara. "Hello again," she rasped, "Remember me from the pool?"

Barbara gave a half-hearted smile and Shirley returned her gaze to Lily, tilting her head sideways. "She your daughter or what?"

Lily shook her head. "This poor young lady just lost her mama."

"Oh my God oh how horrible," said Shirley, "I'm so sorry."

"Her mother played Bridge," said Lily. "Maybe you knew her."

"I know everybody," Shirley said, rolling her eyes, "even some jerks I'd care not to. What was her name?"

"Alice Thunderclap," Barbara's voice was hoarse and low and rang strange. "Sorry," she said, extending a hand to Shirley Hagoden. "It's been kind of a long weird day. I'm Barbara."

"Alice!" Shirley clutched Barbara's hand and wiggled it. "Oh dear God in heaven I'm so sorry for your loss kid. I knew your mother alright. She was a peach."

"Thank you," said Barbara.

"A *real peach*," Shirley emphasized. "A real lady. Cut from the old cloth, if ya know what I mean. Real serious-minded. Had all the manners of a good Bridge partner." She went to a nearby table to stub her cigarette out. "Well," she said, "if you need a good recommendation for a funeral home, Sunnyville Funeral Home. Just outside the gate. Everybody raves about it."

"Actually," said Barbara, "that's where we just came from."

Shirley nodded. "We had an old friend of ours Mimi, passed away last… what was it, January?" she asked herself, furrowing her brow. "Had family over, from France. They treated them like royalty."

While they talked on, Lily glanced around the patio, taking in all the people while remembering Dorothy. It had all came flooding back to her there at the funeral home. Her only surviving sibling laid out in the coffin. That old wound re-opened by mere happenstance. She was beginning to soak herself in those feelings but the spell was broken by Shirley Hagoden finger jabbing staccato at her shoulder.

"That's him!" her voice croaked conspiratorially, "That's your guy." She pointed at a silhouette emerging from the shadows, striding across the patio with fists dug in his pockets.

"Kenny!" She called. "*Kenny!*"

Kenny Fitzroy brought a hand up to shield his eyes from the bright floodlights. Shirley clutched Kenny's elbow and wrenched him over to put on display for the ladies.

"C'mere! I want you to meet somebody. *Somebodies.*"

His glance passed quickly over an elderly woman who appeared much like any of those he saw regularly at Sunny Glen Palms. While Shirley Hagoden introduced one and then the other his gaze remained fixed to Barbara. He shook her hand and then Lily Westfall's. He drew up a chair. This was not turning out to be another night alone in the dark living room, sitting on the sofa watching an old movie or perhaps one of those dirty movies he tucked away deep in his closet, although there was never much chance of anyone discovering them. He wanted to be anywhere other than that house tonight. Suddenly he didn't want to go home.

Shirley was summoned inside and back to the dance floor, leaving the three of them to themselves. Lily cleared her throat.

"So you're Alice Thunderclap's friend?"

"Yep." Kenny sank forward, dropping his elbows to his knees.

"You left a message on Alice's machine. Earlier today."

"That's right," he said, shifty-eyed. "That was me."

Lily glanced over at Barbara and thought how a strange twist of fate had caused her to be here eating dinner late. She squinted at the darkness, eyes barely able to discern the lit houses nearby. "I have some bad news to bear. About Alice. Earlier today. She passed away."

Barbara shook her head in a slow and deliberate manner. This was a younger version of Alice, Kenny thought with his eyes fixed on her.

"You must be Alice's daughter," he said. "I can't say just how sorry I am for your loss." Kenny reached a hand for Barbara but the gesture went unnoticed. He returned his hand to his lap and his attention to Lily. "What horrible news," he said.

This day was full of shocking news, thought Kenny Fitzroy. Kathy on the phone from Connecticut in the morning. When he checked the mail at lunchtime, there was a notification from the IRS that an income document hadn't been included in last year's return and he owed an additional fifteen hundred dollars after penalties and interest. And now this—his Bridge partner, no sign no warning, just there one minute and then kaput.

"I played Bridge with your mom. She was a real nice lady."

His words fell flat. *A real nice lady.* What was that supposed to mean? Maybe he didn't know Alice Thunderclap *that* well. Not much better than any of the other residents of Sunny Glen Palms anyway. He thought he knew his golf partners and just like that they had hardly a word for him.

Lily sighed and excused herself, carrying hers and Barbara's plate to the waste bin at the far end of the patio, near the man-made lake with a fountain in the center gushing water. She was tired and she was ready to leave. Shirley Hagoden grabbed her arm and said it was good to see her, was she going to make Pub Night a habit now that she had a taste of it? Lily replied that driving was a challenge at night but she would do her best, then returned to the table to discover that Kenny Fitzroy was able to get Barbara talking. Or listening, at any rate. He was talking rapid fire and Lily had to dance a pantomime to convey to Barbara she was ready to leave.

"Oh, nice meeting you," he said and turned to Barbara. "I can give you a lift. I've dropped your mom home a few times," he said, as if this lent him a certain credibility, like a job reference. "I know the way. I mean, if you wanted to stay later."

He knew he was only trying to forestall the inevitability of heading home to wrestle with restless thoughts. Barbara had her own reason to linger, given the prospect of returning to that empty house. It wasn't a long walk but she wasn't sure she'd be able to navigate the maze of identical houses. Anyway, she brightened to the idea of staying behind a little longer. They bade Lily Westfall goodbye.

"So," Barbara said after Kenny returned with another round of beers, "tell me about my mother."

*

*Up before sunrise.* (Alice Thunderclap wrote in her journal) *This morning. Unusual. Mind occupied despite the sleep medicine. Getting harder to shut off. Fridge still leaking, hand towel soaked on floor. Have to find warranty. Not getting to little things as fast as used to. Not getting around to much of anything lately. Bridge last night. North Club. Only go when Kenny Fizroy asks. Slow. Saying little to partner. Playing wrong cards. Institutional setting cold next to warm memories of Cohasset on back porch. Screened in. Husband as partner. Mind sharp as a tack. Scrawl so I don't forget. Grandfather Ahearn writing memoirs in third floor attic of the old manse by the sea. Mother chastising him when late for dinner, coming down back stairs to kitchen and entering, face molded in contriteness. Have to call Roger back. Only son in world. Worried about Barbara. What to do with Barbara? My little girl. My little girl in pigtails. Running around the house, always running. Me always telling her to slow down.*

*

Lily Westfall closed the door behind her and began to gather herself, placing her hands flat on the kitchen counter, the grandfather clock in the living room ticking against the silence. Rex began scratching at the sliding doors at the back patio and she realized that in her haste she'd forgotten to let her little compadre back in before she left the house. Lucky for him it wasn't often she left the house for long stretches.

It started after her sister's passing. After many years of operating at full capacity to manage herself and others, she was starting to worry about the things that began to escape her attention. Like forgetting to set the timer when she put things in the oven. Or missing doctor appointments she'd neglected to mark down in her datebook. Forgetting their names. Her eyes fluttering awake some mornings thinking she was in Tennessee. Misplacing important documents. Sometimes it felt to her like the Titanic without a captain in the wheelhouse. She didn't like this sense of vacillating between lucidity and fogginess as if God was playing Jekyll and Hyde with her. In more lucid moments, it was as if she reflected on another person entirely, one who occasionally went on the blink. Her GP poo-pooed her concerns, told her it was *just a part of aging, our memory fades, our brain power lets up a little just like our muscle mass, just like our skin softens.* Worry showed up more and more in the voices of her sons. Without the benefit of good eyesight, would she completely lose touch with the world outside of her? She'd heard that blind people inhabited a rich inner world, one that would be otherwise inaccessible. Would she want to inhabit such a world as her brain weakened and her faculties failed? She tried sleeping more, but she found herself saturated of sleep after five or six hours, so any more time in bed felt gratuitous to her and so she'd give up on the idea of sleep and get out of bed.

She let the dog in and he licked at her hand and she scratched him behind the ears. It was good to be home among the lingering scent of potpourri, vintage trinkets and familiar furniture adorned with decades-old photographs of loved ones. A museum dedicated to the life and times of Lily Westfall. Her life story was a more-or-less standard recipe with not much in the way of spontaneity to spice it up. She saw herself as a simple country girl, born in Madison Tennessee, just north of Nashville. The youngest of seven siblings, the only one alive. She was closest in both age and sensibilities to her sister Dorothy. Lily the housewife with a few forays into the work force. Once as a middle school teacher for a year, then after the birth of her son Jack, part-time receptionist and clerk for a pediatrician.

She had two children. Her husband Dan was a service manager at a nearby auto dealer. She met him when she was sixteen years old and he was dating her sister Dorothy. She adored him then and that adoration hadn't waned. After his death at the early age of fifty-six, Dorothy filled a void for a few years and later implored her to sell the house and come down to Florida. She balked each time, wanting to be near her kids. Her younger son Billy lived only a few hours away in Kentucky but seldom visited. After Jack and his wife Ann left for her hometown in Maryland, Lily decided to leave the house and Tennessee and head to Florida to ride out the rest of her golden years with her by-now-widowed sister in Sunnyville. It sounded inviting, she daydreamed about her and Dorothy in flower print one-piece bathing suits, sprawled languorously on chaise lounges by the pool. Sharing meals at franchise diners, subsidized with clipped coupons. Playing cards in the clubhouse in the early evening, trading surreptitious glances like teenagers over the deck fanned in their hands. No sooner had she arrived, Dorothy got sick. Within a few months she was making funeral arrangements.

Retirement and Florida had very much diminished an altruism she'd managed to tap into over the course of her life, mostly by volunteering at church. Feeding the homeless, teaching the illiterate to read, visiting the infirm, the elderly. A busy mind accompanied her each day going outside to retrieve the mail. A conversant mind full of thoughts and ideas, trapped as they were with nowhere to go. Some of those thoughts were recurrent and often as she walked to the other side of a quiet street, she'd think about how much she wished she'd been granted, alongside those two recalcitrant sons of hers, a compliant and sweet daughter. How much softer her life would have been! How she'd be able to spill the stories, the conversations in her head, to a kind and faithful daughter. How the daughter would have shone baby blue eyes upon her, wrapped in a soft pink blanket in a pink-upholstered cradle. How the daughter would have sought her counsel in feminine matters. How the daughter would bend her ear now with the problems of adulthood. The sister she had lost not long ago shortly after she made it at last to Florida from Tennessee had two daughters of her own. But neither of these nieces were ever very close, not in the way a daughter would have been. After Dorothy passed away, Lily made herself scarce. She lived alone and many days these trips across the quiet street to the mailbox were her only public appearances.

Her next-door neighbor was also making himself scarce lately and that was just fine by her. Their infrequent interactions would commence with innocent small talk before degenerating into odd behavior and remarks. Lily was certain that Ed Wackbender was finding himself in the early stages of Alzheimer's, and there didn't seem to be any family members nearby to address the situation. One morning last week she went to collect the recycle bins from the end of the drive-way and he came out of his house to berate her for littering, jabbering on with insensible complaints to her bewildered ears. She left him lurking beside her driveway in a food-stained tee shirt and boxers, addressing himself and some imaginary friend. A few days later he appeared again, his back to her, talking to himself, prancing around barefoot in her neatly-mulched flower beds. She considered the idea of reporting it to the management. There were things about the world that bothered her and caused her to talk to herself, but by God she had the good sense to do it in the privacy of her own home. And that she did, the self-conversations like static in the background serving as a barrier against the loneliness that lurked just beyond. And when the soft-hued static of loneliness gave way to the hard stuff of a loneliness she tried to avoid but could no less feel in her bones, at her core—that was when she let loose and had a good cry, it was always sitting at the foot of her bed, that seemed to be the place in her house to collect herself. Collect herself and get back to the static. She kept to herself just about all the time and so the element of surprise had greatly hidden itself from her amid the tedium of old age, something that fetching the mail was akin to. This afternoon she went to fetch the mail like usual and suddenly a distressed young woman impelled her to summon thoughts and feelings of empathy she hadn't entertained in quite a while. As if she'd mined the depths of her soul only to discover there still lay nurturing and caregiving diamonds to gather up.

She talked to Rex and poured herself a glass of sherry, collapsing her eighty-seven-year-old body into the recliner, straining her eyes to read the paper, her mind going back to this afternoon on the street. What if she'd gone five minutes earlier to fetch the mail? What if she'd gone for it five minutes later? Fetching the mail, one of those chores you took for granted until you were no longer able to do it. Who would fetch her mail then? Her thoughts went to the funeral parlor. Dorothy laid out in that coffin. Going ahead and dying on her like that. She dropped her head to her hands. Rex kneaded his paws on her lap and whimpered. She drew a finger to damp eyes beginning to fail her. Just when she thought that tears had been carried off somewhere far downriver, sadness exhausted, and crying a lost art.

# 2

Marge Cumberbatch was an early riser, her husband Ted more of a night owl who slept in. She was up earlier than usual, on the patio in a terrycloth bathrobe, clutching a prayer book in her lap. The morning had reliably become her alone time—a chance to gather restless thoughts in an effort to meditate, gazing out on the golf greens beyond the screen. Marge time. Before the first wave of club-bearing men appeared over one of the rises, like the unwelcome advance of soldiers to a battle site.

Beyond the perimeter of her peaceful refuge she heard the sounds of her husband rustling about. Familiarities, old habits. Corn Flakes, no less than whole milk would do. The full set of pajamas no matter the time of year. Picking his nose when he thought she wasn't looking, reprimanded just as he started the deep digging. He went to pee and she could hear him rustling about in the ensuite bathroom. He stood in the frame of the sliding doors, yawning, rubbing at sleepy eyes. "You still sore at me?"

Yesterday he had chastised her within earshot of several residents in the parking lot of the South Club at what he deemed to be her poor parking skills with the golf cart. His face reddened and his voice turned mean enough to draw the ire of another husband who couldn't just stand by and watch without chastising Ted in turn. You oughtta be ashamed of yourself, the man shook his head at Ted and Marge concurred, then as now. She dropped the newspaper to her lap, staring blankly in front of her, feeling the old lump in her throat. It was dangerous topical territory and she knew not only to armor up but to have an escape plan. "I'm just wondering," she said, "if maybe you shouldn't go back on the meds."

"Dammit, you know how I feel about that. The side effects, the awful—"

"I know, I know all that. But maybe a lighter dose."

"Well," he made a face. "They'd have to be prescribed by a therapist, like before. And supplemental insurance doesn't cover shrinks."

Marge sensed she was making headway and had an opening, ruffling the newspaper. "You don't have to hunt down a therapist. The GPs can prescribe them now. It's not a big deal."

"Stop nagging me and telling me what to do."

"I'm not nagging you."

"Yes you are. You're always making mountains out of molehills."

She shrugged and brought the paper back under her nose. Lately being around him made her feel at odds with her real self. It was as if she were somehow debased, waylaid from that curious and happy spirit she marched into the world with to that of his commonality, baseness, and pettiness.

Ted drew a heavy sigh and drew a cup of coffee, perching himself on the sofa in front of the television in the living room while she peered over the paper at him. She squeezed her eyes shut, sighing deeply, her quiet time trampled by the loud and abrasive voices of the Fox News talking heads.

She dropped the paper onto the wicker footrest in front of her while the TV came to life. A golfer off in the distance executed a chip shot over a grassy knoll. Ted sat before the TV as news anchors bantered back and forth with on-site reporters at a massive protest in Manhattan against the Iraq War. "Will ya take a look at this Marge," he shook his head. "Stupid jackasses. They oughtta be ashamed. Every damn one of them. Godamn liberal mental disorder."

She had nothing by way of response while he railed on about the goddamned peaceniks and their show while real patriots risked their lives for the cause of freedom. Birds chirped outside the screen window and she wished she could join their flock for even just a few minutes, could ruffle her feathers and take to the air. She fixed her eyes on the birdfeeder hanging from the oak sapling just outside. "Look Ted," she called out. "A mangrove swallow. And an egret down by the fake pond."

Marge had taken an interest in observing and identifying species of birds because she'd heard that cultivating hobbies and interests was critical in retirement. A Florida bird watching guide sat in the tiny wicker bookcase on the patio. Ted's complete indifference on the matter induced in her a crude amusement in announcing sightings between rooms.

The television dispensed some breaking news about a teachers strike in Michigan and Ted went on shaking his head. Marge passed behind him on her way to the sink with her coffee cup, mussing his hair and saying, what are we gonna do with you?

The talking heads took a break and turned it over to a weatherman who stood before a map of the Southeastern US with long red arrows and wind swirls. A severe weather warning in effect due to the gathering momentum of Hurricane Charley on its way to the Gulf Coast.

"C'mere and look at this Marge. Another hurricane."

"Uh-huh," she said, wiping down the countertops. "Welcome to Florida I guess."

"They say this one's a Cat five."

"What does that mean?"

"Category *five*," Ted craned his neck so as to address her more directly. "The highest strength. It's on the way. We may have to prepare."

"What do we do to prepare?"

"I dunno. Pull stuff inside I guess. Stay away from windows. Hide in the basement."

"What basement," Marge frowned.

"Well," Ted shrugged, "I guess I can ask the people at Home Depot."

Marge showered and began to ready herself for the pool. She threw pool noodles into the back of the golf cart and then backed it outside into blistering heat, stomach churning. The neighbor across the street watered his grass in boxers and a white guinea tee shirt, a cigar dangling from the side of his mouth. She waved and he waved back. On the way, in the golf cart, she thought about Peggy Beamish. The spilled drink. The ladies room. The mirror. Husbands.

*

Kenny Fitzroy reluctantly extracted himself from his comfy bed and a toss-and-turn night, the first in a long while. From the time he awoke in the dead of night to pee, replaying in his head the events of last night. He'd taken Barbara to her door as promised. After Lily Westfall had left them, he'd reached for her hand. She offered it and squeezed back. He'd begun to draw her out a little on her mother. A turbulent relationship, hadn't seen one another in nearly five years. In fact, Kenny had actually seen more of Barbara's mother in the last year than she probably had in the whole of her adult life. He found himself last evening, unaccustomed as he was, in the role of listener, but his ears were not entirely for loan. His mind raced with thoughts of Kathy in Connecticut. Yes, her name for now, because he hadn't yet learned her surname. Or maiden name? He vaguely recalled her mentioning a failed relationship that may have been a marriage. For now she was simply Kathy in Connecticut, pillager of his thoughts. A hostile takeover, a coup d'etat of his peaceful existence.

He loaded the coffeemaker and hit the switch. It took him a few minutes to notice, among sparse furnishings, the answering machine light blinking on the floor beside the telephone. He usually turned the ringer off and volume down. The tiny light seemed to blink menacingly at him. He laid a hesitant finger on the play button and the digital readout indicated the call came in the middle of the night. The voice that issued from the speaker had a lifeless and forlorn quality.

*Hi Kenny?* As if she were addressing him right then and there. *It's Kathy.* Pause. *I'm sure you're asleep but let me know when you get this. I've been thinking. And I think it's best…* her voice lilted confidently… *if we met in person to discuss where to go from here. I'd like to get a flight as soon as possible to visit and, I don't know…* sigh… *talk things over and make some decisions. I don't want to pressure you but, well... there's a lot on me right now. Could you call me back and let me know what works for you? Thank you. Bye.*

He fumbled about a familiar morning ritual absent his usual sense of relative calm. He kept promising himself to incorporate yoga or tai chi or something exotic into his morning doldrums. The laptop he'd purchased with part of the inheritance had become sluggish—pages were slow to load on the Internet and programs opened only after a long spell of the spinning hourglass. He had the number of a retired guy who fixed these things, a local guy who came right to your house. He was anxious about getting this done, hoped he hadn't left a trail littered with those questionable sites he visited sometimes deep into the night. He stood watching the gray screen and then the spinning hourglass as it took forever to boot up and he didn't much care—this minor inconvenience paled in comparison to this new disruption to a jittery life that had only just begun to run smoothly. For so many years in San Jose and then Austin he'd go from one temp job to another, playing in bands, navigating the local art scene, all the while barely scraping enough together to make rent. He entered the nursing program for an associate degree at community college. What with night school and summer classes he finished quickly for a brief career straining his back moving patients, changing bedpans, bearing the snarky remarks of doctors.

His mother's illness was brief, her decline swift. He'd barely made it to Florida and her bedside and then he was making funeral arrangements for a mother he'd kept at a distance both emotionally and geographically. She'd married and bore two sons and a daughter. Kenny's older brother was killed in action in Vietnam. The untimely death served to infuse an anti-establishment spark that was not shared by his patriotic mother, who made a shrine of her son Will's bedroom and went about the business of grief absent any resentment to either the Pentagon or the politicians. Years later, his sister Nancy fell victim to pancreatic cancer, leaving him the sole heir of two generations of acquired wealth. He had no idea what he was doing, living off dividend checks and a pension in which he'd been named a beneficiary. It was a dark and arcane world. He kept meaning to see a financial advisor. Now that, like the yoga mat and the lumbering laptop, was pushed to the rear of the crowded worry convention in his head.

Kenny fetched another cup of coffee, taking it to the back porch and the sun. He lived up front, near the gate, in one of the first settlements of Sunny Glen Palms in the late seventies. The back porch was screened in and as Spartan in furnishing as the inside of his modest duplex condo. He settled himself onto a metal folding chair beside a rusting washer and dryer and a stack of corrugated boxes. An emergency paramedic vehicle passed, sirens off. It disappeared from view as it made its way toward the main road, Sunset Boulevard. He drew a mental image of the Grim Reaper at the wheel of the carriage, bearing a sinister grin.

When he'd dropped her off late last night, Barbara said she didn't feel like entering her mother's house alone and he invited himself in for a nightcap. They talked deep into the night in territory somewhat familiar to him. Alice seldom invited him in—there were boundaries with friends of the opposite sex even with an attendant age gap, but he had nonetheless occasioned to share a few meals or morning coffee and croissants with her. Now here he was helping himself generously to the Chardonnay and her daughter's company into the late hours. He found Barbara very appealing, in fact he felt the stirrings of feelings long absent as here and there he stole a glance of her face. He was beginning to warm up to her, flattering himself to think he may have inadvertently drawn her out of her melancholy. She sat comfortably beside him on that cozy sofa with the sunken cushions, in tight jeans with her legs pulled up under her, a light blue cotton blouse. In this proximity he could inhale her perfume, her minty breath, the tiny gap in her front teeth. When they'd both drained their glasses, she said she'd better call it a night. Kenny said would you like me to tuck you in, leaving the door open as to whether it was a come-on or merely a silly joke. She waved the offer away with a polite smile, and he got up to leave. She saw him to the door and they stepped back into the warm night. Then he leaned forward and planted a kiss on her lips. She playfully pushed him away, grabbed his hand and squeezed it. Turned back toward the door, calling over her shoulder to him, drive carefully.

Last night seemed a long time ago to him as he took another swig of coffee out in the bright sun, deciding against returning the call from Kathy from Connecticut for the moment. He'd give himself the day to think over everything and determine the best course of action. But it was becoming abundantly clear to him that there weren't many options to choose from.

*

*All the glory of the Lord revealed to the eyes of youth. To youth go the spoils. The aged see only the flaws. Design problems. Planned obsolescence. Take Grandfather Ahearn. Rheumatoid arthritis– knees, elbows, wrists. Fingers ached after bouts at typewriter. Writer has vivid memories of him flexing fingers. Piles of manuscript like snowdrifts on attic floor. Typing away. Accumulated wealth of three generations spoiled while father drained the bottles and the money melted. Instructed tenderly by mother not to disturb father beyond door for days on end. Romping through yard on breezy coastal days, making up stories with brother Albert. Siblings. Thinking of Barbara again. Speaking to me only through Nancy. Otherwise no news. Bad news. Substance abuse. Own flesh and blood bent on self-destruction. Want to write about a mother's pain. Can't. Writer singing psalms of praise in Church pews with own mother. Air thick with scent of perfume, talcum powder, gazing up to veiled lip-sticked face. Rustle of garments standing and sitting. Reassuring hand squeezing knobby knee. Same hand grasping for dignity while people talked as people will. Nephew has GF Ahern manuscript. I'm told. Has made rounds of publishers. Don't think it will ever see light of day. Not before I'm dead and gone anyway.*

*

Lily Westfall's neighborhood was one of the newer subdivisions. The yards took on a different standard of grooming and things got repaired as soon as they went kaput. It wasn't as if there were any serious class division in Sunny Glen Palms, but like anywhere else your means determined what neighborhood you could afford to live in. Normandy had included Alice Thunderclap, whom Lily had never gotten to know. Also not far away on Sawgrass Circle were the Hightowers, whom she saw fairly regularly on her brief strolls—Betsy pruning her rosebushes, Jim riding his candy-apple red Schwinn. Occasionally she waved to them and they waved back.

She took Rex out back and tethered him to his chain so he could run around while she cleaned the house. A rapping on the front door pierced the hum of the vacuum. She switched it off and returned her house to the soothing sounds of her easy listening station from the faux vintage radio combination console, an eightieth birthday gift from son Jack.

Through the window's lace curtains she spied the young woman from yesterday on the front walk pacing and glancing about in every direction. By the time she cracked the door open, the girl had turned around and was halfway down the path. She turned and Lily met her appealing eyes.

"Sorry to bother you again."

"Oh now honey," she said, her hand on the doorknob. "It's not a bother. Not a bother at all."

The blazing sun behind made a silhouette of the girl. Hot muggy air briefly pushed its way into the air-conditioned house as Lily stepped aside and nodded to invite Barbara across the threshold into what was essentially Alice Thunderclap's house with different furnishings, exercising what she deemed to be polite social graces, despite a growing sense of unease at deeper involvement in a stranger's problems.

"Are you feeling any better?"

Barbara shrugged and Lily patted the back of one of the four chairs of her kitchen set. She seldom had occasion to use more than the one she sat in that faced the window looking out on the neighbor's garden. She poured a cup of coffee and placed it in front of Barbara, whose face fully bore grief—mouth set grim and determined under hazel eyes gone vacant, dark rings underneath and the beginning of crow's feet to the side of them.

"Have you contacted *any* of your family yet?" Lily asked.

"I don't know where everybody is."

"What do you mean you don't know where everybody is?"

"I haven't really been in touch." Barbara ran a finger along the rim of her cup meditatively. "I'm what you'd call the black sheep."

"I see." Lily shifted in her seat and watched Barbara wipe at her eyes with the back of her hand, rose on creaky knees to fetch a clump of tissues from the bathroom. "Other than… what was his name, Roger? What all brothers or sisters have you got?"

"One sister. Two brothers. One dead, one alive. That'd be Roger."

"Don't you have any phone numbers?"

"No," said Barbara, dabbing at her eyes.

"Well," Lily said, taking her seat and folding her hands in front of her, "surely we can dig more out of her address book."

"That's why I came here. To beg a favor."

"Yes?" Lily squirmed in her chair and fidgeted with her coffee mug.

"There are the phone calls. I mean, I have her book."

"Yes."

"I can make some of them. Most of them."

"Mmm hmm."

"But there are some I can't make."

"Can't make."

Barbara pushed her hair from her eyes. "Yes. Like I said, I- I don't get along very well with my brother. And I haven't spoken to him in years."

"I see."

Barbara dropped her head to her hand. "God," she said. "My brother. Every time I reach for the phone to dial his number it's as if I'm dipping my hand into a jar of poison. I can't bear myself to the task."

"Okay. Well, maybe you'll feel differently tomorrow."

"No. It's been years. One more day won't make any difference."

For a good while there was only the sound of the old wall clock ticking. At last Barbara spoke.

"Would you mind. Would it be an imposition to ask… if you might call just a couple of family members. On my behalf. Something like that."

Lily drummed her fingers on her coffee cup. She'd never been asked to call complete strangers to bear the worst news one could bear. "I'll do whatever I can to help," she heard herself say. "If that means making a few of those calls for you, I guess I can."

Lily rose with no small effort and walked to the kitchen. She'd recently replaced the old percolator with an automatic and started knocking decaf into the mix. While she prepared a fresh pot, she chattered away about her sons Jack and Billy, how she couldn't quite understand exactly what stood between them, although that wasn't entirely true. Hadn't the signs been there all along? From a young age, they waged a war over her attentions, Jack compliant to the stern demands of his father, Billy more sensitive and avoidant of Dan. Maybe it would put her guest at ease to be reminded first hand that other families had seemingly inexplicable strife and that was just the way life was. She was still in her robe and pajamas and her bare wrists bore strange bruises that began to appear more and more all over her arms, absent anything to attribute them to. Barbara walked their mugs to the counter for Lily to refill and they settled themselves at the kitchen table.

"When was the last time you saw your mama?"

"Oh God, it must be over five years."

"When's the last time you spoke. On the telephone at least."

Barbara furrowed her brow. "Couple of years ago. At Christmas."

Lily bit her bottom lip, nodding sagely.

"We never got along real well," Barbara sighed.

"Then what brought you here?"

Barbara shrugged.

"Sorry," said Lily. "It's none of my business and I didn't mean to go pryin."

"No, that's alright. Really."

Barbara traced the table linen with a finger as if to gather her thoughts. It dawned on Lily that perhaps her guest was as puzzled by her pain as Lily herself. Rubbing at old wounds, considering them in the light of day.

"Make amends I guess, maybe make my peace," Barbara sighed. "Too late for that now."

The central air system kicked on, punctuating the silence in the room. Lily reached across the table and squeezed Barbara's hand.

"Maybe it's best to have the memorial Mass next weekend," she said. "That'll give your family time to make travel arrangements. It'll give us a few days to contact them."

*Us.* It tumbled out of her mouth before she knew it—a single word that implied a pact. Participating with someone she barely knew in familial duty regarding the funeral arrangements of a woman she never knew at all.

Lily got up to let Rex back inside. She pulled the sliding glass door open and a strong gust of wind swelled through the porch screens, rattling suction cup decorations, tiny stained-glass alligators, seashells, mermaids.

Barbara stood up, her eyes darting about and then settling on Lily. "God," she said. "I hope I'm not being too much of a bother to you."

"Oh my heavens," Lily batted a hand at the air, stood and tucked her chair in. "Not a bother. Let me get myself ready and I'll head on up to ya."

"I can fix us a lunch," Barbara rose from the table, "or get sandwiches and chips from the Club."

The two silently regarded one another. Barbara folded into Lily's frail arms, her voice muffled by Lily's shoulder as Lily patted at her back. "I really appreciate what you've done but I don't want to be a bother."

At the doorway she paused with her hand on the doorknob. "I can't thank you enough. I don't know anybody. Here I mean."

Lily closed the door behind her and took in the empty room. She couldn't help thinking, *that makes two of us.*

*

Marge was busy fussing the little signpost into place on the tiny patch of lawn in front of her house, which sat side-by-side with the neighbors under one roof. Ted shoved their racquet bags into the wire basket at the back of the golf cart and climbed aboard. "C'mon Marge," he said, "we're gonna be late."

"I'm *coming*," she replied with a measure of irritation.

"Damnit," he said. "I don't know why we need that thing anyway."

The *thing* he referred to was a personalized yard sign that swung on a stand and bore their bronze-embossed names. *Ted and Marjorie Cumberbatch.*

"I've told you a hundred times," she grunted, pushing the stand into unyielding turf. "It's for our *guests*. To pick out our house from the rest."

Ted glanced up and down at the identical houses on Tammany Drive and shook his head. "C'mon Marge. It's already pushing nine."

Marge turned and waved the spade at her husband and then flung it into the garage. The Cumberbatches glanced in both directions to see if anyone was around to notice. A man strolled by on the other side of the street in the easygoing manner of those with a lot of free time on their hands. His khaki pants and Hawaiian shirt hung loosely on a lanky frame with a slight paunch. Ted had seen and waved to him yesterday while unpacking boxes in the garage. They guessed he must have witnessed their little spat. He nodded and smiled at them and then Ted closed the garage door with the remote and Marge climbed in beside him.

"That was the *Hagoden* guy," she whispered conspiratorially. "He's the one cheated on his wife."

"Really," said Ted, rolling his eyes with feigned interest. Here they were only a few weeks at Sunny Glen Palms, he thought, and Marge already grinding away in the gossip mill. But it anyway diverted his thoughts from their impending financial meeting. Marge wanted to revisit their retirement portfolio after the tennis and he was not looking forward to it. Up until he lost his job at BlueCross, he was the primary breadwinner and moneyman. It was Ted who balanced the checkbook and masterminded a way to send both kids to college mostly on their dime. After Marge was forced back to work, she began to control the purse strings Ted reluctantly turned over. Now he wished she'd just leave him out of the money meetings altogether. She'd seek his input only to disagree with every suggestion he gave

The Cumberbatches shot down Tammany Drive in a golf cart bedecked with an American flag and a USMC license plate. All traces of heavy rain from last week had disappeared and they could finally get back down to business on tennis courts clear of puddles. They'd barely broken in their new racquets and Ted was anxious to meet these new friends they'd met one day on the North Club courts, right before all that rain. On the heels of their brief meeting, Jim and Betsy Hightower invited them to a game of doubles. Then it rained for four days straight and each day he'd spoken briefly with Jim to confirm another washout. They were anxious to meet the Hightowers and see if there might be some compatibility with which to forge a friendship, because Marge was bound and determined to establish a social calendar pronto, with events to keep them busy in things other than television and crossword puzzles. That sounded okay to Ted.

They spotted the Hagoden fellow lurking about again at the end of their street where they turned right onto Hammersmith and waved just as an emergency paramedic vehicle passed them, sirens off.

Marge glanced up at a beautiful blue sky with puffy clouds. Ted began to enjoy whizzing along in the golf cart in the sunshine and he smiled over at his wife. "Well," he said, patting her arthritic knee. "Did you get to stretch?"

"I sure did," she huffed. "Putting that sign in."

She'd been toiling among the flowerbeds as well while Ted had coffee and read the morning paper on the screened-in back porch.

"I'll lay more mulch out back for you today," he said while fixing his gaze in front of him. When they came upon the complex, he checked his watch and frowned. Eight minutes past eleven. The Hightowers were already volleying back and forth on the court they'd reserved. He gunned the cart and Marge was thrown back against the seat, and just as fast he braked and she pitched forward, clutching the dashboard. She glared at her husband. He shrugged and brought the cart to a crawl, parking near the chain link fence. They hurriedly went about fetching their racquet bags.

The Hightowers, clad head-to-toe in bleach white, broke their volley to acknowledge their opponents. They appeared to Marge like something out of a TV commercial touting some product promising graceful aging, their faces decorated with the smiles of winning lottery ticket holders.

Ted apologized profusely for their tardiness and Marge suggested that perhaps if she had a little help installing the signpost with their names, they might have been a tad bit on the early side. The Hightowers chuckled while Ted frowned.

"Well," he said, "I'm just glad we finally got a break in the weather for some tennis."

"Oh man, what a gorgeous day," Jim Hightower said, tapping his wife playfully on the ass with his racquet, then shielding his eyes to glance up at the sky.

"Well anyway, nice to meet you both again," Marge smiled and soon they were off and running, volleying the ball back and forth over the net. Jim Hightower finessed the ball with spin on his net volleys while behind him his wife executed careful but effective backhands from the baseline. By the time they'd warmed up sufficiently it was clear to Ted and Marge that the court skills of the Hightowers far exceeded that of their own.

Ted tossed the ball in the air and bent his knees to put the ball into play for what he hoped wouldn't be too humiliating a margin of defeat. Perhaps a commanding but inconsistent serve might be on today and earn them a few points via easy aces. He knew his backhand surely was not there to call upon. That stroke his nemesis, had been ever since he started hitting tennis balls as a boy in Saginaw, Michigan.

The Cumberbatches proved to be no match for the Hightowers right from the get-go, the first set hard-fought but lost within thirty minutes. Not even the powder-blue sky above could lift Ted's spirits as he and his wife guzzled filtered water and exchanged glances. Marge had drilled a few great shots from the net to the gap between their opponents on the heels of her husband's lightning serves, which were few and far between. Ted's weak spot, his backhand, had been discovered early on and exploited by Jim Hightower. No amount of re-positioning or deferring to his wife could compensate for that shortcoming.

The second set had a promising start. A little ways in—an extended volley. Jim Hightower drilled a forehand that Marge lunged at and returned to the other side of the net as she fell down hard on the concrete. Ted dropped back from the net to cover the court while his wife regrouped. Hightower drilled one at his backhand side. He had a mere step to get his racquet on the ball and that he did. The ball shot up from his racquet and over the tall fence. A homerun in baseball, a bungle in tennis. He flung his racquet with all his might at the chain-link fence.

"God *fuckin* dammit!" It was out of his mouth before he knew it and he immediately wished he could summon the words back.

"Wanna call it a day?" Hightower hollered good-naturedly from the other side of the net.

"Nah," Ted grunted, glancing over at his wife, who was glaring at him while dusting herself off. The couples at the adjoining court stopped play and looked on with the blank expressions of mild shock.

"Sorry about that," Ted smiled, turning to face every incredulous face. "I just get a little worked up when I'm not playing my best. Sorry, sorry."

"Okay," Hightower danced the ball on his racquet in front of him. "We'll finish this set if you like."

"Honey," Betsy Hightower looked imploringly at her husband and said loud enough for the Cumberbatches to hear. "I've got more than a few loads of laundry to do."

It was obvious she was trying to be polite, inject some composure into a very awkward circumstance. But a deal was a deal and they dispiritedly finished out the second set absent any further scenes from Ted, although on several occasions he wished wholeheartedly to smash his racquet on the concrete with force enough to mangle its graphite frame.

As Ted packed the spared racquet back into its vinyl cover, Hightower painted a smile on his face and said we'll have to get together again soon, but Marge knew that this would no doubt be the last time the Hightowers would grace them with their presence on the court.

The Cumberbatches sat still in their golf cart, staring in front of them as the Hightowers disappeared around the bend in a cloud of dust.

At last Ted glanced over at Marge. "Honey I—"

"Don't even attempt to apologize."

"No, I wasn't going to apologize, I just—"

"Right in front of everybody. What on earth gets *into* you?"

"I don't know."

"*You don't know*," Marge glared. "Well you better figure it out real soon mister cause we're here for the long haul."

They sat silently a good while and then Marge said, her voice faltering, "Well, are we just gonna sit here all day?"

The sky was beginning to cloud up for afternoon thundershowers. Ted hit the pedal and the golf cart rattled Marge around on the seat as it trundled along the dirt path that led to Sunset Boulevard. They rode along wordlessly for a good while, passing those earliest of Sunny Glen Palms developments, modest bungalows with peeling paint and window-unit air conditioners. From there to the recent builds with their pressure-washed driveways and neat mulch-laden landscapes. When they turned onto their street Marge muttered, guess we'll have to lay off the tennis for a while.

*

The middle of the afternoon, the day gone to a muggy and brutal heat, the AC condenser just outside the window humming along interminably. They lay on their sides facing away from each other on her queen bed. His socks balled up on the carpeted floor along with all the other shed clothing between the bed and her dressing table. Earlier, while she undressed and he eagerly anticipated the exploration of his conquest, he was surprised to discover wrinkled skin under the clothes. This was after all the prototypical younger woman, and he ran tentative fingers at skin gone too soft with an explorer's deflated enthusiasm at having unwittingly come full circle to old familiar territory from another vantage point. He attributed the fine folds along her bronzed skin to the Florida sun. In any case, he was getting old and so were younger women.

She turned over and curled up next to him, draping an arm over his chest, toying with his St. Christopher medal. "What are you thinking of?"

Mike was just then beginning to contemplate his troubled daughter Ellen in Minnesota, who had just informed them she wouldn't be attending the fiftieth wedding anniversary party on grounds that it was a farce. Their daughter had hijacked he and his wife's snowbird scheme to flee these oppressive summers for cooler air in Minnesota. A simultaneous divorce and job loss had her occupying their modest lake house in Minnesota and taking with her a diagnosis of clinical depression. The termination of this arrangement had served as a bone of contention between Mike and Peggy. But none of that was of any concern to his bedmate Isabel Amador and didn't bear mentioning. He turned his head to meet her eyes, his smile unconvincing.

Isabel let go of the medal, her hand coursing through his chest hair. "It's nice to lay next to a man like this. It's been a while."

It had been a while for Mike too. Infidelity. The truth was there'd been indiscretions. A career in sales with IBM, all that time away from home. Women on planes, women in meetings, women in bars, women in frequent travel destinations. He was born with good looks and he maintained them through the years with a steady regimen of tennis and golf between sales calls and boardroom meetings. He was six feet tall and had never allowed himself to cross the two-hundred-pound mark. He had sharp, chiseled features over olive skin and fine dark wavy hair laced with gray that he parted at the side. Blazing blue eyes beneath a dark brow lured many a woman to him.

Philandering at great distances was apt to go undiscovered. The one affair uncovered by his wife was closer to home. The cat got out of the bag by means of a mutual friend. In fact, Jane Henderson and husband Hank were the other half of a package deal—on the tennis courts, on the square-dance floor, in a popular Catholic movement back in the seventies called Marriage Encounter. Mike and Jane's mutual admiration grew over time and one evening on the heels of a few glasses of wine while Hank was away on business and Mike at the Henderson household ostensibly to lend his thoughts to Jane's preparation of a presentation, a *talk,* for one of these Marriage Encounter weekend retreats, one thing led to another and they ended up getting a little frisky on the couch. The Henderson kids were in bed. The pages of her presentation lay sprawled on the dining room table while Mike and Jane emptied a bottle of wine. The content didn't need much polishing, nothing Mike could add anyway—he never was fully on board for the mushy stuff, the pop psychology, post–Vatican II lets-all-let-our-hair-down guitar mass linguistic styling. His Catholic world was one of reverence and silence and ritual—an entanglement of mortal and venial sins, the experience of guilt and atonement for these sins. Man was born to sin and then just get on with things as best he could. This approach extended to extramarital affairs and so, amid the guise of undertaking earnest efforts to bolster the institution of marriage, he and Jane continued their trysts as opportunities presented. Always in the light of day. It was on one of these afternoons that Peggy went to call on Jane and, finding the family station wagon parked in the Henderson's driveway, chose to forego normal protocol and just let herself in the house and up the stairs to the bedroom. They hadn't even bothered to fully close the door.

Now years later Mike Beamish was feeling his old self in a bed not his own, cradling the head of another woman in the crook of his shoulder and fixing his gaze on the ceiling fan. Trysts in a retirement community, he thought, were relegated to the afternoons if you were married. After nine o'clock, the streets rolled up. Absences at events you may have claimed to have attended were likely to be reported to your spouse via the grapevine. Chicanery was relegated to the less romantic daylight hours. Peggy was not inclined to go out by herself at night. Last night, after his wife had left Pub Night, a casualty to Marge Cumberbatch's upended vodka cranberry, he'd quickly monopolized Isabel out there on the patio. Isabel was a magnet for men, married or not. He seized on the opportunity and began to charm her—at first with his wit, then with his physical prowess. He asked her to dance and she accepted and he could sense more than a few people turning their attention towards them. Afterwards, she was talking about how she still did freelance editing and it seemed there was some sort of problem with her computer and its operating system. He declared himself a sort of computer guy, that was his old line of work, he said. There were a few easy maintenance tasks that could help, like defragmenting the hard drive. He'd be more than happy to show her. When? Tomorrow. It was now tomorrow and here they were.

Isabel rolled over on her side and said, penny for your thoughts.

Mike feigned sleep and she shoved at his arm playfully. He wasn't in the mood to spill his guts or bear his heart. Regular interrogations with Peggy were enough and he could do without prodding from other quarters.

"Isn't it enough," he purred, "to just lay next to each other and not think about anything?"

"You didn't tell me you were into practicing meditation," she said, tracing a finger along his arm.

"Meditation?"

"Yeah, you know. Where you empty your mind of all thoughts."

"Oh puh–lease."

"Well then, what else would you call it?" She quit massaging, poked his arm. "What's wrong with meditation anyway?"

Mike checked his watch. "Myself, I *pray*. That counts, doesn't it?"

"*Counts?"* she said. "Like there's some old guy with a beard up in the sky keeping score?"

"Score of what," he asked.

Isabel uttered a soft groan, sighed.

"Well," Mike said, slapping the pillow. "I guess I should be heading. She'll be wondering."

He climbed out from under the sheets, fishing about for his clothes, checking his pants for his wallet, an old habit. When he'd laced his tennis shoes, he walked over to the bed. He debated whether to kiss her goodbye. She'd turned on her side, her back to him.

"Look," he said. "Don't take it the wrong way."

She glanced sharply over her shoulder. "Take what the wrong way?"

"I–I just don't want you getting, I don't know. The wrong idea."

She gave him an odd look then, both startled and amused, brought a finger to her chin. "You don't have to worry about that," she furrowed her brow. "I take things for what they are and no more. Always will."

He had nothing to say to this. He patted her back through the sheets and leaned in to kiss her full on the mouth. She stiffened her lips. "See you around," she said.

A pain-masked smile spread over his face and he knew she could read it. He quit the bedroom and paused at the front door and studied the street scene. A few houses over, neighbors stood on their lawns talking back and forth. He hesitated. Then he pushed the door open, stepping outside and glancing around tentatively in all directions. Above him, gloomy clouds began to overtake a bright blue sky, darkening it to clear a path for brilliant and solitary stars.

*

The library in the North Club, on the other side of town so to speak, had a desk at the head of the room, manned irregularly by volunteers, now unattended. A black spiral bound notebook documented the comings and goings of a book collection mined almost exclusively from the donations of the dead. Marge Cumberbatch was signing out a few books on this honor system. She had just come from the North Club pool, where the Hightowers said they occasionally visited to break up the monotony of the South Club pool. The first round of thunderclaps drove her indoors and she watched the sky darken, a heavy rain lashing against the windows.

The modest library had become a sort of refuge for Marge. It included three full rows of bookshelves, a sidewall with glass encased reference books, two tables with chairs where one could read or write, a couple of cushioned arm chairs where she could curl up and read. At night, absent even the lightest traffic of visitors, the library offered a degree of quietude otherwise unknown in Sunny Glen Palms. Marge had already begun to forge a habit of visiting the North Club in that critical after-dinner time, the lull when the house was beholden to the talking heads and their divisive panels on the Fox News channel. When she returned to the house around nine-o'clock she could count on Ted readying himself for bed and she could reclaim the living room in the recliner, the TV screen gone as dark and dead as the night outside. She would read until her eyes got tired. He'd plant a goodnight kiss upon her forehead and it would go unmentioned that his newly found political fervor, his passionate ideological convictions, were serving to drive his wife from her own house.

She was preparing to leave when the door opened and in came Peggy Beamish, a stack of books under her arm. "Well," she winked, "you again. Gotta stop meeting like this."

Marge gave a snort, put her hand out. "I'm Marge, in case you forgot."

"Forgot? Name kinda sticks when they spill their drink all over you," Peggy winked. "Kind of a protective measure."

They both laughed and it seemed a long time to Marge since she had a genuine belly laugh. Peggy dropped her books on the front desk. One of them was a book on tennis. Marge pointed to it. "You play?"

"Oh," Peggy batted her hand, "That's my husband's. He still plays, me not so much. I prefer pickle ball. Smaller courts. Easier on the knees."

"Yes. I see people playing next to the volleyball court. Looks like fun."

"It is. If only I could drag my schmuck of a husband out for it," Peggy sighed.

"Well I'd like to try it."

"Maybe we can play doubles."

"Oh my goodness," Marge said, "we'd love to."

"If it's nice out tomorrow we can play in the morning. Say nine o'clock?"

"Sure. Let me run it by my husband."

"Well," said Peggy. "I'll be there at nine anyway. If the husbands don't want to play, screw them, we'll just go one-on-one."

Peggy opened the black binder and checked the books in while Marge stalled at the door. "See you tomorrow," Marge said as she pushed on the door to let Peggy pass.

"Toodaloo," Peggy called over her shoulder.

Marge picked up the tennis book and considered her husband's tirade on the tennis court that afternoon, in broad daylight, in front of potential new friends the Hightowers, in full view of the dozen or so other players on the adjoining courts. Ted could get so worked up and throughout their forty years of marriage she often recoiled in fear from a raised voice, or hand. He'd actually hit her once, years ago. Sort of. He went so far as the wind-up and the motion but had pulled back enough so as to curtail what would have been a slap to more of a tap on her cheek. She had long since put it out of mind and forgotten exactly what had ignited the argument, but she sure could remember the fury of that not so precious moment. It was the one time in their marriage she just up and left, not even bothering to pack a suitcase—she just started walking down their suburban street with him at her heels pleading her to come back to him and the kids, what about the kids? She spent the night at her parents before returning the next night and Ted had never been more contrite before or since. Back then there was no anger management as a therapeutic methodology, she just stowed herself and the kids away while he smacked at cabinets or once ripped a door clear from its hinges then spent all of a Saturday replacing it.

Back outside, in the large hallway that led to the lobby, Marge listened to the strains of a jazz quartet playing in the café where lunch was served. The music and the promise of something to appease her appetite drew her left. When she reached the café she could see the waitstaff busily cleaning up behind the counter and she hurried over.

"Am I too late for a sandwich," she asked a tired looking middle-aged woman, her greying straggly hair pulled up under a bonnet.

"Almost," the woman replied. "What can I get ya? We only got hamburgers and hotdogs. Everything else is packed up."

"I'll have a burger and a bag of chips. And a bottled water, please."

Marge paid the woman and took the brown tray over to one of the many empty tables, near the music. No sooner had she settled herself than Peggy Beamish came up from behind and pulled up a chair next to her. "Hope you don't mind," she said. "I think I'm gonna wait out the rain."

"Of course not. Please, sit down."

"Just don't go throwing drinks at me." Peggy gave Marge a playful tap on the arm.

The jazz trio, consisting of piano, upright bass and drums played a loose version of *Summertime* while the rain beat against the windows. There were large screen televisions in the lobby, mounted high in the corners of the ceiling, with the sound turned down. They were tuned to CNN, images from Iraq and then the White House. Peggy pointed at the one nearest to them, breaking the spell the music had cast on Marge.

"Awful," said Peggy. "I don't know why the hell they're sending more kids over there."

Marge nodded and returned her attention to the jazz trio.

"I mean," Peggy continued, "what on earth did these poor innocent Iraqis have to do with nine-eleven?"

Marge took a bite of a cold hamburger. "I suppose there's some good reason they're not telling us."

"Oh horseshit," said Peggy, waving her hand dismissively. "Tell you what, the older I get, the less stock I put in any system of authority. I stopped going to church down here. It's so softened up for the pallet. Just ridiculous. No sense of social awareness, just platitudes to make old people feel good. Now my husband Mike still goes to mass. Every Sunday like clockwork. The priest keeps bugging him about *me*."

Marge nodded. "Were you very religious before?"

"Oh God," Peggy made a face and nodded, as if recalling a bad habit overcome. "Post Vatican II," she said matter-of-factly. "The idealistic era of the Church. At least in America. I think the cultural revolution sort of nudged that. But as far as I can tell it just fizzled out. Anyway, I don't have time for any of that hullaballoo. What a racket."

Marge took a napkin, wiping her hands with it while she swallowed the last bit of her lunch, feeling obliged to divulge a little about herself. "I was raised Methodist," she said. "I go to church services sometimes still. There's a really nice church here just off of Pebble Beach Boulevard."

"That's nice." Peggy was half listening, her eyes cast over Marge's shoulder to the image of the president on the TV screen mounted on the wall. "What a liar," she said. "Anyone with half a brain knows we're killing those poor people over oil. It's all about the oil. And the portfolios of all those Lockheed Martin stockholders."

"What did you do," Marge asked, steering the topic. "I mean, before you retired?"

"I was a high school teacher. For a few years anyway."

"What did you teach?"

"History," Peggy said glumly. "We can learn an awful lot from history. If we're paying any attention."

The muted television had gone to a commercial and Marge hoped that would serve to take Peggy's mind off Iraq and her issues with authority.

"So," Peggy said, "what about your husband? Is he very religious?"

"Ted? Well, he was raised Catholic. He still goes to church most Sundays. I don't think it matters much to him," she laughed. "Sometimes he'll tag along with me to the Methodist service."

Peggy was playing with her curls and bobbing her head to the music. The trio had now switched gears to a more up-tempo number. "So," she said without taking her eyes off the band, "how do you like it here so far?"

"Oh, I think it's great."

"You don't feel cooped up? Sometimes?"

"No, not really."

"Well," said Peggy. "Guess you haven't been here long enough. It's really not a long way to the beaches, or Tampa," she said, shaking her head. "But with most of *these* folks you'd think that was another planet."

"Oh, I see what you mean."

"It's like," Peggy rolled her eyes, "going shopping in Brandon is a big day out for most if not all of these palookas."

"Well, there's so much to do here."

"Inside the gate you mean," Peggy drummed her fingers on the table. "Inside the *gate*," she repeated for emphasis.

The lady from the counter fetched a towel and started wiping down tables while the band wound down and began stowing their instruments away in cases. The rain was beginning to let up and the ladies rose and began walking towards the corridor for the parking lot at the rear of the building. Peggy stopped and pointed to the double doors past the café counter. "Have you been inside the auditorium?"

Marge nodded. "We went to that July 4th gala last month. And we've been to a few shows. We saw Jerry Lewis the week we got here."

"We're having our fiftieth wedding anniversary party next weekend."

"In *there*?" Marge's eyes grew wide.

"No, dingbat," Peggy laughed. "One of the smaller meeting rooms. We couldn't hope to fill that place. The kids are coming down and we're having a few friends from here of course."

"How nice."

"You're welcome to join us if you're not busy."

"Why thank you. It sounds like a real fun night."

Peggy batted a hand at the air. "*I* wanted to have it somewhere offsite. A nice restaurant downtown Tampa near the bay, Channelside, something like that. But *oh no*, Mike wasn't having any of that. He had to keep it inside the gate." She fetched her napkin and wiped at her mouth. "Oh, I feel so old already."

"Fifty years. You must have married young."

"High school sweethearts. Eloped at nineteen years old. Crazy," she said, shaking her head. "Just crazy."

They strolled over to the corridor.

"Lot of ups and downs, God only knows." said Peggy in a tone laced with regret.

"Mostly ups, I hope."

Peggy shook her head. "I don't know. I'll tell you what. I'm gonna let him have his party. Then I'm gonna file for a divorce."

Marge laughed and playfully elbowed her new friend.

"You think I'm kidding," said Peggy.

*

The strains of The Legendary Pink Dots issued from a stereo system nestled in the entertainment center along the wall of Kenny Fitzroy's living room, while the window unit air conditioner rattled along, a chilly refuge from the oppressive heat outside. Kenny stood before the mirror in the bathroom after a shower. He cleared the steam from the mirror and shaved more methodically than usual, in his own reflection he contrived the face of his child. In his visage he witnessed the legacy of his countenance—the sallow cheeks, prominent nose, the knitted brow, the altogether grave and serious face of the cursed overthinker. His forbears refined New England stock, rugged Protestants. The palm trees and sand and even the ground of tropical Florida directly at odds with his physical bearing. Development had served to make it more palatable for the old New England stock of the northeast corridor. There were now strip malls, multiplex movie theaters, long stretches of four-lane blacktop—ample opportunity for the kind of detachment and anonymous commerce that was their emotional domain. More factories sprouting up among the marshland. Perhaps things were coming home to roost.

He dropped a fresh CD into the player, today it seemed that no matter the music his mind wandered back to the telephone call he knew must be made before the day was out. It was the only right thing to do. *What*, he thought, *am I going to say?* He badly needed someone to bounce this off of and there were clearly no takers. Gerry Hagoden was good for only a few words now. Alice Thunderclap was stone dead. Her daughter? He ruled it out, it would seem odd and besides he remembered their close encounter on the sofa last night, the somewhat playful manner in which she pushed against his advance. He didn't want to open his mouth about the situation with Kathy, not one iota, until he had a clear idea just what Kathy from Connecticut wanted to do going forward. Meanwhile, he'd do exactly what Kenny Fitzroy did when he was agitated—fidget. He was wearing a path on a faux wood floor he'd been meaning to cover with rugs for two years.

After some pacing back and forth he noticed the blinking light on the answering machine. With no small sense of dread he mashed a finger to the play button, but where he fully expected to hear her voice, there was instead a different female voice—Alice Thunderclap's daughter.

*Hey Kenny, Barbara here.* First name only. Familiar terms. *I just wanted to say thanks for taking me home last night. Um, if you're not doing anything later. Would you like to have dinner or something?* His heart raced. *Oh, by the way, so you don't think I'm stalking you or something… I got your number from mom's address book. I've been digging through it for– for the funeral and everything. Anyway give me a call if you get this.*

It was nearly four o'clock. The day was waning and dinnertime right around the bend. He'd just drive right over there, that was all there was to it. On his way out, on Sunset Boulevard, an emergency paramedic vehicle passed him, on its way out the gate. He drove the speed limit, twenty-five miles per hour. When he got to her mother's house, she was sitting on the front steps. He pulled his mother's old Dodge Dart into the driveway, clambered out and walked towards her with a slow, plodding gait—hands shoved into pockets and shoulders hunched. A bit of buoyancy injected into this posture by way of arriving at a woman's house at her behest with a dinner invite in the bargain.

"Hello," he said and then he was off and running, perched on the front step, his hand on the railing. Standing before her and talking, talking, talking. Busy feet, his gaze falling everywhere but on her. He went on about how the news was too depressing to watch. All those troops going over to Iraq. The people in this place just don't get it, he said, they're desensitized to it. He'd forgotten to ask how she was feeling.

"Well," she said when he came up for air. "What exactly are the dining options around here?"

"Oh, um…" He looked over his shoulder and shielded his eyes as if seeking a sign for a restaurant. "We don't have a whole lot in Sunnyville. I mean, we could go to the South Club, or…"

"I want to go outside the gate. My pass has expired, so we'll have to take your wheels."

"Cool," said Kenny, wracking his brain for a good dining option. "*I* know," he said, snapping his fingers. "The Seagull. Kind of fancy. Over in the Regency development."

"Whatever," she shrugged. "Let me get dressed."

*

Lily Westfall sat in her recliner before the television for the parade of game shows—Wheel of Fortune, The Price Is Right, Family Feud, and so on. The sound effects—sharp bells, whistles, dings, buzzers—served to beat back the silence. She dropped a copy of the weekly Sunny Glen Palmer to her lap and yawned, Rex already asleep at her feet. The excitement of the previous day now vanquished by a familiar tedium. Someone hit the jackpot. The television audience cheered, bells dinged, the contestant and her family hugged and cried and pogo-ed up and down.

She'd had lunch with Barbara and made good on her promise to help her contact some of Alice Thunderclap's friends and relations. They called it a day after just a few calls and agreed to leave the rest for tomorrow. Lily was glad of that because things were catching up to her and making her sleepy. She settled on an evening of puzzle books and a large-print thriller. In the garage lay bags of paperbacks she intended to donate to the North Club Library, the fine print now a strain on her failing eyes. Another frozen dinner from the freezer to the microwave. She fetched the remote from the side pocket and pointed it at the television, switching over to a Bay News 9 weather alert. Hurricane Charley had now passed over Cuba and resumed a more northerly track, regaining Category 5 strength. Attaining winds of one-hundred and sixty-five miles per hour as it passed within thirty miles of Grand Cayman. The meteorologist looked concerned.

The phone rang and her thoughts immediately went to her new friend up the road. The young woman's unannounced visit this morning caught her a little off guard, then the working lunch on the phones, she didn't feel up to any more. The dog stirred. She lowered the volume with the remote and fetched the phone with the other hand as the dog climbed into her lap.

But it wasn't the young woman, it was her son Jack.

"What're you up to," he wanted to know.

"Just sittin here watchin the news," she said, rubbing Rex behind the ears. "Good to hear from you."

"Looks like you got some bad weather coming your way."

"I know it."

"You gonna be alright?"

"Guess I will. Kind of a wait-and-see I reckon. How are you honey?"

"Hangin in there. You?"

"Oh, much the same. I sure do miss having Dorothy around."

"Yeah, I'm sure you do." A pause on the line and she could hear the familiar labored breathing of her oldest son, it was as if he was always in the middle of something when checking in. "Are you doing any activities," he asked. "Joining any clubs?"

"Oh, you know me. I like my peace and quiet."

"Mom, why don't you at least consider moving back up here?"

"Oh I don't know honey."

"Think about spending time with the grandkids, they'd sure love to spend more time with their grandma."

She sighed into the phone.

"I'm not trying to lay a guilt trip Mom."

"I know."

Jack and Ann had been to visit her last Christmas with the two boys who were her only grandchildren and it cheered her up considerably, but the week went too fast.

"I'm worried about Billy," she said as the dog clambered from her lap and onto the sofa. Her other son was between jobs again–it had been happening to him a lot recently, after a long spell with the phone company. From a young age, he was always pre-occupied, easily bored. She knew he wasn't cut out for regular work. Or marriage–last year his second wife had served him divorce papers just months after the wedding.

"Mom, you gotta do something to take your mind off your kids. He's not a kid anymore."

"I know it. But he's my son and I guess I can't help it."

"Well," he sighed. "I wish you'd try and develop some interests. You know, hobbies. Or come back up here and do it. Be nearer to us."

"Well," her voice trailed off. "Anyway, Billy doesn't sound too good to me. Have you spoken to him lately?"

"No, not really." Jack's tone was even.

"I wish Teresa and him could have worked out their troubles. He needs a wife to look after him."

"Mom, that was years ago," Jack sighed. "Anyway I'm sure he had a big hand in their… troubles."

"Oh my," said Lily, "but she could be a real meanie. Never enough money. Never enough things."

"Now mother, he seems barely able to take care of himself let alone anyone else. You have no idea what it's like to live with—"

"He's a sensitive creature. He's got a good heart."

"Well a good heart doesn't get you anywhere in life if you don't apply yourself. He's had every opportunity. You helped him start at Tennessee State and look what he does with a *two*-year degree. Nothing. Throws away what little education you helped pay for."

"Jack, I've heard all this before."

"And it falls on deaf ears." The heaviness in his sigh was audible and she responded in kind almost as a yawn triggers a yawn in the observer.

"Sorry Mom."

"Anyway, you won't believe what happened yesterday. Neighbor up the street just up and died. Heart attack."

"Really?" Jack said evenly.

"Her daughter came to visit, and would you believe she hadn't seen her in over five years? Anyway, here she comes a running while I'm out to fetch the mail and I had to ride over to the funeral home with her and then back to her Mom's house and Lord I didn't get back home til after nine. Poor Rex was left to himself and—"

"Now Mom, don't get involved too much in other people's stuff."

Lily sighed into the phone and took in her familiar domain—her son's words that meant to protect and assuage rang distant and remote and they failed to penetrate the province of loneliness she'd carved out for herself in Sunnyville. It was territory that he'd, after all, only visited a few times in all these years. The willful effort to hold up the decorum of a concerned son did provide some measure of solace, but she knew that he was in fact far afield from her daily battles, and he was also far afield from the situation that presented itself yesterday at the mailbox. Half-hearted remonstrations were launched from too great a distance to carry much weight. She knew her son had no jurisdiction and so held no sway over her lonely province, and that she would not follow his advice.

"Oh," she said, "it's a nasty business and you'd think people wouldn't have things so bad between them. I mean—"

"Well," he interrupted, "I gotta run. Just thought I'd give you a holler. Keep me posted on that weather."

"You gonna come down and look after your momma?" she chided.

"Tell you what, you keep taking on other folks' problems, I just may have to do that."

"Well, let me know if you want to fly down. Or maybe just the kids. I can always help with the plane fare—"

"Okay. I've got a lot on my plate right now. Running the pharmacy means long hours."

"Oh I know it."

"Well, love you Mother."

"Love you too honey."

She hung up the phone and turned the sound back up on the TV. She could imagine the conversations concerning her between Jack and his wife. She was getting older. When the time came that she could no longer live alone and take care of herself, who other than them would be able to step in and help? Financially, practically. Ann worked part-time as an adjunct professor while Jack's community pharmacy thrived. Billy was doing odd jobs and barely scratching by, and she had no doubt that this fed greatly into her eldest son's resentment towards his wayward younger brother.

Lily switched over to The Weather Channel. Hurricane Charley was now being discussed with the utmost gravity between the regular weather guy and a storm expert. It was building in momentum and force. Viewers were advised to stay tuned, follow precautions, await instructions. Landfall for Florida was predicted for Friday August 13th. There had been a flurry of hurricanes this season, but none with the size and intensity of this new foe Charley. Would the residents of Sunny Glen Palms huddle together in a bunker, perhaps there was one to be found under the immense North Club near the gate? Lily shuddered to think what she would do in the case an evacuation was ordered. The nearest relative she could drive to was a nephew in Alabama. She struggled out of the recliner on arthritic knees for another frozen dinner alone. The dog lay sound asleep on the pullout sofa, the house seemed more quiet than usual. Beyond the sliding glass doors at the back of the house, sunlight had been dispelled by menacing clouds. Nightfall would bring once again the loneliness she'd become accustomed to. These were the days that were left to her, and sometimes she would carry the plastic patio chair from the garage and sit out front listening to the sound of the sprinklers turning on, watching neighbors' grandchildren pedal their bikes along the blacktop, or the fireflies glowing golden in the thick summer air. It was getting harder to lift that chair and tonight she was just too tired to bother. She stared a good while at the Rolodex next to the phone on the kitchen counter. Her sister Dorothy's number was still in there. Would that the dead could bring their phones along with them to the Great Beyond.

*

Mike Beamish's eyes were glued to the TV and the meteorologist in front of the Hurricane Charley map with its high-alert visuals. An attractive young lady in a lowcut dress with lowcut neckline, around which hung rich blond hair of smoothly-ironed straightness and the exotic green eyes of a princess in a children's fairytale book. He may as well have had the sound turned down. These channels, he was thinking, exaggerate weather events for viewership and ratings. His thoughts broadened to the news reporting and the fallacy imbued in anything connected to advertising dollars, wasn't everything hyped into something that couldn't possibly exist? The news reports from Iraq, for example, what was it they were presenting while the facts on the ground were different? He wondered if his skepticism wasn't cultivated from a lifetime squashing about in the bullshit one must shovel in a career in Sales. It dawned on him in the rear-view mirror with greater clarity than it ever could have while he was busy driving and flying around with the smile and the pitch. For all the talking he did, there were a lot of things he didn't tell anybody. There were times he'd wondered whether he was not an introvert rather than the extrovert for whom he exerted so much energy. He didn't feel the need for people these days as much as he once did. There was a territory of his mind he'd mapped out and stuck a private property sign around. There were many things he left unsaid. He switched off the TV but carried these thoughts about the dichotomy between TV and reality to the dinner table.

His preoccupation was not lost on his wife. Between tiny bites of steak she fixed her eyes on him across from her—toying distractedly with a fork at his mashed potatoes. Her conversation starters failed to ignite any words between them to crush a deafening silence absent the TV chatter. She drew a napkin to her lips, set it back down in front of her and cleared her throat.

"Is something wrong? I mean like, more so than usual?"

He looked up and shook his head.

"Well," she said. "We're gonna meet the Cumberbatches in the morning for a round of pickleball."

"The *what* batches?"

"The *Cumber*batches. Marge and… and Ted, I believe."

He sighed and made a face. "What time is this?"

"I told Marge nine o'clock."

"Well damn," he threw his napkin at the table. I wish you'd ask me about these things first."

"Sorry to disrupt your busy social calendar," she said, throwing a palm at the air. "It's just another little game of pickleball. I don't give a rat's ass what you do."

"It's not like we play regularly."

Peggy sighed and rolled her eyes.

"I just wish you'd ask me first," he made a face. "I may've had other plans."

"Like what?"

"I don't know. Golf, er…"

"What did you do this afternoon?"

"What's that supposed to mean?"

"Asking what you did today?" She rose and began to clear a few things from the table. "Just a little polite conversation."

"Well," he said, rolling his eyes, "if you must know. I was over at the North Club tooling around. *Loitering.*"

"Oh," she said over her shoulder from the sink. "I was there too. Funny we didn't run into each other."

"Billiards," he shook his head. "I was shooting pool."

"Uh-huh."

"Don't forget we have a meeting with the business office to firm up particulars for the party," he said. "Monday at… nine o'clock."

"Friday," she corrected him, wringing her hands with a dishtowel.

"Well *any*way," he said with mock exasperation and then perked up. "It'll be fun. The big party. You can invite the Cumberbuns."

"Batches," she rolled her eyes, drawing her chair and sitting once again opposite him.

"What?"

"Cumberbatches. The Cumberbatches."

"Cumber…batches," Mike said, shaking his head. "What kind of a name is that?"

"I don't know." Peggy underlined her curt reply by stabbing her fork at the plate, glancing up briefly to watch her husband draw a napkin to his lips and drop it to the table. He rose to fetch his jacket from the hook by the door to the garage in front. Raindrops tapped against the sliding glass doors at the back of the house. Peggy started to inquire where he was going and stopped herself. He closed the door behind him. Beyond the door she could hear the snapping of the canvas cover onto the golf cart, the whirring of the garage door and the beeping golf cart backing out. He usually helped do the washing up after dinner. Peggy folded her hands under her chin and placed her elbows on the un-cleared table.

It was Mike's idea that brought them here. She mulled regularly over the irony of a man who'd enjoyed a career canvasing large portions of the country becoming listless, provincial and unadventurous. Peggy wanted to buy a Florida bungalow, somewhere within walking distance to the beach. Find an affordable market and buy their beach house. An advertisement in AARP magazine introduced Mike to Sunnyville and Sunny Glen Palms. Little by little, Peggy's beach house plans were dismantled and replaced with the scheme to settle in a community far inland from the shoreline—over an hour to any of the Gulf beaches.

The phone rang and brought Marge Cumberbatch's worrisome voice.

"Have you heard about the weather?"

"Tomorrow?"

"No. Later next week. Hurricane warning."

"Oh we get those a lot this time of year."

"Well they say this one's a real doozie."

"Mike always says they like the TV ratings. You'll get used to it."

"Okay, so I shouldn't worry?"

"Oh I didn't say stop worrying. Just not about the weather."

Marge gave a polite laugh on the other end. "Okay Peggy."

"I guess we'll see you tomorrow morning."

She hung up, turned on the Weather Channel and set about collecting the dishes from the table, rinsing them and setting them in the dishwasher. Her hands were beginning to flare up and she decided to hit the Ibuprofen. After a certain age, she pondered, you couldn't help see your body as an old automobile and what was gonna go next. Her hip hurt and she placed a hand on the small of her back and winced. Sooner or later she'd have to bring it in to the shop for repair. Certain aspects of the onset of aging were nuanced, the deterioration gradual. Others had distinct landmarks. Like the first time she couldn't bring herself from the floor to a standing position without the aid of a chair, a table, maybe a bed. That was on a yoga mat in a yoga class she took shortly after they moved to Sunnyville. She'd done it a few times with great effort—never again after that attempt on a rainy morning, glancing around the room surreptitiously at other mat-dwellers while wincing at a shooting pain in both knees. A young woman who was probably visiting her parents had spotted her and sauntered over with an outstretched hand, but by then Peggy was standing up and massaging her aching hip.

A red severe weather-warning strip along the bottom of the screen announced Hurricane Charley steadily making his way across the deep seas and eying an attack on Florida's shores, exact location of landfall uncertain. But he was closing in, one of the mightiest wind monsters in recent years, already beginning to wreak havoc. Charley. He was now a household name.

Peggy brought a glass of wine to the glass table in front of the TV and sat down on the sofa, sighing and tsk-tsking to herself while the attractive young meteorologist bore more bad news. Charley was now a Category 5. Updates would be provided hour-to-hour. No question there'd be damage. Viewers were advised to begin stocking up on supplies like water and toilet paper to avoid long lines and dwindling supplies at stores.

She got up and poured herself another glass of wine, hardly taking her eyes off of the weather map on the large screen. There was nothing to do for now but watch and wait. The worst, they said, was on the way.

*

The Seagull was in the Regency, Sunnyville's higher-end community—housed within a one-story office building that included a full-length porch lined with white rocking chairs between its white porticos. The restaurant bordered the most impressive golf course in Sunnyville. Plush red carpet covered its floors, plush green drapes adorned its windows. A full bar took up most of one wall. Absent snowbirds there was a light crowd and so they didn't have a wait. Barbara and Kenny followed the maître d' to a table for two beside the window. She hesitated for chivalry and then drew her own chair. Kenny sat opposite her wringing his hands.

"You alright?" she asked.

"I don't know," he shrugged. "I guess so."

She fixed her eyes on him, scrunching her eyebrows.

"What?" he shrugged.

"You just seem… I don't know. Nervous."

"I don't know, maybe the hurricane."

"But it seems you're always like this."

"Okay, I'm always like this."

"What've you got to be so nervous about?"

"I'm *not nervous.*"

He raised his palms and then stuck his hands in his pockets, promising himself not to bite or chew on his fingernails. He'd been on edge since he pulled his mother's Dodge Dart into the driveway beside the lawn, where Barbara was waiting, taking in the sun in a low beach chair. And then on the short drive over he chewed her ear off.

"You're not fooling me," said Barbara with a wink.

Kenny nodded with mock affability. In adding a gesture to the charade he knocked the glass of ice water the waiter had just placed in front of him, soaking the white linen tablecloth. They both dabbed their napkins at the spill, Barbara bringing a hand to her mouth to try and stifle her laughter.

The waitress brought fresh napkins along with their hors d'oeuvres and cocktails. Barbara ran down the details of her life in Asheville North Carolina. She worked part-time at an independent bookstore and part-time at events as a facility host—security, or taking tickets or seating the audience. She occasionally performed herself, singing and playing guitar at small venues like coffee houses with a limited seating capacity. She had a hard time keeping supporting musicians interested. She did sculpture and oil painting and sometimes brought her work to the Farmer's Market in Asheville or points beyond.

"Spent three weeks in Jamaica last winter," Barbara's eyes glowed. "It was amazing."

"Wow, that's so cool. You get to hear some good reggae?"

"Of course. Pretty much everywhere you go," she said. "There's this club Margaritaville that I hung out at all the time. In Mo Bay."

"Mo Bay?"

"Montego Bay. Ya learn to just call it Mo Bay after you're there a bit."

"Oh wow, cool. Man, I really dig that ska thing they got going down there. All the great stuff that came out in the early seventies. Have you ever seen *The Harder They Come*?"

Barbara shook her head and her eyes glazed over while he continued reciting a list of artists she hadn't heard of. By the time he got to the Aquabats she tired of shaking her head no and begged him to cease the deluge of names.

"Where do you go to party?" she asked.

"Party?"

"Yeah, you know. Unwind."

"I guess I used to go to the South Club."

"That all?"

"I went downtown a few weekends back," he shrugged. "There was a music festival. Pretty cool. Lots of bands I hadn't heard of."

Dinner came and they busied themselves to their entrees. Kenny drew a napkin to his lips. "So, what's the deal with the funeral plans?"

Barbara held a forkful in front of her and stared blankly at some space over his shoulder as if it had slipped her mind that her mother had died and there was business to attend to. "I have to get on all that tomorrow," she shrugged, stabbing at her plate with a fork.

"A few phone calls I guess," said Kenny.

"Phone calls," she puffed her cheeks. "I have to call a lot of people. I'm really not looking forward to that."

Kenny glanced up sharply from his plate. "Brothers and sisters?"

Barbara shrugged and made a face. "I haven't spoken to my brother Roger in years."

"Where's he?"

"Boston," she frowned. "I have an older sister Nancy who's kind of hard to keep up with. Worked in the defense industry. Met her husband that way. They lived in the DC area up until a few years ago. Now he works for some company in Chile. I think it's a CIA front and the husband's a spook. And my brother Charlie passed to the great beyond."

"I'm sorry."

"My mother tried to get all of us together in one place a few years ago, before Nancy moved and Charlie died. Here in Sunnyville. I was in rehab."

"Wow. Again, sorry."

"Anyway, those calls are tomorrow. Meantime let's go hit some bars."

"Now?"

Barbara nodded and her eyes lit up. "I wanna see Ybor City. They say it's the happening place."

Kenny gulped. It seemed far away. He was nervous about going any distance by car when drinking, and he was already two cocktails in. He fidgeted with his napkin. "I– I um… I guess we could."

"What's wrong? Gotta get up for work in the morning or something?"

Kenny dropped his napkin to the table, leaned back and massaged his tummy. He wasn't used to sitting in restaurants with good-looking women, in fact he wasn't used to going to restaurants. He hoped he'd remembered his table manners. He regarded the woman before him.

"Well," he shrugged. "I guess I'm game."

"My goodness," said Barbara, making a face. "Curb your enthusiasm."

It was with a good measure of reluctance that Kenny passed the gate for Sunny Glen Palms on Pebble Beach Boulevard and continued to the entrance ramp to the interstate. He would have preferred returning to Alice Thunderclap's house for a night in. Low key. Glass of wine and some more conversation across the cozy sofa. Instead it was pushing nine and the Dodge Dart seemed to exhibit its own objection to the evening's plans as he pushed the pedal to the floor to try and match speed on entering the madness of the Florida interstate. He preferred not to drive at night. An angry pack of automobiles moving at a rate of speed far beyond his liking put him on edge. He chattered. Barbara drummed her fingers on her jeans and glanced over occasionally.

They reached Ybor City after a few wrong turns, and he found after-hours street parking. Parallel parking the Dodge Dart was accomplished only after several maneuvers, Kenny turning the wheel this way and that, huffing and puffing while Barbara glanced from her window at the curb. The routine seemed to prove the same challenge one might face attempting to dock a gigantic yacht into a slip. Barbara was about to get out of the car after a good bit of finagling, when at last he cut the ignition and clambered out to check whether he was too near or too far from the curb.

"I think you're good," she said, not even bothering to look.

"Let me just pull it in a little closer."

She shook her head and started down the sidewalk toward 7th Avenue, Ybor City's main thoroughfare. Throngs of people strolled along sidewalks adorned with those old-fashioned streetlights one sees in historic districts. The sound of music mixed with the voices of the street revelers. He caught up with her in front of a head shop. In the large storefront window were shelves of various smoking implements. Glass, porcelain, marble, metal. He stood beside her to join the window-shopping.

"Do you get high?" she asked.

"Not as much as I used to. It sometimes makes me paranoid."

"You seem to have a hard time relaxing."

He shrugged.

"Sorry. Is everything okay?"

"Um, yeah. Pretty much."

He'd neglected to call Kathy in Connecticut and now it would have to wait until tomorrow. To dispel the anxious thoughts, he drank in the sight of the Friday night throng along the street and to his companion he gave it his blessing—this is so cool, said Kenny Fitzroy. In mock gallantry, he locked her arm in his and whisked her along the sidewalk. They passed historic clapboard buildings in one of Tampa's oldest neighborhoods. It was cigar town—founded in the 1880s by Vicente Martinez-Ybor and some other cigar magnates and populated by thousands of immigrants, mainly from Cuba, Spain, and Italy. For the next fifty years, workers in Ybor City's cigar factories rolled hundreds of millions of cigars. It slowed to a roll in the thirties with The Great Depression. Currently it served as a place where young people gathered to drink themselves silly in bars and nightclubs alongside music of a decibel level far above conversational. And in one of these Kenny Fitzroy found himself now, his high spirits quickly diminished after standing in line for what seemed an eternity while the beefy security guy did his best to regulate the population inside to the fire code limit.

Barbara kept shouting and Kenny leaned in, straining his ears. Techno music issued from the mighty PA system. With a flurry of hand gestures, she extended an invitation to dance. He balked but she took him by the hand anyway, guiding him to the middle of the fracas on the dance floor. Kenny's dancing had all the animation of a corpse. It bore the identifying stamp of the middle-aged guy—shuffling his feet, hips frozen in a very un-Latino white guy way. Barbara gave up on the prospect of bringing him to life and they sauntered back to the bar at the far wall.

For all the time he did in tiny clubs playing with or listening to indie punk bands, tonight he felt out of his element. This music only served to punish his ears and ramp up his anxiety. His mind went to the dead-quiet streets of Sunny Glen Palms and another night at home, one of the library items he checked out for company. He frequented the North Club library, essentially a repository for the clearing out of the dead, an inheritance of mostly pulp fiction and dime-store novels with a smattering of thoughtful and provocative literature. From shelves laden with paperback romance novels, campy westerns and cheap thrillers he'd plucked the odd treasure—last week he'd discovered a nicely-bound hardcover edition of Cheever's *Bullet Park*, waiting there for him beside his recliner. Glancing around the dark environs of the club, Barbara swaying to the music, he was beset by the discomforting thought that perhaps his clubbing days were over and he was either heading towards or had already passed the border of old fart territory—a real stick in the mud, a crossword-puzzling deadbeat.

"I'm bored!" he shouted over the din. "I get bored in places like this!"

"Okay," she said, pulling his head toward her and pressing her mouth to his ear. "We can go somewhere else."

The lobby had filled considerably since they entered. She squeezed his hand and again drew his cheek to hers. "I've got some really good weed and it won't make you paranoid, I promise."

Out on the street the noise of traffic and walking conversations was music to his ears. They walked side-by-side back over to the car. He badly wished to hold her hand but he wasn't going to try any of that stuff and risk an awkward drive home on that infernal speedway called Interstate 75.

They cracked the windows. Barbara drew a lighter and a tiny marble pipe from her purse. There was no wind outside and the pungent odor immediately filled the car. *Not a good idea*, he thought, *drinking and smoking and driving*. Kenny preferred to smoke pot in the comfort of his own home. Nevertheless, sharing a high carried a new level of intimacy—he accepted the pipe and drew on it calculatedly, just enough to get a taste. He passed it back to Barbara. She pulled on it and offered it back. Against his better judgment he took it and inhaled deeply. They fell silent, gazing through the windshield at the lonely side street. A couple strolled arm in arm on the sidewalk. Kenny fumbled the pipe back over to Barbara and clumsily rolled up the window. Started to speak and reined himself in. Ordinarily words flowed as natural as a river but not now.

Barbara said, "I don't know what to do about funeral preparations."

He nodded silently while the words tumbled from her, as if they'd been damned up and now the levee broke and Kenny's only job was to catch them.

"I keep thinking about the prospect of having to see my brother in person. My family makes me uneasy enough at a distance, how much more so up close. Roger merely a blank face on a body, along with the rest of my family, and I try my best to keep it that way."

Her story wound on and as stoned as he was he tried to stay focused on it. Into the tapestry of her life she'd knitted a family out of those whom she'd cultivated friendships. A cavalcade of characters in an ever-changing cast, this had saved her from walking the path of life alone. All too fluid as opposed to the constant that is family. Now there was a nagging sense that the present was all that mattered. Those fortunate to have long-standing marriages and familial relationships had, she thought, an easier time staying grounded in the present. No matter how much the trail behind may have been littered with kindred spirits, she felt left alone in the present.

"Look," she sighed, "I'm not four months away from the breakup of a relationship on the long side, for me anyway, roughly three years. Not the healthiest relationship and not the best guy. Yet I'm still beating myself up over my shortfalls, angry at him for his own. But mostly angry at him for deciding to walk away that last time. Because no matter how many ways I might try and analyze things, rationalize our relationship as fundamentally flawed—in the end I'm left with the fact that he chose to give up. Like the relationship wasn't worth the struggle, the effort, call it what you will. I tell myself morning after morning waking up with thoughts of him that I was simply unworthy."

The vision of her mother lying dead before her very eyes on the floor washed over her, another wave of grief. He could tell from the lump in her throat that she was likely on the verge of tears. He reached for her hand and she offered it, squeezing and releasing before returning it to her lap.

"I guess I feel myself completely untethered. When I turn to look back on the path of my life, I realize there isn't a single one of the kindred spirits who'd come to walk beside me from time to time. Some for five years, some three, some just one. Some just a few months, or a few weeks, or a couple of days or a mere few hours. There's only myself on the path now."

The sadness imbued in her commentary left Kenny Fitzroy ensconced in a tomb of shared loneliness, with the sort of numb detachment one feels when observing oneself from outside oneself. Kenny already carried a sort of loneliness that was palpable and he wished very much he could offer her something otherwise, wished like hell he were more of a popular man about town with a bundle of friends and a reassuring nature.

Barbara took a pull from the pipe and sighed the smoke into the car. "I still can't believe this. I mean, I was on my way to… I don't know… heal some wounds I guess… something like that."

"You said you weren't real close."

"No. We weren't close. She was controlling and I'm not exactly the easiest person to control."

"Was it always bad between you?"

Barbara shot him a glance and sighed. "Jesus, it's not as simple as that is it? All good or all bad? There sure is a lot of gray area between people."

"I only meant, you know, generally like–"

"No. We were… connected when I was a little girl. My father never had anything good to say about mom or us or anyone else for that matter. She kind of shielded us from the bastard."

"Was he violent?"

"Yes he could be." She nodded emphatically.

"Do you want to go dance again or something?"

"We can just walk around a bit."

In his imagination he conjured up a cozy bohemian café on the streets of Ybor City. They strolled back towards 7th Avenue, he feeling woozy but at the same time light on his feet, bouncing along the concrete, taking in the crowd they were now ensconced in, this time embracing the hullabaloo all around them. He attributed it to the second-hand smoke in the enclosed space of the car's interior back there. He'd have to roll down the windows and give it a good airing out before they hit the highway.

Alongside the wash of euphoria, he pictured Kathy from Connecticut sitting by the phone, emptying a bottle of wine and waiting for it to ring, getting more distressed by each ticking minute. He stopped himself in his tracks and began taking deep breaths as his therapist had instructed him years ago when he felt these panic attacks coming on, shaking his shoulders as if the problem were something attached to his body.

"You okay?" Barbara massaged his arm.

"I'm fine. Just give me a second."

There was no bohemian café—the coffeehouse kept daytime hours, and so he treated her to an ice cream. At the park they sat side-by-side on a bench. Barbara slumped forward, her shoulders shaking. He reached across and when she turned to him he could see her cheeks were streaked with tears. She folded into his side and he sighed and massaged her arm.

"I'm sorry," he said. "Your mom really was a nice lady. She was super nice to me."

They stood up and walked the few blocks over to where they'd parked. After he started the car and hand-cranked the window down she reached across and squeezed his hand. "Thanks Kenny. You're a good guy."

He shrugged. Alice Thunderclap had once opined that he was a good guy and now her daughter—the only souls to dispense such a favorable judgment on his character lately. He drew the car onto the road into traffic. Her hand was warm. She gave his hand a squeeze before letting go, turning her face to the window, ostensibly to survey the historic surroundings, quivering and drawing the back of her hand to her eyes.

There was nothing to offer but an ear, but she had emptied herself of words. To his relief, signs began to appear for the interstate. Across from him on the bench seat she appeared vulnerable to him—sniffling, dabbing at her wet eyes with a Kleenex. He imagined Kathy in Connecticut in a similar state. Quite a paradox, he thought, that Barbara could be as brought to tears by death as Kathy could by life.

# 3

A morning without wind, the air thick with moist heat under a pale blue sky. Hurricane Charley was the furthest thing from Peggy Beamish's mind as she snipped away at some rose bushes in a modest front yard while Mike showered and dressed. She waved to the neighbors across the street and agreed that it was a beautiful day. The screen door at the side of the house slammed shut and out came Mike, sporting a loose Hawaiian palm print shirt. She shielded her eyes from the sun, the better to size him up.

"You're gonna wear that shirt again?"

"Well," he said. "It's less laundry for you if I get some wear out of it."

"But you've already worn it like four times this week."

"Hey, I like this shirt."

"I know. Everyone's starting to notice."

Mike tugged playfully at the fabric. "A remarkable shirt," he said.

Peggy shook her shears at him. "Hop to it. We gotta be there in like five minutes."

"Well then put those big scissors away," he said, rolling his eyes, "and I'll warm up the golf cart."

"Warm up the golf cart he says," she muttered to herself.

Pickleball was all the rage at Sunny Glen Palms. The courts weren't overcrowded, with all the snowbirds having packed off for more agreeable northern climes. Peggy liked to arrive early nonetheless to beat the heat if not the crowds. She usually played with her friend Cindy, Sunny Glen Palms resident and real estate agent, although she was never above approaching a total stranger for a pickup game. With no small measure of reluctance Mike had agreed to participate in this contest of marriages. They had no inkling of the abilities of their adversaries. But pickleball afforded a more friendly competition. It was somewhere between tennis and table tennis, played with paddles and a whiffle ball on a small-scale court. A less strenuous cardiovascular workout, but no less punishment on the knees and more so the shoulder. Aging bodies were beginning to show up at the offices of orthopedic surgeons with rotator cuff issues related to this new pickleball craze. No such correlation was indicated for any of the nearby shuffle-boarders.

Marge Cumberbatch earnestly hoped that this game, played on a smaller court among amiable adversaries, would better serve her husband's athletic prowess and accommodate his limited capacity for patience. She knew there would be no second tennis date with the Hightowers, the scene Ted made yesterday still fresh in her mind although she hadn't mentioned it on the ride over in the golf cart. When he turned off Wingate Loop into the South Club parking lot he tried to make light of it while she folded her hands mutely, fixed her gaze straight ahead and prayed Ted might contain his fiery and unpredictable temper. Play nice. Whatever it took to avoid a derailment of her burgeoning friendship with Peggy Beamish.

She had a keen eye for parking spots and hastened to point one out near the courts. Ted grumbled while piloting the cart to the spot. "What's the point in saving a few steps of exercise when we're gonna be running around like crazy jackrabbits anyway?"

Marge glared at him, shaking her head puzzledly at the odd use of a term typically alluding to another kind of physical exertion. They were running late and every second counted.

When they approached the courts, there was no sign of Peggy and her husband. There were only two courts, and one of them was taken by an elderly couple dressed head-to-toe in white tennis garb. They were having trouble getting to the ball. Ted sighed and remained standing while Marge seated herself on one of the benches in the shade of the trees that separated the courts from the pool deck area.

Ted glanced at his wristwatch. "They said nine o'clock, right?"

"Relax. They'll be here."

"You sure you got the right people?" He gestured at the slow-moving octogenarians.

"Yes dear," she made a face. "I can assure you Peggy Beamish isn't a figment of my imagination."

Ted paced back and forth checking his watch while Marge watched the players volley on the court. However lacking they were in speed, energy and prowess, it was obvious to her there was no deficit of love and good will between them. They were sweethearts. They laughed at their mistakes. He made some joke upon her swing-and-miss, then coached her on the mechanics of the pickleball forehand stroke.

At last along the brick path from the parking lot came the Beamishes. Peggy waved and scooted in front of her husband.

"Sorry we're late. Getting him up and at em on a Saturday morning is like trying to wake the dead," Peggy said, rolling her eyes and nodding over her shoulder. "I can't imagine what on earth he coulda done to tire himself out yesterday."

"Oh now really, c'mon my dear," said Mike, glancing sheepishly at the Cumberbatches and extending a hand to Ted.

"You'd think he played five sets of tennis," Peggy said, "the way he conked out last night."

Hands shaken all around, the Beamishes went to fetch paddles from the closet nearby. The old couple had apparently decided to pack it in, and Marge informed them they were playing teams and needed only one court. The old woman was red in the face, out of breath and hunched over. Her partner smiled at Marge, saying they'd had enough and were headed to the bar at the club. How long had they been married, Marge wanted to know.

"Us?" The woman looked at her partner, who hobbled towards them. "About five years I guess."

"Wow," said Marge. "Looks like you've been married for fifty years. I-I mean, the way you get along so wonderfully."

"Right," said the old woman, "I get you. Third time's a charm. My first two husbands could be the most awful sons of bitches."

Marge was a little taken aback at this genteel old woman's choice of words. She smiled amiably at the woman and then the old fellow, who took his lady's elbow and said with a pat of his paddle on her behind and a wink to the newcomers, "She just might make one out of me yet."

Peggy's eyes lit up at this and she brought a hand to her mouth and snickered while Marge shook her head slowly at the retreating couple. The old codger tossed a wave over his shoulder and said, enjoy yourselves.

Ted started jogging in place, bouncing the plastic ball on his paddle. Peggy ran down the rules of the game, Marge nodding her comprehension at every detail from scoring to placement of players while Mike told Ted collegially *it's essentially tennis on a smaller court for us old folks.* Ted nodded and said, well then let's get on with it.

So they got on with it. A little ways in, Marge could tell her husband was enjoying himself, getting in some good strokes, the Beamishes giving him the benefit of the doubt on a couple of close calls at the lines. The Cumberbatches found themselves leading their hosts after two sets and Ted was happy, if not gloating a little.

In the third set, Mike Beamish seemed to have found his serve and began to work Marge's side of the court. To each and every one of his wife's mishaps Ted made a sour face.

The Beamishes, having redeemed themselves and managing to force a tie going into the fifth and final set of the match, paused for a breather and show of goodwill. Marge slapped her paddle playfully and Ted shuffled his feet like a boxer between rounds.

A young couple stepped onto the adjacent court with their paddles. The fair-haired young man wore a tee shirt bearing on the front an image of President Bush and VP Cheney with the red No symbol overlaid. On the back the slogan, *No More Oil Wars.*

Ted rolled his eyes, nodding toward the other court. "What a jackass," he said.

"What?" Mike Beamish hadn't yet noticed the tee shirt, his attention drawn instead to the tanned and lithe legs belonging to the man's partner.

"Hey," Ted faced his perceived enemy, "you can take that shirt off pal. You're in America."

The man stopped dribbling the ball on his racquet and regarded his agitator with a puzzled expression. "Oh I'm sorry." he said. "I thought we can wear whatever shirts we like *because* we're in America."

"Smartass," said Ted, staring him down. "It's guys like you are gonna take this country down."

"Honey please," Marge approached her husband and he waved her away.

"Go back to your game and we'll go back to ours," said the young lady, raising her chin and staring daggers at Ted Cumberbatch.

"Damned liberals," Ted muttered. "If you don't like our country, why don't you just go somewhere else."

Scorn displaced a great deal of beauty on the young lady's face. "We do love our country and my nephew just returned from Iraq. Damaged, I might add."

Her partner's composure seemed to have ebbed. "Why don't you stop watching shit news channels," he said, "and quit trying to bully complete strangers."

"Come on Ted," said Marge, frowning apologetically to the spooked couple on the neighboring court. "Leave them alone for godsake. Let's put the ball in play."

"They're disgraceful," he scrutinized the racquet in his hands as if it were that he was addressing. "Their opinions are abnormal," his voice now dissolved to muttering. "Rude and disrespectful. I cannot abide by these wishy-washy touchy feely sissyfolk…"

"Put the godamn ball in play," said Peggy, rolling her eyes and then shaking her head convivially at the young couple.

The man, having deemed the ugly business finished and not wishing to engage any further, served the ball to his partner, and Ted Cumberbatch refrained from hurling further insults.

When play resumed on their court, the Beamishes seemed to have lost a little steam. Ted seized on the opportunity and began to understand that he could lash a serve over that net with enough force to make a return a challenge. Peggy had to remind him more than once that serves were *underhand*, and he begrudgingly took the ball back and swept it into play.

It was deuce in the final game of the set when Ted took a volley and smashed the ball directly at Peggy Beamish's face. She was unable to get the paddle up in front of her in time and took it right on the nose. The ball dropped to the ground. Marge hustled around the net to attend to their opponent, glaring at her husband while she rubbed Peggy's shoulders and asked are you okay, are you okay?

Mike glared at Ted and then scrunched his face at his wife, the better to assess the damage.

Peggy's nose was bleeding. She pinched it and tilted her head back.

"Sorry," said Ted. "Didn't know my own strength."

The apology elicited no response from any corner. "I didn't mean it." Ted said. "Guess I just got too hopped up."

Peggy gathered herself and Marge took her by the elbow and guided her to the restroom. In the mirror Marge watched Peggy tilt her head back and press tissue paper to her nose, a bruise forming under her eye.

"Here we go again," Peggy's voice was muffled. "Maybe I oughtta stay away from you."

"No no, really. Please. Oh God I'm so sorry," said Marge, dabbing at Peggy's forehead with a wet paper towel.

"He always behave like that around complete strangers?"

"I'm so sorry," said Marge. "He can be difficult."

"Does he have any *redeeming* qualities?"

Marge pondered this while Peggy's eyes remained fixed to hers in the mirror.

"I'm so sorry about this," Marge moaned. "He gets so wound up."

Peggy shook her head and sniffed. The bleeding stopped. The two ladies looked at one another's images in the mirror.

"I'm sorry," Marge repeated. "I hope this doesn't put you off playing with us again."

"You and I can play singles, honey."

When they returned, the young couple had vacated the neighboring court. Ted was speaking animatedly to Mike Beamish and tapping the net with his racquet to emphasize a point.

"It's the goddamned liberals ruining this country. And I don't see how they contribute one iota to it."

Mike shrugged. "I guess I'm just too old to get worked up about such things."

"Well," said Ted, "maybe y'ought to start now."

He met his wife's stare and looked over to Peggy. "You alright?"

"*I'm* alright," Peggy replied.

"Well I guess we'll just pack it in then," Ted smirked. "Anybody want to hit the club for lunch?"

"*Bull*shit," said Peggy, tossing the ball at Ted Cumberbatch with a little extra zing. "We're not finished here yet mister."

Ted smiled crookedly and shrugged at the others, and they resumed their place on the court.

"Who's serve?" asked Mike.

Peggy held her hand out and beckoned the ball back from Ted. She bounced it on her paddle and then whipped it sidearm over the net at Ted. He returned it to Mike at the net and Mike drilled it back over the net at the ground with such force that it bounced over Ted's head and he chased it back and nearly fell in the bushes.

"Deuce!" Peggy hollered and Mike served it into play again. The ball went back and forth and then Peggy saw her chance on a ball that bounced on the net. She ran to the net and swiped at the ball with the conviction of a judge bringing the gavel down for life without parole on a serial killer. The ball smashed against the ground and bounced far to the side and out of play. The Beamishes had prevailed.

Ted shuffled up to the net to shake hands with his opponents. Marge hoped this might serve to put them back on a more amiable course, but it was apparent to her that the Beamishes were not on board.

*

*Summertime in Cohasset. Open windows, much clamor in house. Scuttling feet. Shrieks. Chitter chatter. Radio in kitchen with weather warnings on New England Coast. Grandfather Ahearn in coveralls, chastising. Father another bout with drink. Running shirtless out front door to road. Mother calling after. Went to town in rusty old car clicking and clanging. Seek him out. Usual haunts. Local bar. Uncle Billy's. Everyone shaking heads. Missing. Florida. Hot today. Windows closed up in summer heat. Entombed in quiet chamber. Imagined visits from grandkids. Nobody. Roger, two kids busy. Charlie, left this earth too soon. Nancy off in some godforsaken land. Barbara missing. Spoke my mind to Roger about her rehab. Maybe cured, money owed, so what? Roger says if she wants to kill herself let her go ahead and do it. Too hard on my little girl? Mind goes everywhere now. Can't shut down for sleep. Regrets fill thoughts like demons. What to do? Barbara drowns in drugs. Roger too mad to speak. My little girl. Found laying on street. Almost dead. Too many pills.*

*

Lily hadn't yet gotten the coffee started when the doorbell chimed. A guest at the door was somewhat of a novelty and it got Rex barking. At the door she shushed him and met Barbara, fidgeting her feet and glancing up apologetically. Her cheeks were sunken, her eyes red and so Lily could tell she'd been crying a lot and had slept little.

"Sorry to bother you again."

"You're not bothering anybody," Lily said, beckoning her inside. Rex stood up on his hind legs balancing against Barbara's thighs with his paws while she rubbed at his ears. Lily drew one of the chairs at the kitchen table and shuffled over to fetch another mug. This morning while housecleaning her thoughts had strayed to Dorothy and Dan, and once again she'd been walking with the dead. Much as she'd have liked to empty those thoughts from the space they rented in her head, there was no one to share them with. Billy and Jack always changed the subject when she broached it. Now it appeared there was an obliging ear to spill them to, but in deference to Barbara she refrained from doing so.

"Cream? Sugar?" Only one day later, and she'd forgotten her friend's preference.

"Both."

"Well," she said, setting the mug on the table in front of Barbara, "how are the arrangements going?"

"Not too well," Barbara heaved a sigh and wiped at a tear.

Lily rose to gather a clump of Kleenexes from the guest bathroom. "Have you heard from your mother's Bridge friend?" she called over her shoulder. "The young man we met at the Pub."

"We had dinner last night. Out by the fancy development."

"Oh, you must mean the Seagull. Over in the Regency community."

"That's right."

Lily had dined at the Seagull a few times with Dorothy before she got sick, and then a lady from the pool who'd been recently widowed. She'd thoroughly enjoyed it. It was about the fanciest dining you could hope for in Sunnyville, and the prices weren't too steep. She recalled an expansive natural view beyond floor-to-ceiling length windows on all sides, and the tables had votive candles. It was a long time ago and no opportunity had presented itself since.

"He's kind of a strange bird, isn't he?"

The dog shifted from one paw to the other at Barbara's feet while she blew her nose. "Yes," she said. "Kenny Fitzroy is a strange bird alright."

"So," she said to Barbara, "is this a love interest or—"

"Oh no," Barbara shook her head, her long auburn hair flaying about. "I mean, he's nice enough and everything. Just—"

"Not your type."

"Just not my type."

"Well," said Lily.

"I was going to ask if you wouldn't mind helping me tackle a few more calls. Family, mom's friends, the funeral home. I just feel weird doing it all alone."

Lily pursed her lips thoughtfully. "Why, I guess I could come over to you for a little while."

"Thanks," Barbara wiped at her eyes.

"It's very difficult to lose a mother."

"We were hardly best friends."

"Well," Lily rose, gathering the cups from the table, "if you had been, it'd be hard enough. When you're not, the reasons why are as much a cause for grief in their own strange way. I don't know which is worse."

"Are you sure you don't mind coming by?"

"It'll be one less worry for you I reckon. I have a few things to do around the house and then I'll drop over and help you make some calls."

"Well let me make it up to you somehow."

"Oh heavens. That's not necessary."

"No really. How about dinner? I'd love the company. I can't bring myself to cook. I'm really not a bad cook. It's just… going through her things. The thought of using anything in those kitchen cabinets…"

"Well. I'd be happy to join you."

"Where would you like to go? You name the place."

"Well," she said, "if you don't mind a repeat, I guess I'd like that place you went to last night. The Seagull."

*

One of the components of Kenny Fitzroy's spartan furnishings in his humble abode, a two-bedroom/one bath in its original form, unrenovated, a real time capsule—was a card table with foldout legs that constituted a makeshift desk. On this desk of sorts sat a laptop he'd swapped for his old clunky desktop with its colossal tower and monitor, in the interest of lightening his load in the move just a few years ago. To this end, he took on the cumbersome task of consolidating and transferring numerous Word files that constituted his literary output—he assumed upon himself from a young age the gift of the muse. He took upon himself the endeavor of scratching out a novel-length work the magnitude of Tolstoy's *War and Peace*, with equal aspirations in regard to content. Alongside this tome lay a digital record of numerous false-starts, single page sketches, fleshing out ideas for short stories or essays or novellas. He actually made it to the end of the novel-length work-in-progress in perpetuity for which he never could settle on a title, this conundrum was directly related to the problem of extracting some unified theme from a fragmented narrative with long rambling expository passages that mimicked his penchant for verbosity in the real world outside the borders of his imagination. He joined writers groups and those in attendance bore the brunt of his long-windedness, centered around his own work-in-progress. After all the rewrites, the added fluff, the trimming of added fluff, the painstaking task of sculpting and refining, there simply was no story.

He'd spent an enormous chunk of time throughout his adult life alone plundering a forest of words to gather and assemble the great American novel, swore he wouldn't wait for retirement to do so. The truth of the matter was that he had more fun playing at being a writer than being one. The ritual of getting the soft-focus study music going, setting the cup of coffee in front of him, rolling up his sleeves, readying himself to get down to the business at hand—all of this superseded the actual process. And so, the sessions got shorter by the day, the week, the month, the year. Early retirement now found him greatly resolved to finish that digital legacy that resided on that modest machine on that unimpressive card table in that unimposing condo in a community of what he regarded mostly corporate cows put out to pasture.

Kenny rose from this makeshift desk with the morning's last cup of coffee to turn the volume down on the stereo. He fetched the phone from the dusty floor and dialed her number, pacing back and forth until she answered.

"I'm just calling you back," he said.

"Right."

"And I got the news."

"Well. I um– guess I wanted to… to talk about… where to go from here."

"Right. I think that's fair. For both of us."

"Fair?"

"Yeah, I mean…" Kenny's voice trailed off. A fly had found its way inside the condo villa and with a growing disdain he watched it flit about haphazardly and knock itself into the sliding door to the patio, drawn by some impulse to light, seeking a way out of the murky dark to the daylight that beckoned from the other side of the glass. "Have you thought about… all the options?"

"Kenny," she said, her voice imbued with new confidence, "I think I want to keep the baby." After a pause she said, "But I want to talk to you."

Kenny collapsed onto the sofa. He'd vaguely figured on a discussion of options—now it seemed to him options were off the table. His feet went to tapping and he began to fan his legs.

"You think it's wise? To go through with it? I mean, given as we hardly know each other. Bringing a child into the world…"

There was silence on the line and for a moment he wondered whether she'd hung up.

"There are options, you know," he said. "I mean, I think, at this early stage."

"I know." Her voice lost some of the authority it had marched in with.

"Have you thought about, maybe it's just not the best time. For you, for me."

Kathy said, "I'd like to come down and talk. In person. The sooner the better. What does your schedule look like?"

*Schedule?* thought Kenny. *What schedule?* His life was one morning after another absent any plans. Leisurely strolls, reading, listening to music on the stereo system, resignedly tapping on the practice putting green given his futile attempts to retain golf partners.

"Um," he said, "let me check the calendar."

An audible sigh issued from the other end of the line. "I'm looking at flights next weekend," she said.

"Can I get back to you?"

"Get back to me?"

"Um, yeah… I-I can confirm, a–after I look…"

After what seemed an interminable pause, she rallied herself back to a businesslike tone. "Would you please get back to me soon. Like today?"

"Sure," he said, "I'll let you know."

He tried to make his voice sound casual, unaffected, as if they were trying to nail down plans for a concert or sporting event, maybe a hobbyist convention. He waited for a response, a goodbye, something—but the abrupt click on the line when she hung up speared him with anxiety.

He sat a good while sipping that last cup of coffee. Then he rose to stand before the tall bookcase that housed his music and movie collection, most of them music documentaries in VHS format. Music, music, music. For many years, in Oakland and then Austin, Kenny dabbled in music. He had played electric guitar in bands that pushed eclectic boundaries, bands with scarce musical ability, sparse rehearsal time, bands that did multiple-act shows where the audience was a handful of people at best. There in front of his collection absent the usual admiration, today an unexpected sense of indifference. No impulse to reach for a Rolling Stones LP, an Iggy Pop cassette, a Violent Femmes CD, or a VHS Beta Creedence Clearwater

Revival documentary. Suddenly he had no use for any of this assembled hodgepodge of packaged pop culture. They sang only a song of boredom. Maybe, he thought, it'd be a good idea to go outside for a walk, get some fresh air and sunshine. Drop the cultural artifacts and gather his thoughts. Stroll beyond the gates and see what was going on out there in the great wide world.

*

Peggy Beamish drove along Sunset Boulevard at well over the twenty-five-mile-an-hour speed limit. She was doing more and more of that now on long stretches of Sunset Boulevard where there were no crosswalks, it had become difficult to control herself. Nearing the gate, she slowed her roll for an emergency paramedic vehicle. She thought she might head for the family-owned Sunnyville Café for a bite to eat.

Both she and Mike had declined Ted Cumberbatch's invitation to lunch at the South Club after their thorny pickle ball match. After shaking hands all around, Ted wondered aloud if perhaps Peggy's winning smash was just outside the line and the point might be replayed at some future date. Peggy couldn't tell whether or not he was joking. Mike went off to do Mike things, whatever that was, whatever he got up to when she wasn't looking. Marge returned the paddles and gave Peggy a conspiratorial look of apology. Peggy took her arm and said we must get together for lunch sometime soon though, *just the two of us.*

Now she was off by herself and looking forward to the peace and tranquility of a solo lunch—absent polite responses and efforts to keep the conversation going. Her plan was foiled shortly after being seated at a booth by the picture window at the front of the restaurant. The café was always more crowded on Saturdays, and close on her heels was another patron in search of a table for one. He wore beat up tennis shoes, old jeans and a wrinkled golf shirt. He asked if she minded company. Suit yourself she said, glancing up sharply from a laminated tri-fold menu. He slid into the vinyl-upholstered bench and rested his elbows on the Formica table. The waitress brought them both menus and cutlery rolled in napkins. He ordered coffee and the waitress returned with a saucer and cup. Into this he dashed an exorbitant amount of sugar before spilling in half-and-half creamer minis one after another, and Peggy thought it might never end.

"Like a little coffee with your cream and sugar?" she said.

He bore a blank look but took this no less as an invitation to converse, reaching a hand across the table to her. "Oh, I guess so. By the way, my name is Kenny."

*By the way*, she thought. As if they'd been talking for twenty minutes without exchanging names. The waitress returned with a pad and took their orders, their appetites stoked by the aroma only such greasy spoon diners afford drifting in from the kitchen.

"I'm Peggy," she said, "and I'm not giving you my last name, so we'll just agree to know each other on a first-name basis. So, what brings you out and about on a Saturday afternoon Kenny?"

*What indeed*, he thought, *where do I even begin*? Kenny's worrisome thoughts were now banging around that noggin of his like a bunch of flies stuck in a light globe. Kathy from Connecticut was coming to pay him a visit—where would she stay? The prospect of her staying at his place was daunting to say the least. His second bedroom was more of a closet and didn't even have a bed in it. So absorbed was he in his thoughts, he was nearly blind to the expectant face across from him.

His distraction had piqued Peggy Beamish's interest, a curiosity of sorts sat across from her in the booth there at the Sunnyville Café—an unshaven, balding, oval-headed character right out of a comic strip, the bushy eyebrows animated in the array of expressions that danced across that cartoon face. She'd come here for a little peace and quiet, but this character stirred her curiosity enough to forego it.

"I guess I kinda needed to get out of the gate," he said, his eyes darting everywhere and not meeting her gaze.

"Out of the gate," she echoed. "You make it sound like a prison."

His face lit up with something between a grimace and a smile. "I guess I do make it sound that way."

"That's okay," she said with a dismissive wave of the hand. "I feel the same way myself sometimes. Actually, more often than not."

"Really?" He leaned in. "I-I mean I like it here, but sometimes—"

"Where's here? Which community?"

"Sunny Glen Palms."

"Oh, me too. *Us* too. My husband and I."

Kenny nodded and the waitress came upon them, tray in hand. Peggy clutched a knife and fork, one in each hand, over her plate, hesitating. She said, "So at the risk of being nosy. What's got *you* so wound up?"

Kenny shrugged. "I don't want to burden you with my problems."

"Me? I'm not gonna lose sleep over *your* problems bud. I got enough of my own to keep me up at night."

He laughed politely. She lowered her voice to a more conspiratorial tone, "Sometimes it's easier to talk to a stranger. You know. About things."

"Well," he said, leaning in. "It seems I've gotten a girl in a family way."

"A girl?" Peggy nearly dropped her fork.

"No. I meant, I- I mean… a woman."

"Well now. That sounds better." Peggy waved her fork after taking a bite of her steak. "She from around here?

"No. Connecticut."

"That where you're from?" Peggy asked while scooping a forkful of mashed potatoes.

"No. I grew up in California. Lived in Oakland for a while and then I moved to Austin, Texas for a good number of years."

"So where the hell does Connecticut come in," Peggy said, carving at her steak.

"That's where she's from."

"I got that," Peggy shrugged. "I'm just trying to get the connection," she said, fanning her wrist. "Elaborate."

"Well, I was up there for a family reunion. A few months back."

"She's not related to you, is she?"

"No!" Kenny's outburst broke the gravity imbued in their hushed talk.

"Careful now. You're drawing attention to us," Peggy said, glancing around and smiling politely to onlookers at nearby tables.

"Sorry." Kenny leaned in with enough gusto to cause Peggy to recoil and repeat, *you're drawing attention to us.*

"I meant no," he tapped the table. "Kathy's a friend of my cousins."

Peggy nodded. "So now you've got family in the know… of getting someone… in a family way? Isn't that what you said?"

"Yes."

"That's kind of an old-fashioned way to put it," she said, playing with her fork at arranging the food on her plate. "Do you have any children? I mean, besides what's on the way."

Kenny shook his head vigorously.

"Sounds like you've been trying to avoid the inevitable. And it's finally caught up with you."

"Yeah," Kenny shrugged. "I don't think I'll make much of a father."

"Why the hell not?"

"Too old," he said matter-of-factly, as if it were an athlete or an actor they were discussing and not Kenny Fitzroy, early retiree with one stroke of the pen in an attorney's office settling his mother's estate.

"Anyway," he said, "it's very upsetting."

"Kinda throws you for a loop doesn't it?"

"You can say that again."

"I remember all too well having anxious feelings." Peggy returned her attention to her plate, shaking her head.

"What? Just antsy about becoming a mother?"

"No. Not at all. More like antsy about remaining a wife *and* mother."

Kenny let that sit a while. "How long have you been married?"

"Well," she drew a napkin and wiped at thin determined lips. "We're *celebrating* our fiftieth wedding anniversary," she said, rolling her eyes. "Next weekend."

"That's cool," he said noncommittally.

"Mike Beamish and Peggy O'Malley fall in love," she said. "In high school. Never even had a chance to date anyone else. Overnight I become Peggy Beamish. Whole other identity. The Beamishes begat two sons and a daughter. Whoop dee do."

"Have you been drinking?"

"No," Peggy rolled her wrist. "Why, am I slurring my speech?"

"So you're thinking, don't get married? For *me*, I mean."

Peggy frowned. "I'm not saying anything. I can only speak for Peggy Beamish. Follow your heart, honey. Do you think you love this gal?"

"I don't know. I haven't thought about it."

"*Thought about it?* It's not upstairs in your noggin," Peggy tapped her forehead then held a hand over her heart. "It's something you either feel here or not."

Kenny's face clouded over.

"Have you been in regular touch with her? Since—"

"I haven't been in any touch with her. Not since then. That night."

Peggy scrunched up her face.

"I-I mean, except for her phone call a few days ago."

"Well," she said, arranging her napkin. "You sure as hell don't love her. Not a chance. If in fact such a thing does exist. You'd not have been able to help yourself picking up the phone and calling the girl… I mean *woman*."

"So what are you suggesting I do?"

"I'm not suggesting anything. I barely know ya."

Peggy straightened her sleeves and fussed with her hair. "But," she said, "I will tell ya one thing. Don't break this poor woman's heart. Be honest. Don't try and pull any fast ones."

"Fast ones?"

She pointed her fork at him. "Don't try and pretend to feel some way you don't. But you better man up and take responsibility."

"I-I don't even know where my finances are. I mean, I know I'm barely scraping by."

"That's not her problem. Don't you make it her problem, mister."

"Jesus," Kenny said, "Can I get a few comforting words here? A little more empathy? Some, I don't know, words of wisdom maybe?"

Peggy reached across the table and clutched his arm. "Listen… what's your name again?"

"Kenny."

"Kenny. You gotta meet with… what's her name?"

"Kathy. Kathy from Connecticut."

"Kathy from Connecticut."

"That's right. Kathy from Connecticut."

"You don't even know her last name?"

"Sorry, I–"

"Oh dear God," she sighed. "What is with you kids today?"

"I'm not a kid."

"Okay then, what's with you *middle-aged men* today? Kenny. Listen to me. You gotta have Kathy come down, or else you hop a flight up there. As soon as possible."

"She's threatening to come down next weekend."

"Threatening?"

"It's an expression," he shrugged, "an odd phrase."

"Not a very nice one." She said, shaking her head and glancing around to see if anyone was eavesdropping. "Anyway. Kenny. I hope everything works out for the best. I'm sure it probably will. But take my advice, a woman wants to know she's not all alone when it comes to this. You gotta assure her you're going to play some part in this child's life."

Peggy's face went softer, her eyes gazing upon him with a new glow.

Kenny said, "Can I ask you a favor?"

"Oh God, what?"

"Nothing much. It's just, I- I don't have anybody… I mean I haven't told anyone else. Would you mind if I… if I needed to talk. Could I call on you?"

"Well," Peggy shrugged. "I guess there's no harm in that."

"You don't golf, do ya?"

"I have a set of clubs. I never use them. They're collecting dust."

"Would you play a round of golf with me? It'll help take my mind off things."

"I don't have a membership. I let it expire."

"I have one. I haven't used it since, like, January."

"Well you might think twice about renewing it," said Peggy. "I'd steer you to my husband, he's more the golfer. But I sure as hell wouldn't want *him* giving you any advice on women."

"So whad'ya say? Play a round of golf?"

"It might serve to make him a little jealous. But he's made it his life's mission to make *this* old lady jealous. Oh what the hell, why not."

"Do you have a golf cart?"

"We *do*."

"Good. We'll have to use it."

Peggy frowned at him. He shrugged, throwing up his palms. "Unless you wanna walk."

"Okay, fine."

"Wanna go tomorrow?"

"Sunday? No way Jose. Have to wait til Monday."

"Why not Sunday?"

"Because Sunday is sacred."

"You religious?"

"Oh God no," she batted a hand at the air. "I just like having one day I don't even have to think about going out the door for anything."

"Oh, okay." Kenny scratched at his stomach. "Monday then."

They paid their tabs at a podium up front. Outside Peggy stood next to the Beamishes Lincoln and asked if he wanted a lift back inside the gate.

"No thanks," he said. "I thought I'd just sort of loiter, er linger around town, get a little exercise."

"You might want to hunt for a little job while you're at it. You know, help with the finances, now you got a kid on the way."

"I guess I'll have to do something."

"You go to college? Got a degree?"

"Yeah. Fine Arts."

"Well," Peggy said, rolling her eyes, "that'll sure as hell come in handy right now."

"Well," he grimaced, "thanks for lending an ear."

Peggy waved dismissively then said wait. "Gimme your address so I can come and fetch you on Monday."

"I can meet you at your house. S-so you don't have to–"

"No way, Jose. Mike might get funny ideas. Although I don't think my husband has a jealous bone in his body."

She scrawled his address on a sheet of paper. "See you at, what, nine-o-clock sharp on Monday?"

"Okay. Nice meeting you."

Kenny looked on as Peggy climbed into the Lincoln—in that moment she appeared to him strangely glamorous in the hot sun with her oversized sunglasses, glossy lipstick and dyed-blonde curls. She clambered into her car and checked her lipstick in the visor. Put the car in gear. Waved through the open window and smiled, said too-da-loo.

*

Mike Beamish hastened over to Isabel's after the pickleball. He knew she'd be waiting. They'd arranged it yesterday and confirmed it later that evening in phone whispers, after Peggy had turned in for the night.

Isabel's house was impeccably neat and ordered, a décor at odds with the typical Florida kitsch Sunny Glen Palms fare. There were heavy chests, a huge oak dining table, a pair of immense Queen Anne chairs, an oversize sofa with the most exquisite hand-embroidered cushions. A thick Turkish rug over which hung an elaborate Moroccan mosaic chandelier light. On the walls, original works, leaning toward bright color explosions of natural settings and landscapes. Earth tones. Everything hung on custom-made frames, of a significantly higher value than the wall art at Casa Beamish, which consisted of an unremarkable array of prints. Isabel's bedroom was adorned with heavy velvet curtains that served to keep it in darkness against even the harshest sunlight, the space dominated by a heavy oak four-poster bed upon which they now lay. Mike imagined it must have cost a fortune to ship her belongings a few months ago.

She lay on her side facing away from him. Mike alternated toying with jet-black hair that ran almost to the small of her back and massaging a small frame, tanned and dark and slightly freckled. They'd made love several times. He was beginning to feel the stirrings once again, accompanied by a stomach churning interminably over Cialis, the magic pill that would make these afternoon trysts possible. He racked his brain to conjure up words, Isabel having been far more conversant yesterday, oddly reserved today. The tone of her voice, the sophistication imbued in the words amid her home's exotic dressings served to magnify how very different their interior worlds were. She had travelled widely and extensively as a journalist. She had no children. She'd married much later in life, into a significant amount of money. The marriage was brief and she had mixed feelings about it and suddenly she was a relatively young widow who could pick and choose what free-lance editorial work she could take on. She had contacts all over the world.

Mike's own backstory was vastly at odds with hers. He and Peggy had married young and wasted no time in having children, in fact their first child Jeff was what drove them to the altar at nineteen-years-old. A career in kitchenware and then IBM sales. Church, active members in a Catholic organization called Marriage Encounter. So now here he was in steamy hot Florida attempting to conjure up words with the sense he was climbing a rockface to a new plateau of a worldly sophistication and refinement. What he said was, *you okay*?

She turned around fully to face him. "Of course, why shouldn't I be?"

"You just seem, I don't know, unusually quiet today."

"Mike, we've only known each other for two days."

"Oh, we've known one another longer than that. Where did we first meet? Oh yes, Pub Night. Weeks ago."

"You know what I mean."

She was toying with his St. Christopher medal again and he took her warm and delicate hand in his. He said, "Well anyway I'm glad to know you better."

"Your wife made a point to remind me about the big fiftieth bash. Do you suppose I'm on the guest list?"

"That might be awkward."

"I don't see why."

"Hmm?"

"We're not children," she mused. "I don't see why either of us would act beneath the appropriate level of social decorum."

"Do you want to come to the party?"

Isabel shrugged. "It's of no consequence to me. I suppose it might be amusing, in a kind of perverse way."

Mike withdrew his hand from her fine silky hair and Isabel let the St. Christopher medal drop from her fingers back onto to his chest.

"Do you like my wife?"

She stared at him quizzically. "Why are we talking about your wife?"

*

Barbara dropped Lily off at the front door of the Seagull under a light drizzle from a gloomy sky. There came a rumble of thunder and then the heavens opened as she went to park the car. She grabbed her tiny umbrella, hot-footed it through the heavy rain, and met Lily in the lobby. Inside the restaurant was a much larger crowd than the previous evening. There were half-price drink options and after they were seated Barbara ordered a glass of Merlot, Lily a glass of Zinfandel. It was five-thirty and they were exhausted after a long afternoon taking turns on the phone. Barbara had a long call with her Aunt Eleanor, her mom's only sister, always extremely talkative. A safe call—a lot of tears, a lot of catching up. Her uncle was also eager to talk.

"I'm glad there's just a memorial service," Lily said over her menu. "That's enough really. Especially with people coming from out of town."

"What out-of-towners? From what I gather, there's only my brother Roger." She sighed, "I'm just sorry she didn't write any local people into the address book. I guess with a Sunny Glen directory she didn't have to."

"Did she belong to any clubs?"

Lily had asked her that not an hour ago but had apparently forgotten. Barbara was starting to notice it more and more, the forgetfulness.

"Like I said, Bridge. It's not like I was on speaking terms with her."

"Well anyway," said Lily. "Everyone here reads the obituaries. You have to call the paper."

Lily folded her napkin neatly in front of her and patted it. "I hope you don't mind me asking, and it's really none of my business, but what came between you and your mama?"

"Oh," Barbara shook her head and looked wistfully around the room. "I don't know. I guess we just kind of grew apart."

"Oh?"

"Well. She's very religious, for one thing. I'm not."

"Now that's foolishness," said Lily. "You gotta believe in something."

"I do. I have a whole spiritual thing going on, but it springs from a positive place, not guilt and shame. Mom was raised strict Catholic. Wacky. Then she met my father and became even more devoutly Catholic, even more wacky. The whole guilt trip thing, and my old man would sin mightily against her and hurt us and he'd just show up at Mass and it'd all be okay. I hope I'm not offending you. With the Catholic thing and all."

"No," said Lily, "but you're close. I'm Episcopalian."

"Oh God I think Episcopalians are so cool! Y'all are like Catholic Light."

"In any case, God has been my rock through many a hard time."

"Thing I've found with religious people," Barbara tapped a finger on her wineglass, "is that for all the engagement with something that's meant to provide confidence, comfort… you know, the take it on faith thing, they can be the most fearful people. They operate, ironically enough, out of fear and doubt. It's as if their true self knows it's all just a fairy tale. They're still as uncertain as the rest of us. It ends up not doing the job intended. It's all just bullshit to me."

Lily cleared her throat at Barbara's expansiveness and glanced around warily, but the din of conversation in the dining room provided a cover for their conversation and any expletives in it. "I will say, to fear God doesn't necessarily mean to be afraid of him."

"Well that's beside the point."

Lily's face was that of a kid whose hand is slapped at the cookie jar.

"I'm sorry," Barbara frowned. "I didn't mean to offend you."

"Oh that's alright. We're just talking."

"Sometimes I think the whole purpose of conversation is to get us thinking, widening the field of our consciousness."

Lily had nothing by way of response. Barbara gazed around a dining room that was beginning to fill up with guests.

"Oh," Barbara sighed, "the long and short of it, me and my mother… is that we just live in two different worlds. *Lived* in two different worlds."

"I see," said Lily.

"I hope I'm not scaring you."

"Heavens no," said Lily.

"Do you have kids?"

"Two sons."

"Are they close?"

"They don't keep regular contact with each other."

"How about with you?"

"Me? Not much. I keep trying to get them to visit. My grandkids too."

"I'm sorry."

"You know," Lily sighed. "After I lost my sister Dorothy, I went to the pool a few more times. But I'd just get sad watching the younger people visiting their parents. The grandkids splashing around in the pool."

"I'm sorry. But it shouldn't have put you off going."

"It's okay. I guess every family has their… *things*."

"That's a gentle word for it." Barbara placed her hand over Lily's and squeezed. "Thanks for helping me. On the phone."

"It's nothing," said Lily. I can't imagine it's an easy thing to just… stumble upon. I can't imagine what you're going through. Still in shock."

"I'm strangely calm. Maybe *that's* shock. I don't know."

"You'd never been to visit her before. Here I mean."

"Nope. This is my first and last visit."

"I might need your help calling your sister. I can't seem to figure out that foreign number in your mother's address book."

"Nancy's is in South America. I'll do that. She's at least civil to me."

"Your brother sounded nice."

"Nice enough to strangers. Sure."

"Your other brother—"

"Charlie, right. My younger brother died."

Lily had heard this a few times over the short time they'd known each other and now Barbara was certain she had pretty regular memory lapses.

"My brother," said Barbara, "sees me as, like, a ne'er-do-well. Settling for a simple life of scraping by. I've been held in pretty harsh judgment for that. I wonder if I *didn't* do precisely what they thought I *should* do merely out of spite. Stubbornly sticking to their rotten script as the years went by."

"And you just stopped speaking to them?"

"No," she shook her head slowly. "For many years, I returned to the family fold with grandiose expectations. Each time, I imagined me and my family might grow into loving and supportive relationships. I don't know, maybe from our own processes of maturity. I'd turn up at family functions and holidays expecting everyone might suddenly be genuinely interested in each other's news."

She shifted her gaze from Lily to some middle distance. "I'd visualize scenes of goodwill and harmony. Sharing memories, good and bad, with the light banter of a Hallmark movie. When things didn't turn out that way, when I met only indifference, ineptitude, and intolerance, I just stopped turning up."

"It must be hard. Not talking to your mama."

Barbara sighed. "The phone calls just got more and more difficult. I'd hang up feeling the worse for them."

"Why?"

"I don't know. I always thought she didn't have much of a life for herself. Not here, not before she came here. Her whole life was her kids."

"Mamas have a strange connection to those we bear into the world. Almost like a sixth sense I reckon. It never goes away."

"I really wish I was nicer to her," Barbara's voice cracked, her face reddening. Lily looked around surreptitiously. But the few sat at nearby tables seemed not to have noticed. The waitress was not on the floor and the bartender seemed deep in his own thoughts as he dried glasses and set them on the bar in front of him.

Barbara glanced up. "Can I ask you one more favor Lily?" she paused, tapping distractedly at her glass. I just don't want to be alone in that house tonight. I could hardly sleep last night. Would you mind staying over?"

Lily brought her napkin to her mouth and massaged her brow. "Well," she said, "I guess I could. I'll just have to fetch a few things from my house. And let the dog out."

"Oh man, thanks. There's a deck of cards and a Scrabble game. It feels silly, I haven't played board games or cards since I was a little girl. But for some reason all I want to do is sit down with someone. Sit down and play some game."

"Well," Lily said, coughing and glancing around her, "It does help take your mind off of things."

She hadn't spent a single night anywhere but her own house in all the time at Sunny Glen Palms. She could pack a bag. *God*, she thought, *it's not miles from home, just a few doors down.* She could pack a toothbrush and pajamas and that'd be about it. A real slumber party.

Barbara brought her head to the palm of her hand, shoulders heaving, her eyes blind with tears. Lily glanced around once again and saw that they now had the attention of a few of the diners at nearby tables. She smiled abashedly at a white-haired woman in golf garb and rose to fetch a napkin from a setting at a table nearby. She handed it to Barbara and stood beside her, a hand on her shoulder. Barbara composed herself, fetching her purse to pay the check despite Lily's objections. Lily linked an elbow in Barbara's and together they walked to the car. Lily thought to ask for the keys but it was getting dark and her eyes would not likely oblige any night driving.

"Don't you drive till you're all cried out," she said.

Barbara nodded, sticking the keys in the ignition but not turning it. They settled themselves mutely in their seats.

"I feel like I don't have a friend in the world," Barbara said at last to the windshield.

"Well now that can't be true," Lily glanced over at Barbara. "Good-hearted girl like you? Pshaw."

"I may have a good heart," Barbara's voice was thin, "but I've burned so many bridges. Moved around too much. Never laid down any roots."

"Fiddlesticks," Lily said. "I spent my life laying down roots and look where it got me."

"There's nobody for me to call. The older you get," Barbara said, "the harder it is to make new friends. Everybody already has their circle."

Lily drew a tissue from her purse and wiggled it at Barbara. "Guess you're onto something there."

Later they sat across from one another at Alice Thunderclap's kitchen table, a low hanging lamp hung between them with muted light. A board game was laid out between them and they hunched over it with the focused intensity of two generals studying a map. The rain had subsided, the wind baying through the palm trees, a choir of crickets sang outside the open screen window. A bottle of wine from which Barbara poured. Lily allowed half a glass before raising a halting finger.

Barbara said, "I've moved around so much. My whole life. Never put down any roots. Just left a trail of people who go away, little by little after I've gone. The older I get the more I feel like my life is one big mess that has to be cleaned up."

"I'm sorry."

"My aunt, my Mom's sister… I had a good conversation with her on the phone today. We were talking about Mother of course. My brother got sick when I was like… two I guess." Barbara shook her head and took a swig of her Merlot. "I don't know why I'm telling you all this."

"Go on," said Lily.

"She was talking about how hard it was on my mother. Dad got worse, coming home drunk and often in a rage. He and Mom split up when I was about twelve. I've been told that I have insecurity and abandonment issues. Stems from a very turbulent home when I was a child."

Lily nodded and moved a piece on the board and Barbara wondered if unravelling her story and embellishing it with popular psychology would come off like a foreign language to her counterpart. A generation gap, she thought, to herself, ours being the overanalytical generation.

"I've never had money to speak of. I guess when we settle the estate, there might be something. I don't look forward to it. Dealing with Roger."

"Well, sometimes it can be very unpleasant."

"How do we do all that," Barbara asked, "I mean find the will and—"

"I'd almost bet it's in the same place I found the other documents."

Barbara shook her head. "I feel like a burglar, to tell the truth. Like an imposter."

"That's how I felt, fishing around in your momma's dresser when it… happened. And then again later for her checkbook."

"And to think it had to be me, the family failure, to be the one to walk right into an importunate situation when her… time came."

"Oh now, quit being so hard on yourself."

"It's a weird thing, an awful irony," Barbara said, draining her glass then emptying the rest of the bottle into it, "not measuring up to the very same authority figures that you in turn regard as failures. I'm a failure on their terms, they're failures on mine. Makes us dead even."

"You make it sound like a game."

"Well it is a game, isn't it?"

They began packing the board game pieces. Lily went to change into her pajamas and Barbara cracked the sliding doors on the patio, her head swimming with the effects of too many glasses of wine. She met the warm summer night. Crickets sang. The neighbor's yard furniture glistened with the dew. Palm trees bayed in the wind. Lily came beside her and told her it would get easier and time really does heal all wounds.

Barbara's words were slurred. "I try to imagine myself a little girl with a nurturing caregiver and nothing to fear and my mother could hug on me the way others have. Like you have. I wanted that. I thought maybe I still had a shot at it."

She wiped at the tears with her sleeve and Lily put an arm around her.

"There there."

"I just wanted to let her know I was alright. Even if I'm not."

They went back inside. It was just past midnight. Lily shuffled over to the sink to wash and rinse their glasses. Barbara had already set herself up in the guestroom and began making up the bed up in her mother's room. She was groggy and stumbled around executing the process. In the master bath she pulled the medicine cabinet open and rummaged around. There was a bottle of Percodan and she seized it. Spilled a few in her palm, drank it down with a little Dixie cup.

From just beyond the cracked door came Lily's voice. "Oh honey, you didn't have to fuss with all that."

Hastily she stuffed the brown bottle in her pocket and met Lily on the other side of the door. "It's no bother, really."

"I can sleep out here on the couch or the pullout."

"Nonsense," said Barbara. "You may as well be comfortable."

"Well, it does seem kind of funny. And I don't mean ha-ha funny." In the doorway Lily scratched at her neck as a bashful child might.

"That's how it felt to me last night. I can pull out the couch in the den if you prefer."

Lily shook her head. "Nah, better not to go to all that fuss."

"Well, goodnight then." Barbara flung her arms wide open. When was the last time, thought Lily, she'd hugged anyone for more than a quick pat on the back? Held a crying man, woman or child in her arms? Barbara rested her face on Lily's shoulder and said, "I can't thank you enough."

Lily closed the door and prepared to crawl into the bed and under the covers of a dead woman she never knew. She eyed the dresser against the wall opposite the queen bed, trying to quench an odd impulse to rummage through its drawers. Hadn't she just minutes ago declared to the young woman that it seemed an intrusion? It did, under the same roof and in the presence of an heir to whatever monetary assets Alice Thunderclap had accumulated in her lifetime.

In the ensuite bathroom, she gathered her cotton pajamas from the overnight bag, and drew from a bag of toiletries a toothbrush and a tube of Polident. Her entire set of teeth had been replaced one by one over time and left her with only dentures to remove and brush. She drew them from her mouth and gazed reluctantly upon a whole other face entirely, with the collapsing bite of an old crone. Like Jeckyll and Hyde—perhaps to match this strange impulse to go on the prowl, so contradictory to what she had expressed only minutes ago to Barbara. In the mirror she saw the face of a vagrant or a criminal, or perhaps a witch. She dumped her heart pills into a hand and gulped them down with a little Dixie cup of water.

In the mirror over the dresser appraising an aging body as one might an old automobile. Things were bound to go bad and need replacement and you did your best to keep the parts going as long as you could. Maintenance and quality fuel. Sometimes with food and sometimes little pills. She reached over to the bedside table to switch out the light. The moon's bright light shot through the blinds, creating random patterns on the ceiling, fuzzy to her naked eye. How many times, she thought, the words *love you* had been quick-mumbled between her and her sons. So hurriedly. Vacantly. Carelessly.

The propensity to draw into herself began after Dan's death. How easily she had slipped into the habit—relegating herself to the comfortable confines of home. It became harder and harder to push herself out the door. Before she knew it, human interaction had become a challenge. Just when she'd begun to warm up once again, Dorothy went and left this world. It was difficult to leave the house sometimes. A fish out of water. Strangers appeared before her every day she went out to collect the mail or go to the grocery store. However odd the circumstances, this woman with whom she'd just broke bread and shared wine and a game for two had summoned something from the depths. The joy of companionship. Imaginary Hearts partners on the computer could never compensate for a real person across from or beside you.

She sat up against the headboard, absent the drowsiness she'd felt all night. She became restless, eying the dresser and considering the personal effects likely inside. Plundering at the bidding of the recently bereaved did feel odd, an invasion of privacy. She considered waiting until the morning as planned. But curiosity got the better of her and she pushed the covers back, planted her feet and tiptoed like a burglar over to the dresser to fish around. Two piles of papers under the bathing suits, the left side formal, the right side more casual. The end-of-life instructions folder lay on top just where she'd replaced it. Underneath that more manila folders and after a few of those her hand met a blue legal-sized folder bearing the inscription in gold *Last Will and Testament*, with fancy gold trim bound by a golden thread. It may as well have had a padlock attached, for Lily Westfall and her sense of propriety anyway. She'd leave that one to the daughter now camped out in the guest room. On top of the other stack was a peculiar Kancu leaf and bamboo-bound book. She held it in her hands and marveled at the binding, three little string ties holding the pages. Its unique texture served to stir her curiosity far more than the formal folders that lay alongside it bearing the legal papers. She extracted an envelope placed in its pages like a bookmark and went to fetch her glasses from the vanity in the bathroom.

A letter addressed to Alice Thunderclap, the return addressee was one Melissa Beauregard. As carefully as one might a specimen, she drew the letter from the envelope.

*30 May 2004*

*Dear Alice,*

*You're the last real person I know. I don't know anything about anybody anymore. Everyone resides in his or her own world more and more and I see that true hearts are few and far between. I'm sorry to hear about your heart and your visits to the doctor. I love you more than words can say. I wish your children felt the same way. The good Lord swept down and took your Charlie too soon and you know I'm praying for your heavy heart. Your Roger seems eternally anxious and depressed despite his affluence, and I'm sorry I call it no less than affluence- my measuring stick for that level of wealth is the two-car garage. My own son Chris still hasn't found a job. It seems he's always looking for a job, but what with the market and the way companies just go laying people off there's no loyalty anymore! Geez, I remember our husbands and how hard they worked and how much they gave of their lives to their companies, and how much those companies valued them and how we reap the rewards in retirement. How is Florida these days, my friend? Has Barbara been to visit yet? My God, you've been waiting for years, haven't you? I don't know what's come over young people these days. So many without any direction. I'm sorry she's caused you so much grief and worry. Who knows where her trouble sprouted from, but God only knows you were a great mother, as good a mother to her as you were (are) a friend to me. She was such a sweet little girl and God only knows where she went wrong, but it seems like things like job and family and responsibility have gone completely out the window.*

*I look forward to seeing you up here in Cohasset next month and then down in your warm nook this winter. You're the last kind person I know, everyone's died off and I don't understand the young people nor they I (my own kids included). Nobody is real anymore, everyone puts on pretenses and the people in the supermarket work for some large conglomerate and they say have a nice day but they don't really mean it, it's just part of their job. Everything is so impersonal and each to their own business. Maybe that's what Barbara saw in the drugs and the alcohol- a means to escape a very lonely selfish world. But isn't it our responsibility to play nice and make it a little better of a world, like it was when we were kids? I've known you just about all my life Alice Thunderclap and you're the nicest friend anyone could wish for. I won't bother to spell out all the times you were there for me and for my dear late Bob- we'll just take that little trip down memory lane when you get here. I love you with all my heart old girl.*

*Missy*

# 4

Lily Westfall drifted out of deep slumbers to an unfamiliar room. The morning sun pierced the blinds, slivers of light cast onto mint green walls with floral prints, framed oils of brightly lit botanical gardens. She shifted from her side to lay on her back and rub at her eyes, refreshed and with a little less of the morning aches in her hips and lower back. She thought, I must get a new mattress. Propping herself against the headboard of Alice Thunderclap's expansive bed, alien surroundings served to contradict her comfort with an uneasy and profound sense of guilt. She lay in the bed of the most private chamber of someone who'd risen unfailingly until a mere few hours ago, with a sense of having desecrated the inner sanctum of the dead. Throwing her legs over the side of the bed and not finding familiar slippers to slide her feet into, she went barefoot on the plush carpet to the bathroom ensuite to pee. Then she drew the blinds, the sunlight like a lamp that brought to life all the bright colors imbued in the flowers of the wall art. She shuffled over to the bedroom door and pressed an ear against it. No sign of life, only the hum of the central air unit. She turned the knob slowly, walking barefoot along the plush carpet into the living room. The door to the guest room was still closed. She tiptoed into the kitchen area, the tile floor cold under her feet until she reached the area rug in front of the sink where she fetched a glass and drew water from the tap for her meds. Blood pressure, cholesterol, heart. The statins put her off grapefruit and she regretted that. Her stomach grumbled and she considered a quiet exit and home for breakfast and to let the dog out, glancing at the large refrigerator. She couldn't bring herself to open it and rummage around—food intended for someone now unable to eat, to walk, to breathe. The stainless-steel door was riddled with magnetic clips and the papers they held. Activities schedule. Scrawled reminder notes. Doctor appointments. Doctors' prescriptions. The little ornaments bore logos of local businesses. One larger magnet bore a sketch of a rustic wooden fence, a pastoral meadow beyond it with the inscription, *Learn to prize silence. Embrace and appreciate stillness. Sometimes you hear more when you speak less.*

She scratched at an itch and walked back over to the master bedroom, standing again before the dresser, stooping to pull the bottom drawer, the one with all the papers. She extracted the peculiar Kancu leaf and bamboo-bound book. Inside on its pages she saw scribbling in the same hand as the notes on the refrigerator door. She brought the little book over to the bed and climbed back into it, perching herself knees up against the headboard. Outside the birds were singing in the early light. All else was quiet. And in that stillness she pored over the cursive scrawling that comprised Alice Thunderclap's epistolary journal.

*

*Remembering Cohasset and the house and those awful unclean smells. Humid and close, foul odor of the unbathed. Mother now neglectful. Father going through vodka like water. How fast everything changed when the flow of money dried up like water supply does when a city main bursts or a well dries up. No food for days sometimes. Father's coughing echoing down the stairs to the dusty hallway. Curses in between. Steering clear of him. Hiding in the empty pantry. Foraging for blackberries. So young and uncertain. How vulnerable. Like a hatchling fallen from its nest. Ready for Harold to swoop down and gather me up, flutter his wings and carry me skyward.*

*

The dimensions of the Cumberbatch open floor plan living area were being carefully calculated. Ted tamped down one end of the tape measure in the floorboard near the curio cabinet and crept, hunched over, toward the wall at the other side of the room. The doorbell rang before he could steady the unwieldy tape measure and get an accurate tally of the room's square footage to verify the contractor's estimate. They were replacing the carpet, how he hated carpet. Who liked carpet these days? It demanded an upkeep and maintenance that did little to prevent the accumulation of dust mites. A hotbed for allergies—collecting dust and deeper down… dirt. The Cumberbatches wanted good old faux-wood flooring they could run a dry mop over every so often and polish maybe once a year.

The contractor had agreed to make a special trip out on a Sunday. He arrived ten minutes early. This irked Ted Cumberbatch as much as if he were ten minutes late and Ted made no attempt to mask his annoyance. After barking at Marge to stall the guy while he finished taking his measurements, he all but shoved his wife out of the way to face a young man in jeans and a yellow collar shirt with the company logo. The shirt fit him tight and put on display an enormous belly. The man stuck out a beefy hand. "Good morning sir, I'm Mark. Nice to meet you."

"Well Mark," said Ted with a loose-grip handshake. "Running a little early today aren't we?"

Mark shrugged, a smile opening his face enough to display a wide gap between front teeth, and said he didn't want to get behind on his calls on a Sunday with a wife and new baby at home.

Ted opened the storm door to admit him and trailed behind the large man, frowning at his back. "I'm fed up with this carpet," he said, glancing over at Marge. "So's my wife."

"Well then. Let's get it fixed," Mark said amiably, dropping a thick binder to the kitchen table. Ted watched while he measured out the living area. "Now," he said, retrieving the big black binder from the table, "let me show you what we've got to offer in the way of our wood flooring."

"*Fake* wood flooring," Ted said.

"Well now," Mark remained standing and Ted didn't invite him to sit. "We do have real wood options too, Mr. Cumberbatch."

"I know. They're way too expensive."

"Now hold on hold on. We can work with ya. I'll show you something along more economical lines."

Marge retreated to the back porch and her Robert Ludlum paperback, unable to focus, given a husband not predisposed toward politeness and civility when engaged with anyone in the service industry.

"I hope," Ted was saying, "you can understand we're on a very fixed budget. We have a house under water up in Michigan and a deadbeat son falling behind on the bills. Of course we'd prefer to have *real* wood. I don't mind if I have to do the staining myself."

"Ted," Marge called from the porch, dropping the book to her lap, "I will not have you on your bad knee staining the floor and–"

"–Marge—"

"–speeding yourself towards knee replacement–"

"–Marge keep quiet—"

"—Not to mention having to clear all this heavy furniture–"

"–Marge leave this to me."

"I'm only telling you–"

"I'll take care of this."

He was speaking in the taut and quiet manner that preceded a fit. She brought the book back up from her lap, knowing full well that reading was now an exercise in futility.

The phone rang.

"Would you get that please," Ted shook his head at the carpet.

She glared at him. "I was fully intending to."

It was their son Ted Jr. Teddy. Up in Michigan.

"Teddy," she said, "your father was just talking about you."

She glared once again at her husband but he was fully engaged with the contractor. The woodenness in her son's voice promised no diversion from the tension around her.

"What's wrong? What's the matter honey?"

"I don't know, I just can't get out of bed in the morning sometimes," Teddy mumbled.

"Are you boozing again?"

"No. I just can't take this much longer. I'm losing my grip. It's getting hard to do the smallest things."

"Where's Ellen?"

"She wants me out of the house."

"She wants you out of *our* house?"

"Um, let's not split hairs over this."

"No one's splitting any hairs Teddy. If anybody's leaving it's her."

"I couldn't do that to her."

Marge sighed in response. There was silence over the line a good while and then she could hear her son crying.

"Look," she said. "Why don't you come down for a few days? Maybe you just need to get away. See things from a fresh perspective."

"I don't know. I have job applications out and–"

"Any interviews?"

"Nobody gets back to me. I'm fifty-two. It's age discrimination."

"Maybe so," said Marge. "Maybe so."

"I feel like such a failure."

"Nonsense honey. You just need to get back on your feet. You were not so bad before the layoff."

"My kids don't even talk to me."

"Nonsense. Kelly said she saw you last week."

"*Saw* me, but didn't talk. Not the way people should. Definitely not the way fathers and daughters should anyway."

"Teddy listen. I'm going to get online and book a flight for you if you're not going to do it yourself—"

"Mom I don't need—"

"Nonsense. I know what you need. A mother knows best."

He sighed. "Look, I can book a flight when I want to book a flight. I don't need people telling me what to do."

"Well," Marge sighed. "You just let us know when you're coming."

"Mom, I can't even get the electric bill paid. Dad's gonna go through the roof when he finds that out."

"He's busy going through the floor right now," said Marge, glancing over at her husband hassling with the contractor.

"What?"

"We're having our floors redone. Ridding ourselves of that hideous carpet."

"Well *that's* gonna cost a pretty penny."

"Your father's doing his level best to have it done for a song."

When she hung up the phone they were wrapping up. She shook her head and sighed while her husband shook their guest's hand and said he'd get back to him after looking into a few more estimates.

*

Kenny Fitzroy lay awake tossing and turning most of the night. When he finally gave up on any chance of sleep, he climbed out of bed and went to draw the blinds. His thoughts went to church. He hadn't been to church in years. He'd attended Catholic services with his mother as a young boy. She was a devout Catholic until she befriended a Buddhist at UCLA where she was on faculty. Then a Hindu, and from there one belief system at a time her scope broadened—his mom had a curious mind that led her away from singularities. He'd inherited this curiosity, but unlike his mother he couldn't channel his intellectual absorption into a career. His father was a Christian Scientist. The handful of those services he attended as a young boy were ordered and solemn. He and his father would polish their shoes alongside one another and then they'd drive downtown along quiet Sunday streets. When his father died, a distraught mother sent him to live with her sister in west Texas. The Evangelical services he attended there made the Christian Scientist services seem like a picnic. The vacation-like quality he sensed at the sight of vast stretches of flatland dotted with cattle and oil drills was quickly snuffed when he crossed the threshold of the Baptist Evangelical church. An enormous congregation of humans stuffed into such a small cramped space. The odor of sweaty bodies, hopping about and flailing their arms, speaking in tongues. Solemnity and decorum went out the window. It was disgraceful and it scared the hell out of him. He cowered from those gathered in the pews, flinched when one of them reached out to touch him.

He considered seeking out a church this morning because he didn't know where else to go with his restless thoughts, suddenly all was not right with the world. He had commitments now. Perhaps it was redemption he needed to seek for himself. All that time wasted getting high and listening to music, starting and ending rogue bands that played for paltry crowds in cramped clubs for meager sums. Flopping into a chair for hours on end to devour biographies. The exploits of others. Studying course schedules with the intent of going back to school but never acting on it. Procrastinating and killing time like nobody's business. Maybe what he needed was to turn his back on his lifestyle over the entirety of his adult life and begin grinning and bearing it like everyone else. Perhaps he might consult Frank Alsatian on how to do this. Frank with his cut-and-dried opinions, his patriotism, and his faithfulness. Dutiful to the last with his wife—driving over to that extended care facility every day without fail. Maybe he should talk to Frank Alsatian. Whatever the case, he knew things had irrevocably changed and his premature retirement had been abruptly upended.

He put the coffee on and went about fixing instant oatmeal, retrieving the little plastic tubs of blueberries and strawberries from an overcrowded refrigerator, as he did each and every morning. The same breakfast habit. This morning this ritual was laden with sadness—it seemed pathetic to him as did every other aspect of his life. Kenny Fitztroy pulled the usual chair from under the Formica table and considered the empty seat across from him. Glanced over at bookshelves lined with the achievements of others. Collections of his favorite authors. Books on art, design and architecture. His enormous music library culled from hours on end combing the aisles of Tower Records when CDs were all the rage. Kenny dropped his spoon into the bowl of oatmeal and he began to weep. He was grieving a lost life, this was crystal clear from the first tear. He'd glided along through life, heedless of the warning signs, negligent to the folly of trying to perform life without a rehearsal.

His phone still hadn't found a home since he'd arrived with all his boxes—it sat mostly lifeless on the floor. It did bother him that nobody called much. Now Kenny dreaded the shrill ring—notice that someone was trying to reach him, because that someone would very likely be Kathy from Connecticut, and they had the business of life to work out between them. Talking to someone other than her was of the first order today. He badly needed to move his mouth and spill all those things flitting about in that noisy noggin of his. Peggy Beamish came to mind, but she'd already claimed her quiet alone-time Sunday and they'd arranged a golf outing for tomorrow. He considered calling Barbara, then dismissed the thought. She had enough on her hands. He sure as hell didn't want to hang around the house like usual. He had to get both his feet and his mouth moving.

He didn't have far to go, walking in the immense heat in khakis and a golf shirt, to a church just beyond the front gate on Coral Beach Boulevard. At the immense front-door he hesitated. He'd have preferred to really go out on a limb and try something extreme, but there were no extremes in Sunnyville. So he found himself standing before a more familiar landscape, Our Lady of Lourdes Catholic Church. Climbing the concrete steps and tugging at one of the tall wooden doors that opened onto a neo-modernist building of wood and earth tones, a far cry from the concrete behemoth of childhood and his mother. Perhaps, Kenny thought, there might be new ideas to be found underneath these high vaulted ceilings, the stone interior of yesteryear supplanted by cozy wood.

Mass was underway and a few heads turned at the entrance of the latecomer. The priest was reading from the gospel of Luke and was in the middle of the parable of the lost coin. *Or what woman, having ten silver coins, if she loses one coin, does not light a lamp, sweep the house, and search carefully until she finds it? And when she has found it, she calls her friends and neighbors together, saying, 'Rejoice with me, for I have found the piece which I lost!' Likewise, I say to you, there is joy in the presence of the angels of God over one sinner who repents.*

The ensuing words given in the priest's homily were based on the gospel. Kenny's thoughts went to the structure of the Mass and he felt a tinge of comfort to know the memory hadn't escaped him. Nor had the metaphorical nature of parables, the allegorical nature of the coin. The priest went on to say that the coin represented not only the repented sinner but the missing piece, for that woman, of a spiritual life and her joy at having re-discovered it.

So here was Kenny the Coin, pondering Kathy from Connecticut. Mister non-conformity himself—unobtrusively ensconced in just another pew among the rows of pews, seeking answers like everyone else. A Sunday among the congregation. He'd come to idle, to people watch from the best vantage point, the rear of the church. He was afforded a view of an enormous structure filled to far less than capacity. He took in every man, woman and child, and imagined comfortably settled lives populated by abundant family and friends. Lives that left in their wake rewarding careers, memories distilled in family albums, pride-inducing progeny. Things that were the stuff of dreams to Kenny Fitzroy. Those who sat on the pews in front of him also brought their own fears and worries, but he was sure none of these bore the gravity of his own. These people had invented clever retirement schemes that vouchsafed them a life of leisure—where most often there need be nothing more on the day's itinerary than lounging around the pool. True, they had health issues he had yet to face, but their children were raised and the bills were paid. None of them faced any more sudden financial setbacks, none dreaded the prospect of that unexpected layoff, none lost sleep over a decline in the market value of their house, none faced the grave responsibility of parenthood at fifty-seven years old.

Still, he beheld the solemn faces and thought, were they any better off than he? With their singular lives, focused on a calculated career and suffering from burnout for the majority of it. He had spent nearly a lifetime condemning anyone who submitted to work for The Man, played such condemnation over and over in his mind like a mantra. But lately it began to dawn on him that some of the congregation may have actually enjoyed much of their careers. This thought returned his somber mood to him. He continued to brood, tuning out most of the remainder of the sermon.

He was seated next to an elderly woman dressed far better than he for the occasion—a long-sleeved floral print dress with pearls and a brooch at the neckline. She smelled of talcum powder and perfume. The time came for the sign of peace and he took her wrinkled hand very briefly, neither of them troubling themselves to put much of a smile on. When the Mass was finished and the congregation began to gather their things and file out of the church, he remained seated.

Among those shuffling out, he recognized Ted Cumberbatch from Pub Night and imagined Ted's prayers centered around his woebegone unemployed son up in Minnesota sitting beside a troublesome girlfriend in an empty dark house. Cumberbatch shot him a look of recognition and Kenny got up and followed him out into the vestibule to shake hands. The beefy guy crushed Kenny's hand, making him wish he'd left his rings off his fingers. "Haven't seen you around this place before."

Kenny caught a whiff of a strong cologne.

"No, I-I mean, this is my first time out."

"Oh. Good. Hope you enjoyed it."

The remark struck Kenny as odd—he thought church services were more to be endured than enjoyed, and Cumberbatch's face and much of the others didn't exhibit much enjoyment.

Up behind Ted came someone that Kenny didn't recognize, beaming at them both. Cumberbatch turned and seemed to be racking his brain for a name.

"Beamish," the newcomer said after a beat. "Mike Beamish."

Another handshake that swallowed Kenny's hand. They started in on some small talk and no sooner had Kenny got his mouth moving both men began checking their watches. Cumberbatch bowed out, leaving Mike Beamish alone with Kenny. As Beamish turned to leave, Kenny took him by the elbow and looked at him imploringly. "May I ask you something?"

"Sure pal. Something on your mind?"

"Yeah."

"Something troubling you?"

"Well, yeah."

Beamish glanced over his shoulder to an almost empty vestibule. "There's a priest," he said. "I– I mean if it's something serious. They hear confessions."

"Yeah. I know that."

Beamish rolled his eyes. "Lord knows I sure as hell could use one."

Kenny tilted his head in curiosity.

"*Oh* yeah," said Beamish, gesturing at a pair of cane-backed chairs in the vestibule next to the staircase leading up to the organ loft. "But that's a long story."

They settled themselves and after an awkward pause Beamish said, "What's yours anyway?"

"My *what?*"

"Your story."

"Well," said Kenny, "it's just that it in many respects I um, never grew up. I mean never really grew up and there's so much I missed out on."

"Yeah?"

"Like fatherhood. At least until now." Kenny drooped his head.

Beamish leaned in. "You're gonna be a dad?"

"Looks like it."

"You're a little old to be a dad. If you don't mind my saying."

"Yeah. I know. It's a mess." Kenny felt a lump in his throat. "I don't know why I'm telling you all this."

Beamish took his elbow. "How old is she, kiddo?"

"Late forties, I think."

"You think."

"I seem to remember her telling me that."

"Okay. How old are you. If you don't mind me asking."

"Fifty-seven."

"Okay."

"It was one night. A one-night stand."

"She have kids?"

"Two. They're grown."

"You know much about them?"

"No. We only spent the night together. We didn't have much time to talk."

"Right," Mike Beamish splayed his hands and nodded, acknowledging the obvious. One-night stands were old hat to him.

"I don't know what she wants to do," said Kenny. "I hinted at having an abortion and I feel horrible about that."

"Sure," Beamish pursed his lips and glanced at the altar, the Virgin, the Child, the saints.

"I'm thinking," Kenny lowered his voice to almost a whisper, "I can't take my words back, but I gotta do, I don't know, some sort of correction. I gotta make her know it's not my decision. I gotta tell her something to balance out my seemingly pushing her towards—"

"I know—"

"—a decision she may not want." Kenny lowered his head, wrung his hands.

Beamish clapped him on the back. "You'll do fine."

Kenny had more to say, but Beamish clearly had to get going.

He re-entered the enormous innards of a church now gone silent. The kneeler squeaked when he turned it out. He dropped to his knees and rested his elbows on the pew in front of him. Squeezing his eyes shut to conjure up a meditation of sorts. Trying to remember from those classes at the spiritual center in Austin. Attempting in vain to return his mind to silence. Kenny the Gabber—the king of verbosity, the guy who could chew your ear off with a seemingly endless supply of words, Kenny the Idler—the King of Killing Time, Kenny the Inheritor, Kenny the Impregnator, Kenny the Avoider. Kenny the Lost Coin.

*

In a dead woman's bed reading the dead woman's journal Lily said her morning prayers. She got up a few times to use the ensuite bathroom. With a heavy sigh, she returned the journal to its place in the bottom drawer of the bureau. Then tiptoeing to the kitchen, vacillating between putting the coffee on and foraging the cabinets for breakfast or returning to her house. Rex would need let out and so she dressed and put her shoes on, scribbled a message on a notepad and left it on the kitchen counter.

People were already out and about watering their grass or tending to gardens. The central air units hummed along, the day already gone hot and humid. Feeling very much an indigent, unaccustomed to stepping out in public unwashed and unfed, she waved at the neighbors.

Rex greeted her as soon as she crossed the threshold, standing against her on his tiny hind legs and panting. Calm down little man, she said. Calm down.

She fed the dog and took him out to the patch of grass that constituted her back yard. In the kitchen she fixed herself instant oatmeal and orange juice and put the coffee on. She showered, had a cup of coffee and decided to go look in on Barbara. She got the dog's leash and she and Rex headed back up the road to her former neighbor's house. She knocked lightly on the door and got no answer. She hitched the dog to the light post out front and let herself in. The house remained as quiet as a museum after hours.

At first she thought it was the refrigerator, but it soon became clear that the moaning and groaning sounds were human and very real. When she walked across the kitchen to the guestroom the door was still closed. She turned the doorknob and cracked the door enough to see the end of the bed and under the bedcovers a mass, oddly menacing in its inertness. A lumpy thing that didn't belong there. She cracked the door open wider. The young lady lay curled up on her side on the bed, the pillows and sheets strewn about in a manner that suggested violence and struggle. Next to her on the nightstand, a brown prescription bottle, its lid on the carpet.

"Barbara?"

The room had the musty smell of skin and sweat. Lily placed a hand on the young lady's bare shoulder, tugging her onto her side. The face she met was pallid and wet and chalk white, mouth open and eyes closed, hair strewn about her sweaty neck and forehead.

"Oh my God!" Lily shouted, trying to lift Barbara up by the shoulders. The limp body kept collapsing back in dead weight. She seized Barbara by the shoulders, shaking her and slapping at her face. Barbara's eyes opened briefly and closed. Lily slapped her again in a panic.

"What on earth happened?" Lily panted.

Barbara's response was muffled and incoherent.

"I'm calling nine-one-one."

"No." Barbara's speech was faint and slurred as she propped herself up on an elbow and collapsed back down on the bed. "No need."

Lily fetched the prescription bottle. Percoset. Oxycodone.

"How many of these did you take?"

"I… I on't weemembuh."

"Try."

"Have to throw up," she whispered weakly.

Lily scampered to the guest bathroom just outside the door. The light was on and there was the lingering stench of vomit. She snatched a hand towel to run under the cold-water tap, deliberating between attending to the young lady or calling nine-one-one. She returned with the cold towel and pressed it to Barbara's forehead.

They sat still for a spell and then she helped Barbara to her feet and took her by the elbow and they staggered toward the bathroom, pausing at the threshold. When the young lady went to crouch once again beside the commode, Lily supported her weight as best she could. Barbara began to retch and when nothing happened, she stuck a finger down her throat and the vomit gushed from her like a waterfall. The stench was vile in that enclosed space and Lily switched on the exhaust fan. She watched Barbara pant before the toilet bowl, beads of sweat on her forehead.

"Oh God," Barbara panted, sweeping damp and stringy hair from her face. "Oh my God."

"Where did you get those?"

Barbara lifted an arm limply to the medicine chest above the sink.

"How many did you take?"

"Six I think. No… maybe eight."

She held her head over the bowl and once again began to retch.

Lily bolted to the kitchen and picked up the phone. Her son Jack, the pharmacist. He'd know what to do. She rang the number and paced back and forth as it rang unanswered. She left a hasty message on his answering machine, realizing upon hanging up that she hadn't given him the number at Alice Thunderclap's. Rex pawed at her feet. Then she rang her son Billy, with the sobering thought that he might have some experience with these things. What she could only guess at, but didn't want to know. After a few rings, he picked up. Hastily, breathlessly, she filled him in.

"Your *neighbor?*"

"Her daughter, Billy. It's Oxycodone."

"Oh man."

"What should I do?" Lily rolled her eyes at the ceiling, as if her question were directed to heaven and the Almighty.

"Is she coherent?"

"She wasn't but I think she is now."

"You have the bottle?"

"Yes."

"Is it empty?"

"Yes."

"Where did she get it?"

"The medicine chest. Her mother's."

"Try and find out how much she took."

"She said six or eight."

"Six or eight," he echoed back.

"I tried to get a hold of Jack. I got his voicemail."

"Uh-huh. Well, it's a good thing she's throwing up. That's what she needs to do. Make sure she throws up until she can't throw up anymore."

"Okay."

"Keep her talking and make sure she makes sense."

"Okay."

"Keep her hydrated. Plenty of water."

"Okay. Do you think I should call nine-one-one?"

"Not if she's coherent. Gotta check the dosage on the bottle. Per pill."

Lily brought the bottle up close to her eyes and read the small print. 10mg per tablet."

"She take them all at once?"

"I guess so. We went to bed at midnight."

"That's a pretty high dose. Alcohol?"

"Wine. Let me see, the bottle is empty."

"Did you help empty it?"

"Yes," said Lily, "I had my share. Couple of glasses."

"Mom."

"I know."

"Anyway, that's good. She's not passed out right? She talking to you?"

"I'm okay," Barbara uttered feebly from the bathroom. "Just weak. Sick to my stomach."

"Right. Hold on a minute."

Lily dropped the phone and returned to the bathroom with a glass of water. "Do you want me to take you to the hospital?"

"Uh-uh," Barbara's voice was still thin and weak. "I got this."

Lily paused at the bathroom door a moment, arms folded, watching Barbara sip at the glass before returning to Billy on the phone.

"Keep her drinking lots of water Mom. That'll flush it out, as good as having your stomach pumped. As long as she's coherent you're probably okay."

"*Probably*?"

She hung up the phone and returned to Barbara. "Are you sure it was only eight?"

"That's all there was left," Barbara said hoarsely.

Lily poured another glass of water and when she returned Barbara was lying on her back and massaging her belly.

"Here," she said. "Sit up. Drink this."

Barbara propped herself up on her elbows. "I got this." Some color was restored to her face and she started mumbling.

"Speak clearly," Lily pleaded.

Barbara's speech was slurred. "Back to the land of the living," she murmured, raising the glass to her lips.

"I'd say you nearly killed yourself."

"Sorry. Damn." Barbara drew a deep breath, propping her head up on the pillows against the wall.

"I'm an old woman and you ask me to stay and keep you company and then you go and do something like this."

"I'm so sorry," she muttered, arm turning to rubber after an attempt to gesture. "I feel so stupid."

"Give me that glass. Sit up."

Lily hadn't spoken to anyone like this in years, not since chastising the mischievous little boys that were now her full-grown sons. Barbara pushed herself up and sat on the edge of the bed, collapsing her head to her hands, rubbing her temples. "I think I have to throw up again."

"Do it," said Lily, tapping Barbara's hand. "Empty out."

She went to take Barbara's elbow once again, but Barbara waved her away. "I'm so sorry. I got this," she said again.

Lily wrung her hands while Barbara pushed herself up from the bed, still wobbly, grabbing at furniture and doorknobs to steady herself along the way to the bathroom. "Please don't call nine-one-one," she muttered.

After she'd made a few trips, Lily refilling the glass with water, the two sat wordlessly beside one another on the bed a good while.

"Well," Lily said at last, "you've done a fine job of disrupting this old lady's peaceful existence. Death in the first act. Family trouble. Attempted poisoning after the intermission. Near death in the final act? I mean, what do you do for an encore, go on a killing spree?"

Barbara dropped her head to her hands. "I'm so sorry. I had no right to invite you into this. Please go, you've done enough for me."

*Soon's I get home*, thought Lily, *I'm going to check my blood pressure.* She patted Barbara on the shoulder and rose from the bed. Rex lay just outside the door with his chin over his paw, eyes darting about nervously. She took his leash and they went outside for some air.

When she returned Barbara was in the kitchen steadying herself over the sink. There was only the sound of the wall clock ticking. Lily pursed her lips, her eyes welling up. "I read your mother's journal," she said.

"What?"

"She kept a diary of sorts."

"Did she?"

Lily gave a slow nod. "You're mentioned quite a lot."

Barbara said, "Probably all bad."

"Some of it, yes."

Barbara nodded resignedly.

"But she loved you."

"I don't know about that. If she ever did, she sure did a real good job of hiding it."

"She didn't know how to show it. But she loved you." Lily placed a hand on her shoulder.

Barbara heaved her shoulders, began sobbing. "I'm so ashamed."

Lily rubbed her shoulder. "When did you start doing drugs Barbara?"

Barbara coughed. "I mean, we smoked pot when I was in high school, some other harmless stuff. But I didn't run across the painkillers until after college. After a surgery."

"Did you know your mother wanted to help? Again? She was looking into a rehab center. Again."

"I didn't know that."

"Won't you even consider it?"

"No need. I've been clean. I've managed to stay away from them."

"Till now."

"I'm under a lot of stress," Barbara shrugged, "I opened the medicine cabinet and there they were."

"There's none left."

"No. But maybe I need to find a meeting."

"What kind of meeting?"

Barbara closed her eyes and said nothing.

"Like, for drugs?" Lily asked. "I mean addicts, that sort of thing?"

Barbara brought her face to her hands and nodded forcefully. "I was doing so well. And now for you to have walked in on this."

"It's not an easy thing to have stumbled into," Lily said, wringing her hands and thinking she didn't know the right words, they were odd to her ears, sounded painfully off-target from what this woman needed to hear.

"Sorry for all the mess," Barbara unburied her face from her hands. "I don't want you to feel like you have to do anything for me anymore."

"I want you to walk with me and Rex," said Lily, fetching a clump of tissues from the box on the desk. " Just a little. I want to know you're okay before I leave."

"Alright," Barbara said. "Just let me try and throw up one more time."

Lily returned to the bathroom, fetched the pine-scented air freshener from the commode and sprayed generously into every nook and cranny of the tiny space. Then the guestroom, frantically trying to cover up a foulness that hung in the air like a demon, herself a shaman with an aerosol can as a talisman. Covering the ugly stench of unhealthy choices, thinking would that there were an aerosol that might obliterate loneliness, hopelessness and despair.

*

It had been three years since the Beamishes pulled up the stakes in Michigan for Sunny Glen Palms and sometimes it felt as if it were three weeks to Peggy. She spent over a year cultivating friends as one would a garden. Establishing a social network as one might sow the seeds and see which ones might take and bear fruit. The Michigan Club, the Thursday night Pub Nights, the pickleball court—all these venues served as fertile soil on which to scatter seeds. For that first year or so, she carried herself with a buoyancy, an optimism that quelled the still but turbulent waters of her long marriage to a man whose detachment and avoidance knew no bounds. The initial excitement waned, gave way to the doldrums she found herself in now, pouring her third cup of coffee while flipping through the pages of the Sunny Glen Palmer community newspaper. She'd spent, she reflected, a lifetime as a person fabricated from others' wants, needs and desires, pretending over much of her life. She looked forward to being her true unfiltered self, it was late in the game and why the hell shouldn't she? From now on her human interactions would be unfettered and unfiltered—there would be a genuine quality and in this way the output of her garden would be real and colorful and pure beauty would spring from the dirt. But instead she'd discovered much to her chagrin that not many people around her were similarly inclined to change up the game plan this late in life. The pretensions, self-consciousness, the adherence to social norms continued. People were polite, if guarded, trading their frowns for a smile when they met a stranger. People talked behind one another's backs. People regularly complained. After three years, there was not much in her garden for Peggy Beamish to take in and admire.

The phone rang. It was her son Tom in Minnesota and she could tell right away he was wound up. "Where are we gonna put all these out-of-town guests Mom?"

"I don't know, ask your father. This was his idea," she sighed. "The party I mean."

"Okay. Put him on the phone then."

"He's not here."

"Where is he?"

"I have no earthly idea. He's been disappearing a lot lately. Just like old times."

An audible sigh at the other end of the line and a long pause before she said, "They're all adults, they'll figure it out."

"How many have RSVP'd they're coming?"

"I don't know."

"Hey. Mom. You don't sound too enthusiastic about this."

"I'm not. Like I said, it wasn't my idea."

"Oh really now."

"I don't know why we have to make such a big deal of it."

"Fiftieth wedding anniversaries *are* a big deal. A cause for celebration."

"Yeah, to all appearances. Put on a show for a few hours."

"Dammit," Tom grunted. "This thing sure seems to be turning into a colossal failure."

"Well," she said, "a suitable tribute to the marriage."

"C'mon Mom, stop talking like that. I hate it when you talk like that."

"Well I've been holding it in for years."

"No you haven't. You've been bitching about it like crazy the last ten I'd say."

"Well maybe it's a sort of catharsis."

"I *knew* we should've had the party up here. Patty and I could've done all the organizing."

"You mean Patty could've done all the organizing. You men are all alike."

"Well, when Dad gets home, have him call me. How big is this room anyway?"

"What room?"

"The *party* room. C'mon Mom, focus."

"Enough to hold fifty, I'd say," she said impassively.

"Not that huge auditorium they held the New Year's bash in?"

"Oh God no. It's one of the meeting rooms nearby."

"Okay."

"I know my cousins from Utah are coming. They winter in Sarasota."

"Well, there's a few guests, anyway."

"How about your son Jeff?"

"Yeah, Jeff's still coming."

"I'm looking forward to seeing my favorite grandson."

"Jeff's made us proud."

"You see less and less of that these days. He married well too."

"Yes he did. She's a peach."

"Wish I could say the same."

"You *are* a peach Mom. A real pain in the ass. But a peach no less."

"I didn't mean that. I meant the part about marrying well."

"I wish you'd stop airing your dirty laundry."

"Well, I'm just glad Jeff and his lovely wife are going to stay with us."

"This may be the last time they do for a while Mom."

"Don't be so maudlin."

"No. I mean you don't have the space to have great grandkids running around. We just got the news. Ella's pregnant."

Peggy drew her breath. "Oh God, that's wonderful news!"

"I'm going to be a grandfather. A grandfather! Can you believe it?"

"Oh that's impossible," Peggy said, with a tinge of sadness at feeling old beyond her years at sixty-nine, "I'll have to call them and congratulate them."

"Well, I gotta run over there right now Mom. Talk to you before the weekend. Tell Dad to call me."

"I'll let him know whenever he turns up."

Peggy returned the phone to the base and drummed fingernails with worn and cracked polish on the counter. Fingers that once held rings now unornamented. Wrists that once bore bracelets of fine gold and silver. The unremarkable wooden box that lay buried in the top drawer of her dresser merely a vessel for unused fine jewelry. Into a more decorative mahogany box on top of her dresser she crammed her costume jewelry. Perhaps, she thought, that's what she'd avail herself of for the big wedding anniversary party—costume jewelry, because costumes were for shows, and the whole thing was, as she'd just told her son Tom, a show.

*

Mike Beamish was at that moment dressing himself in the locker room of the South Club after swimming a few laps in the indoor pool. Wringing out a mushy Speedo and stuffing himself back into his Sunday best for a few cocktails at the clubhouse, going from church pew to bar stool.

His wife had dropped the church routine before they left Michigan for Florida. She did accompany him one Sunday, shortly after they arrived, to Our Lady of Lourdes Catholic Church. On the ride over and entering the tall and imposing doors of the church, Mike found himself in the way one might on a first date—in the grip of that anxiety that presents when one hopes for a good outcome, like hoping she enjoyed the movie because she would always associate the movie with him and the date. Out of the corner of his eye he spied his wife scanning the pews and fidgeting from time to time with the contents of her purse, clearly on a fact-finding mission. At the end of the Mass, it was obvious to him she was no longer a match for these rituals and no change of venue could change that fact. And so, each Sunday he shaved and dressed for church, while she remained on the back porch sipping her coffee and cutting coupons out of the Sunday Tampa Tribune. He would leave without saying goodbye, with the sense his wife held mild contempt for his having upheld an old habit she no longer attached any reverence to. As if it were not a corporeal being but a phantom of their past that shaved and dressed and slipped wordlessly out the front door, climbed into the car and drove off for some kind of redemption. Or perhaps appeasement to an invisible, ineffable, distant and unsympathetic God. It was as if his wife was afforded a moral superiority without having to rally herself each Sunday morning. Despite his best efforts to hold them at bay, these thoughts continued to plague him for the entire duration of every Mass.

*

Lily Westfall keyed the door to her house, Rex barking out a greeting, nails scraping the linoleum, at her feet as she placed her overnight bag onto the counter and checked the answering machine. Her son Jack had left a message, his usual even tone now laced with worry. She called him back to tell him everything was fine.

"Well I'm glad to hear that Mom," he said, "As a pharmacist, I'd have had to advised you call an ambulance immediately, no matter what. As a son, I hate to hear about all this trouble."

"I know," she said.

"What on earth are you getting yourself involved with?"

"Everything's fine. The girl's okay, after all."

"Well that's good. Just don't go and mix yourself up too much in other people's stuff."

"Well, I like this girl," she said. "She's very sweet, she's just had a few bad turns I reckon."

After she'd hung up, Rex followed her into the den, panting at her feet while she flopped into the recliner, then jumping into her lap and she petted him and said *easy there, not so rough for goodness sakes* as she always did and where she'd have expected it to return her to comfortable habits, it failed to. Rex kept sniffing and snorting with uncommon emphasis. When he'd settled down her eyes grew heavy, where normally she'd soon be fast asleep, she found herself restless between the ears. Jumbled thoughts that lent nothing towards the comfort she took in the usual predictability and order. Things were making less and less sense to her as she'd increasingly kept to herself. Kept to herself. It had become a way of life to Lily Westfall. Now it seemed, just like that, she'd lost all perspective. Where did one draw the line between common decency and overcompensating?

The phone startled her awake and she let it go ringing. With a sigh she realized she'd forgotten to remove her hearing aids. It was a rare occasion to have the phone ring and she seldom came home to a blinking light on the answering machine. The machine clicked on and she listened while the disembodied voice droned its default factory greeting. She pushed the dog from her lap and began to extricate herself from the chair, pausing to catch her breath, almost leaning back against the headrest before deciding better to check it in case something was wrong. She stood up and steadied herself on the armrest.

Barbara's voice pierced the silence. *Hello Lily, it's Barbara. Listen, I just wanted to say I'm so sorry and thanks for all your help. I just don't want you to feel like you owe me anything right now. You've done enough. I just think you don't need all this excitement at your age. Thanks, um, bye.*

*

The Cumberbatches returned from the supermarket, where a run on toilet paper left a row of shelves bare. Every Sunday Marge skimmed the articles of the Tampa Tribune while fervently clipping coupons—most of the items inside their cabinets were got at a discount. At the supermarket she was subjected, aisle by aisle, to her husband's dogged iteration of the flooring replacement issue. She shared his desire if not urgency to have the carpets up. While he rambled on, she hummed along distractedly to herself without indulging him even the briefest acknowledgement.

He carried his anxiety back to the house along with the groceries and once again a home whose colorful décor cast in bright beams of sunshine, pregnant with possibilities for joy, were befouled with his very un-joyous presence. No amount of tropical plants, stained-glass art, or neatly framed watercolors of broad beach landscapes could suffice to put him at ease.

When the last item was stuffed away and the plastic bags set aside for recycling, Ted left the kitchen and linoleum for the living room and that bane of his existence, the carpet. He flopped into the recliner and switched on the news. A severe weather alert. Charley was marked as a Category 5 hurricane and there was no sign of degrading. It was bearing down on the Gulf Coast, the Tampa area now on high alert for the coming weekend. Ted bit his nails, his eyes glued to the screen.

"I don't know what we're supposed to do, Margie. Pack?"

"I don't know. Pack what? For where to?"

"Well," he said, "we'll just have to wait. It's a wait and see I guess."

"I'm worried about Teddy," she said.

"He'll be alright. No hurricanes up *there*."

"No, silly. I mean about… well, you know. Everything."

"Oh. Yeah."

"He didn't sound too good this morning."

"He never sounds too good."

"I mean he sounded extra not too good," Marge frowned, tapping her fingernails abstractedly on the counter. "Maybe he should come down."

"Come down *here*?"

"Mm hmm. Might brighten his spirits. He could grab a cheap flight."

"On whose dime?"

Marge sat across from Ted on the sofa in front of the meteorologist on the big screen, wringing her hands and trying to gather herself. "Maybe if we could just put off having the floors done a little longer."

His attention quickly turned from the severe weather alert to his wife. "What?" he scowled. "Put off having the floors done?"

"Yes, I just thought–"

"Put off having the floors done!"

His face had gone beet red. It was getting damn close to purple as he rose from his chair and stomped up and down on the carpet.

"I'll be goddamned if that kid will cost us one more dime! I've had it up to here!"

"Oh for godsakes, calm down and listen to me."

*"No!"*

He paced in circles while Marge kept wringing her hands. His voice grew soft. "I am so tired of our… retirement years being trampled by the problems of a grown man."

Marge knew the inevitable monologue, practically word for word—how he'd served his country as a marine, scraped and saved and worked hard only to be shown the door by Blue Cross. When he'd regained some of his composure, she addressed him from the corner of the room, where she'd taken refuge.

"Ted. Can I say something?"

"Okay. Go ahead."

"I can live with this carpet if it means knowing that–"

"No!" Ted charged her and she made a beeline for the door. But he quickly had her by the elbows and started shaking her. "It's time you stopped babying him! Listen! Listen to me! You spoil that kid–"

"He's not a kid," she felt a lump in her throat and her eyes began to well up.

"Exactly! He's a man! A man owns up to his responsibilities! We had to pay our own granddaughter's tuition–"

"One year. It was *one year* Ted. We chipped in–"

"Stop defending him! You're always defending him!"

"Ted," she looked at him imploringly, "You're hurting me."

He released her from his grasp, breathing heavily and rapidly, bringing his hands to his head. Marge dusted herself off and said one of these days you're going to give yourself a heart attack. Ted stormed off, slamming the screen door shut behind him.

Marge shook her head, eyes closed, lips pursed. There was more time to think these days, and think she did. If her marriage were a garden, she thought, it was overrun with weeds and had become untidy. How easily we give ourselves license to speak to one another with less propriety we would afford a friend, a boss, or any stranger. How carelessly we drift into a space devoid of that modicum of decorum that protects our mental well-being.

Become derelict in our duty to nurture and care, heedless of long-ago oaths of loyalty and kindness. Simply because we take for granted that the partner will always be there, will never simply get fed up and walk away for good.

The phone rang. Teddy. He'd thought over everything. Found a cheap last-minute flight. He would be down to Florida by tomorrow afternoon.

*

There was tension on the line when Kenny called—her voice laden with a wariness, fraught with the guarded vigilance of those in trouble. She would fly down this coming weekend. When he hung up he sat for a good while out on the back porch and watched the sun go down over the man-made lake alongside the North Club. With a heavy sigh, he pushed himself out of the plastic patio chair, laced up his battered Converse high tops and went out the door. On the walk to the South Club he and Gerry Hagoden's paths crossed and they exchanged a few words, Hagoden rocking on his heels, staring down at the sidewalk, repentant for having been complicit in Kenny's ousting from their golf team. "You know *Frank*," he said.

"Yeah, I know," said Kenny. "It's okay. See you around Gerry."

The South Club was sparsely populated by a few daytime stragglers. He glanced over at the bar and immediately recognized Beamish from this morning at church. They'd already forgotten each other's names and had to re-introduce themselves. Sat next to Beamish was a very dark-tanned brunette. She stuck out an elegant bronzed hand with long slender fingers and a wrist bedecked with several fine gold bracelets. He grasped it too tightly, it was soft and tender, and straight away he knew he'd overwhelmed both the hand and the woman attached. He didn't go much for eye contact but this woman seemed to command it. He found himself gazing into her hazel eyes beneath sharp-penciled eyebrows as she introduced herself with a polite smile as Isabel. Beamish pulled the barstool out and tapped its seat in invitation. While he settled himself, Kenny couldn't help but notice the dark-tanned thighs that went with the black miniskirt. This was a woman who obviously exercised regularly.

"You look a little young for Sunnyville," she said. "Just visiting?"

"Nuh-uh." Kenny shrugged. "Been here for a couple of years."

Beamish tapped playfully at her bare knee and said, *you* look a little young for Sunnyville. She batted his hand away, flashing a mischievous smile at him before her face went serious and her gaze returned to Kenny. She said, "I'm new. Just moved here from Chicago."

"Wow," said Kenny. "That's a big jump."

"Yep," she sighed. "I did extensive research for a project that had me flying in and out of Tampa several times. I just love Tampa, I mean it has incredible diversity. Lots of cultural amenities. And the beaches and resorts are so accessible."

Kenny was expecting a somewhat deprecating tone from the missus but she didn't appear to have altered the straightforward and somewhat sophisticated tone that he deduced by now was her nature. While Isabel continued speaking, he greatly exaggerated his level of interest.

"I'm a documentary journalist. I was co-writing a book series on the history of Tampa and I became so enamored of it, the whole Gulf Coast region. I wrote extensively about Ybor City and the cigar trade at the turn of the century."

"Oh my God," his eyes bulged, "I was just down there Friday night." His overenthusiasm for an unremarkable coincidence seemed to take the wind out of her sails for a moment. Then they were off to the races, jabbering away while Beamish leaned back in his barstool so as to better allow the flow of conversation between them. Isabel was in an extremely expansive mood and while this served to tease Kenny out of his somber mood and get his own mouth moving, it was obvious to him that Beamish was beginning to regret having invited an encroachment on their exclusive and valuable pleasure time. She paused to draw a glass of wine to her full crimson lips, nodding at him. "Are you retired Kenny?"

"Well," he said. "Sort of. For now at least."

This woman was clearly sophisticated and cultured and he thought the better of imparting to her any information about the easy windfall that preceded his early retirement. But he had to say something so he said, "I've dabbled in a lot of stuff. Did some copy editing in Austin."

He had in fact done some copy editing in Austin—unpaid, for an undergraduate student for whom he had a crush that, like her book, didn't materialize into anything.

She squinted at him, as if she'd lost her train of thought or couldn't quite make her mind up about something. He took a swig of his beer and glanced up at the TV screen behind the bar. A baseball game with the sound turned down. Then Isabel bent down to fetch her purse near the foot rail. Mike Beamish put his hand over hers and said I got it and when she stood up she placed a hand on his shoulder for what seemed to Kenny a rather long duration for friends having run into one another by mere happenstance. She excused herself, saying she had a lot of catching up to do from the weekend, and Kenny once again accepted that slender hand into his own, this time with a little less firm a grip, and bade her goodbye.

That left the boys to themselves. Mike ordered another round. Kenny had barely touched the pint of Yuengling before him. He accepted Mike's offer for a second one, deeming it bad manners to protest a pal buying a pal a drink. Could he call this fellow next to him a pal, he wondered. He was lousy with names and had forgotten that of the attractive young lady who glided gracefully away from them.

"Boy," he said to Mike. "She's a real looker." He nodded at the double doors she'd just exited through. "Isabel, is it?"

Mike pursed his lips and nodded his head gravely as if considering a weighty moral issue. "So," he tilted his glass, "any news from the lady?"

Kenny cleared his throat. "I just talked to her. Before coming here."

"Uh-huh."

"Thanks for asking."

"Don't mention it. You figure out her age yet?"

Kenny shrugged. "Young enough to be pregnant."

"Aye," Mike said ruefully, running a thumb along the rim of his glass. "What do you think you're gonna do kiddo?"

"We have to… I mean, she, she wants to have the baby."

"And you?"

"I don't know," Kenny sighed. "I really don't know."

"Sounds pretty sketchy."

"Well," Kenny took a gulp of beer. "I wouldn't say we're real close."

"Aye. One night sure doesn't add up to much."

"That's right." Kenny glanced around for anyone in earshot. "We got up the next morning and it was very awkward man, very awkward. She didn't fix breakfast and I didn't hang around too long."

"No pillow talk."

"Uh-uh."

"I hate those."

"Hate what?"

"One-night stands." He nodded at the door Isabel Amador had just exited through and winked. "Sometimes I like when they have sequels."

But his drinking partner seemed pre-occupied in his thoughts and he wondered if his revelation even registered.

"If you don't mind," Kenny said, "I wish you wouldn't tell anyone any of this stuff I told you. About the baby."

"Your secret is safe with me."

There was a commotion out on the patio and they turned their heads. It was evident there was an argument under way between an elderly man and woman, their voices raised far above conversational level.

"Dammit!" shouted the man. "I'm cutting off the damned cable and that's that!"

"The hell we are!"

"I can't stand that goddamned idiot box!"

"Maybe you should try watching. It might smarten you up a little!"

"Hah, that's a laugh! All it's done is make you stupid!"

"Who you calling stupid!"

"Stupid!" He thumbed his nose at presumably his wife and one of the staff hurried over in a uniform of black trousers and white golf shirt as if to officiate a match. Mike rolled his eyes and nodded over his shoulder.

"Now there's another happily married couple."

Kenny shivered and Mike wondered if it were the air conditioning or something else entirely. The commotion having subsided, Kenny and Mike fixed their stares dead ahead, speaking in low conspiratorial tones with no eye contact.

"We're gonna talk this weekend," Kenny said. "She's flying down."

"She gonna stay with you?"

"I guess so." Kenny frowned.

"Maybe she'll cook you breakfast this time."

"I really don't know about this baby," Kenny spoke to a solemn-faced Mike Beamish. "Does that make me bad? I guess in the eyes of the church it would make me a murderer."

"You haven't killed anybody yet."

"But I might. If she decided to… terminate the pregnancy, I can't honestly say I'd be disappointed.

"Well," Beamish leaned back in his chair and flexed his fingers. "It isn't so cut and dried. In the Church I mean."

"But doesn't the Pope say–"

"There's mixed opinions among Catholics."

"What's your opinion?"

"I don't know. I don't think about it much. I mean, we *had* our kids."

Kenny shook his head and gazed ruefully at the beer in front of him. "Remember I told you I haven't grown up in many ways?"

"I think so. Over at church."

"Yeah… Well what I mean to say is… there's something about my life. Looking back on it I mean. There's this sense of, I don't know, failure? Mom left me a good sum of money and this house here and not everyone knows that."

"I'm sure some people do. If *she* lived here I mean."

"Well, that's the thing. I never came to visit her."

Kenny wanted to spill his guts right then and there and Beamish could sense it. He needed to stay the momentum of this confessional speech with one of his own. It was out of his mouth before he knew it, a kind of quid pro quo of secrets. Or maybe it was the beers in him loosening up his machismo, and its accompanying sense of bravado. Perhaps he could see that his new pal was both impressed and interested with the exotic lady and he needed to mark his territory. Whatever it was, he elaborated broadly on the true nature of their relationship.

"That's my secret. Just don't tell my wife," he said as if to seal the deal.

"I don't even know your wife."

"Well. Just in case you meet her. Bound to in this place."

"Like, as in… we never had this conversation?"

Mike winked, raising his glass and clinking it against Kenny's.

"Well," Kenny returned his voice to conversational level. "I just hope your wife–"

"Sssshh." Now it was Mike's turn to glance around for eavesdroppers. He drummed on Kenny's hand and brought a finger to his mouth, his lips curling into a smile.

"*I* gotcha," said Kenny. "I'm none the wiser."

Beamish flinched. "You mean *you know nothing*."

"Huh?"

"You know nothing. *None the wiser* would mean for all our talk you've learned nothing."

"Oh, okay." Kenny said, a little dispirited at standing corrected on a turn of phrase. He prided himself, after all, on his intellectual capability, considering it a mark of distinction among those who surrounded him. By his estimation, a rather pedestrian slice of middle-class corporate America. After they finished their beers he shook Mike's hand and said he'd see him around, balking at the invitation of a lift home, saying he could use the walk. In the heat he trudged along in his Converse high-tops—a fifty-seven-year-old man with a tiny hoop earring in each ear. For all the day's heart-to-heart and soul-searching, he was none the wiser.

*

Peggy Beamish was a binge eater and that's what she was doing when Marge called. She'd made a pretty good dent in a package of Oreo cookies watching another rerun of Mary Tyler Moore on the oldies channel when the phone rang and Marge asked did she catch her at a good time?

"I'm good. What's up?"

"Oh, nothing really."

"Something wrong?"

"Well, not exactly… I– I mean, not earth shattering or anything–"

"C'mon spill it. You can tell Peggy."

"It's my husband."

"You don't say."

"He just left the house upset. I'm afraid of what might happen when he comes back."

"Yeah?" Peggy lowered the sound on the TV and sat up straight.

"I– I hate to bother you with this. We don't even hardly–"

"Look, why don't you put some shoes on and come over here."

"Oh, I– I wouldn't want to impose on you."

"You were an imposition, I'd hang up on you right now. C'mon over."

Peggy switched off the TV and went to put the kettle on. She stashed the Oreos away and brought out some crackers from the cabinet, cheese from the fridge. She had some Chardonnay chilling and she removed that. She had everything ready by the time Marge's tentative knock came at the front door—or side door, depending on how you looked at it.

At the door Marge was a bundle of nerves, wringing her hands in the manner of apology. Peggy ushered her over the threshold with a broad sweeping gesture of welcome. She could tell her new friend was doing her level best to paint a cheerful picture on her face.

The phone rang and Peggy deliberated, said let me get this and took the cordless.

"Oh, Emma," she said. "How are you?"

Peggy went on with some small talk and it was clear to Marge that this was someone who badly wanted to catch up. Peggy made a face at the phone and nodded for her to sit down at the kitchen table. She traipsed around the house, her cues to bring the conversation to a close apparently falling on deaf ears. The conversation rumbled on painstakingly and at last made a soft landing on the topic of travel arrangements for the big wedding anniversary party. After Peggy shook the call, the two of them sat across from one another, bottle of wine before them on the table. Peggy poured generously to a large wineglass despite Marge's mannered protest. "What a pain in the ass," she shook her head. "This goddamned party."

"But it's your anniversary. Shouldn't that something be something to look forward to?"

Peggy rolled her eyes. "It wasn't my idea."

Marge scrunched her eyebrows.

"So," said Peggy, "what's all the fuss about at your house?"

"My husband has such an awful temper." She shook her head ruefully. "Lousy temper."

"I'll say," said Peggy. "We all got a pretty good sampling of it out there on the pickleball court."

"I just don't know *what* I'm gonna do," Marge squeezed her eyes shut.

"Does he… I-I mean he doesn't go batshit crazy and hurt you does he?"

Marge shook her head and fussed at her wedding ring.

"Does he hit you?"

"Oh God no," Marge said, shaking her head. "Only objects get the brunt of his anger."

"Inanimate ones I hope."

Marge nodded with an air of solemnity.

"All the same," Peggy said, "I'm sure it's pretty upsetting."

*Did it count*, Marge thought. That one incident years ago, when she'd packed it in and left on the heels of his lashing out then restraining himself, staying his hand for it to end up a light almost playful slap the cheek? Did it count, earlier this morning when they'd been bickering once again about something so insignificant as to have been forgotten, and he'd rushed her and then stayed his hand? *Stayed his hand.* As she recoiled in fear.

She was a good way towards telling Peggy about redoing the floors and Teddy flying down tomorrow when the door opened and in came Mike Beamish. He gazed upon the ladies as if sizing them up, bestowing a smile upon Marge in the manner of a benevolent and kindly king. "Evening ladies. Nice to see you Marge."

Marge warmed at his having remembered her name. This guy was clearly a charmer who could work a room. She watched him as he playfully bound over to his wife to massage her shoulders. "Long day," he said.

Peggy rolled her eyes. "Me? Or *you*? Just what have you been up to?"

"Oh, this and that," he said, releasing his grip, drumming his fingers on her arms.

"This and that," Peggy repeated. "Kinda leaves you wide open. Our son called, by the way. I told him you'd gone missing in action again."

Mike glanced over at Marge and winked. "Well," he said smiling, "I'm back from behind enemy lines. And they didn't get so much as a word out of me."

"Well that's a comforting thought," Peggy said, shaking her head and waving him away.

"C'mon," she said to Marge. "Let's move this party to the porch. It's starting to cool off a little outside."

Mike started for the kitchen and called over his shoulder. "You ladies want some company?"

"Nope," Peggy mumbled. "Girls talk. Lady stuff."

"Right," he said, drawing a glass of filtered water from the fridge, the ice maker grinding and clunking. "Nothing on the topic of men, I'm sure."

"Only those nearest and dearest," Peggy glared at him.

"Well," he gave his wife a mock-startled glance, took a swig of water and said to Marge. "I saw your other half at church this morning."

"Oh," said Marge. "Hope he didn't make a scene."

"No," Mike smiled. "Very solemn. Quiet as a church mouse."

"Much like us martyrs," Peggy murmured. "Suffering in silence."

Mike shook his head perplexedly. "I beg your pardon dear?"

"Oh nothing," said Peggy, ruminating over the husbands' meeting at church. *The saints convene in church while the martyrs compare notes in the comforts of our home.* Peggy and Marge gathered up the glasses and snacks and started for the screened porch.

"Well then," said Mike. "I think I'll stretch my legs." It would be a pretty long walk to Isabel's, he would go and surprise her. He opened the door and stepped into a light drizzle. At the end of the driveway he turned around and started back to the house, his mind working to conjure up an excuse for his wife, who'd returned to the kitchen for the rest of the things on the table.

Peggy glared at him. "C'mon, in or out. This isn't a bus station."

"I was just thinking I'd take the golf cart over to the library before they close."

Peggy shook her head perplexedly while her husband shrugged.

"I have to return a book and I want to take one out."

"They don't have due dates."

"I know but I've had it long enough. Someone else might want to enjoy it."

"How very thoughtful of you."

She shut the door behind him, lingering, running a finger along the wainscotting before returning to the porch and her guest. Amid the palm trees and manicured lawns, she'd managed to keep a muted loneliness at bay for the first year or so. Now it seemed to be creeping back like some vapor seeping through the freshly-painted walls.

Out on the back porch she found Marge standing before the wicker bookshelf, hands clasped behind her, studying the framed family photos.

"That's from my son Tom's wedding," she said, glancing over Marge's shoulder. "They're up in Minneapolis."

"What a handsome groom. Beautiful bride. My goodness Peggy but aren't you the picture of beauty?"

"Aw shucks, that was a long time ago."

"You look like a movie star."

"Well," Peggy tossed her shoulders playfully, "beauty is but fleeting."

"Oh, come on now."

"Their son Jeff and his wife Ella, these two," Peggy pointed at another framed photo propped up on the bookcase, "they're staying here for the big shebang. And she's pregnant. That'll make me a great-grandmother."

Marge pulled a face of mock surprise.

"Now doesn't saying *that* out loud make me feel like a spring chicken," Peggy said, shaking her head.

"What a cute couple, these two," Marge drew another framed photo from the shelf and brought it up under her nose.

"Jim and Chrissie."

"Where do they live?"

"In Michigan. In separate houses."

"Oh," said Marge. "I'm sorry."

"Don't be. They're better off that way."

"What keeps *us* together? Do you ever wonder?"

"*Wonder*? I've been scratching my head about it for fifty years."

"Mike seemed so gentle with you."

Peggy frowned. "Yeah. That's because you're here. He hasn't touched me in the most important way in years."

"Must be difficult."

Peggy settled herself in a wicker chair and gestured to the one opposite her. "What it was, at least what the therapist told me, and then the both of us years ago. Mike's childhood shaped his behavior. The therapist used the term *emotionally unavailable*. An alcoholic mother and a workaholic father. Caretaking depressive parents. Left him to his own devices for emotional coping and going forward it would be a difficult task for anyone to get close to him. Avoidant attachment style," she batted a hand at the air, "something like that."

"How did you survive fifty years like that?"

"Well," said Peggy, picking distractedly at a piece of flint on her shirt and flicking it to the floor, "how does anyone? It was easier... well, I don't know if *easier* is the word, let's just say less... noticeable? When we were raising kids. Or, more like, when *I* was raising kids."

"You had to work, didn't you?"

"Off and on. We had Mike's salary. He did well. I always had that umbrella to live under."

Marge nodded. The air was warm and sticky on the screened-in porch without a breeze.

"Anyway," Peggy pointed to the framed photos on the shelves of the wicker bookcase. "The kids, the grandkids. I guess the ultimate distraction is just to make babies. Fill up the empty space with people."

"I guess that's one way of looking at it."

"Well, we're down here what, three years maybe? And now we have no one but ourselves."

"You have friends. I can see that."

"Sure. We socialize a little. But *these* walking zombies?" Peggy rolled her eyes. "Anyway, nobody lives with us. It gets pretty damn quiet around here."

"What do you argue about?"

"Are you kidding me?" she snickered. "We hardly talk."

"Sounds pretty awkward to me."

"I'll tell you what. If it weren't for that stupid box," Peggy pointed beyond the sliding doors to the television, "it'd be stultifying. The silence would kill me."

Marge cleared her throat. "Have you made any *good* friends here?"

"I tried," Peggy said, puffing her cheeks. "There's Cindy Goodman. But people being people, I've kinda run out of steam. Mike doesn't really let anyone get too close. Not his style. But he sure has been flirting lately, and I can assure you it ain't with yours truly. But that husband of yours, phew. If you don't mind me saying, he's a real piece of work."

"I don't know what's worse," said Marge. "Being sentenced to silence or too much noise. At least your husband doesn't have a temper."

"Everyone's got a temper," said Peggy.

"Not like Ted's."

"No, definitely not like Ted's. Thank God for that."

"I read somewhere," said Marge, staring vacantly and bringing a finger to her lips, "that anger is always rooted in fear."

"Our therapist," said Peggy, "said anger is really just fear. It's acting out fear, or some shit like that, I can't remember exactly."

"When did you go to a therapist?"

Peggy waved a hand dismissively. "Years ago. When it was the thing to do." She took a healthy gulp of wine. "What triggered it was Mike's affair. The shit. With my best friend. *Our best friends.* The priest said we could work it out. Save our marriage."

Peggy's voice began to crack. She wiped at her eyes with the back of her hand. "Sorry," she said, "Old wound."

*

Lily Westfall slept right through dinner. The den was pitch black save for light from streetlamps through the blinds that cast an eerie glow. She glanced over at the clock, startled to see it was nearly nine thirty and her stomach not grumbling. The dog sat at her feet panting and pawing at her leg and she guessed it was he who'd woken her up. She patted him on the head and pushed herself up.

"I don't know what's got into me little fella," she said to Rex. "You musta thought I'd gone and died on you."

She was surprised at her own words—she usually didn't talk like that. After she'd filled Rex's bowl, she took a small portion of leftover chicken casserole to heat up in the microwave. She checked the answering machine and after the girl's message was a new one from her son Jack saying he was just checking up on her and hoped things turned out alright and she wasn't involving herself too much in the girl's business.

Her appetite hadn't shown up for the leftovers and she took meager bites from a modest portion. Her mother always told her she ate like a bird and now she reflected on this and wondered aloud at how she'd come full-circle—from a little girl to a little old lady, having carried much the same characteristics and tendencies. The dog cocked his head at her. While she ate she thought of the girl down the street. Sure it was none of her business, but something still tugged at her sense of propriety, moral duty. She again addressed the dog. "I don't know what it is Rex. It used to be, back when I was teaching, biggest problem we faced was running down the hallways. Copying homework. Cheating on tests. Maybe a fistfight once in a blue moon. Things like that. Now they tell me it's drugs. Families split up. Single moms. Suicide. I don't know Rex. I really don't know."

Once she'd cleared the remains of the casserole to the garbage bin and finished washing up, she laced up her tennis shoes and fetched the leash. Rex leapt about, perching his paws on her thighs and then scampering in circles at the door. She fetched his leash and together they stepped outside to go and check on Barbara.

*

Isabel had just settled herself comfortably in bed with a good book–propped up against the pillows under the covers when the doorbell rang. She dropped the book to her lap with no small measure of annoyance, pushing the comforter aside and extracting herself from the cozy bed. In her silk pajamas and a pair of faux fur slippers she hastened to the front door and the peephole. The fisheye lens made his face distortedly wide and lent a sinister aspect to his grin.

"Who is it," she said evenly although she already knew who it was.

"It's me."

She tensed her grip on the doorknob, bringing a tiny fist to her mouth, running a curled finger along her teeth.

"You remember me, don't you? Mike Beamish?"

She opened the door, leaving a hand on the doorknob. "Yes?"

"You don't look exactly thrilled to see me."

"It's ten o'clock at night."

"And?"

"*And* it's my bedtime."

"Maybe I could liven up your bedtime."

"Maybe I don't want it livened up. Maybe I'm dead tired."

"Can I come in for a second?"

Isabel glanced over his shoulder, her eyes panning the neighborhood, the cul-de-sac. "If I let you in I don't think it'd be for just a second."

"Would that be so bad?"

She stepped aside, bringing a hand to the top of the door and shaking her head at his back as he walked in. "Look. *Mike*," she said. "Can we rain check this?"

"It's not raining."

"No. It's not raining. But it may as well be. I was just getting ready to put the light out."

He looked her over from head to toe, all the cheer gone from his face. "Well, I just thought I might, I don't know. Surprise you."

"You have."

"Wouldn't you like some company?"

She rolled her eyes at the ceiling and addressed him as one might a petulant child. "I love company Mike. Just not now. I don't want company right now."

"Okay, okay." His charming smile was back, if somewhat affected. "I was *just* leaving."

He leaned in to kiss her on impulse but she recoiled and merely took his kiss on stiff lips. "Goodnight Mike."

He left the cul-de-sac and turned the golf cart onto Sunset Boulevard. An emergency paramedic vehicle lumbered along, sirens off. The streets were otherwise completely dead and above him the blanket of clouds had lifted. There were no streetlights in the cul-de-sac, per referendum by the neighborhood association. The light of a nearly full moon cast a somber glow that dampened his spirits. What was this unfamiliar feeling of his that seemed to spring from some new region of his mind perhaps carved out of old age? What was this sadness sprung upon him from a mere glance at manicured grass fresh with dew, or was it just the sprinkler system? Even the flowers that bordered the yard he stood in front of out there by the golf cart seemed to evoke only feelings of emptiness, a hollow pit in his soul. He saw himself dying alone, no one to hold his hand as he passed from this life. He had been rebuked, refused, but never like this. Isabel had clearly made a case that there should be neat restrictions on their level of intimacy. He accepted the verdict like a gentleman. He would be alone tonight. There would be none of the kind of affection that comes with a deepening knowledge of the person whom you lay down with, you are a lamb and you will be accordingly meek. There was no one whom he could actually say was overjoyed at his phone call or his surprise visit. No one, not even his wife, was invested in his emotional well-being. He turned the wheel of the golf cart and hit the pedal—it jerked forward, and then Mike Beamish whirred along empty streets, bound towards a sort of home.

# 5

Unaccustomed as he was to setting an alarm clock, Kenny overslept. He'd set the time but neglected to set the switch to the on position. The oversight had allowed a dream to play itself out. The details were fading, carried out to sea with the tide as it were. Dark hallways, castle, mist. A tiny cubbyhole room nearby. Someone sobbing. A tinny clacking sound.

Someone was rapping on the back door. He sat bolt upright in his makeshift bed with a sense of foreboding, this was not going to be a good day. Something had tagged him in the dream and cloaked him in anxiety and remorse. Carrying this into the real world, summoning himself to action—throwing his legs over the side, scrambling about in boxers, scrounging up a tee shirt, wrestling himself into it. Bright sunlight spilled into the living room from the back porch and he saw Peggy Beamish peering through the jalousie windows, tapping on them with her keys. She wore large leopard print sunglasses and a green plexiglass visor. She spied him and waved, the keys in her hand jingling. "Hey! Did you forget about me or what?"

Kenny feebly raised a finger in acknowledgement and approached. He opened the door and then Peggy Beamish stood in his modest dwelling, unfamiliar territory—she'd never occasioned to view the inside of any of these units, the first settlements of Sunny Glen Palms. The pioneer houses, the forerunners—with peeling paint, window unit air-conditioners and problematic plumbing. She wore impeccably clean white golf attire that included a short skirt and Kenny saw a very fit pair of legs, if a little on the stout side. Peggy jiggled her keys and glanced around at all the clutter. "God what a mess. How can you live like this?"

"Sorry, Kenny rubbed his eyes. "I overslept. Do I have time to put the coffee on?"

"Go ahead. Knock yourself out."

In the tiny kitchen Kenny poured gourmet grounds into the coffee-maker while Peggy paced around the living room for a closer evaluation of the mess that constituted his environs. Unopened boxes lay stacked almost to the ceiling beside walls lined with bookshelves.

"You just move in or what?"

"No," Kenny replied. "I've been here a few years. I just haven't got any more space to put these things."

"What *are* these things?"

"Oh, some collectibles, things like that."

"No body parts, I hope. Or dead bodies."

"What's that?"

"Dead bodies," Peggy jiggled her keys. "I was joking. At least I hope so anyway."

"Oh," Kenny affected a laugh. "Do you want a cup of coffee?"

"Honey, it's after nine in the morning and that's Peggy's cutoff time. Or else she'll be up all night tossing and turning. Or maybe *extra* tossing and turning." Peggy continued to take in her surroundings. "There's this TV show called Hoarders," she said. "Have you seen it?"

"No," said Kenny. "What's it about?"

"It's about people who just can't seem to get rid of shit. Some sort of psychological factor to it. Being stuck, unable to move on, that sort of thing. Just wondered if it might've inspired you."

The dig was lost on Kenny or maybe he was only half-listening as he hurriedly threw together his morning oatmeal ritual. "Sorry I'm making us late."

"*Late*?" Peggy said. "There's no such thing as late around here. We get there when we get there. Well, as long as I make my lunch date anyway."

"Lunch date? I thought you told me you were married."

"*Ladies* lunch."

"Oh okay. I just hear what I hear from the gossip mill and nothing would surprise me."

"Well," Peggy said, plucking an oversized hardback on the Sex Pistols from the bookcase. "who'd be interested in an old lady like me anyway?"

"I would."

"Careful mister."

"I only meant it as a compliment," Kenny said, carrying his bowl of oatmeal from the small kitchen to the living room.

"You gonna sit down and eat that?"

"Oh. I thought we wanted to get going."

"So you're gonna eat it over nine holes?"

Kenny shuffled his feet and laughed and when he glanced up at Peggy she shrugged and then he farted.

It was out of him before he knew it. His morning flatulence normally played to an empty room but not so this morning. There was no music on to cover it up. He was blushing and he knew it. "I'm sorry. It must've been the beer last night."

Peggy brought a hand to cover her mouth, laughing and shaking her head. "God," she said, "if that isn't just like a man. Blame it on the beer."

"I'm sorry. Really," he said while she folded herself over laughing. "I won't do it again."

"It's not as if it's a capital offense."

"I know, but it's a clear lack of manners. People go to jail for less."

Peggy gathered herself and they regarded one another silently, until they both broke out in fits of laughter.

"Well," Kenny said. "Would you like to hear some music? I've got just about everything you can think of. Even Big Band, Sinatra, swing—"

"Big Band? What do I look like, an old lady? Oh no, let's not start that again." She waved her hand at him. "We better get going or we'll end up here all morning. You sure your degree wasn't in procrastination?"

"Alright, let me get dressed."

"Go ahead. I'll read about the Sex Pistols while I'm waiting."

When they reached the links in Peggy's golf cart, there were already a good number of golfers and a group of four elderly people were slowing progress. The men were dressed in plaid golf knickers, argyle sweater vests, over-the-calf argyle socks and tweed wool caps. The ladies wore long skirts, arm length wool sweaters and saddle shoes.

"Looks like Halloween came a little early this year," Kenny puzzled, gripping the roll bar as Peggy's cart trundled over the bumpy grass off the blacktop path.

"They must be sweating their you-know-what's off," Peggy muttered. "Upstairs *and* downstairs."

Kenny chuckled, his golf attire hardly a fashion statement —unwashed polo shirt, khaki shorts, dirty socks, sneakers and a battered golf hat.

The air was not yet thick with humidity and held the scent of morning dew and fresh-clipped grass. They found a bench and sat down side-by-side. "So you haven't said anything about your lady friend," said Peggy, staring straight ahead. "The baby. How's that going?"

"Um," Kenny cleared his throat, "she's coming next weekend. We're gonna talk."

"Well that's encouraging."

"Yeah." He pursed his lips.

Peggy shot him a sidelong glance. "You better shape up there, mister. If you're gonna do right by this kid."

Kenny nodded ruefully. The dream slipping further from him, but the emotional state it had produced hanging around stubbornly. The sobbing alongside the clack of some mystery machine, perhaps an implement for a medical procedure? He wanted to pour his heart out, instead he reined in his anxious words while his stomach made funny noises.

"How many kids have you got?" he asked.

"None," said Peggy. "I've got *adults. Big* adults. With *big* problems. Two sons and a daughter. Two out of three divorced. My daughter's one of them. Single mom, raised two kids. She tells me once, know what she says? 'Mom,' she says, 'I don't know how you did it even with Dad around.' Let me tell you something, I said to her. Your father wasn't around much. Out *fooling* around is more like it."

Kenny nodded and Peggy continued. "But I will say, at least I only had to work mostly part-time. My daughter held down two jobs most of the time and had to put her kids in day care." Peggy shook her head. "Man, what a difference that makes. Day care kids, shew."

"What do you mean?"

"What do I *mean*? I mean drug problems, trouble with the law, unwanted pregnancies… Sorry."

"That's okay."

"Well," Peggy said. "You better know what's in store is all I'm saying. It's only getting worse."

Kenny shook his head ruefully, and then he spotted his old partners Gerry Hagoden and Frank Alsatian finishing up on the adjacent ninth hole. He hoped they hadn't spotted him but it was too late. After Gerry finished his putt, he sauntered over to Kenny—easygoing Gerry Hagoden, one of the few Sunny Glen residents who, though not sharing much in common, wasn't run off by Kenny's long-running monologues.

"Hey," Gerry said. "Good to see you on the links again. Haven't been out much myself lately. Kind of losing interest."

It was obvious to Kenny that Gerry was lying only out of the goodness of his heart and so he chortled good-naturedly.

Gerry nodded at Peggy. "Who's your lady friend?"

"I'm Peggy. Peggy Beamish. And it's strictly platonic, so you can just unplug the gossip mill."

"Hey," Gerry threw up his palms and shrugged, "I wasn't suggesting anything otherwise."

"I'm old enough to be his mother."

"I'd never have guessed," Gerry said.

"My oh my, but aren't the compliments coming in droves today."

"Well don't let this guy flirt too much with you," Gerry winked. "He's dangerous."

"Honey," said Peggy, "as soon as I meet dangerous in this sanctum of boredom and ennui, you'll be the first to know."

Gerry shrugged. "See ya round Kenny. Next beer's on me."

Peggy held her gaze on Gerry while he walked back over to Frank. "I see you've got some friends here after all."

"Yeah," Kenny shrugged, "I guess you could say that."

*

The indoor pool at the South Club didn't lend itself to lolling about in the sun with discreetly smuggled cocktails inside thermoses, as did the outdoor pools. It was roped off into lanes, delineating the sole purpose of exercise. Beside it was a four-foot pool with warmer waters conducive for soothing aching bones.

Mike Beamish was doing extra laps when a round of voices exploded from the pool deck and reverberated around the tiled room, causing him to pause and lift his goggles to discover what the commotion was all about.

A young man in a white-collar dress shirt with a gold-black Windmere name tag was conducting a tour of the premises to prospective residents. He waved to Mike and Mike waved back.

"So as I was saying, there are happy hours here at the South Club," he beamed. "Thursday night is Pub Night and you get the full whack. Deejay, dancing, cookout."

A woman in tow wanted to know if the drinks were on the house. The rep's typewriter laugh bounced around the room. "I can't promise you that. But you'll make so many friends here, it's likely they'll pick up the tab for a few rounds anyhow. Haha. Hahaha."

Mike resumed his freestyle, gliding towards the wall with outstretched hand meeting the lower ledge, coming up for air and pushing himself from the wall. He'd forgotten exactly how to execute the flip turn and he figured he could live without the rush of chlorine up the nose that resulted from a botched one. He committed himself to forty laps, three or so times a week, to try and rein in the spare tire around his waist. A skinny tire, but a tire no less and he was 198ish pounds banging on the door to 200. He'd never weighed over two-hundred pounds in his life. Now there was a younger girlfriend in the picture. Well, maybe she didn't qualify as girlfriend status, but here he was anyway doing overtime in the lap-laned pool.

He dried himself off and quit the pool for the locker room, donning a pair of open-toed sandals and tying the towel around his waist to cover a bikini Speedo he wouldn't be caught dead in outside the lap pool at his age. There was a steam room housed within the locker room and when he pulled on the handle, he was met with a steam fog so thick he couldn't see an inch in front of his face. With what little cloud rolled out he could barely discern the single occupant sitting on the bench against the far wall of the completely tiled compartment.

*I hope it's not too high for ya*, a soft and low voice uttered in the darkness. Mike said it was just fine and the door closed. An absolute silence returned to that tomb—an air of solemnity and sacredness settled on two men sat naked on a marble bench, elbows on knees, heads drooped in a prayerful and supplicant manner.

*Sure does a body good*, the voice was gentle and gravelly at the same time. Mike grunted agreement and the two voices bounced around softly in the dark until they'd both run out of steam and silence returned to the vault. The steam jets fired up and then quit, leaving a thick fog with the sound of the drip drip drip of the water from the jets onto the tile floor. Mike took in the steam with deep breaths and rose at last, a little light-headed, palming along the wall to find his way to the faint light of the glass door and the locker room beyond.

He'd just finished showering and was toweling off and assessing his physique in the long mirror when the sauna door opened and out of the billowing steam emerged Gerry Hagoden stark naked—belly pouch, liver spots, white legs and all. Mike recognized the face, having been introduced a while back over at church. "Oh it's you," Mike said somewhat bemusedly. "Haven't seen you at church lately."

"We go Saturday nights," Gerry rolled his eyes. "In-laws schedule."

"Aha," Mike said. "Well at least you can get *your* wife to go with you."

Hagoden chuckled and began whistling as he stepped into the shower. "Hey," he called from beyond the glass door. "You don't play golf, do ya?"

"Not lately," Mike said as he clambered into his boxers. "I have a set of clubs but I'm kind of rusty."

"That's okay. We need a partner. Always losing them."

Between his wife and the new love of his life, Mike saw nothing but scheduling conflicts. "Check back with me when the weather starts getting a little cooler."

Gerry stepped out from the shower, reached for his towel, and began dabbing at his face. Mike zippered up, fastened his belt and bade farewell to his steam room comrade, his voice sounding all of a sudden distant to his own ears, as if belonging to someone else entirely. The air was thick and close and his head went light and then all at once he was gone from that room before he could even reach for the doorhandle.

When he came to, Gerry Hagoden was slapping him hard in the face. The locker room ceiling came into focus and then Gerry Hagoden's panic-stricken face in near point, so close he could discern whiskers, the pores in Hagoden's clean-shaven chin, cheeks and nose. Hagoden's Listerine-laced breaths swept across his face.

"There you are! You alright? You okay buddy?"

Mike Beamish felt reduced to a helpless infant with all the attendant vulnerability—absent swagger, clever retorts, chiseled chest laden with the hair of masculinity. He began to attempt to push himself up on his elbows.

"Wait, wait," said Gerry, pressing Mike's broad shoulders gently but firmly back to the cold tile floor. "Not too soon."

From behind Gerry's shoulder a voice boomed. "Everything alright?"

"Yeah," said Mike. "Think I just had a little too much of the steam."

"Okay, just checking," the voice said, and the door thudded closed.

With an iron grip Gerry Hagoden hefted him from the floor and then sat beside him on the wooden bench, dabbing at his forehead with cold paper towels and asking are you sure you don't want to call the paramedics. No Mike said, telling Gerry repeatedly he must've had a blood sugar crash or something, maybe too many laps. Gerry suggested he get up and walk around a little, he wouldn't leave his side until he was sure Mike Beamish's body wouldn't fail him again. They sat at the edge of the outside pool in the hot sun, fanning their legs in the cool water. Mike joked about getting some drinks in him from the bar and having a good reason to pass out. Hagoden laughed politely. After plunging into the water, pinching his nose and going under, he dusted himself off and told Mike he better get going before the wife started wondering. Had his wife Shirley been there, she'd be waving number 30 sunblock at him like a cheerleader with a baton. But Gerry never carried the stuff himself. "Don't stay out in the sun too long," he said to Mike. "Don't let it get under your skin."

Left to himself, Mike was up to his old tricks, scanning the pool for youthful tanned bodies. Spring Break's young mothers were long gone and given the thinning out of the population in summer, there was little in the way of sightseeing. No sign of Isabel, and he was strangely relieved at this. Her rebuff didn't bother him today as much as it did when he returned to the house last evening. It only meant the chase hadn't ended with a roll in the hay, and he could continue his pursuit absent the trappings the catch brought. She would never suddenly cease her sprint and let him crash into her at full bore with the deep weight of intimacy. It meant she wouldn't cling to him, become needy and appeal to him to leave his wife. She was doing him a favor in keeping him at arm's length. He wouldn't let her get under his skin.

*

The golfers in front of them moved at a snail's pace, parading around in vintage golf attire. Peggy kept checking her watch and by the seventh hole she told Kenny they'd have to call it quits so she wouldn't be late for her lunch date. Kenny's game was off anyway, he was no match for Peggy and her repeated self-deprecating remarks about her own poor golf game didn't serve to alleviate his frustration.

"I haven't played in a while," he said.

"I know," she said. "You've said it like eighty times, I get it."

"Sorry. Lot on my mind I guess."

"Well," said Peggy. "It's a sunny day on the golf course and the idea is to focus on getting a tiny ball into a tiny hole. All your worries cast aside. That's the idea anyway."

"Yeah yeah," he said. The dream left a sort of hangover, an odd sense of guilt not attached to anything specific but leaving him, despite the fresh air and the sunny spirits of the golfers ahead of and behind them, tethered to a *bummer*.

"You gotta stop dwelling on that mister. You don't even know what's gonna happen until you talk to her."

"But I have. Talked to her. She wants the baby."

"Well then have the baby."

"I'm too old for a baby."

"Oh," Peggy frowned, "don't be such a baby."

Kenny made a face and Peggy took him by the elbow and steered him toward a nearby bench. They sat side-by-side and nobody said anything for a while. Peggy cleared her throat.

"You know, nobody's ever ready for a child. Listen to me real good. Whether it's a burden or a joy is entirely up to you. I'm not the most… say philosophical person. And God knows I'm not religious, although I was at one time. But I'll tell ya there's something special about bringing a life into this world. Sure I've had problems with my sons, my daughter. But there's a pride I can't put into words. I don't know what else to say. I'm not very good at this."

"In so many ways," he said. "I've never really grown up. Somebody told me once that having children makes you grow up."

"Maybe that's true for some more so than others."

"Well, what about me? Where do you think I stand with that?"

"You?" said Peggy. "You're just a big kid Kenny. I mean I don't know you that well, but you strike me as a big kid with a lot of play time."

"Shit," said Kenny, as if his own worst suspicions were confirmed.

Peggy pinched him on the cheek. "It'll all work out, you'll be fine. Maybe this is just what you need."

They stacked their golf bags on the back of the cart and trundled along the narrow path beside the greenway. Kenny tried to steer the conversation to politics and his passionate opposition to the Bush administration and its perpetual war doctrine in the Middle East. The War on Terror, he said, had no end and was a dangerous propaganda game for a free society. Peggy stared at the path in front of her and said, "I don't do politics much mister.

You're gonna have a whole lot more on your plate to worry about real soon."

Where the path met Cocoa Palm Court, Kenny spied Barbara on foot, in shorts and running shoes, swinging her arms and gazing at the well-landscaped scenery of the houses she passed. He tapped on the dashboard, summoning Peggy to stop, waving his hands and calling *hey there* to Barbara.

Barbara's face brightened and she strolled casually across the road to the cart, extending a hand to Peggy. "Hi, I'm Barbara."

"I saw you at the pool. You always remember the pasty white ones around here," Peggy tapped Barbara's arm playfully. "Looks like you still got some rays to catch."

"Yeah," said Barbara. "I guess you could say that. Fair-skinned Irish."

"You managed to avoid the security guard checking badges at the pool I guess," Peggy chortled.

"Oh yeah, I think he got distracted with that crabby lady."

"Derelict in his duty. You're not from around here, are you?"

"No," said Barbara. "I'm here under extraordinary circumstances."

Kenny nodded solemnly. Peggy leaned forward, the better to address Barbara. "Can you elaborate," she said. "I mean, I'm not nosy or anything, but it was you put it out there."

"My mother died."

"Oh I'm sorry, forgive me please." Peggy thumped the steering wheel. "I can be such a dolt sometimes."

"That's okay, really."

"No, I mean it honey. What an awful thing to lose a parent."

Barbara lowered her head and nodded at the black-top while Peggy shook her head mournfully and tsked-tsked. "I'm so sorry."

"That's okay. Just part of life I guess."

"Now don't go giving yourself platitudes. Just let yourself feel what you feel," said Peggy. "Where are you going honey?"

"Just out for a walk. I underestimated the heat though."

"Want a lift back?" Kenny offered, then turned to Peggy, "She's not very far from here."

"Hop on," said Peggy.

Kenny shifted over to allow Barbara just enough seat room to squeeze beside him and now he found himself squished against Peggy's bare arms and legs.

"Well now look at you lady killer," said Peggy. "Sandwiched between two ladies. You're gonna get us all a bad reputation."

Instead of playing along a flirtatious line of discourse, Kenny returned to the subject he'd raised before they'd encountered Barbara.

"Like I said," Peggy turned the wheel hand over hand and bumped elbows with Kenny. "I don't go much for politics or politicians."

"But," Kenny said, fanning his legs, "how can you be apathetic about the atrocities these rich men in suits perpetuate every day on the rest of humanity?"

"You think it's all lost on me? Just a few months ago we're up North and they're having a sendoff for my daughter's stepson. He's eighteen and enlisted in the Army. To go and fight the terrorists. Now in this country we have a built-in reverence and respect for those in uniform. Those who serve. But there's still half of you wishing him good luck and praising his patriotism while at the same time the unspoken words are 'are you fucking crazy? What the hell are you doing? Go to college and keep out of rich men's fights.' But you can't *say* that. It's the unwritten rule. You don't say that. Not my generation anyway."

"I guess I can see what you mean," said Kenny.

"You don't sound too convinced," said Peggy, "But that's just the way it is. The law of nature. But Peggy's gonna enjoy what's left of her time on this earth mister. Cause there isn't much left to enjoy and I'll be damned if I'm gonna spend it agitating about things I can't change. Whether it's my husband or guys in suits I don't know from Adam."

"That's just the kind of apathy that—"

"Look, you wanna change things, then do something." Peggy took her hands off the wheel to gesture for emphasis. "Vote em out, I don't know, march for peace and love. There was an anti-war rally downtown St Pete about a month ago. We were just coming back from a rare trip outside the gates. Pull over, I said to my husband, we're gonna stand with these people. There were people of all ages. Some older than us."

"Yeah?" Kenny perked up.

"I didn't have a sign so I borrowed someone else's."

"Wow," said Barbara, leaning forward to glance over at Peggy, "good on you."

"He stayed in the car the whole time while I joined that crowd. Nice people." Peggy nodded her head ruminatively. "You know something?"

"What?" said Barbara after an expectant pause.

"I could have stayed there for hours, just talking. About all manner of things. You sure as hell don't get conversations like that in Sunny Glen Palms." Peggy shook her head, frowning.

"What did your husband think about the rally?" asked Barbara.

"He says he doesn't know enough about the subject. But I think he's just playing dumb. Sometimes I think we're all just playing dumb."

They came to the intersection at Sunset Boulevard. Peggy checked her watch and said she was now running late.

"Late for what?" asked Barbara.

"Lunch date. I'm taking one unhappily married friend to the beach."

"Got room for one more? Not me, I have an appointment with the priest about the funeral at two. But I have a dear friend who could really use a break."

"Sure, why not?" said Peggy. "She unhappily married? We could call it the miserable wives group."

"No," said Barbara. "She's many years a widow."

"She'll fit right in."

Kenny nudged Peggy and pointed at Fairway Drive. Barbara pointed out her mother's house and Peggy pulled the golf cart up to the end of the driveway.

"Lily's just a few doors down that way," said Barbara, hopping out of the cart.

"Hand me that scorecard," Peggy poked Kenny and nodded at the tiny glovebox under the dashboard. "Give me her address honey so I don't knock on the wrong door of these cookie-cutter houses."

"Hey," Kenny said after Barbara waved goodbye and started up the driveway, "just go to straight to your house. I can walk from there."

"What about your clubs?"

"I can come back for them. Or just drop them off when you can."

"I can drop you off. Just put your clubs in the car. I'm beginning to feel like a taxi."

She brought the golf cart to a stop in her driveway. Kenny gathered his clubs as the garage door clunkity-clunked open. She opened the trunk and he placed the golf bag inside it.

"You thirsty?" she asked. "Come on in and have a drink while I get changed."

Kenny followed her through the door from the garage to the kitchen. Everything in there was neat and ordered, the marble countertops shiny and new. Peggy pulled the stainless-steel door to the gigantic fridge open and called out the options.

"Lemonade? Orange juice? Gatorade? Sparkling water? Water?"

"I'll just have water, thanks."

The dream she'd tapped him out of this morning came rushing back as ice tumbled from the magnificent stainless-steel fridge and clinked into the glass. The dark corridors in his dream, a room from which sounded a machine clank. He imagined, standing in the antiseptically clean environs of the Beamish's kitchen, some medical apparatus engaged by a technician to do the dirty work, a medical procedure for which not she Kathy, but he himself, had planted the seed.

Mike Beamish appeared from the guest room and Kenny's eyes hadn't fully adjusted to the dim interior from the bright sunlight. The voice rang familiar and soon the form took shape and then he stood speechless before the man Peggy introduced as her husband.

"Well, my goodness, hey there my friend," Mike Beamish did a better job of masking his surprise.

"You two actually know each other?"

"We met at church," Kenny said.

Peggy glanced sharply at him. "I didn't have you pegged as a church person."

"I went once. Yesterday."

"Crisis of conscience?"

Kenny shrugged at this, his eyes hadn't left Mike, who tapped his wife playfully on the shoulder. "Maybe you should try it. Might do you a world of good."

"Nothing to confess," she puckered her lips, shrugged. "Not a thing on this old gal's conscience."

"That's Confession. Not what Mass is about my dear."

"*Isn't* it?"

Peggy poured lemonade in two tall glasses and glanced at the clock, thinking *won't I have something to tell Marge about.* She drained the lemonade in one gulp and went off to shower and change clothes, leaving Kenny standing alone with Mike.

Mike motioned Kenny over to the kitchen table. "What a surprise," he said. "My wife told me she had a golf partner this morning."

"Well," said Kenny, "I'm no match for her. She's got quite a drive. And her putting game is pretty damn sharp."

"I used to play," Mike shrugged. "Kinda lost interest in the game."

Kenny nodded, glancing around to take in the Beamish household. A living room in impeccable order. A coffee table before a deep-cushioned sofa. Two matching chairs and a leather recliner. Beneath small windows high up near the ceiling, a widescreen TV that took up a good portion of a wall lined with tiny shelves adorned with family photographs right down to the grandchildren. Ocean-themed wall art. At the back, flowery stained-glass ornaments hung on sliding glass doors that opened onto the screened porch. While Kenny's back porch was a nondescript cement floor with not much space after the rusting washer and dryer, Peggy and Mike's had fresh paint, a bamboo rug and tropical plants around the white wicker furniture. Beyond the closed bedroom door, he could hear Peggy turn on the tap for the shower. He hoped it would be brief and that they'd be on their way in a jiffy. *Maybe*, he thought, *I'll just bug out for the dugout and come back for the clubs later.*

"So," said Mike, "any word from your girl?"

*So now*, thought Kenny, shaking his head, *this couple, independent from one another, knows my sordid business.* "Not since we… talked."

"Well," Mike rapped assuringly on the table. "I'm sure everything will turn out okay."

So now, in addition to their shared knowledge of his affairs, he had a vote of confidence from both Mr. and Mrs. Beamish, neither of whom he knew very well or very long.

The dining nook off the Beamish kitchen was an oak table with four cushioned rolling caster chairs. While the seating was more comfortable than the bare wood barstools they'd sat next to each other on just last night, their conversation was less comfortable in the light of day. Kenny utilized his gift of gab, kept his gob moving, lest any lapse in the onslaught of words might allow Beamish to interject and direct the conversation to a shared masculine knowledge, men stuff, keeping it hush hush. Their vow to secrecy.

Peggy ran the shower and cut the water before Kenny Fitzroy ran out of words. Just as he was preparing himself to launch a lengthy polemic on the Bush administration and its ties to oil landlords and illegal wars, Peggy Beamish strode into the living room in denim shorts, a plain black tee shirt, a flowery print silk scarf draped around her neck. She pinched the scarf.

"I know it looks funny wearing it in summer. But it actually helps keep me cool. And besides," she tapped Mike on the shoulder, "my boyfriends tell me I look great in it."

While Mike racked his brain for a clever response, she swiped her keys and sunglasses from the table and said hop to it Kenny I'm running late.

"You guys going to lunch?"

"Oh no," said Kenny. "Mrs. Beamish is just dropping me home. Girls' night—er, day out."

"Aha."

"What are you gonna do with yourself today sugarplum?" Peggy asked her husband with a smirk.

"I don't know," he said, and he wasn't lying. He was unsure of what direction his emotions might steer him as he listened to the sound of the car doors slam shut and the keying of the ignition in the adjacent garage. He drummed his fingers on the table, sat still and listened to the sound of his own breathing. He'd done his laps. Done his *extra* laps. He imagined a girlfriend for himself in Isabel Amador, but last night's rebuff continued to nag at him and he couldn't shake it off. Different generation. In his day, relationships were forged fast and that was that. This, he'd heard, was the dating age, all about the individual. Women's lib. Empowerment. Hooking up. Playing the field. You could still play games, only the rules had changed.

He considered picking up the phone and dialing her number to set up a lunch date of his own. He lifted the cordless, hesitating about whether to dial. Paced about the living room and flopped into one of the wicker chairs on the back porch. Watched a gathering of egrets by the man-made pond that served as a water trap for the golfers. The porch was always a little warmer than the rest of the house. It was more Peggy's space than his.

The big party loomed. Peggy hadn't stepped up and taken care of the arrangements after he'd rented the room at the North Club. He'd got some invitations out himself, very late. They hadn't received an overwhelming response, by phone or email. Now here was his wife going to have lunch with this lady Marge, whom she hardly knew. Peggy was up to something. He was sure of it.

*

When Lily had gone to check on Barbara the previous evening after supper, she saw the car missing and left a note. A customarily humdrum evening was clouded with worry. About nine o'clock the phone rang and it was Barbara saying she'd just got back from one of those meetings she had to attend. Lily went to bed greatly relieved and slept soundly. Her son Jack called early this morning and she told him the latest news on Barbara. Jack wasn't used to hearing news about anyone but herself and he worried she was getting too deep into someone else's affairs. Maybe, she told him, it will take my mind off your brother. Stop obsessing on family, he said. I keep telling you. Join a book club. Or arts and crafts. Or Bingo. You gotta get out of the house more Mom. I *am* getting out of the house, she said. I'm going to check on the girl. She's not a girl, Mom. She's a grown woman. With problems. Lily said, she's a sensitive soul. She needs help right now. I'm here and I can give it.

She dressed and stepped outside with Rex to go and check on Barbara. The air was thick with afternoon heat and by the time they reached the end of the driveway, the dog was already panting and so was Lily. They started up the sidewalk and there came Barbara, strolling casually in the middle of Fairway Drive towards them. Such a marked difference, thought Lily, from the frenzied manner in which they'd run into each other the first time in this very same spot. She spied the neighbors across the street from Barbara casually going about trimming rosebushes, the same couple who'd only a week ago looked on at the EMT scene with worried faces and asked Lily if everything was alright.

"Hi," Barbara beamed. "I tried calling but your line was busy."

"I was on the phone with my son Jack," said Lily, catching her breath.

Barbara walked over to them on the sidewalk and crouched to pet Rex with both hands. "I've got some good news for you, I think."

"Well c'mon let's get out of this heat and you can tell me." Lily turned back to the house and Barbara followed her up the sandstone driveway.

Lily poured two glasses of filtered water from the fridge. When they'd both caught their breath, seated across from one another in the living room area, Barbara reached over and tapped Lily's knee. "Tell me. When was the last time you went to the beach?"

"Oh heavens. Must be years ago now. Dorothy and I went a few times before she got sick. Once to St. Petersburg, once further down south over the Sunshine Skyway. Sarasota, I believe it was."

"I know this is short notice," said Barbara. "But I've invited you to a lunch and beach day."

"Oh my."

"Unfortunately, I won't be able to join the fun. I have a meeting with the monsignor over at the Catholic Church."

"Oh. Well, who's going?"

"Two lovely ladies whose company I think you will immensely enjoy."

"Today?"

Barbara nodded, again tapped Lily's knee. "That's why I rushed over here to tell you. Kenny's friend Peggy and her friend."

"Who's Kenny?"

"My mother's old Bridge partner. You remember, the oddball?"

"The one you had dinner with. At the Seagull."

"I just ran into him. And his friend Peggy. Coming back from golf. She's just getting changed and then she's going to pick up her friend and then come by here to pick you up."

"Oh my heavens. Now?"

"C'mon. I'll help you pack a beach bag. You got a swimsuit?"

"Sure. I've got a few stashed away."

"Well let's *un*-stash them."

Barbara followed Lily to the garage and they fetched a straw woven beach bag and stuffed a beach towel into it. Lily fetched a pair of floral-print one-piece swimsuits from the depths of her closet and they settled themselves on the sofa, the front door wide open so as to keep a lookout for Peggy's car.

"I still haven't dug into my mother's papers."

"Why not?"

"I don't know. It just feels… icky." Barbara grimaced, seating herself beside Lily. "I was going to bring them with me for you to look over and I forgot. Maybe I can bring them over later. If you don't mind."

Rex scampered over to Barbara and stood up on hind legs, placing his paws on the edge of the sofa. A couple of pats on the head and he jumped up onto the cushion and crumpled beside her.

"It's a good thing I'm not all about money," said Barbara, petting the dog, "because I expect she wrote me out of her will."

"Now why do you think she'd go and do a thing like that?"

"Because she said she would."

"Oh my goodness, did she really say a mean thing like that?"

"I don't know. Once or twice. In anger."

"People say a lot of things they don't mean when they're upset."

"I'd say people say *exactly* what they mean when they're upset," said Barbara. "In those moments, the truth comes out."

Rex brought himself up on all fours, shook himself and dismounted. Barbara gathered her long auburn hair to unclasp a fine gold chain with an emerald pendant from her skinny neck. Lily reached for it and draped it in her fingers before placing it in her palm to study a bright-cut silver round setting, ten round pavé-set diamonds flanking an emerald with a cut that bespoke elegance.

"What a unique piece of jewelry," Lily said. "I didn't notice it on you until just now."

"I just found it this morning. Going through mother's things."

"Oh."

"My birthstone. She gave it to me years ago. A graduation present."

"So how did she come to be in possession of it after giving it to you?"

"I gave it back to her. Actually I threw it at her."

"At graduation?"

"No," Barbara laughed, "Long after that. In an argument about how I didn't turn out the way she might have hoped when she gave it to me."

"Did she *say* those words? Put it to you like that?"

"More or less. I was a pre-law political science major. Straight As."

Barbara's lucidity was a far cry from the condition Lily had found her in just a day ago. The contrast lent her a sense of both relief and concern—if Barbara could fall so deeply and recover so quickly, who could tell when it might happen again? She returned the precious gem and Barbara clasped it around her neck.

"I never went to college," said Lily, shuffling over to the kitchen table. "There was a shortage of teachers. I studied, took the certification test."

"Were you a good student?"

"I was obedient, if that's what you mean. My grades were so-so."

"You were the shy little girl who sat at the front of the class," Barbara settled herself across from Lily at the kitchen table. "Didn't speak unless spoken to."

"Well, I guess you might say that."

"Kept you nose clean."

"Well."

"Did you *ever* get in trouble?"

"I did my best not to."

"So you *did*. Get in trouble. A time or two."

"Yes. I guess I did."

"Well, spill it. What did you get up to?"

"What does it matter? My gosh, all these years later."

"It's just a story," Barbara shrugged. "I like stories. Oblige me."

"Well," Lily frowned, "there's not much to tell."

Barbara tilted her head inquisitively.

"It's a little embarrassing, really."

"Well *now* you've stoked my interest."

"I don't remember exactly how old I was. Maybe twelve or so. There was this boy in my class."

"Started with the boys a little early, did we?"

"Oh please."

"Sorry. Go ahead." Rex was sprawled out on the kitchen floor, and Barbara rose to rub his belly.

"Anyway," Lily sighed, "I guess he was what you'd call a bully. Yes. A bully. Made fun of me. My… glasses. I had crooked eyes and a stigmatism and my coke bottle glasses. I wasn't about to win a beauty contest, with or without them. My brother Tom… Tom was older than me, always looked out for me. When the other kids… well. You know how kids can be."

Rex had found a new toy—one of Lily's pot holders and Barbara was sitting Indian-style on the linoleum floor playing tug-of-war with him. "Go ahead," she said. "I'm listening."

"Anyhow, this boy. Peter Sellers. Not the actor."

"His name was really Peter Sellers?"

"God as my witness. No relation. Nothing like the actor. Big, brawny. Freckle-faced. Ran the show with the boys. Mean as a snake. Made me his object of ridicule right from the beginning. Started a rumor I wet my pants. He'd come up behind me and pull my hair."

"Pigtails?

"No. No pigtails."

"Okay, just had this picture—"

"Anyway, one bright fall afternoon Tom and I were playing by the river. You know, like kids do."

"Sure," Barbara gave up on the tug-of-war with Rex and sat across the table from Lily.

"Tom was showing me how to use a slingshot. Always had that thing, those days. Stuck in his back pocket. There we were, down by the river, shooting pebbles at floating Coke cans. Tom'd found a good stick and he fashioned a slingshot right before my eyes, with a pen-knife and a rubber band. While he whittled, I was telling him about Peter Sellers. How he just wouldn't let me alone."

"Right."

"Tom tells me he'll pull that bully aside and warn him, threaten to beat the snot out of him if he doesn't quit bothering me."

Lily was very still. She licked her lips and bit her bottom lip and stared into some middle distance. "I guess maybe I thought that might only invite more trouble. I don't know. Who knows the way our mind works behind the curtain sometimes? Anyway, I started carrying that slingshot in my little purse."

"Like a twenty-two-caliber. Your lady's gun," Barbara said, gathering the dog up and into her lap.

"One day," Lily squinted as if to conjure up a distant past, "we were sitting in class, waiting on the teacher. Kids laughing, a few of em shooting spitballs at each other. Sellers had insulted me again, said something in the hallway." She scrunched her eyebrows. "He wasn't bothering me right then and there. Wasn't saying anything. Wasn't *doing* anything, come to think of it. Just sitting there, staring off into space. I was just watching him. His freckled face. His pug nose. His crew cut. How I hated that ugly crew cut."

Barbara petted the dog with long slow strokes, listening intently.

"I drew the slingshot from my lap. Lifted my desktop just enough to draw a paper clip from the inkwell. Loaded it the way you would a pebble. I was a pretty good shot by then. I aimed for his chest. I didn't mean to hit him in the eye."

A tear rolled down Lily's sunlit cheek. "That boy was in the hospital for three days. Lost the sight of that eye."

"I'm sorry."

"Still haven't forgiven myself," Lily wiped at her tears with the back of her hand. "Don't reckon I ever will."

*

Thirty miles south of Sunnyville lay the bottom lip of the mouth of Tampa Bay, Anna Maria Island. Long stretches of white sandy beach, the turquoise water graduating to teal, then to a deeper blue where it meets the horizon and a pale blue sky that darkens in shade with altitude.

Marge had assumed their lunch date was both local and exclusive until Peggy pulled into her driveway, lowered the window, told her to step it up because they had one more to fetch, and asked her if she'd packed a beach bag and a bathing suit.

The map she held in front of her was folded to show all parts south—through Fort Myers down to the Everglades and the long string of Keys. Ted enjoyed where he was and would say so—why go anywhere when we got it all here? He'd always been that way. Marge was pretty sure that wasn't the way she felt as they turned onto the interstate leaving Sunnyville behind them. The open expanse of highway, the uninterrupted stretch without towns or exits seemed to evoke an elaboration on Peggy's wanderlust with a rumination on all the places she'd never been. In her excitement she kept removing her hands from the wheel to make gestures and this put Marge and Lily a little on edge. Her plans were vague and magnificent and her husband never showed up in any of them.

Lily closed her eyes and took in the ocean breeze under the shade of the table umbrella. From the moment they'd picked her up in her driveway, she'd taken a backseat, literally and proverbially, on the drive over the Sunshine Skyway and past Palmetto, craning her neck this way and that and taking in a Florida she'd not come to know much. Much of the ladies' talk back and forth over the front seat of Peggy's expansive Lincoln was lost to her ears without the hearing aids she'd forgotten to pack in her haste. She gave a smile and nods of acknowledgement to both ladies when they glanced over the bench seat to her, snuggled up in the corner of the passenger side so as not to obstruct Peggy's rear view. Her own social skills were well in the rearview mirror. Much as the young woman had drawn her out, a crisis was woven into the fabric of that drawing out. This casual socializing was a whole different animal. She was glad of the backseat as it afforded her the benefit of testing the waters, rather than diving in with muscles long unused.

When they crossed the Manatee River and drove through downtown Bradenton, it dawned on Marge there was a whole other world out there and she and Ted hadn't yet ventured beyond the gate to explore it. Peggy cut the air-conditioning and let the windows down. Marge closed her eyes and took in the gush of salty air across her face. She could sense they were near the beach and became charged with excitement about the day ahead of her and the promise of sand and the great big sea.

Peggy said let's do lunch first and then hit the beach and that was just fine by Marge—her paltry breakfast seemed an eternity ago as the hostess at Island Beach Cafe led them to a table and dropped menus on the table.

They had a spectacular view of the Gulf and three plates with grouper sandwiches and French fries arrived to them in short order. A salad to spilt three ways. Marge and Lily sipped water with ice and a slice of lemon while Peggy dawdled with her margarita. She toyed with a fork at her salad and sighed, puffed her cheeks and addressed Lily.

"So Lily, tell us about your love life."

"Me?" Lily leaned in, the better to hear. "Oh, not much to tell really. Married young."

"High school sweetheart, eh?"

"Well, not exactly. My sister Dorothy's high school sweetheart."

"Ahh. Fella with a rovin eye."

"Well, I guess it all turned out for the best. Dorothy and Dan dated in high school. Then she met the love of her life in the end," Lily shrugged. "And I reckon I did to."

"So what happened after that?" Peggy sipped at her margarita. "Years of marital bliss?"

Lily shook her head ruefully. "He died too young. Fifty-six years old."

"Oh, I'm sorry." Peggy cocked her head sympathetically.

"So you came down here all by yourself." said Marge.

"Well, it took me years to take the plunge. Dorothy was here when I finally did. Not long after *she* was widowed."

"Well, it's good you've got family nearby anyway," said Marge.

"She died."

"Oh my gosh," said Marge. "I'm sorry."

"Not long after I came down." Lily gave Marge an appreciative nod, having forgotten, to her chagrin, her consoler's name. Another social skills muscle she'd long been exempt from exercising—remembering names on introduction. It was awkward, to Lily anyway, to ask again this far into their shared company. She coughed politely and excused herself the restroom, leaving the other two ladies to their exclusive company.

"So," said Peggy, "we both have shitty husbands and grown kids living rent-free in our real estate. My youngest is the reason we're down here in the sweltering heat and not up at the lake house we'd counted on for a summer home. But at least he's not shacking up with a kooky girlfriend."

Marge chewed and swallowed hard. "I wish I could just wave a magic wand and make her go away. My Ted isn't such a bad egg. You know what he told me this morning when we were waking up? He told me—"

"Wait a minute. You guys actually talk in the morning? In bed?"

"Sure. All the time."

"You sleep in the same bed?"

"Of course. Don't you?"

"We have twins," Peggy sighed. "Evil twins."

"*Oh.* Anyway," Marge said, "he apologizes for the way he talks to me sometimes. Out of the blue. I say how long have you been thinking about this? And he says he just got the idea from one of his new pals over at the computer club. He tells me there's so much to be angry about, but he's tired of being angry. He wants to go back on some meds and I'm trying to talk him into therapy."

"Yeah well, let's see," Peggy said, waving her sandwich at Marge. "I wouldn't hold your breath."

Marge stilled her fork in midair, her buoyant optimism speared.

Peggy shrugged. "*Mike* has promised any number of times to change over the past fifty years. And now here I am stuck with the same old galoot and the same problems."

"What kind of problems? If you don't mind me asking."

"Okay, you sure you want the list in its entirety?"

"Maybe just the highlights."

Peggy wagged her fork. "Cute. Okay. Top of the list. Philandering. Or adultery if you want to get downright biblical."

"You told me that awful story."

"Yep, the one I witnessed firsthand. But he's done it more than once."

"God," said Marge. "I can't imagine what that must be like. To go through. To have to deal with."

"Deal with? We don't deal with it. Don't talk about it. We just pretend it isn't there. Anyway, that's Mike's way of dealing with it."

"Haven't you ever challenged him?"

"Of course. Years ago. Like I said, I caught him with my best friend. *Our* best friends. We had to go through it as couples. Called the priest in, the whole shebang. He was real contrite. Real penitent. Kind of chilled out after a while, over the years. I don't know, ran out of steam I guess."

"Uh huh."

"At least until recently. Since we moved down here. I noticed he's got his flirt back on. And it ain't with yours truly, I can tell you that."

"I'm so sorry for you Peggy."

"Sorry?" Peggy said, bringing a napkin to her mouth. "Don't be. This lady's got a plan up her sleeve, while she's still got some spark left in her."

Marge squinted across the table, Peggy nodded her head. "*Oh* yeah," she said. "I'm gonna hit the road. I started pricing everything from RVs to sleeper vans. That's what I'm gonna do, after the divorce goes through.

Find my own little hideaway. Somewhere out west. In the high desert, I think. It's too damn hot here."

"The *divorce*?"

Peggy waved a hand dismissively. "Honey, I've already contacted an attorney. I'm going to file. After he has his little party."

"But why even have the party?" Marge knitted her brow.

"Aren't you supposed to, when you hit the big fifty mark? I guess I want the kids to have a chance to celebrate us, the grandkids to have a nice memory of us. Before the end of us. Hell," she shrugged, "I'm celebrating *endurance.* I'm celebrating my incredible capacity to abide the craziest shit. I'm gonna enjoy my party. And after the dust settles, when all the hoopla is over, I'm gonna hit the road jack. Gonna hit the road."

"Just like that," said Marge, drumming her fingers on the table while gazing off into space.

"Just like that," Peggy repeated. "And let me tell ya something, it's not the first time I've hatched an escape plan. I've harbored secret plans for years, even brought them out in the open a few times. He once threatened to kill himself if I left him." Peggy drew a heavy sigh. "Once I had my bags packed, a guest room at a friend's house all lined up, and then his dad goes and gets sick. My father-in-law. Terminal illness. Suddenly it's not the right time. Seems like every time I find the right time, one life event or another gets in the way. Postpones the inevitable."

Marge shook her head slowly. "Life event. As in a fiftieth wedding anniversary."

"Yeah," Peggy rolled her eyes. "Only this is the last one. I'm not going to wait on the next crisis, or grandbaby, or whatever else might keep me from leaving that lovable jackass."

Lily returned to the table and Peggy turned her frown into a polite smile of greeting. They finished their lunch amid light banter about the great weather and how wonderful it was to be out of the gates and at the ocean and there was nothing disingenuous among the three of them in this shared sentiment. Peggy picked up the tab and said one of you get the next one—leaving Lily to think, for the second time in just a few days, someone had treated her at a restaurant. At the car, she fished around in her beach bag for a swimsuit and started for the restaurant and a restroom clothing change, something she couldn't recall ever having executed.

There was nowhere else to change into their bathing suits so the other ladies settled on taking turns in the back seat of the Lincoln. While Marge wrestled into her one-piece, Peggy hollered out from her lookout post.

"Why does he get so upset anyway, that husband of yours, about the godamn liberals this the godamn liberals that? What the hell does he care?"

"He has principles," Marge grunted as she struggled into her suit. "He believes in a kind of code to live by I guess."

"Live and let live, that's what I say. Jesus if I wasted any time stewing about why other people don't think like I do, I'd go batshit crazy."

Marge clambered out of the Lincoln, waving Peggy invitation to the back seat. She stood with her back up against the car and glanced at the shoreline. "Ever get the feeling," she called out to Peggy, "you married the wrong person, the wrong guy?"

"Yes I do. On a daily basis."

"I guess I just never dwelt on it much. Until lately."

Lily returned in her one-piece, toting her beach bag. They carried their gear to a sparsely populated beach. Marge unfolded the chairs, Lily spread out the blanket and Peggy cranked the umbrella open. Lily walked to the water's edge and dipped her toes in the surf. She got ankle deep, then knee deep, the waves splashing cold drops of water up to her waist. She shivered and hugged herself, went in waist deep, splashing the cold water about her shoulders, deciding to wade no further into the crystal-clear sea. She tried to recall just how far back in the years it was that she and Dorothy had their one and only beach outing. Jack and Ann and the grandkids balked at her requests to pack the car and have a day at the beach, derailing plans she'd so looked forward to. The pool, it seemed, was enough for them.

She swirled her arms and lowered herself into the seafoam, crouched, wiggled her toes in the sand and tiny shell fragments. The curl of a wave loomed in front of her and she rose, closed her eyes and lifted her face to the sun. The other two watched, having settled themselves side-by-side on the blanket, hugging at their crossed legs while gazing out upon the breakers, listening to the sound of waves crashing one after another. Even in the shade, it wasn't long before they were good and hot. Marge followed Peggy into the ocean. She fanned her arms through crystal clear water and when she'd swam out beyond the breakers she rolled over onto her back, having her own private joke about how those extra pounds she'd gained in Florida came in handy for flotation. She watched Peggy swim along the shore, her tanned arms rising up out of the water in smooth even strokes and she was very grateful for her new friend and hoped that she might change her mind about leaving town after the big party. Perhaps, she thought, this was just some kind of late-marriage crisis and the party would be just the thing to snap her out of it.

Because the truth of it was, no matter the ten-thousand and growing population of the Sunny Glen Palms community, true friends were hard to find. And no one seemed to be warming up to Ted very much. Perhaps he might temper his temper, trim his principles so as to widen the net they cast for friends. Because the emails from friends up north were dwindling, phone calls initiated mostly on her end. She had hoped things might take root in Florida. She needed someone besides Ted to bat words back and forth. She and that principled husband of hers badly needed friends. They simply could not go it alone. *Why do I always just go along with whatever he says*, Marge thought, biting her lip and watching Peggy floating out on the water, eyes closed, soaking up the sun much like a little girl in the halcyon days of summer when nothing else mattered but the moment one found oneself in, the past something forgotten, having rolled out with the tide, the future as vague as that distance beyond where the sea meets the sky.

*

Ted Cumberbatch checked his watch at the Arrivals terminal of Tampa airport, on the lookout for parking officials. When he saw his son, he waved his arms with a look of recognition and Teddy came rushing forward with his bag in tow. Ted stuck out his hand while his son initiated a hug. He took this and after a few manly claps on the back, he released his son and grasped him by the elbows. "Ya lost some weight," he beamed. "Looking good kid."

"Thanks Dad. Stress will do that sometimes, I guess."

"Well, better than overeating. C'mon let's put this in the trunk."

He hefted his son's suitcase and they hustled so as not to be ticketed in the no-parking zone.

"So where's Mom," Teddy asked after they'd got onto the interstate.

"Oh, she had a lunch date today."

"A lunch date?"

"Lady friend."

"Oh, that's cool. Hey, thanks alot for flying me down Dad. I really appreciate it."

"Our pleasure." He tapped his son on the knee. "Good to see you."

"I really could use the break."

"Well, we're not gonna put you to work. You still play tennis?"

"Been a while, but I could."

"We'll have to get you a racquet," Ted said, smarting at the thought of the one he'd mangled on the court a few days ago. "Walmart usually has them cheap."

"I almost missed my flight. The airport shuttle got slightly delayed," Teddy said, staring out the window abstractedly. "Some anti-war protest downtown."

"Anti-war?"

"Yeah, the whole Iraq thing. I don't know."

"Those kids better not be parading our streets with their hogwash."

Teddy gave his father a sidelong glance. "You wanna go up there and run them off single-handedly?"

His father squeezed the steering wheel and huffed. "They don't know the sacrifices our men in uniform made to give them their freedom."

Teddy steered the subject back to Florida and his rusty tennis game, because he knew his father's sermons by heart and it didn't take much to draw them out.

When they arrived at the house, Marge still hadn't returned. Ted went to help his son hoist the carry-on out of the trunk.

"I got it Dad."

"Mom has the guest room all ready for you."

Teddy wondered what all it entailed, preparing a guest room. Wasn't it in a state of perpetual preparedness? Unless you arrived on the heels of a previous guest, or perhaps his mother had taken up a new hobby that required a dedicated room. He set the small suitcase on the bed. Folksy framed embroidery on the walls. An unexpected wave of contentment, fantasizing once again about the idyllic family. To wake up each morning to the bright sunlight and the sound of his mother in the kitchen rustling up a hearty breakfast of bacon and eggs. To spend afternoons playing golf with dear old dad. To rip through a John LeCarre paperback at the pool between dips. It sure beat reporting to work in a cubicle every morning to be browbeaten. It would sure beat waking up in a dimly lit house with another argument just around the corner. Cotton clouds drifting along calm blue skies sure as hell beat the gray winter skies back north.

"Why don't we go get us a beer," he heard his father calling from the kitchen. "Your mother didn't have anything to say about dinner so we can eat at the club. You hungry?"

When they reached the South Club on the golf cart it had just begun to rain. The club was packed and Ted recognized his tennis partners from just a few days ago. The man at the corner of the bar with the sun at his back and somewhat silhouetted and alongside him his wife, rays of sunlight coursing through her jet-black hair. He'd already forgotten their names. After scanning the room for anyone else he might know and seeing none, he sauntered over to them, his son in tow, and Jim and Betsy Hightower reintroduced themselves.

Hightower grinned broadly. "Where's the wife today?"

"Ladies day out," said Ted as Hightower pumped his hand. "Friend of hers."

"I see."

"Well," said Ted, glancing around him, "I've never seen this place so packed. What's the occasion?"

Hightower shrugged. "Maybe the last hurrah before the bad weather. Quite a hurricane season."

"Guess we get a few of them here in Florida," Ted said, bouncing on his heels and doing his best to display a level-headed and happy-go-lucky retiree to contradict the racquet-smashing lunatic they met on the court a few days back.

Betsy Hightower shrugged. "Tis the season. Part of the package." She squinted one eye closed and raised a warning finger, "Bad one on the way though."

To this Ted stretched his face in mock astonishment and gave a smug patronizing smile. "This place is packed," he repeated, glancing around.

"Actually," said Jim, "we were just leaving if you'd like our seats."

The Hightowers settled their tab and then the Cumberbatches settled themselves on the vacated barstools. Teddy watched the TV screen above the bar and half-listened to his father chatting easily with the staff member tending bar as he ordered a pitcher of beer. The weather forecast. Every day of the week beyond today marked with a lightning bolt and raincloud icon. *That's just great*, he thought to himself. *Come all this way to be cooped up inside the whole time.* The west coast of Florida was getting the residual effects of Hurricane Jeanne. Meanwhile Hurricane Charley bore down on the Gulf. Teddy didn't like that look on the weatherman's face.

*

While he'd only managed a meager savings, something Kenny Fitzroy could count among his lucky stars was his good fortune regarding health. Until now he'd been plagued by no major ailments, no diseases presented as dissonance to his corporeal harmony. A bout with the measles as a tyke, a broken arm as a teenager. There were of course, the ulcers. He was plagued by a problematic digestive system, largely due to a lazy diet that didn't incorporate much in the way of healthy home cooking.

His dental health was a whole other ball of wax. Four crowns, three fillings, two root canals—a result of a childhood over-indulgence in sweets. The proverbial sweet tooth to which his mother dispensed—Easter was a chocolate feast largesse, Halloween a candy orgy, an overall steady diet of all things saccharin.

He was fortunate not to have seen the inside of a hospital too often. He had his tonsils out at a young age and that was a night. An emergency appendectomy as a teenager and that was a night. That was a good thing, because for most of his adult life Kenny had rolled the dice, going without health insurance. At present he'd neglected to attend to this by taking on even the most bare-bones catastrophic coverage. He wondered about the baby. Kathy worked for some large corporation or another—he'd have to assume she'd be covered for the birth, maybe had maternity leave. It was new territory for Kenny—this thing of having to concern himself with the plight of another human being.

He was sat on one of the vinyl-upholstered seats at the Formica table in his modest kitchen, thumbing through old family photographs that his Aunt Eustice had brought with her from Punta Gorda on her visit to him shortly after his mother's death. He drew an old black and white print with scalloped edges. The three sisters, in formal wedding dresses, big smiles, shot very casually at an angle—his mother Margaret and Aunt Eustice sat in front of a mirror at a vanity, his Aunt Charlotte hovering behind them. Aunt Charlotte's wedding—it bore out later that she was already pregnant with her first-born daughter.

He could imagine his Aunt Charlotte phoning him from Connecticut, an authoritative voice taxing his overworked mind. *Nephew*, she would say with her distinctive tone of authority, this was the term by which she most often addressed him—nephew, as if they were relations and she were stuck with the fact. *Nephew*, I got the news—*we* got the news, about Kathy. I know it's probably none of my business but for what it's worth I'll put in my two cents. There are responsibilities that have been introduced to you at a rather advanced age no doubt and that's just the way life is sometimes.

He'd hold the phone at a good distance from his ear as his aunt droned on, studying the back of his hand, its coarseness, deepening wrinkles, the marks of aging. Her speech would run its course and he in return would loft words of reassurance that he would not fail in his duty, would do right by Kathy. He returned the photo to its place, and with it his imaginings.

After a good bit of lumping around the golf greens, after Peggy had dropped him to his door, wiggled her fingers and said toodaloo, he'd taken refuge from the sticky heat in his air-conditioned haven. Where ordinarily he'd be drawn to the couch as if it were a magnet and he heavy metal, he was shifty and restless.

He traded his golf shoes for a pair of punished Converse high tops, and along with them cooler air for hot and humid. He started walking at a leisurely pace towards Sunset Boulevard, no destination in mind. He let his feet guide him to the Meadowbrook subdivision, and followed the road until he came to Alice Thunderclap's house. He lingered at the end of the driveway, under the palm trees, balled fists crammed into his jeans pockets. The door opened and Barbara called out to him.

"Are you just gonna stand there?"

She held the screen door open and he shuffled over.

Inside the kitchen he leaned on the granite countertop while Barbara drew him a glass of filtered water from the fridge.

"I hope I'm not barging in at a bad time."

"Uh uh, you're fine."

"I just happened to be walking by."

"Well good timing. Just got back from the church."

"I didn't know you went to church. And weekday mass. Wow."

"Oh stop it. I had to meet with a Monsignor John Davis. About the memorial service."

"The funeral Mass."

"Memorial service. There's a distinction when it's a cremation."

"Oh. How'd that go?"

"As good as these things can, I guess. What've you been up to?"

"Just laying low beating the heat after all that sun on the golf links."

"With your lady friend."

"Yeah, with my lady friend."

"So, was that a date?"

Kenny made a face. "She's married, remember? Probably old enough to be my mother."

"Doesn't ever keep you lady killers at bay."

"So," he said, rolling his eyes. "Got any plans? This evening?"

"Actually, I was just packing up some board games."

"Oh?"

"Cards and whatnot party at Lily's."

"Where does she live?"

"Just a few doors down," she said. "We'll deal you in if you like cards. You play rummy?"

Kenny shrugged. "Been a while. Kind of a bridge guy."

"I know. You played with my mother. Now you get to play with her daughter."

"Okay."

"What was she like?"

"Your mother?"

"Yes. My mother."

"Well. I mean… you're her daughter."

"I know. But I want to know your impression of her. Was she nice, was she grumpy? Did she lose patience easily, quick to temper? That sort of thing. Sit and talk to me while I pack."

"Okay."

He followed her into the guestroom and sat on the bed watching her heft a few board games from the shelf in the closet.

"Your Mom," said Kenny, "was really nice to me. She was one of the few friends I have—*had* here. A skilled Bridge player. She didn't talk much. While playing Bridge I mean. But sometimes I'd see her at the pool and we'd sit and talk up a storm. We'd have lunch at the South Club."

"Did she ever talk about me?"

"She mentioned you every now and again."

Barbara zipped up the sports bag and glanced up at him. "*And*?"

"I think she was frightened of you."

"Frightened?"

"I mean that in a sort of… flattering way. I mean she considered you highly intelligent, if a little misguided."

Barbara smiled, shaking her head. "A *little* misguided? She thought I was batshit crazy."

"N-now that… that's definitely not true."

"You're just saying that to make me feel better."

"Uh-uh, no way."

"You can't put words in the mouths of the dead."

Perhaps, he thought, he was treading dangerous waters. He rose from the bed and stood in the doorway as if doing so might change the subject.

"Well," she said, "she despised me anyway."

"No she didn't. I wouldn't say that. She said you were the brightest of all her kids."

A look of surprise came over Barbara's face. She stepped around the bed with a handful of board games and he backpedaled into the kitchen. "Anyway," she said, "I'm curious how others saw my mother."

"Sure, I understand," he said, looking on as she folded the board games into a shopping bag, following her to the front door. "Anyway, I think she loved you. I'm pretty sure of it."

She stopped in the driveway, swinging the bag with both hands in front of her. "So, you coming over for cards?"

"Yeah, I guess so," he said. Games and cards, he thought, would serve as a welcome distraction to the thoughts that plagued him.

"While I can't say I espoused her political views," he said to her back, "I can't say your mother was inconsiderate in her expression of them. At least she was curious about my own. She was one of the few people I could share them with who didn't get angry, didn't get red in the face."

Barbara turned around briefly to display her puzzlement.

"Don't get me wrong. Nobody was out to change anyone's mind. She seemed curious about my generation and how we thought about things, as if an entire generation can speak unequivocally as one voice."

"Maybe," said Barbara when he caught up to her to walk alongside, "she was just trying to get a glimpse of *me* through you."

*

*There are pennies in the attic. Heard father counting them early this morning. At first writer thought father stumbling around up there. Up to usual no-good. Pressed ear to closed door, heard tin can rattle then clank wobble and ring of coppers on hardwood. Grandfather Ahearn shaking head. At writing desk. Shook head much in those days. Shook head at most anything said by anyone. Us running off to school at crack of dawn. Hungry. Taking extra notes in schoolroom. Afraid I would forget. Like now. Mother long days at tile factory. Too tired to cook. Brother and I serving up scraps from kitchen. Grandfather at head of table. Shaking head.*

*

The house had darkened, what with all the lights switched off. In the living room the large screen television cast a soft glow, the sound muted. Mike Beamish's voice wafted in the darkness, addressing a pal he'd known most of his life. "I don't know what she wants to do. All I know is I can't stop thinking about her. I think all she wants is a little dalliance. You know, casual...No no, you don't understand. Listen to me Stan, she's the most fascinating woman I've ever met... Well, maybe it's me looking for the fountain of youth, shoot me... I don't know what Peggy's got to do with any of this... I know she's my wife, Jesus... Sure it complicates things... No, but I swear to God I've never felt this way about any of the others... what's that?... I know I'm sounding like high school... okay okay, mooning over Peggy... I guess so. I mean, Isabel has to protect herself... I *am* all in... oh, who invented the idea marriage anyway, I'd like to strangle him... I *am* happily married... Well I mean, you know Peggy. You gotta let 'em think they're running the show, right?"

He heard the door being keyed and hissed into the phone, *Hey Stan, she's back*, steering the conversation to baseball and what a lousy season the Twins were having, frantically rummaging about the sofa cushions to fish out the remote and turn the sound back on—it came back to life a little too loud and then he was practically shouting into the phone while he thumbed the gadget to tamp down a four-way argument between talking heads.

In the doorway, Peggy watched silently. The sun left her tired, woozy. She listened as her husband wound down the phone conversation. "Well God, Stan. We sure look forward to seeing you and Nancy. It means a lot to both of us, you making this trip down to share in our celebration."

Her husband's tone sounded just a little stilted for Stan Higginbottom.

"Well God almighty," she said, dropping her beach bag on the counter and switching on the kitchen light, "are we living in the dark ages?"

"Oh hi hon. I was just talking to Stan."

He listened to his wife putting things away, getting settled in. All he could think was that the day was gone, slipped through his hands while he could've been out having his own parade. With his what, girlfriend? All he knew was she hadn't invited him along with her friends to the Art Expo in Tampa, what would have been an opportunity to steal some time with her while Peggy was away.

Peggy sat at the far end of the sofa and he switched over to the local weather channel. Rain ahead, nothing but rain. And a severe weather alert. Hurricane Charley's projected landfall now late Saturday night, evacuations along the Gulf Coast already underway.

*

The prospect of entertaining company put Lily's house in a different light—the four matching chairs around the kitchen table made sense, as did the glassware and plates, and the nonstick baking pan she scoured before digging out a box of brownie mix buried deep within the cupboard. The glorious day at the beach with the ladies had left her tired and energized at the same time. All these things brought an old pleasure back to life. The extra wicker chairs on the back porch might now, like those in the kitchen, become useful accomplices to the one which she sat on every morning and dropped a book to her lap now and again to gaze out upon the golf greens.

When her guests arrived, she drew extra tall glasses and rinsed them in the sink with the buoyancy of a schoolgirl. Kenny's eyes lit up at the sight of brownies just out of the oven and cooling on the counter. Barbara cut pieces and he bore them over to the kitchen table on a serving plate with the care and attention one might a precious cargo.

The table had been cleared of its decorative faux flower centerpiece and replaced with a pile of un-played cards still in the shrink-wrap. Barbara broke the plastic and soon the three of them had their cards fanned out in front of them, studying them while they spoke between themselves. Kenny planted an elbow on the table and propped his head on his hand.

They played the first few hands in silence, organizing the cards in their hands while savoring home-made brownies that melted in their mouths.

"Weather's turning ugly starting tomorrow," Lily said.

"Really?" Barbara toyed with her pendant.

Lily drew a card and nodded. "Hurricane and I-don't-know-what-all. They're calling for evacuations in some places."

"Evacuations?" Kenny's eyes bulged. "Where?"

"Hard to tell exactly where it's going to land. Or how strong the winds are gonna be. Seems like it changes up to the minute."

"Do you think flights will be cancelled?" Kenny asked.

"Oh, I don't know about that," said Lily.

Barbara glanced over to Kenny, and then Lily. "He's nervous about a certain… guest."

"Oh, family?" Lily plunked down a discard, glancing over at Kenny.

"She soon *might* be," said Barbara, drawing a card from the deck and rearranging her hand.

Kenny pouted. "Just a friend from Connecticut."

"Kathy from Connecticut," Barbara said, her eyes glued to the hand of cards fanned out in front of her.

"We don't need to go into all that," muttered Kenny.

Lily cleared her throat and glanced over her cards at Barbara. "How did it go at the church today. With the monsignor?"

Barbara drew a sigh. "My brother's already meddling with the church and the funeral service. What all did he say to you, anyway? On the phone."

"Oh, your brother? He said he's flying in Wednesday."

"There's a flight I wish they'd cancel. Did he say where he's staying?"

"He didn't say. Have there been any more responses to your calls?"

"A few," said Barbara. "Most-if-not-all can't travel for the funeral. Offering condolences anyway."

"Well, all you can do is let them know. It's a long way for most people on short notice," said Lily, and couldn't help but wonder how ill-attended her own funeral might be.

Kenny drew a card, frowning at it, drumming his fingers at the table. He was careful and deliberate with each and every draw, and after a few plays Lily and Barbara exchanged knowing glances and Lily even brought a hand to her mouth to shield a playful grin.

At last, with a sigh of resignation he plucked a discard out of his hand.

Lily drew a card from the deck and then laid her hand out on the table for all to see. Three aces and a run of hearts.

"I'm out," she said. "Add em up."

Kenny groaned. He had all high-point cards in his hand that he had to subtract from his score and he was already in the hole. Scorekeeper Lily diligently scribbled on the scratchpad beside her. While Barbara shuffled and dealt the next hand, she rose to offer refills on the milk. Playing cards with friends after a full day at the beach watching the ladies laugh was a far cry from what she might have imagined a week ago, as unlikely as riding a camel in the Saharan desert. In an instant, she thought, the verdict of a predictably dull life might be overturned at the whim of whatever imagined judge might preside over the affairs of man from the heavens. Just when she thought destiny might send her to the grave without anything more to savor at the joyful feast of fellowship, here she was giggling with Barbara, feigning interest at Kenny's long monologues, and sharing her memories with both of them deep into the night. This and Kenny's deliberating over every move made for a long game of rummy and it was after eleven o'clock until at last Barbara hit the five-hundred mark. Barbara said she'd leave the board games behind for another night and the promise of future gatherings served to further warm Lily's thoughts.

After seeing her guests to the door and bidding them goodnight, Lily collapsed into the recliner and turned on the Weather Channel. Images of Hurricane Charley swirling off the coast of Cuba, leaving destruction in its path. The gravity of the situation was not lost on her and she worried about having to drive anywhere, particularly at night. Rex climbed into her lap. While she petted him, she tried to push such thoughts from her mind. She wouldn't let them have her tossing and turning. She wouldn't let a simple thing like the weather ruin the best day she'd had in a good many years.

*

Marge and Ted were propped up against the headboard side-by-side, books in hand. In hers, one of those quick-read romance paperbacks with a provocative title and cover art that suggested clandestine romantic trysts, betrayals, sly maneuvering. In his, *The Way Things Ought To Be* according to Rush Limbaugh, to which he tsk tsked at regular intervals.

Marge dropped the book to her lap as he fumed and flipped another page. "You're just going to get yourself whipped up into a frenzy."

"I like to read before I go to bed," he said evenly. "Nothing wrong with that."

"Depends on what you're reading," she said. "I like light fluff. You might try something a little more soothing at bedtime."

Ted dropped the book to his lap. He usually sat in the recliner and read and went to bed after Marge, but tonight they'd made space for their son in the guestroom. Teddy had a late-night TV habit and they could hear Letterman chuckling through his monologue and getting laughs.

"Anyway," said Ted. "You girls have a good time at the beach today?"

"Yes," Marge sighed. "we girls had a good time at the beach today."

"Do I detect a hint of sarcasm?"

Marge made a face, without taking her eyes off her book. Ted squinted at her. "That woman. What's her name?

"Peggy. Thought you already knew that."

"Peggy. Right. She's sort of an odd bird isn't she?"

Marge sighed, bringing the book to her lap. "Aren't we all an odd bird at the end of the day, Ted? You're a *very* odd bird to some."

"Did *she* say that?"

"Say what?"

"That I'm an odd bird."

"Well, if she had, I guess that'd make you even."

"Well anyway," he fanned the pages of his book. "I'd be careful with that one."

Marge set her book down on the nightstand. "I think," she said. "I'm old enough to pick my friends."

"I'm not suggesting otherwise, my dear. Just a little friendly advice."

She flung back the covers and threw her legs over the side of the bed. "When I need advice, I'll ask for it."

"Hey, hold on dear. I wasn't trying to tell you what to do. Just looking out for you."

But he was talking to her back as she thrust her arms into a terrycloth robe and closed the door quietly behind her.

Teddy was burrowed deep in the folds of the sofa with a beer and a bag of pretzels. On the big screen, a commercial for Acme Flooring. Teddy lowered the volume.

"Hi Ma."

"How's things?"

"Okay. Can't sleep?"

"It only gets harder as you get older."

"I'm having a hard time at my young age."

"Well you've got a lot on your mind."

"Wish I was working. I keep sending out resumes. But at my age."

"You'll find something."

"Yeah," he said, shooting her a glance." I'm just afraid of what that something might be. Like flipping burgers at McDonald's."

"Well," she said, patting him on the knee. "Just enjoy yourself while you're down here."

"It's good to have a break from a break I guess."

"Maybe everything'll clear up a little when she's out of the way."

"Still haven't made up my mind about that," he said to the television.

Marge tilted her head back and sighed heavily at the ceiling. "You need to move on."

"I told you, she's dragging her feet on the divorce. I just don't know if we're there yet."

"It's killing you in the meantime. And I don't think this other gal—"

"Stop trying to tell me what to do."

Letterman went to a commercial break and Marge stepped outside for some fresh air and a break of her own. Outside the sky had clouded over, the night still thick and hot. She drew the sash and opened her robe. There was a little table with a set of plastic chairs by the porch near the side door. With the bottom of her robe, she wiped beads of moisture from the seat of a chair and sat down. She pushed herself from the chair and stepped warily along the cement that led to the driveway, on the lookout for gecko lizards and garter snakes. A sudden impulse—to shed her robe and walk naked through the streets, how liberating it might feel to fly in the face of the dull and lifeless ennui of those streets. How primal, an aching for nudity that she hadn't seen coming when she stepped out of the house and into the driveway. She would have acted on this impulse, she thought, if it weren't for the possibility of her son stepping outside to soothe his own restlessness—or perhaps he still smoked in secret.

When she got to the end of the driveway she stood and looked at the house. A light illuminated the address number 1020. Tammany Drive. The exterior lights were a bone of contention between her and her husband. He insisted on their use as a crime deterrent. She argued in vain that these lights were pointless, in fact a waste of electricity in a community with a guarded gate and financially stable residents without any motive to go and rob their neighbors. He made the case nevertheless for the chance of infiltration from beyond the gates or the outside chance of a kleptomaniac inside the gates. The glow these lights cast into their bedroom served as an intrusion to perfect darkness. Leave the light off, she said. Leave it on, he said. They went back and forth like this from day one.

The street was quiet and she guessed there was nothing but boredom for the men at the gate, or was it just one man overnight? Nothing but boredom for Peggy Beamish, anyway. Peggy talking about hitching her wagon and heading out West. Leaving her husband, her friends, everything she knew. But what did anybody know, thought Marge, glancing at the palm-lined street of houses that replicated one another in every aspect right down to exterior paint color. What was there to be gained, now that the shackles of working life were removed from both of them? Ted worried incessantly about the state of the market and their retirement funds. Every morning upon waking, Marge tested her brain with the crossword puzzle and rued the day when the letters and words might cease to make sense, when she'd forget the simplest things in a matter of seconds, when she'd lose her motor coordination to the extent of an inability to use the bathroom unassisted, when her body simply might not respond to motor impulses, when her mind might simply fail her.

The porch light came on at a neighbor's a few doors down and across the street. She waved at the silhouetted figure rolling the garbage bin to the curb. What if her son wasn't here and she'd stripped down to nothing and been observed outdoors in her natural state, rendering her in an instant an exhibitionist, the object of gossip? Whoever it was didn't see the wave and once the scraping ceased and the bin settled, the figure paused and glanced over at her standing there at the foot of the driveway in her robe, and then turned to walk back to the house, closing first the screen door and then the heavy oak door behind them, there was the click of the lock and then the street returned to silence.

When she returned to the house and their bedroom it was dark except for the glow of the floodlight through the heavy curtains. Wordlessly she peeled back the covers on her side of the bed and crawled under them, curled up on her side to face away from Ted.

She held out hope yet—there were clubs she could join. There were like-minded people everywhere and surely it wasn't any different here. The vibrant life depicted in the Sunny Glen Palms brochure merely something she had to construct out of the puzzle pieces around her, but finding the pieces proved a more difficult challenge than she'd imagined a year ago up north in the daily struggles of work and family problems and bad weather. She and Ted had left the suburbs of Minnesota behind for this haven of peace and yet oddly enough she felt herself more at war than ever.

# 6

Under gray heavens a torrent was unleashed, the sun hidden behind ominous clouds, with brief spells of drizzle and mist. The neighborhoods in Sunny Glen Palms went mostly un-trafficked. Sales at the supermarkets were slow—scheduled employees lolling about near the sliding glass doors in front by empty carts, gazing out upon the downpour, smoking cigarettes and cracking jokes to pass the time. Like sentries at the front doors of a fort. Waiting on the forecasted break, the calm before the storm, when they would be invaded by armies of shoppers stocking up for the weekend and the big hurricane.

Lily Westfall poured herself another cup of coffee and collapsed into the recliner, listening to the white noise of heavy rain overhead on the roof while she switched on the Weather Channel. Passing Cuba, Hurricane Charley resumed a northerly track and regained Category Five strength, due for landfall on late Friday or early Saturday. In high winds, find a small space without windows like a closet, they were saying. A basement was the most favorable space. Steer clear of the windows.

Jack called, urging her to evacuate inland. She balanced the suggestion against staying on to help Barbara with the funeral arrangements. A far as she knew, neither the funeral home or the church had cancelled the funeral on Saturday.

The phone rang and it was Barbara. "I've got some news," she said. "My brother called. I picked it up and he's telling me he's flying in tonight. He intends to stay here."

"Oh," said Lily.

"It's gonna be interesting to say the least."

"Well, what else did he have to say?"

"Not much. His usual cold and distant self. He mentioned he talked to my sister Nancy. She told him not to wait on her and her family. She'll send flowers. In the middle of some big assignment. She's always in the middle of some big assignment."

"What does she do?"

"Right now she's raising her kids I guess. Her husband is a CIA spook, I'm convinced. Defense and intelligence. Some job, some line of work the particulars of which mother knows nothing about. *Knew* nothing, that is."

"Honey," said Lily. "I don't know if there's going to be a funeral this weekend. We're now in the projected path of the hurricane."

"What?"

"Haven't you been watching?"

"I don't watch TV."

"My son is practically begging me to evacuate."

"You're making me nervous."

"Maybe you should call the church."

"Yes."

"But first come help an old lady finish a pot of coffee."

"Sure," said Barbara.

There was a break in the deluge of rain. Lily brought her coffee to the couch in the living room, muting the sound on the TV, switching on the radio to the soothing sounds of WAMB. While the Sandpipers sang their silky-smooth harmonies alongside lush orchestration, the TV displayed a map with swirling red arrowed lines. Lily's mind raced. She kept a supply of emergency valium in the medicine chest, but Barbara's scene with the pills put her off the idea. Oh why not, she said to herself at last and shuffled over to the bathroom to gulp down two tablets with a Dixie cup. A light rapping sounded on the door and where she'd expected to find Barbara, her next-door neighbor stood before her in rain-drenched sweat pants and a plain tee shirt. Being perched one step above him afforded her a bird's eye view of a bald head dotted with freckles, a few strands of hair strewn across haphazardly. She invited him over the threshold and into her home for the very first time.

"Have you heard about the weather?" he pouted, and she met his stare from beady blinking eyes, thinning hair drenched.

"Yes Ed," she spoke to him as if addressing a child. "Got the TV on right now. It doesn't look good."

"Well," his eyes darted about the room. He brought a shaking hand to his mouth and gaped at her. "We've got to take cover."

"Yes Ed. We'll keep an eye on what the weatherman says."

Neither the music or assurances managed to win over his sensibilities. He shifted his weight from one foot to the other, his eyes darting here to there in the manner of a squirrel. "Everyone," he declared, "has to hide."

"Let's just see what happens. Things change."

"Now," he insisted. "We have to hide right now."

"Oh now, it's too early," she said, not wishing to invite any exchange of nonsensical ideas.

Occasionally she could hear the clang of Ed's garage door and then him backing the car out. She'd worry he might find himself waking up in the ER, she wondered if his driver's license was current and valid.

"Well Ed," she patted the door with an air of finality. "Let's keep each other posted."

Ed sauntered along the concrete path to the driveway, heedless of the rain. She deliberated over offering him an umbrella or following him home to make sure he didn't linger outside until he was drenched, no one there to towel him off. He turned around, beads of rain dripping about his chin and nose. He said, "I'm going to find a place to hide."

So intently focused as she was on her neighbor, she hadn't noticed Barbara approach in her blurred peripheral vision.

"I'm not interrupting a secret tryst with your neighbor am I?"

"Oh for goodness sakes don't be silly," Lily chastised, tapping Barbara playfully. "I believe he's losing his senses, poor man."

"That's what a man does when he falls in love."

Lily made a face and beckoned Barbara inside. They gathered their coffees and Lily nodded at the television. "You have to help me make sense of all this. I don't know what all to do. My son Jack keeps telling me to just pack everything and get a hotel somewhere inland. Well anyway, they haven't cancelled my eye appointment."

"Well," said Barbara, "let's see what they say."

"Honey, I think you might better call the priest and put off the burial until next week."

"Really?"

"Better to be on the safe side."

"But my brother's already coming. Probably in the air already."

"Well maybe you two can sort everything out. Go from there."

"We can't sort out so much as a shopping list between us. How are we going to deal with a funeral, an estate? For a week?"

Lily fidgeted her fingers, her eyes darting back and forth.

"I'm sorry," Barbara said. "This is not yours to worry about. There's enough going on already with the storm."

Lily patted her hand. "You've got a great big heart."

Barbara shook her head. "You're the one with a great big heart."

Lily shook her head ruefully. "I just turned a man away from my door who's all worked up about the storm. Someone with no one to look after him."

"You can't feed every bird," said Barbara. "Anyway, my family'd say I've got one cold heart. A self-absorbed jerk."

"Oh don't pay any mind to that."

"Well, just ask my brother what he thinks of me. Mom would've said the same."

"Sometimes it's hard to see a mother's love." Lily folded her hands, watching the hurricane arrows move on the screen.

"She would sabotage everything I said into her own story," Barbara continued. "For the purposes of telling her own story."

"Like how?"

"Okay, like, once I was going through a real bad breakup. I called her. I don't know why. I called her, maybe because she's my mother, simple as that. Anyhow, no sooner do I get into what's going on, my feelings about it she's going on about this man who's just broken her heart. At her age, wanting marriage again. It's like, she can't set aside her own shit to listen. Just to listen. But she's been like that all her life. Everything's always about her. Well, *was* anyway. I felt so short-changed when I hung up the phone. So deflated. Cheapened."

Lily shook her head. "I'm sorry."

"Why is it," Barbara said, "I can talk to you and not my mother? By all appearances you're not much different than her."

"I don't know. It's somehow different with family. Same way for me. Worked that way with my mother, I guess. My sons."

Rex pawed at the sofa and leaped up between them. Lily rubbed at his floppy ears while Barbara slunk back in the sofa cushions and pondered over her family and conversations that leaned more towards banality than profundity, the mundane over the existential. Speaking tentatively between each other in the codification of the damaged.

The drizzle gave way to a heavy rainfall and they sat in silence listening to the heavy droning white noise on the roof. The room fell dark. A severe weather alert band streaked across the bottom of the television screen as a glamorous and sharply-dressed meteorologist brought more bad news. Hurricane Charley was gaining momentum and was projected to kiss the tip of Florida and then hug the Gulf. These things were dynamic, said the attractive blond on the screen, were unpredictable. Anything could change.

*

From beyond the guest room door, the sound of her son clearing his sinuses triggered a memory, the way little things often do from a mother's perspective—that fateful day when there was another argument, escalation of anger, a flaring of tempers between her sons that she'd arrived too late to quell. In the backyard, shouting from a flurry of sheets on the clothesline that billowed like ghosts in the breeze. From within the drying linens the hollering abated and then a flurry of fists, thumping, the ground rumbling beneath her feet as they tussled in the dirt. John straddled Teddy, fists flailing, and there was already blood. A single punch had consigned him to a lifetime of sinus problems, along with a lifelong resentment of his sibling.

There were times when tensions came to a boiling point and the two of them would not speak to one another for days, months, now sometimes years. She'd want to intervene. Ted would say let them settle it between themselves. But they seemed able to achieve a tentative peace, and then the tension would build up again.

From the guestroom more sniffling, hacking and blowing. The door cracked open and Teddy waved half-heartedly, shuffling into the guest bathroom.

Ted came in from the garage. He poured himself a cup of coffee and sat across from his wife. "How'd you sleep," he asked.

"Not so good."

"Why don't we all go to lunch somewhere today."

"What's a good place?"

"I don't know, Denny's?"

"How about that seafood restaurant off Pebble Beach Boulevard we keep talking about?"

"Schooner's. Good idea."

Teddy yawned, he never was much of a morning person, pouring himself a cup of coffee and sitting between them at the head of the table.

"What can I fix you," she said.

Teddy scratched at his belly and said, "No need. I eat light in the morning."

"Just like your father," Marge frowned at Ted. "Why don't you let me fix you a vacation breakfast."

"Don't worry Mom. I'll just fix myself some cereal."

"You ought to have some fruit," Marge started for the fridge. "We get fresh grapefruit."

"I'm good. I'll have cereal. Not now."

"Oh-okay." Marge returned to her seat. "So," she said. "What are you doing with yourself these days?"

Truth was, Teddy wasn't doing much with himself other than walking to the liquor store to fetch a fifth of vodka for his bedraggled girlfriend, who waited at home to receive it without filling his purse. He'd bought himself a composition notebook, a throwback to his old schooldays with its black and white marbled cover. He began to scrawl poetry between its college-ruled lines. But this was a piece of news about himself he didn't intend to impart to either Marge or Ted. Instead, he replied, not much. Not much Mom.

After he'd left the house in the golf cart to visit the computer lab, ostensibly for the purpose of catching up emails and sending resumes to job postings, Ted and Marge sat on the porch and watched the rain.

"Maybe he should move down here," said Marge. "Maybe we should just sell the house, kick that lay-about girlfriend out and let him come down here and stay with us awhile. Just til he gets his feet back on the ground."

Ted leaned in, elbows on thighs and hands clasped together, shaking his head at the floor. "I don't know," he said. "You see what happened to the Martins."

The Martins, their new neighbors a few doors away who had a forty-something son who'd come down from Georgia with his beat-up Ford pickup to get back on his feet. That was over a year ago. Now all the kid did was sit. Sit around the house, sit up at the South Club drinking under the glares of his elders, retired people who'd earned their rightful place to just sit.

"Well," she said, "You can't compare that guy to Teddy. He wouldn't do that. You wouldn't permit it."

"Marge," said Ted, "as much of a hard-ass I may be, it's an impossible thing to do. Throw your own son out of the house."

"Well, that house can't be sold anyway, it's under water and—"

"Maybe we should sell it anyway. We wouldn't stand to lose much."

Marge sighed. "I never would have imagined we'd have this shit on our plate at this point in our lives."

"Me either. But here it is."

"That girlfriend of his," she sighed.

"I know, I know."

"It's a rebound. He's just afraid of being alone."

"Well who isn't?" Ted said, shaking his head. The phone rang and he swiped the cordless from its base. "Oh. Peggy." He scowled at the phone and handed it to Marge.

"Am I interrupting something?" Peggy's voice crackled.

"No, not at all. How are you?"

"I'm bored as hell. I'm gonna have to find a boyfriend or something. My husband takes these extended absences. I mean, don't get me wrong, I've had about enough of him for a lifetime, but with all this rain what's a woman to do?"

"I know," Marge muted her response under the watchful gaze of her husband.

"Well, how about you? Got cabin fever or what? You wanna get out for a spell?"

"Sure," said Marge, gauging her son and husband against where she might fit Peggy Beamish in.

"This big hurricane is about to hit," said Peggy, "and it'd be just fine by me to put the kibosh on the party. Wipe the slate. Sort of a cleansing."

"Uh-huh."

"In the meantime, why don't we shoot some pool."

"Pool? I'd be surprised if it were open. With bad weather on the way."

"No silly. Billiards."

"Oh."

"Do you shoot pool?"

"No, not really. I mean, it's been years. Since I was a little girl."

"Well, come tag along with me. I can teach you what I know."

Marge glanced from her watch to a wary husband. "Okay, I guess so. I'll have to check on the car situation here. My son's down to visit and he took the golf cart."

"I'll pick you up."

"Okay."

"Fifteen minutes."

She passed the phone back over to Ted. He scowled at it again and replaced it to its base.

"Well?"

"Well what?"

"What'd she have to say?"

"Not much. We're going to go play some pool."

He frowned. "Pool?"

"Billiards. Over at the North Club. I better get ready," she sighed, pushing herself up out of the wicker chair. "She's coming to fetch me."

"I wish you wouldn't," said Ted, rubbing his palms together.

Marge left the porch without a word.

"Oh God Margie, she's… there's something I don't like about her. About *them*."

"Well you'll just have to get over it," she called over her shoulder. "I like them just fine."

"Why can't anybody do what I say? Just once!"

"Why the hell should it bother you so much, me having a friend of my own? We're batting zero as a couple, thanks to your damn temper."

"That's enough!" His hand came crashing down on the wicker foot rest in front of him. "I've had just about enough of this nonsense!"

"I've had just about enough of *you* mister."

Marge closed the bedroom door and leaned against it, shook her head with a sigh. Then she went into action, snaring a pair of khaki shorts from the dresser, hopping about while dropping one leg and then the other into them, ripping a Bermuda shirt from its hanger in the closet and thrusting one arm and then the other into it. Clutching her swimsuit, she stormed off to the garage, gathering up a few other items into a straw beach bag, praying it wouldn't be long until Peggy turned up.

*

Isabel Amador straddled Mike Beamish, massaging his chest with long dainty fingers, brushing her silky hair aside, curling up against him, nestling her head in the crook of his arm. He ran his fingers along her back.

What was she thinking, he wanted to know. She just shrugged by way of response and they lay in silence, the room darkened by heavy drapes.

"I could lay here all day," he said.

"I'm gonna have to kick you out soon," she said. "I have work to do."

Mike heaved a sigh, he'd been thinking about the party in front of him that the hurricane threatened to nullify. He liked parties and he missed the kids and grandkids. It was the first big event to come along in years and he wished there were vacations to look forward to, but there didn't seem to be any need for vacations for either he or Peggy. His lover was occupied not only with freelance editing, but friends and cultural events and travel. He wondered what he'd done to draw her attention. He couldn't imagine what she saw in him and he didn't dare ask.

After another bout of love-making she slid out from under the sheets of the giant four poster bed to run the shower. She didn't call out for him to join her, didn't invite him to eat, nor linger. She half-heartedly indulged an embrace and didn't invite a kiss goodbye. Mike said goodbye at the door and she abruptly closed it behind him, leaving him to walk disconsolately down the path and then her driveway in the misty rain.

He didn't feel inclined to go home, and the North Club wasn't too far a walk. He glanced at the sky. Drizzle was one thing, but if the heavens unleashed a downpour he was screwed. He considered returning home to fetch the blue windbreaker, immediately dismissed the thought. The streets were quiet and the sidewalks eerily bereft of walkers or bicyclists. An EMT vehicle passed him, sirens off. By the time he reached the North Club he was nearly drenched, shivering in the air-conditioned hallway, hair standing on end, like a cat dragged in from the rain. He hastened to the Men's room and stood before the electric dryer, bringing his head under the airflow, facing forwards then backwards and hoping no one would enter to witness a fool drying himself in this manner. In just a few days presumably he'd be the toast of the town dressed sharply in a suit and tie, just down the hallway in one of those conference rooms. He decided to head for the pool area at the far end and hit the dry sauna and possibly the pool or hot tub in his boxers. He might beg steal or borrow someone's towel. Coyness and stealth seemed to be the order of the day.

In the pool's locker-room he stripped himself naked and beat a hasty retreat to the dry sauna. Pulled at the thick wooden doorhandle, and where he expected a wave of moist heat, there was nothing. An elderly gentleman lay fully dressed and curled up in the fetal position on the wooden bench, beside the bin of cooling steam coals. He lifted his head to glance at Mike, his hands shaking, lips quivering.

"Are you alright," Mike furrowed his brow.

"We're doomed," the man said.

"What?"

"We're doomed," he repeated, settling himself back into the fetal position. "Take shelter here brother."

Mike paused and wondered at the odd man's strange words. Doomed? Take shelter? Was he speaking to life in general or some kind of immediate perceived threat?

"Hey buddy," he said. "It's a dry sauna. For heat. You know, sweat."

"It's a bomb shelter," the man said.

"There are no bombs," Mike said. "No bombs here pal."

"As good a place as any to take shelter from a hurricane."

"Oh," said Mike. "I see." His first impulse was to sit beside the man but his nakedness precluded this and so he sat down at the other end of the wooden bench, folding his hands in his lap to cover his balls.

"You don't need to take shelter *here* pal. Your house is just as good. I definitely don't think we're gonna get hit anyway."

"Oh yes we are." The man turned, sat up and drunken-shuffled over to Mike and then Mike met a gaunt and whisker-stubbled face, eyes red-rimmed from lack of sleep. His breath stank to high heaven. Sharp facial features, a chiseled chin, a torso so thin as to be near emaciated underneath a tee-shirt riddled with food stains, chicken legs protruding from a baggy pair of khaki shorts.

"We *are*," he shot darting glances about the teakwood floor walls and ceilings, what appeared a bank vault constructed of wood and not cement. "Charley," he said. "On his way."

Mike decided it was futile to try and contradict the man any further, and the dry sauna would just have to be off limits today.

"Bring back some food," the man said. "A sandwich or something."

Mike stood for a moment outside the door, peeking in at the feeble man through the tiny window, shaking his head. He would alert security, but not just yet. The old man wasn't hurting anyone anyway. A thin white-haired man who'd been within earshot of their exchange was stooped over packing his belongings into a gym bag in the customary mannered fashion. Seizing the opportunity to restore an air of orderliness and sensibility, they spoke of the weather as if this were just another storm, this was the season for it after all and the pools would be closed and just as well leave it at that. The door closed behind him, leaving the locker room free of onlookers. He scanned the wooden benches and then went rummaging about in the lockers for a towel. He found nothing. But he was anxious to hit the indoor pool and the hot tub. Stripping down to his boxers, he draped his wet shorts and shirt over one of the locker doors in the hope they might begin to air dry. He moved about stealthily, peeking through the window of the dry sauna and finding the strange man still there. He turned around and nudged the louvered door just enough to afford him a view of the pool. A group of ladies gathered in one of the roped off swimming lanes, swirling their arms and kicking their legs in the water. In the lane next to theirs, a wizened old man in a Speedo did his laps. Mike paused there in the locker room, weighing his options. He could simply put his wet clothes back on and walk home in the rain, or he might chance going unnoticed to the hot tub for a good long soak.

Mike was a physics major, initially a tech guy before IBM moved him into Sales. He had the know-how and, they must've figured, the charm. Early on in his career, a mentor gave him a tip that would be repeated more than once over the ensuing years. When you walk into a room, said the seasoned seller, imagine your audience in their underwear. This advice to mentally undress his audience was occasionally heeded, but he always ran the risk of getting distracted with some of those before him of the opposite gender. Now here was Mike Beamish, in his underwear, hands pressed against the white slats of the door to a public venue. He wondered whether the boxer briefs he wore, of a plaid print pattern, and a size too small (for Isabel) might not be mistaken for some new fad in swimwear. He dallied, gathering courage, turned to peek again at the odd man in the dry sauna who'd addressed him as brother. The door to the locker room opened and then a small gaunt man hobbled in with a gym bag and a towel draped around his shoulders. Now or never. In his haste, Mike pushed the door open with enough force to draw the attention of a few of those scattered about the indoor pool environs. He didn't recognize anyone and didn't expect to out here, on the other side of town so to speak, at the North Club. He lowered his eyes and hastened his step to the far end of the room and the hot tub, all-the-more conspicuous without a towel around his neck to augment his puny costume and perhaps draw attention away from his midriff. The voices of the swimmers and loungers echoed around the large room with its concrete floor, tiled walls and high ceilings. He reached the hot tub and, amid the spurting bubbles of the giant bowl, a young couple and a spinster. As he lowered himself hastily into the tub, he sensed three pairs of eyes on him and his underwear. The old lady made a face, while the couple pretended to ignore and go about their business.

While the couple across from him muttered their private conversation he glanced somewhat furtively at the elderly neighbor to his right. Her skin had wrinkled and freckled with moles here and there on her arms—all the imperfections that showed up along the path of aging. Her lips fluttered with noiseless words sprung from private thoughts as she scrutinized every part of the large room and threw toxic thought darts at its occupants, while avoiding any eye contact with those at close range.

Once he'd settled himself comfortably, his underwear out of sight but not out of mind, Mike decided rather than try to assimilate himself into the private conversation in front of him, he might have a go at some light banter with the prunish-faced lady to his right, but in the wake of her initial startlement lay a clear disinterest. At his offhand remark about the coming hurricane (which still plagued him with anxiety and so the craving for more dismissive assessments) her eyes ceased scanning the room to regard him briefly before darting about once again.

His thoughts wandered back to Isabel and the giant four-poster king bed that claimed most of her bedroom space. Isabel's face hadn't a hint of wrinkles and he considered that sharing her bed was like taking a dip in the fountain of youth—the elixir to any propensity to wrinkling, accumulation of unwanted weight, random medical problems. In the hot tub among the strangers he wiggled his toes, ducked his face in the water and pinched at minor fat folds around his midriff. He spread his arms out over the rimmed wall behind him, rested his neck upon it, and gazed upon an aging ceiling riddled with blemishes—white paint discoloring and peeling, rust among the beams. He guessed hardly anyone would notice, after all how often did people in here look up over their heads? He'd just shut his eyes when he heard the soft clink of sandals and the arrival of a newcomer to the tub.

It was the Hagoden fellow, from church. From the South Club, most recently slapping him in the face and urging he come to in the locker room. Now here was somebody to talk to.

"Hello there," Hagoden said. "Steering clear of the saunas?"

"Oh I think that was some kind of fluke. Blood sugar, overexertion, that kind of thing."

"You okay?" Hagoden gripped the handrail and looked him over as a doctor would a patient and Mike self-consciously brought his hands to his lap, the boxers.

"Yeah Gerry, I'm fine. C'mon in. Plenty of room in here."

Two outlaws on the outskirts of town, Mike thought to himself. Could he impose upon Hagoden to impart some advice concerning his marital indiscretions? It was common knowledge, what had transpired last winter at the South Club, the moment that had served to usher disharmony into the Hagoden household. The lingering and soulful kiss, in a room full of spectators, between Hagoden himself and a visitor, the French woman who'd come to visit her ailing sister. That story had made the rounds and lent an awkwardness to any interaction with the Hagodens. Perhaps, Mike thought, a heart-to-heart, a baring of the soul might serve to forge an alliance between himself and Hagoden, might even cause some of the foul air of infidelity to evaporate.

Hagoden eased himself into the bubbly water and they volleyed small talk back and forth. Mike weighed this against more confessional matter but perhaps the one with Fitzroy was enough, or more like one too many. He'd nearly fallen over when Kenny appeared with his wife. Out of nearly ten thousand people inside the gates of Sunny Glen Palms for a confidante he'd managed to pick the very same oddball his wife had chosen as a golf partner. What were the odds of that? Did she manage to drag anything out of Fitzroy?

"So," said Mike, "what brings you to this side of town?"

"I was gonna ask you the same thing."

"Well," said Mike. "Change of scenery."

"Yeah," said Hagoden. "I think they do a better job of maintenance over here."

Mike nodded, although he wasn't sure what exactly Hagoden meant. Were the pool waters clearer, were locker rooms cleaned more regularly? Had the hallway floors a more luminous glow to them from having been waxed more frequently? What was maintained over here, he thought with amusement, was Gerry Hagoden's reputation. Because nobody knew him from Adam on this side of town and it was highly unlikely any word had spread about his transgression in front of a crowd last winter at the South Club. Some were convinced his no-no went no further than a public kiss, others conjectured about the likelihood of a full-blown romantic tryst.

"By the way," said Gerry. "Have you given any thought to joining us on the links?"

"Well, I've paid my membership, but this heat has seriously put me off the golf lately."

"Don't I know it. I'm just... we're just... always looking for partners. We like to team up in pairs."

"Why's that?"

"I don't know. The more the merrier I guess."

"Uh-huh." *I'm not signing on*, thought Mike. *More interested in leaving time open for indoor activities at the moment.*

"Anyway, we'd love to have you on board. It's been me and Tommy D'Antonio mostly. Our buddy Frank has been occupied with his wife, she's in an assisted living facility over in Tampa. We're looking for recruits I guess you could say."

"Oh," said Mike. "Sounds like it's all boys."

"Guess you could say that. Kind of like when I bowled. Years ago."

"Well then my wife's out of the question. Wait, here's a thought. You know that skinny young kid? Kenny, is it?"

"Fitzroy?"

"That's it. Anyway, he's looking for golf partners. My wife shot a few holes with him the other day."

"Not a bad fella," Gerry shrugged. "He played with us a few times."

Mike shook his head inquisitively. "No good? What, he hold you up between holes?"

"He ah… kind of found himself at cross purposes with Frank."

"Who's Frank?"

"Just one of the guys."

"Cross purposes over what? If you don't mind me asking."

"Politics," Gerry shook his head ruefully. "Lousy *politics*." He lowered his voice and emphasized the word as if it were some fatal disease. "That's why I never discuss politics."

"Hey," Mike said, "can I ask you something?"

Gerry ceased swirling his arms in the bubbly hot water. "Sure."

"You wouldn't by any chance have a towel I could borrow a second? I seemed to have forgotten mine."

He wondered if Gerry had figured out his swimsuit was his underwear through the tiny bubbles he hoped muted transparency.

"Sure," Gerry said. "I have a towel. It's in locker… one of the lockers to the right, when you walk in. At face level."

"Thanks," said Mike, weighing the propriety of asking Hagoden to fetch his own towel and bring it to the hot tub. He dawdled. The elderly woman pushed herself up and tottered over to the handrail and the steps. The couple remained snuggled in their private discourse. The elderly lady crept slowly, lips quivering, settling herself on one step at a time, her tree-stump thighs distressed with wrinkles like fish gills a thousand-fold and dotted with a road-map of varicose veins. A young couple stood waiting, a teenaged daughter in tow. They took their seats and right after that, two old ladies, all skin and bone, lowered themselves in their modest one-piece flower print bathing suits. Their heads were adorned with rubbery bathing caps, the straps attached to nodules and fit snugly under their chins. They oohed and aahed as Mike Beamish agonized over his leave-taking. Perhaps, he thought, he could wait them all out. But that might take all day, it might be dinnertime before the place was emptied enough of people for him to make a clean getaway. Well, he couldn't stay in a hot tub forever. Like the odd fellow in the dry sauna. Just how long did that goon intend to hole up inside that cell of solitary confinement?

He was getting antsy besides, having run out of things to say to Gerry Hagoden and the newcomers, and joined now by two more wrinkly old ladies chattering familiarly between themselves.

"Well Gerry," he said, bracing himself. "Guess I'll be seeing you out on the links. Once the heat lets up a little."

Gerry Hagoden nodded and said, "Yeah buddy. This heat kinda cuts my walks in half."

And then Mike grabbed the handrail and lifted himself enough to where his waist was below the waterline and under cover of the surface bubbles. He stalled, collecting himself, watching those in the circle of bubbly heat turn their attention to the outgoer. When his waist appeared, the paper-thin boxer briefs clung to his privates, leaving nothing to the imagination. He turned his back on the onlookers and knew that the crack of his ass and every contour was visible, he may as well have been naked.

Lo and behold there were newcomers waiting to greet him at ground level just outside of the hot tub. Jesus, he thought, is the entire population of Sunny Glen Palms making a run on the North Club hot tub?

"Looks like you forgot more than your towel!" Hagoden hollered after him, arms casually draped over the brick bordering of the hot tub. He may as well have cupped his hands around his mouth for all the bark of his voice—the remark reverberated around the immense room for even the deafest of ears to hear.

No IBM presentation, no matter how nerve-wracking, no matter how much might be on the line, exceeded the anxiety of this moment standing here before his audience in his underwear. What was this odd thing about panic in being exposed, like a bad dream you cannot wake up from? There is a waking up of course, but it's not to a warm bed—only the cold reality of having been found out. All those years ago with Janey Williams. The anger, the hurt of betrayal in his wife's eyes. Right in the middle of their marriage, smack in the middle of the warm parameters of a couples' kinship. After a round of marital counseling, she never subjected him to a conversation about the indiscretion but it would forever be embedded in their mutual history. He'd never been let off the hook. Nor was he now, stepping with a feigned nonchalance on the concrete deck in the immense indoor pool of the North Club. His audience had grown and now there were plenty of more bathers to meet along the way to the locker room, it was as if he'd met a reception line. Just on the other side of the glass walls, another downpour. He tugged at his wet underwear and tried his best to appear casual, striding towards the locker room door. He could feel all eyes upon him as he fixed his gaze on that white slat door that harkened to mind all things nautical— yachts, buoys, rope dock lines, life preservers.

When at last he pulled it open with the full expectation of returning himself to privacy, he encountered a locker room now busily occupied by old men and their aging bodies, the sagging balls and developing tits of the fraternity of the elderly. He peeked inside the dry sauna. The stranger still lay curled on his side on the bench in the wood compartment. Mike rifled through a few empty lockers until he found one with a pair of tennis shoes, a Bermuda shirt and a pair of shorts, with a towel draped from its hook.

One of the naked, a distinguished-looking man, rubbed at a thick head of white hair and a protruding belly upon yanking open the door to the dry sauna.

"Hey pal, c'mon," he muttered conspiratorially. "What are you still doing in here?"

Mike could barely hear the muffled reply. "Waiting out the hurricane."

"Well wait it out somewhere else. C'mon, some of us wanna use the facilities." The naked man gripped the door handle, peering over at Mike while nodding at the sauna. "Think we should notify security?"

Mike shrugged. "That's about all we *can* do. Tell you what. I'm leaving and I can tell them on the way out."

The man frowned and looked unconvincingly at the exit door to the pool. "Are there many in the hot tub?"

"Too many," said Mike, dabbing himself with Gerry Hagoden's towel. He stepped out of his wet boxers and into a vacated shower stall, wringing out the boxers, deliberating over whether to don them under his dampened shorts or just leave them behind for the lost and found.

*

Just two doors down in the North Club, Mike Beamish's wife busied herself with another kind of pool with Marge in the billiards room.

"Eight ball, corner pocket."

Peggy Beamish hunched over the felt cloth tabletop, pumping the cue stick between ring and index fingers with an eye shut to sight a shot. Marge looked on as she sank the last ball and took the game.

The billiards room featured walls freshly painted in hunter green and burgundy, elegant thick-cushioned chairs with rolled arms and nail-head trim, elegant overhead lamps glowing above six full-sized tables covered in green felt cloth, a stately sanctum of quiet calm and piped-in muzak—one might believe the room belonged to a country club in the Hamptons. No other chamber in that enormous building exuded such graceful formality, not the model railroad room or the crafts/pottery room or the Bingo room or the computer lab or the lobby with its café and its daytime live entertainment or the business office or even a neat and orderly library dominated by mahogany. The nearest kin to the billiards room was the auditorium, that expansive and windowless hall, its walls lined with crush velvet burgundy drapery, its high ceilings supporting enormous and regal brass chandeliers. The gigantic hall hosted events ranging from ticketed concerts for stars of yesteryear and the revered New Years Eve bash to private functions like Flora Wheeler's one-hundredth birthday party last winter that featured a bluegrass band, a good spread on the buffet table and a surprise visit from the EMTs in response to a medical emergency.

"C'mere, I'll show you how to rack 'em up good," said Peggy, dancing the colored balls around to get the right arrangement of stripes and solids. Marge's only other visit to the room came as part of the tour of the Sunny Glen Palms community she and Ted had been given last year on their visit to Florida, when it was one of many places to consider in choosing the setting in which to ride out the remainder of their golden years. After that, she rarely visited the North Club except on official business at the offices.

As Peggy was lining up her break, the door opened and a young couple sauntered in. While the young lady's eyes took in luxurious surroundings, the fidgety young man was sizing up cue sticks, testing the heft of one and then another in his hands. When the balls had settled without one dropping, Peggy's concentration left the table and fell upon the young lady and her partner.

"Oh hey there Kenny." She smiled at the girl. "It's Barbara, right?"

Kenny looked over at Marge, and she gave a quick wave of the hand. "I'm Marge."

He nodded with a brief smile on what appeared to her a pained face.

"So," Peggy said, glancing him up and down. "In addition to golf pro you're a pool shark."

"Well, I'm not very good."

"Oh sure," Peggy needled him, shooting a glance at his pool date. "I'll bet that's what you tell all the girls before you fleece them." She winked at Barbara. "Better watch out honey. This shark is more than a pool shark. Real lady killer. Break your heart in a New York minute."

"Well, I'll stay on guard," Barbara said with a wink. She marched up to Peggy and extended a hand. "Thanks for taking Lily along to the beach."

Marge walked around the immense billiard table and held a hand out to Barbara and Kenny in turn. "Marge, in case you forgot. Nice to meet you both."

Introductions made all around, Peggy finished cleaning Marge's clock again and then the four of them agreed to play in teams, young against old. Following Marge's dismal break, Kenny leaned over Barbara to instruct her on how to hold the cue stick and Peggy chortled, tilting her head at Marge. "See what I mean? He's putting the moves on her already."

Kenny made a face and backed away from Barbara, only to watch her dink the cue ball off center, barely grazing another ball to avoid a scratch.

"Your friend Lily is such a sweetheart," Marge said, thumping her cue stick lightly on the carpet after scratching, the cue ball dropping into the side pocket. "She told us about your mother. Sorry for your loss."

Barbara gave a smile and nod of acknowledgement.

"Anything we can do, you just say the word," said Peggy with a firm and resolute nod. "Even if it's just baking stuff for the funeral gathering."

While the ladies chatted away, Kenny Fitzroy was running the table, sinking one ball after another.

"Hey buster," said Peggy. "Not very good? Everyone look over here at mister amateur's little run of luck."

Kenny frowned, began lining up a shot with lots of green between the cue ball and the object ball. Fueled by Peggy's remark, he drove the cue ball with a newfound authority. The balls made an enormous crack and the object ball caromed off the rail and spilled out onto to the floor. He hustled over to pick it up and return it to the table.

"Uh-uh mister," Peggy teased him. "It's like golf. You gotta play it where it lands."

After the billiards had run its course, they strolled around the hallways and watched the rain on the other side of the glass. Marge said, "I want to stop by the Business Office and see if there's an evacuation plan in effect for the hurricane."

"I know of a fun plan that's on for the hurricane," said Barbara.

"Do tell," said Peggy.

"Well, at the pool this morning during that sunny spell. I ran into this young couple from New York. In the hot tub. They're having a hurricane party. Two actually. One tomorrow night and one on Friday when it's likely to hit."

Marge furrowed her brow. "A *hurricane* party?"

"Yep."

"What's a hurricane party?"

"Well," said Barbara, "it's a gathering of people during a hurricane. I guess it's sort of like moral support. I guess it's collective anxiety to distract away from individual anxiety. Something like that."

Marge made a face. "Sounds a little odd to me."

"Actually," Peggy chirped, "sounds like fun to me. Assuming drinks are involved. Because let me tell ya, if we get caught in the middle of this monster, I could sure use a drink or two. Or three, or—"

"Well," said Barbara. "Why don't you join us then?"

"Maybe tomorrow, but I definitely can't on Saturday," said Peggy, "as much as I'd like to. I'm already committed to my own celebration of the death of my marriage."

"Can you elaborate," Barbara winked. "I mean, you put it out there."

"Touche," Peggy scrunched her face and waved a hand. "Sounds like ole Peggy is rubbing off on you. Anyway, that's a long story that'll have to be told over a few too many margaritas."

Barbara smiled and tapped at Peggy's arm. "Then why don't you come tomorrow night? They invited Kenny and I'm sure they wouldn't mind if we brought an extra guest or two," she said, glancing over to Marge.

"Hey," said Peggy, "you're not talking about that young fella prances around in the Speedo are ya?"

"No, I don't think so." Barbara squinted her eyebrows. "I forget their names already."

"It's those Canadian snowbirds I'm thinking of," said Peggy.

"That's the Gastons you're thinking of Peggy. Snowbirds. They won't come down until the holidays," said Kenny matter-of-factly. "Fun people."

"My hubby's always making derogatory remarks about them." Peggy still had her mind on the snowbird Gastons, who had closed up their house of many parties in June for their home country way up north.

"Mine too," said Marge, remembering Ted scoffing at Philip Gaston lounging around the hot tub at the South Club in his Speedo.

"Oh, I'll bet," said Peggy, shaking her head. "I can only imagine what that hothead of yours has to say about a man walking around in public clad in a bikini."

"Hey, hold on a minute," Marge half-heartedly protested.

"Well, what's it gonna be?" Barbara said, poking Peggy's arm playfully. "You gonna join in the fun or sit home and bite your nails in front of the weather channel?"

"Oh, what the hell, count me in," said Peggy. "In the meantime I guess I'd better see if our shindig is on for Saturday."

The four of them strolled over to the Business Office and approached the receptionist. She ushered them past her desk along a narrow corridor and they found themselves facing Activities Director Ellen Everitt, a buxom middle-aged woman with sharp fashion-design glasses of turquoise and jewelry to match. Her voice matched the neatness of her attire.

"As of yet," she declared, "we have no firm plans for evacuation as a community. At the moment, we're leaving that up to the discretion of our residents."

Peggy shot a bewildered glance to her cohorts. "So it's kind of a wait and see? Three days out? What about the party? We're supposed to have a wrap-up meeting with you tomorrow."

"Oh yes, the anniversary party in the Armstrong room." said Ellen Everitt. "Well, I can appreciate your concern Mrs…"

"Beamish," said Peggy. "For now, anyway."

"Mrs. Beamish," she repeated, tweaking the fashionable eyewear on the bridge of her nose. "I can appreciate your concern. But this is Florida and it's hurricane season," Ellen unfolded her hands, threw up her palms and shrugged. "We've had an unusually high level of storms this season. If there is a definite imminent threat, of course we have a protocol in place. But this one doesn't present sufficient danger to mass evacuate, at least not right now. We're monitoring and by tomorrow we'll know for sure."

"Like every major life decision," Peggy said, shaking her head. "Leave it until the last minute. Guess it all comes down to Friday."

While Marge and Peggy sat in the twin chairs in front of Ellen Everitt's desk Kenny stood in the doorway bouncing on his heels, Barbara looking over his shoulder. "Do you think," he asked Mrs. Everitt, "there's a chance flights might be cancelled? To Tampa airport?"

"Chicken shit," Peggy snapped over her shoulder.

Ellen Everitt glanced sharply over her designer eyeglasses from Kenny to Peggy and then back to Kenny. "I'd say you'll have to check on flights up to the minute. We don't monitor that info here. Now if you folks'll excuse me, I have some things to wrap up before calling it a day."

Back outside in the hallways of the North Club, they walked through the café. Kenny asked if they cared to join he and Barbara for lunch. Marge said she had a date with husband and son at Schooner's. Peggy twirled her keys and said, guess that leaves me out since we came in my cart. She and Marge looked on while her youngers sauntered off, Kenny Fitzroy's voice carrying all over that long hallway until they passed through the glass double-doors at the side exit.

*

A strange new car was parked in the driveway when Lily passed Alice Thunderclap's house on her way to the eye doctor. A new Ford Taurus, most likely a rental, she thought. She'd nearly forgotten about the arrival of Barbara's brother and it seemed to her as if Barbara had also. A portly middle-aged man she assumed to be Roger sat in one of the plastic chairs at the side door to the house, fanning himself with a newspaper. He was dressed in a starch white-collar shirt and he had loosened the necktie. The grey trousers he wore were sweat-stained. He didn't look too happy.

Lily slowed the car and decided against stopping—she didn't have a key to the house so there wasn't any point. She'd already turned right onto Hammersmith Drive and decided to double back. When she pulled in the driveway a smidgeon of hope washed over a mean and despairing face. He met her at the car before she could step out of it. Lily introduced herself and offered her hand. "I believe we spoke on the phone the other day."

"Right. Any idea where my sister is?"

"I don't know. I saw her this morning."

He looked at her quizzically.

"She stopped by my house."

"Oh. I left her a message last night. On my mother's machine. You wouldn't happen to have a key to the house, would you?"

"No. I haven't." Lily tried to disarm him with a smile. "It's hot out here. Looks like more rain on the way. You can wait it out at my house if you like."

"No thank you. I'll just wait here."

"Okay," she put the gearshift in reverse.

"Thanks for your help. And thanks for looking after my sister. I know she can be quite a challenge."

Lily nodded, kicking herself while backing the car out for failing to dig in her heels and contradict him, defend her new friend. Her wits had failed her and she hoped for another chance to speak in Barbara's defense.

Lily's dilly-dallying could not be attributed solely to concerning herself with a neighbor's irritable brother. A compounding anxiety inside of her leading up to the two o'clock appointment with the ophthalmologist. By the time she parked her car and took the elevator up to the seventh floor it was already ten minutes past her two o'clock appointment time. She approached the receptionist with an apologetic frown. The smile and reassurances of the young lady behind the desk and shelves of paperwork only slightly soothed her anxiety, because Lily Westfall was nothing if not a punctual person. She gave the receptionist a contrite nod and took a chair and a magazine.

Her eyes were under attack from all sides. The war had escalated over the years, now the diagnosis of uveitis joined ongoing problems of macular degeneration, type-2 diabetes, and glaucoma. And she was still feeling the effects of two cataract removal surgeries. The doctor wasn't very optimistic at her last visit and she didn't imagine any further testing would brighten the outlook. Her corrective eyewear simply wasn't doing the trick anymore and the she was beginning to dread the prospect of driving, even during daylight. She ought to have asked Barbara to drive her, she thought as she squinted at the windshield, leaving the calm streets of Sunny Glen Palms onto the heavily trafficked Pebble Beach Boulevard just outside the gate. Her poor eyesight had begun to rob her of the pleasure she took in reading books and the day when that would prove impossible was not far away. She tried the audio books, but preferred the experience of having a book in your lap. The doctor had already delivered the unpleasant news that total blindness was imminent. When that came to pass, who'd do her shopping and take her to doctor appointments? How would she move about in the dark of night? Who would be her eyes when she could no longer see?

*

They were halfway through lunch until it dawned on Barbara to check the answering machine at her mother's for news of her brother's arrival. She glanced at her watch and saw it was pushing two-thirty. She assumed he'd have an evening flight after a full day of business.

When Barbara pulled her car into the drive-way she found her brother in much the same manner as Lily had, underneath the eave near the side door or front door, depending on how you looked at it. It had begun to rain, a light drizzle that he was barely shielded from.

When he rose from the chair she could see he'd clearly gained weight, particularly in his face—it had grown puffy jowls and a double chin. He frowned at her and she frowned at him—an immediate quickening of her senses, her breath taken, a knot in her stomach. A squirrel scurried across the power line attached to her mother's house and she wondered if it had siblings to compete with, whether they'd failed to understand one another over their brief lives. Was every species, every form of wildlife, subject to those wiles of expectations and disappointment? Or were such things the exclusive domain of the human experience? Roger unfolded his arms and gestured at the rain-filled sky and then the door to the house.

Reluctantly she pulled the latch to open the car door, deciding against the umbrella. She met him at the door, fumbling in her purse for the keys.

"I've been waiting over an hour," he said, his tone imbued with a predictable and familiar terseness. "Didn't you get my message?"

"No," she said. "I'm afraid I didn't."

"I left a message on Mom's phone. Last night."

"Sorry. Been kinda busy with funeral arrangements," she said evenly.

When they stood inside, Roger brushed at his wet shirt. "Haven't you heard about the hurricane?"

"Well yes, I-I mean I've just been over to the business office and—"

"What business office? The funeral home?"

"No, this place. Sunny Glen Palms and—"

"What have they got to do with anything?"

"Well, there's been talk about evacuating… this place and—"

"Evacuating? With a funeral on Saturday? What about all these people who've made arrangements to be there at the burial? I only got the weather news this morning at the airport waiting on my flight."

"There's been lots of hurricanes down here this summer. It doesn't necessarily stop things from happening. Anyway, it's not exactly as if we're expecting a crowd."

Roger walked out the door, shaking his head. Barbara put a hand out in front of her to gauge her nerves by how bad it was shaking. He returned with his small suitcase in tow.

"You can have Mom's room," she said, at the same time recalling with a tinge of regret she'd forgotten to change the linens after Lily's overnight. "I'm already in the guestroom."

He wheeled the bag over to the master bedroom. In the living room he flopped into the recliner, removing the tasseled loafers and rubbing at his feet through silky socks.

Barbara glanced over to the door of her mother's bedroom. The legal papers. "Let me just gather a few things from her bathroom."

She whisked past her brother and when she entered the bedroom, she tiptoed over to the dresser and reached in the top drawer to extract the papers Lily had noticed. She gathered them and stuffed them into an old pocketbook on the shelf in her mother's closet.

When she returned to the living room she found her brother squinting at her as a doctor would a patient.

"So what are your plans?"

By his tone she could surmise he wasn't merely referring to the next few hours, or days.

"I have several crafts fairs lined up and I'm bringing out a new idea incorporating small bulb lighting into some of my outdoor pieces. That alright with you?"

Roger made a face.

"Did you get *my* message," she asked. "Over a month ago?"

"No, I didn't."

"I left it on your mobile. On your voicemail."

He shook his head and fished around for the TV remote.

"So," said Barbara, "is there a good purpose for showing up or did you just come here to make me feel like shit?"

Roger flung the remote at the couch. "I can get a hotel. Probably what I should've done in the first place."

"No, no, I insist," Barbara threw her hands in the air. "Just stay right here pal, because I don't want anything. Never did and still don't. I don't care if I have nothing to walk away with after you've executed her affairs. You can have this house, so you may as well start living in it now!"

"Godammit Barbara! Why is it always about *you*?"

"About *me*?"

"Yes *you*!"

"I have no idea what you're talking about. In fact I—"

"It's all we hear about," he bellowed. "Barbara this and Barbara that!"

"What the hell are you talking about?"

"Where were you when Mom got sick? Where were you when she had her back surgery?"

"I tried to work with you all," her voice was beginning to crack. "You had me going up there for *my* shift when she least needed me. She was in round-the-clock care. She needed more than company, more than a visit, she needed help around the house when they released her, she needed laundry, she needed cooking done for Chrissakes!"

Roger waved his hand dismissively. "Oh here we go again."

"You're such a jerk. I changed my flight arrangements to better serve her. And then you just say *have a nice day* in that smug manner of yours and hang up on me! But that was like three years ago, why are we talking about it now?!"

"Because you never co-operate with family. You show up for nothing! You missed our kids confirmation parties, baptisms, graduations—"

"I'm not Catholic anymore. And if memory serves me correct, I was miles away a good chunk of those years. So what's your fucking problem?"

"Godammit Barbara, what the hell are you doing anyway? Why didn't you stick with pre-law in college and do something sensible with your life?"

"What do *you* care?"

Roger leaped from the recliner, his face red, daggers in his voice. "I'm only your brother for Chissakes! You've done nothing but disappoint!"

"Well this just might come as a surprise to you!" Barbara gripped the couch. "I don't care what you think! I'll live my own damn life as I choose!"

"Unbelievable," Roger muttered, shaking his head. "You go and drink and drug yourself nearly to death and we have to bail you out!"

"Nobody's *bailing me out!* I'm paying that off every month out of my own godamn pocket! And where was my *support* when I needed it, huh? All I got was the harsh judgment from you miserable people!"

"I paid a good chunk of that money up front! So did Mom!"

Barbara brought her fist down onto the counter. "And you'll never let me forget it, will you! Well I don't need your money! Take it out of the inheritance!" Her voice was failing and she was losing her breath, shuffling to the kitchen to steady herself against the counter. "You bastard."

"Oh yeah. I'm a bastard, real cute. Tell me, what exactly is it you do?"

"And what exactly is it *you* do that's so noble Roger. Peddle drugs?"

"Oh Jesus, what's that supposed to mean?"

"Last I knew you were selling drugs. Pharmaceutical industry?"

"How distorted. Talk about a stretch."

"Is it?"

"Stop being so melodramatic."

"Melodramatic? Those painkillers sure as hell did me great harm!"

"Look, I'm not going to defend what I do to make a living."

"So then why the hell should I," said Barbara with indignation. "I may be poor, but at least I make an honest living."

"Oh quit the bullshit," he frowned and waved his hand dismissively, 'Why don't you get off that self-righteous high horse? We do a lot of good to make a lot of people's lives better."

"Well I'll be damned, there's a sense of altruism that comes with all the sick amounts of money you make."

"Hey watch it sister!"

"I don't know how you sleep at night!"

"At least I've made something of myself! I worked hard for everything I've got and don't you *ever* forget it!"

"Oh fuck you!"

He'd started for the bedroom and turned sharply to face her. "Oh and just for the record. Why wasn't an autopsy ordered by the coroner?"

"What?"

"I know mom had heart trouble, but all this was still unexpected. And then you show up out of nowhere—"

"Is this an investigation? You want to interrogate me? Because the police already have. But you wanna open your own private investigation go right ahead mister." She was shaking, not having anticipated this ugly turn in the argument, never would she have imagined such words uttered from her own brother's mouth.

"I guess that's how they do things down here in this backwoods place full of old people. Just cart them off to a funeral home and—"

"You didn't have to be here for any of this! I'm the one who's made all the arrangements and you come down here like Hercule fucking Poirot making the most hurtful insinuations. I hate you! I truly hate you!"

"When are you ever going to grow up!"

"You go to hell!" Barbara marched into the guestroom to gather her belongings—ripping her hanging clothes from the closet, stuffing clothes into her suitcase. "Just go to hell Roger. Cause that's where you belong."

"Screw you! At least I try to live a good life. My kids know that, my wife knows that, and just listen to you!"

Barbara couldn't gather up her things fast enough from the guest bath, sweeping some of the contents in the medicine chest into her travel bag.

"I am *through* with this discussion," Roger called from the living room.

"Good! I don't want to speak to you ever again."

She entered the kitchen, clutching her luggage and glaring at his back as he leaned forward on the sofa, his eyes glued to the Weather Channel. She wiped at her eyes, glancing around her mother's house before heaving her luggage over the threshold and slamming the door shut behind her.

In the car she sat panting and clutching the steering wheel. It dawned on her that she didn't get the chance to see the copy of the will as intended, and she deliberated over returning to the house to retrieve the document. At last an impulse overtook her dread at the thought of facing her brother. As soon as she crossed the garage and stepped into the kitchen, she wished she hadn't. Her brother leaned against the counter before the answering machine, playing messages. She slinked around him and went directly to her mother's bedroom, stealthily retrieving the old handbag from the shelf of the closet and clutching it protectively under her arm, hastening her step to the side door amid the garbly voice of Yvonne from Sunnyville Funeral Home, *I'm sorry about this but we wanted to give you enough notice in advance. Please call us as soon as possible to reschedule.*

Roger glared at her. "You missed *that* one last night too," he said, his voice now almost a whisper but no less acerbic. "Funeral's off."

"You son of a bitch," she muttered, her back to him, her hand on the doorknob.

"What?"

"You heard me."

*

A good-sized crowd at Schooner's, a few of them with walkers beside their tables. Marge glanced from husband to son, dabbing at her mouth with a napkin. Teddy was already on his second beer and they hadn't been there fifteen minutes. Ted nursed a gin and tonic. Marge was having a glass of Chardonnay. Their waiter started them off with a few appetizers while they started off with small talk between them. It seemed a hard time going from there, it was as if the cat had everybody's tongue. And so they talked about the weather, only now with good reason.

"If I had waited a day longer to fly," said Teddy, setting his beer down on the white linen and smiling at the glum faces of his parents, "I wouldn't be here now."

Marge acknowledged him with a faint smile, toying with her napkin, shooting a quick glance at her husband, still smarting from his outburst this morning and wishing like all the other times it simply hadn't occurred and they might find themselves dining peaceably as a sensible and morally upright family.

"So," Ted said to Marge. "There's no evacuation protocol, or…"

"That's what they said this morning. Over at the office."

Their waiter, a heavyset mustached man, arrived with their entrees.

"So," Ted asked, sizing the man up and down, "any plans to close up over the weekend? With the storm and all?"

He smiled and shook his head, setting the plates down. "Oh God no. We've been through a few of these already. Life sort of goes on around here. You get used to it."

"You from here?" Teddy the younger asked.

"Born and raised. Over in Ruskin."

The waiter bowed and Ted nodded and then shook his head. "To listen to the television, you'd think it was the Apocalypse."

"They always do that. It's all about the ratings."

"We'll fix that," said Teddy, pointing a fork at his father. "Tigers and Yanks in Detroit."

"Well," Ted sighed. "guess if we're cooped up with the weather that's about all there is to do."

Marge cleared her throat. "There's a hurricane party tomorrow night I guess I've been invited to. Maybe I'll go do that while you boys watch the game."

Ted paused the cutting of his steak and cocked an eyebrow at his wife. "Hurricane party?"

"Well, I don't know. It doesn't sound like something that'd interest you anyway. I just thought I'd tag along. Just for an hour or so."

"What on earth is a hurricane party?"

"Well," she shrugged. "it's a party during a hurricane I guess."

"And who may I ask is putting this on?"

"Oh, this young couple over in the Timberlands. I don't even know their name."

Ted pursed his lips. "Not those crazy Canadians is it? The young fella with the Speedo?"

"I-I don't know."

"Because if it is, I've heard all kinds of things about them. And none of it good."

"Well, you can't always go on gossip."

"I heard it straight from their neighbors." Ted waved his fork before taking a bite of his steak. "Seems they have loud parties. Let their dogs run amuck. And the police have been over their a few times with the neighbors' complaints. So I hope it's not them."

"Well," said Marge with a shrug. "I guess I'll just have to find out."

"How did *you* get invited anyway?"

"I… well, Peggy and I were shooting some pool at the North Club."

"I knew that."

"Some young lady whose mother died. Here. Recently."

"Yes?"

Marge had her husband's undivided attention, it felt as if she'd been brought in for questioning.

"Honey, it's nothing really. Let's change the subject."

"Dad," Teddy shrugged, "We'll order a pizza or something. Did you guys drive up to Land o Lakes for any preseason games?"

Ted was still glaring at his wife and slowly returned his attention to his son. "What's that?"

"The Tigers. You told me you were gonna try and make a preseason game or two."

"We were too busy unpacking." Ted turned his attention to his wife. "Maybe I'll join your mother tomorrow night. At the hurricane party."

"Maroth is on the mound tomorrow dad and—"

"The Tigers are in last place for godsakes!"

Ted brought a fist crashing down onto the tabletop and the silverware hopped and rang out on the fine linen. Marge smiled apologetically at the nearby tables, then glared at her husband.

"If you're going to make a scene," she said evenly, "maybe we should just pay the tab and leave."

"I'm not making a scene."

"Yes you are dear," Marge smiled and batted her eyes. *"Making a scene."*

"No," he said through gritted teeth. "I am not."

"Much ado about nothing," Marge said, darting her eyes about the room with more polite smiles to the onlookers.

They took turns making small talk with their son for the duration of the meal. The bill came and Teddy made a polite if disingenuous attempt to pick up a tab he could ill afford to put on the credit card.

On the drive home Marge sat stiff and silent beside her husband, her mind made up she would for sure be ready tomorrow night when Peggy Beamish came to pick her up at six for the hurricane party. Her thoughts went to Peggy and her plans to terminate her 50-year marriage. They stayed there as Ted pulled the car into the driveway and the three of them walked disconsolately into the house, as the men turned on the sports channel and she washed her face and readied herself for bed prematurely, as she tried unsuccessfully to concentrate on the plot Robert Ludlum had concocted in the paperback she held before her on her side of the expansive king bed.

Ted's temper so often got the best of him and he could be a lion you could not tame. Why didn't she answer Peggy's question honestly, tell her that her husband had almost hit her on two occasions? One in yesteryear and then one time just last week. Why did she persist in this foolish attempt to mitigate her anxiety, downplay what was intended as a slap before he stayed his hand while she recoiled in fear? He'd lashed out in anger for the first time in years. It left her wondering if she'd be so lucky the next time.

*

Lily was fast asleep in the recliner when a knock came on the door. The house had darkened, the sound turned way down on the television, which cast an eerie glow about the room. She rubbed her eyes, gathering herself before prying herself with great effort out of the recliner. At the door, she knew who it was before she parted the curtains.

"I'm sorry," Barbara said, stomping wet feet on the mat and collapsing her umbrella. "I didn't know where else to go."

"Has your brother gotten settled in?"

"Yes, he *has*."

"Well, come on in and sit down."

Lily took Barbara's jacket, draping it across one of the kitchen chairs. "I'll put the kettle on.

She switched on the kitchen light and began laying out the tea service. Barbara collapsed her head to her hands. "I'm sorry," she sobbed, her voice muffled. "We had an argument. I can't stay in that house with him."

"Well maybe you just got off to a rocky start. It happens in the best of families."

"This is the *worst* of families."

"I'm sorry, honey. I-I don't know what to say."

"And this was the worst argument," Barbara said, closing her eyes and pursing her lips. "The argument to end all arguments. And we haven't even buried her yet."

"Well," Lily mused, "at least he'll be gone soon."

"The funeral home called and I missed their message too. We're going to postpone the memorial service with this hurricane alert."

"How will you let everyone know?"

"There's only a few who were even going to make the trip," Barbara shrugged. "Let him call them if he hasn't already. I thought about heading inland in the meantime, to take cover."

"Well," said Lily. "You may's well stay with me until everything blows over. I don't mind the company. Things turn ugly maybe we can get out of dodge together."

Barbara's eyes lit up. "You really mean that?"

"Well sure."

"I can't tell you what this means to me," Barbara said, her eyes welling up. "I can't tell you just how badly I didn't want to go back to that house."

"Well, I know you didn't."

"I feel so helpless."

"Well, there now." Lily reached over the table, patted Barbara's hand.

Barbara glanced up and their eyes locked. "Everything is spinning out of control right now."

"Yes. But it'll pass. Just stay strong. I know you'll get through this."

"Thanks. For everything."

"No need to thank me," Lily tsked. "You're gonna be alright."

Barbara rose from the table. Lily met her halfway around it to gather her in an embrace, thinking maybe she needed Barbara around as much as Barbara needed her around. Her chin resting on Lily's frail bony shoulder, Barbara thought to herself, *I have to get to a meeting again. I need to stay off the pills and the booze.*

Lily patted her on the back. "Everything will work out."

Barbara gave Lily's shoulders a squeeze, and stepped back. "I'll go and fetch my things."

When she stepped outside the wind had picked up, a roar of thunder in the distance. By the time she returned to Lily's front door the wind was whipping a heavy rain around. The phone rang. Lily picked it up and it was her son Jack. "I'm worried about you," he said. "Maybe you should get out of there."

"We're going to give it a day," she said.

*"We?"*

"My friend and I. Barbara."

"The one that had the *overdose?*"

She palmed the mouthpiece and shuffled off to the garage, her voice barely above a whisper. "Everything's fine Jack. Trust me. I'm just grateful I have someone with me right now. I'm a bundle of nerves."

"What are you going to do Mom?"

"I'll stay here tonight. See where the hurricane's going tomorrow."

"How are you going to drive if you have to evacuate?"

"My friend will be my eyes."

When she stepped back into the kitchen, Barbara was standing just inside the front door with her luggage.

"Get yourself settled," said Lily, nodding at the guestroom.

Barbara wheeled her luggage and lifted the bag onto one of the twin beds that Lily said her grandkids slept on. Lily poured them each a cup of herbal tea and said, "I know this is a bad idea and I'll be up all night running to the bathroom, but somehow it's comforting."

They settled themselves on the sofa in front of the weather channel.

"How was the eye doctor?" Barbara asked.

"Oh honey listen to me, don't go and get old." Lily shook her head. "Not good news."

"I'm sorry," Barbara said. "Anything I can do?"

"Maybe find me the fountain of youth for a start. My eyes have gotten so I can't hardly see anymore. Don't even think of driving after dark."

"I didn't realize it was so bad."

"It won't be too long before I'm legally blind."

Barbara reached and touched a bony hand, wrinkled and riddled with age spots. "Have you told your son?"

"I don't want to worry him," Lily dropped her head to her other hand and massaged her temples. They sat in silence with the sound muted on the television, listening to the wind roar and the thunder growl outside the walls. Then the power went out.

"Do you have a flashlight?" said Barbara, letting go of Lily's hand.

"There's one in the garage."

"Stay put." Barbara stepped tentatively in the darkness, without so much as the glow of streetlights through the windows, just a few flashes of lightening to go by. But she made it across the kitchen and to the garage. "Okay," she called out. "Where in the garage?"

"Oh, silly me," Lily called out from her spot in the darkness. "There's one in the drawer there in the utility room. Next to the washer."

"This little table?"

"Yes. That's it."

Barbara groped around a drawer full of knick-knacks until her hand fell upon the knurled metal grip of a compact flashlight. She nudged the switch and a beam of light cast a glow around the tiny room.

"Okay," she called out. "Do you have any candles?"

"Some tea lights in the drawer where the phone sits. In the kitchen. I like lighting the house with them sometimes. There's lighters in the drawer by the coffee pot."

Barbara trailed behind Lily, who pointed the decorative candle holders out one by one, and soon the house was illuminated in a soft golden glow. They heard the voices of neighbors calling out to one another in the night. When Barbara cracked the door for a glimpse outside the rain had let up and there was a muggy darkness. Her thoughts went to her brother up the street and her impulse was to go and check on him. That's what family did in a crisis. When they were teenagers and Roger could be protective of her. It felt odd to be standing so nearby one another in a blackout, a potential hurricane on the way. It was not something she'd have figured on a few days ago when she rolled into Sunny Glen Palms for a chance to make her peace with her mother. It was doubly strange to be left incapable of pulling a family together in a crisis.

Lily announced from the kitchen that the outage had knocked out the cordless phone "I guess I wouldn't want to worry my sons," she said. "But I don't know about my next-door neighbor. He's not in his right mind. Do you mind to check on him?"

"Not at all," Barbara said. She traipsed across the wet grass, umbrella in hand, to the neighbor's house. Several knocks on the door yielded no response. Hard of hearing and fast asleep, Barbara thought. On the way back a middle-aged cleanshaven man holding an umbrella approached her and Lily stepped out to join them under Barbara's umbrella.

"I wouldn't worry too much," said the beefy mustached man. "We get power outs every now and again. They'll probably have it up and running in no time."

"I do worry about this hurricane," said Lily.

Barbara cocked her head to one side. "Do you think we should leave, even though they're not making us?"

"Last I heard the hurricane's s'posed to land south of us on Saturday. Down Fort Myers way. We've been watching the weather channel. Up until a few minutes ago anyway. But like I said…" He droned on in a soothing matter-of-fact tone that worked like a sedative for both of them.

The wind was still gusting and the rain had begun to pick up as they walked back inside. Lily went to her bedroom to change into pajamas.

When she returned to the kitchen she stood in front of the refrigerator and shook her head. "I'll be darned," she said, "a whole order of groceries, and now they'll only spoil. Did you meet my next-door neighbor?"

"No," said Barbara, "Dark and quiet. Nobody answered the door."

"I wonder if he's evacuated."

"Can we play rummy?"

"What?"

"Can we play rummy?"

"*Now*?"

"It's soothing. Calms me down."

"Oh."

"There's another way I deal with pressure and I don't think I wanna go that route. Not tonight. Not ever."

"Well," Lily puckered her lips and shrugged, "I'll get the cards out."

"Great."

"Guess we can try and play by candlelight." Lily fetched her reading glasses from the kitchen and when she placed them on the bridge of her nose, the immediate effect lent her an air of studiousness and intelligence.

The house grew quiet and gradually, without central air conditioning, warm and stuffy. Lily fanned herself with her cards, deliberating over her next play, her eyes growing tired while she pored over the cards in her hand with every turn. They had forged a sort of language over the hands they'd played, a secret code between them. Three-of-a-kind and four-of-a-kind combinations of sevens were called lucky sevens. Eights were crazy eights. Twos were terrible twos. Thirsty threes. Fantastic fours. Fabulous fives. Sexy sixes, that was Barbara's. Face cards were royalty. When someone was about to empty their hand, they'd say "add 'em up" to the chagrin of their opponent, who had then to subtract the points of any cards in their hand. A burgeoning portfolio of expressions that would appear gibberish to any onlooker. Barbara noticed the gibberish to be dwindling along with Lily's enthusiasm. She cleared her throat.

"We can always finish the game tomorrow," she glanced around the dimly lit room at the abundance of trinkets with which Lily filled out her home. On the end tables were framed family photographs, and Barbara reckoned that for all her loneliness, Lily was not plagued by many familial resentments—there were problems between her sons and both of them felt she ought to get out more, but nobody was shouting at anybody. An old familiar feeling crept across Barbara right then and there in the darkness, it was a lamentation of the highest degree and it said, why wasn't I born into another family? But here she was once again doing that which she'd done all her life—making friends her family. The glow from tea lights neatly aligned between them not only illuminated their game of five-hundred gin rummy, but also threw light on the comfortable silence that lay between two friends who'd simply talked themselves out.

The old handbag from her mother's closet sat on the chair beside her. With the papers. The copy of the Will. I'll look at it tomorrow, she thought. I'll pull it out of the envelope and look at it tomorrow.

"Is that your bag?" Lily asked.

"It's my mother's. The papers are inside. The copy of the Will."

"Aren't you curious?"

"I don't know. I feel strange just thinking about it. Like it's an invasion of her privacy."

"I guess I see what you mean."

"Oh hell. Let's have a look," she said, fetching the laminated folder from the handbag. "I guess I'll have to do it sooner or later."

Lily replaced her reading glasses to the bridge of her nose, lending her the appearance of higher acuity. Barbara moved from her spot across the table to sit beside Lily. She removed the contents and in the dim light she pored over the first page. *I, Alice Anne Thunderclap, being of sound mind and body…*

Roger Thunderclap was listed first as Executor. Further on down the page her name appeared underneath his in the family details. She thumbed through the legalize and when she turned the first page over and squinted at the content, she dropped her head to her hands.

"What is it?" Lily asked, picking up the page and drawing it closer to her face. "Even with these glasses I can't see a durn thing." She squinted at the words. Her gasp was all the more profound in the quietude of the room. "She's leaving you the house. Here in Sunnyville."

Barbara, her arms crossed on the table with her head dropped to them, gave a barely discernable nod.

"Accept it," Lily whispered, placing an arm around Barbara, squeezing her shoulder. "A mother's love is sometimes beyond explanation."

*

Kenny paced his threadbare living room clutching a cordless phone with backup battery. A single blinking message on the answering machine and he knew who it was before he hit play and heard her voice—fragile and emotional. It sounded as if she'd been crying. She said she was calling to check on him. The hurricane and all. To see if he was alright. Something quite out of the ordinary, someone calling to check on him. He'd not acted on an impulse to call her after his confession to stranger Mike Beamish, in the pews at Our Lady of Lourdes Catholic Church. She was also calling to let him know her flight for Friday had been cancelled. In the darkness he sat on the floor, dialed her number. They warmed up with hurricane talk.

"I want you to know this is our decision," she said, changing the subject after a pause. "I don't want to foist this upon you. I don't know if I'm ready myself."

"Ready?"

"To have a kid."

"I know I'm not." He wanted to scare back the words as soon as they left his mouth. There was silence on the line and he imagined her on the other end, his words sinking in.

"I've just been thinking," she sighed at last into the phone. "I've been thinking so much on everything. What to do."

"Of course."

"I've been praying, but not worry prayer. Does that make sense?"

"Um, I'm not very religious or anything–"

"Nor I. I'm a practicing Catholic, but I'm not preachy about it."

"I remember you telling me that when I was up there." Kenny said, and then after another long pause, added. "Maybe it's not the right thing to- to… have the child."

The only sound on the line was that of her breathing. "Well," she said at last, "we can talk more about it in person soon."

"Yeah," he said. "we'll figure something out when things blow over down here… Yes, yes I'm sure. Well, you know, I think we got along pretty well when I was up there… Yes, yes I know… it's just to um, talk about everything, everything we need to talk about… No, I'm not sorry all this happened, look can we talk when the dust settles with the storm and all? Right now there's a hurricane to get through… No, no that's alright, you're not being insensitive… I'm going to be okay."

He hung up, mulling over his words. *I'm going to be okay*. Sometimes Kenny Fitzroy, he thought, you can be the greatest of pretenders. Maybe that was okay. Maybe he'd had enough years to just let his hair down and be himself. Maybe he'd spend the rest of his life pretending, in the manner that most people do.

*

Later that evening. Just up the road. Roger Thunderclap cracks his knuckles, rubs at aching feet and yawns, thumbing through his mother's address book and calling only the close family members he would tell the bad news to, that might consider making the trip down for the burial, not imagining that his sister and her friend had already beaten him to the chore. Marge Cumberbatch lays sprawled out on the king-sized bed in shorts and a tee-shirt, a battery-operated oscillating fan blowing a current of warm air over her. Wrestling with the idea of remaining in Sunny Glen Palms until the day it was herself that the EMT vehicle came to fetch. Wondering aloud to the ceiling if that was all there was for her to look forward to. Her husband in the next room, the carpet getting warmer under his feet as he sits beside a hand-cranked battery-operated emergency radio he picked up at Walgreens. From the tiny speaker comes the static squawking of the Fox News radio network. Updates on the severe weather warning in effect locally for both Hillsborough and Pinellas County and all points north and south. His son sat next to him on the sofa, hands pressed together with his chin resting on thumbs, as if in supplication to the weather gods. Peggy Beamish sprawled out on one of the twin beds in her bra and panties, the air thick with heat, no fans anywhere in the house. Her husband sprawled out on the couch in his boxers. Calling out to her, honey, I think I'll get dressed. Go for a walk now that the rain's died down. Maybe check in on friends. At this hour? she replies. Across town, Kenny Fitzroy in the metal folding chair before the PC on the foldable card table. In his sort-of living room. Another night all alone, stupefied after the monitor display flashed and the little white ball in the middle of the screen shrunk to nothing. Up late checking flights out of Tampa to Hartford Connecticut in case there was a better deal to be had. And not too far up the road in the most modern of the Sunny Glen Palms developments, the Masterpiece subdivision—the Malaprops. Up in the modest loft of the two-story affair, Wayne Malaprop cutting the white powder on a vanity mirror with a razor blade then rolling up a hundred-dollar bill. His wife Marjorie downstairs tidying up the living room for their hurricane party.

# 7

Somewhere in the middle of night, power was restored to Sunnyville. Peggy Beamish stirred awake, laying on her back in her underwear over a fitted sheet dampened with sweat. Across from her on his single bed, Mike lay sprawled on his back snoring, the sheet twisted around him like a toga. She gathered her sheet over her and turned onto her side watching him, his face set not in its usual cast of calm repose but instead one of anguish. Her mind went to worry. An old instinct. Years ago, around the holidays it was. She figured it was just his year for holiday blues. It went on for weeks. The moping. Even the kids noticed it. What's wrong Dad? It wasn't until months later, when spring arrived with all its openings, its bloom of clarity, that she realized he'd had his cold heart warmed and then broken. Like all of the goings-on in his shadow world, she filed it away, an unsolved mystery. He went on long sales trips and sometimes things happened and sometimes they didn't just end abruptly. They kept up appearances. With their friends. From church, from the neighborhood they resided in for thirty years, out in the suburbs. Cookouts. Little League. He was the kind of friend who turned up at happy hours but didn't visit you in the hospital. That was Peggy's forte.

He stirred and then gathered the sheet into a ball, curling a fist around it, tucking it under his chin. Maybe he had a broken heart, she thought, staring up at the rotating ceiling fan blades in the semi-dark. Maybe she'd had a broken heart, all these years. Maybe she had a broken soul.

A impulse to rise and fire up the computer to search for deals on RVs, make arrangements to look at these things next week, but her body and mind were cloaked in exhaustion and it would have to wait until morning. She dozed on and off, her mind vacillating between enduring and a resolution to leave. When she threw her legs over the bed, Mike had rolled over on his side and now faced away from her. She tiptoed across the wood floor and threw on her robe. In the bathroom she splashed water on her face and studied its imperfections. No amount of cold cream over the years could keep the wrinkles at bay, but she had high cheekbones and she'd managed to keep her weight at bay and she thought she looked pretty good. Maybe there'd be men who'd find her attractive at the roadside attractions. Maybe they'd be easy to meet at the RV parks. Maybe it was her turn to be loosey goosey. Maybe it was time, maybe she was tired of sleeping alone.

The rain slapping against the roof grew heavy and then came peals of thunder and flashes of lightening. She flung back the covers and threw her legs reluctantly over the side. Started the coffee and shuffled into the guest room to switch on the computer. On Craiglist there were an abundance of recreational vehicles for sale. This was Florida and people were regularly dying and leaving things and there was no shortage of deals to be found.

The phone rang and she picked up the extension from the base there on the desk in the guest room. The dispirited voice of her grandson Jeff, with the news that they'd gone ahead and cancelled their flight. They'd seen on the Weather Channel that Hurricane Charley's predicted landfall had changed from Saturday to the early hours of Friday the thirteenth.

"News to me," said Peggy, saying we'll be in touch before replacing the cordless to its base and thumping her hand lightly on the desk.

The rain eased, leaving the room bathed in the blue hue of dawn. The phone rang again and she sprung up from the swivel chair to retrieve it from the extension on the table. It was Activities Director Ellen Everitt from the Business Office.

"Good morning. Listen, Mrs. Beamish, I hate to be the bearer of bad news but we've decided to cancel all events in the North and South Club this weekend, what with the extreme weather warning."

"That's alright," Peggy sighed. "A lot of family and friends called last night and told us they weren't coming. Wouldn't have been many there anyway."

"Okay. Let's see what the weekend brings and then we can reschedule the room for another date."

"That's quite alright," said Peggy, rising abruptly from the desk chair to shut the door of the guest room. "That won't be necessary."

"Oh?"

"Maybe it just wasn't meant to be."

Mrs. Everitt went quiet at the other end of the phone.

"Do you believe in fate Mrs. Everitt?" Peggy stared at the wall and the framed family photographs. "Destiny, y'know. Serendipitous events–"

"Well–"

"–that have meaning. If you're really pay attention," Peggy whispered at the phone.

"I do, there are sometimes reasons for–"

"My husband wanted this party. He wanted a big shebang."

"Oh?"

"I'm going to leave. Fifty years in. I'm going to leave."

It was out of her mouth before she knew it, intractable—and she knew it was foolish to spill the beans in light of how people talked in Sunnyville.

"Well," Ellen Everitt cleared her throat to summon a more business-like tone. "Have you really thought this through?"

Peggy laughed and brought a hand to her mouth. "Do you think I'm crazy? For doing this?"

"Well, with all due respect Mrs. Beamish, it's hardly my place to offer an opinion."

"Yes, but there are signs. If you pay attention."

"Signs?"

"This storm. The hurricane."

"And?"

"Do you not find it ironic it just happens to land on the very day we were to celebrate the most farcical of marriages?"

"All marriages," said Ellen Everitt, "have some element of falsity and pretense to them Mrs. Beamish."

"I know. But some more than others. And I've just about had my fill."

"Look, I'm sorry Mrs. Beamish but I have a few more calls to make. Events to cancel. A lot of people who need to know."

"Of course, I understand. Just tell me if you think this old girl has lost her wits."

"Would it change anything? You strike me as a determined woman who makes up her own mind and does what she pleases—"

"Well, you don't stand corrected there."

At the other end, Ellen Everitt gazed at the call sheet in front of her. Last night security had to deal with a confused man over in the dry sauna seeking shelter from the hurricane, one of several issues on her plate, tracking down the next of kin. "Well," she said, "I really must get to these calls. I don't mean to be rude."

"You're not being rude at all. Thanks." She replaced the phone to the receiver and heard Mike coming out of the bathroom. She stuck her head outside the door. "Party's off," she announced to her husband, still in his boxers and pouring himself a cup of coffee.

"I figured as much," he shrugged. "They've grounded just about every flight to Tampa."

She drummed her fingers on the doorframe, considering spilling the beans about everything, including the legal termination of their marriage. It was too early and he'd just gotten up, she thought. It'd be cruel. Instead she said, did you sleep well? He grimaced and said, you know I never really sleep anymore. It's either the bladder or the brain overworked.

"What's on your mind," she asked, her words ringing odd to her ears, it'd been years since she'd probed into the well-being of her husband.

"Nothing really. The storm I guess."

He brought his coffee to the kitchen table and drew a chair. "I hope we don't get hit too bad. But they said last night on the weather channel if it makes land fall it'll be further south. Fort Myers. Punta Gorda."

Those places didn't mean much to Peggy other than they weren't here where she was and that gave her cause for relief. She was more preoccupied with the dissolution of a fifty-year marriage than any damage to property.

*

In the pale dawn he made himself bacon, eggs and toast—listening to Jonathan Richman and the Modern Lovers with the sound turned down so as not to disturb the neighbors. Outside it was grey and overcast. The coffee was bubbling on the old-fashioned percolator, something he drug out of the boxes from time to time. He'd just sat down when the phone rang. Her voice sounded small and unsteady, but perked up when he told her he'd booked a flight to Hartford for the following week.

"We'll have plenty of time to talk about everything when you get here next week. How long are you staying?"

"Um," he gulped, standing up and beginning to pace the room again. "I booked a couple days, but it's a changeable ticket."

"Oh. Uh-huh. Great."

"I have a friend or two I can ask to stay here and watch my place. But there's not much to worry about in a gated community."

"Well, it's still nice to have friends nearby to check on it."

"Yes," he said, wondering could he count any among them as friends, what constituted a friend? "Some of them," he said, "could use a vacation from their spouses."

A light-hearted laugh over the line, the first he'd heard since that one night they shared, an abeyance in the gravity of the fallout of that one night.

"We've kinda had a lot going on down here this week. Lotta drama."

"Well my goodness," she said. "A hurricane is no picnic."

"Besides the storm. People stuff," he said, willing that the mention of other people's troubles might serve as a diversion to their own.

"Oh. I see."

"Well listen, thanks for calling. I'll call you before I leave."

"Send me your flight info. I'd be happy to pick you up. And you can stay here if you wish. Or your cousins. Whatever you're comfortable with."

"Thanks."

"I just hope you stay safe. Be careful."

His eggs had gone cold. He mopped at them with the toast, savoring every bite of the crisp bacon. Maybe it would be nice to have someone to cook breakfast for and share it with. He would make do, he was thinking, with whatever might come his way as an unlikely parent. A peace coursed through his veins, covering him as if he were dipped in a vat of vanilla. As much as he basked in the experience, he knew it would wax and wane over the coming days, weeks, years. He finished up and piled new dirty dishes on top of the old ones in the sink. The early morning storms had passed, the rain had now tapered off to a drizzle. He climbed into his mother's old Dodge Dart, cranked the window down and glanced up at the sky. It was calm now, but he knew the forecast was very dire for the coming hours. When he pulled up in front of Alice Thunderclap's house, he saw a newer model car where Barbara's car had been. He fetched his mother's battered umbrella, worse for the wear with its broken metal ribs, severed tips and torn cloth. He clambered out of his mother's old clunker, somewhat warily approaching the house. Roger Thunderclap scratched his head from where he watched at the window in the den, at the front of the house where his mother lay dead just a week ago. Who was this gawky skinny guy? One of his sister's deadbeat friends from Asheville? He hesitated behind the door, waited for the knock and then a shaky voice.

"It's me, Kenny."

Roger undid the doorknob lock, then the deadbolt and then he got a view of Kenny Fitzroy up close, beneath a punished umbrella, his mussed hair wet and beads of moisture on his unshaven cheeks.

"Can I help you," he said evenly.

"I'm a friend of Barbara's. And your Mom's. Are you family?"

"Yes I am."

"Well," Kenny said, head down, shuffling his feet, "I'm really sorry about Alice. She was a fantastic Bridge player and at times she had a keen sense of humor."

Roger looked on incredulously at a shabby-looking creature and his odd eulogizing of Alice Thunderclap.

Kenny shrugged. "Is Barbara around?"

"No," Roger shook his head slowly, "she isn't."

"Do… do you know where she is."

"No I don't. But if you see her, please tell her the funeral's definitely off. For now."

"Oh… I see. The weather."

"Yes," Roger said. "The weather. Now if you'll excuse me, I—"

"Is she alright? B-Barbara I mean."

"My sister? Alright? No, I wouldn't say that."

"She seemed alright when I last saw her."

"When did you last see her?"

"Let me see… kind of a lot going on here lately… it was… yesterday I think… or, or maybe the day before last?"

"Do you live here?"

"Yeah," said Kenny.

"How'd you meet my sister?"

"When your mother died."

"How'd you know my mother?"

If Kenny had more gumption, more chutzpah—if it were in fact a Ted Cumberbatch that Roger Thunderclap were addressing, Roger might have summoned the wrath of God with his persistent and dizzying amount of questioning. He may even have received a tap on the shoulder or a punch in the face. But it was Kenny Fitzroy that stood before him, and while the very unwelcoming interrogator before him had truly gotten under his skin, things would stay there, he'd do his best to remain polite on the surface. But the man who blocked the doorway to Alice Thunderclap's abode had him rattled enough to open his mouth and speak just a little louder in an even tone.

"I knew your mother because *as I told you* I *live* here. My condolences."

Kenny started back to the car, then turned around to face the man in the doorway. "Would you be so kind as to ask her to give Kenny a call when she turns up?"

"*Kenny?*"

"Kenny. Kenny Fitzroy."

Upon identifying himself yet again, a voice went off in Kenny's head. It said, *I'm sorry, I didn't catch your name, jerkoff.* But while his lips were moving as he stepped away, no words issued from them, only vague mutterings as he climbed back into his Dodge Dart. Instead of continuing down Fairway Drive he turned back in the direction he came. His friend's brother made him jittery and he was sure he was being observed. He circled around and approached Lily's house from the opposite direction.

*

Ted Cumberbatch cursed the thick carpet upon which he paced back and forth, on hold with the Pinellas County Sherriff's Office. At last a woman's voice came on the line.

"Yes, yes!" he shouted. "Yes, I'm still here!"

Marge peered over the pages of her day-old newspaper to observe her husband shaking his head and holding the cordless phone at a distance and speaking at it as if it were a microphone.

"What? People are evacuating? Well, what's the official line? Are we to stay put or should we start packing? God, this is horrible! They do a better job in Cuba for Chrissakes! Is there no official order to evacuate? I'm sick and tired of all this wait and see!"

He slammed the phone down and said, "C'mon Marge, start packing, we're going."

She dropped the paper to her lap. "*Going?* Just exactly where to?"

"Anywhere! We'll get a hotel inland," he said, starting for the door to their bedroom. "Come on Teddy," he called to the den. "We're heading out. Hurricane's on the way. We're leaving."

"But what about the hurricane party?" Marge flung the newspaper at the coffee table in front of her.

Ted came charging back from the bedroom. "Screw the goddamned hurricane party!"

"But Peggy said—"

"I don't give a rat's ass *what* Peggy said! Let's go! Get packing!"

Marge drew a heavy sigh and shook her head. "I'm not going."

"*What*?"

"Nobody told us we have to leave and I'm not going. I'm staying put right here and—"

"Goddammit!—"

"—enjoy the storm and we'll just hear all about the damage further south in the morning. They just said severe weather here on the news."

"A hurricane can do anything! It's unpredictable!" His face was getting redder by the second.

"Well," Marge held out her hand, spread her fingers and counted out hurricanes on them one at a time, "we didn't get hit by Ivan, we didn't get hit by Francis, Hermine missed us, we didn't get hit by Jeanne—"

"Well then maybe it's our turn now!"

"By Charley? Hah, sounds as harmless as a favorite uncle."

"God*dammit* Marge," he gritted his teeth and lowered his voice. "Start packing. Now."

She shook her head. "You're just overreacting."

"This is a fucking emergency and you're being a smartass!"

Marge stood and slapped her thighs. "I'm staying put and that's that."

"I'm with you Mom," Teddy emerged from the den and trailed behind his mother to the master bedroom. "You guys always get these severe weather warnings, don't ya?"

"Goddammit!" Ted's face went crimson. He stomped on the carpet, punishing it as if it too was conspiring against him. "It's a Category five!"

"I'm telling you," Marge said impassively on her way to the bedroom, "it'll be a heart attack not a hurricane that will get you in the end."

Ted turned his fury from the floor to his wife, rushing her, raising a hand and then staying it as she recoiled, spilling backwards onto the bed. He turned to face his son. "C'mon get packing. She wants to stay here with her kooky friends, that's her headache. Fuck it."

"No, Dad, no. I-I don't wanna go. If only we just sit down and talk calmly among the three of us–"

"*Him* talk *calmly*," Marge said to her son, "Don't hold your breath."

Teddy shook his head and threw his palms up in exasperation before retreating to the back porch, closing the sliding glass door behind him.

"Godammit!" Ted bellowed.

"Will you please calm down, for Godsakes!" Marge pleaded.

A gust of wind slapped rain against the bedroom window.

Ted kicked at the king-sized bed and Marge scurried on all fours to the other side of the mattress. He started for the closet and began thrashing about, ripping shirts from their hangers. Ripping at drawers and flinging clothes over his shoulder.

"I am so fed up with your lousy temper," she said from the foot of the bed, her voice taking on a new command. "You're behaving like a two-year-old."

It seemed an anomaly in time and space, it was as if his fury propelled him towards her with such velocity as to cause him to leave the ground and take flight, across the king bed, crossing a line he'd heretofore managed to stop just short of. This time he failed to stay his hand. Much more painful than the sting of the slap on her face was the sting of betrayal, a transgression far worse than any amount of adultery. A line had been crossed and she could make all kinds of excuses for him–the barometric pressure, Mercury in retrograde, the onset of senility–or simply too much too soon regarding Marge's newly found chutzpah, backbone, pushback, call it what you will. His open palm hit the side of her head so hard it was a split second before she hit the soft mattress, her face throbbing, vision blinded by tears of pain and shock and sorrow. He wheeled his luggage over the linoleum floor of the kitchen, through the utility room and then wrestled it over the threshold of the garage and into the car. The automatic garage door rumbled along its track and then the ignition sounded. Teddy ran out the front door to the driveway, while Marge lay staring at the plain white ceiling, too frozen to bother herself with the freezer and an icepack for the bruising.

*

Peals of thunder and flashes of lightning had stirred her out of heavy slumbers somewhere deep in the night and she lay on her back listening as the heavens pelted a hard rain down on the roof, until the curtains dulled the sunlight in gradients, and when at last she'd got out of the bed it was almost eight o'clock.

Last night before bed they'd had to shift boxes and move the golf cart out to the driveway to make room in the garage for Barbara's car, so as to hide her presence from her brother.

Lily was unaccustomed to a heavy breakfast in the morning, and more so, company to fix it. Barbara had already made a pot of coffee and after Lily sat at the table she brought a cup to her and continued fixing breakfast.

"Full service," said Lily.

"Well," said Barbara, "I've waited on a table or two in my time."

"I'm sorry there's only eggs and toast and no bacon."

"Well then, we'll have eggs and toast. And I've got some marmalade and homemade jams I brought for Mom."

Lily's eyes lit up. She reined in her enthusiasm at the thought Barbara's eyes might well up, as she set the table and then cracked open the jars so they could tease out a taste of everything. The doorbell rang and it was Kenny Fitzroy, folding a tattered umbrella, shaking it before stepping over the threshold. He glanced around him at another tidy and neatly arranged home in stark contrast to his own. He followed Lily over to the back porch where she said he could open the umbrella to let it dry. Her family appeared in framed photographs around the living room on end tables and a bookcase—children, nieces, nephews, grandchildren, husband. Every face a blood relative, he guessed—like Alice Thunderclap's and Peggy Beamish's and almost every other house in Sunny Glen Palms. Except, he ruminated with a tinge of sadness, that of his own. His friends beckoned him to the kitchen table with enough enthusiasm that he might shelve this sadness to be expounded on later.

"I expected I might find you at home," he said, settling himself at the head of the table, a cup of coffee and a slice of toast laden with blackberry preserves before him. "I had the gravest misfortune of encountering your dear brother instead."

"Why," Barbara squinted, "have you adopted the tone of Sherlock Holmes?"

"Happens sometimes when I'm all keyed up," Kenny sighed. "Sort of a coping mechanism."

"Oh," Barbara played abstractedly with one of the jars before her.

"So the funeral's off?"

"Yes. Unfortunately, the hurricane is not."

"Uh-huh." Kenny puckered his lips and shrugged, the tropical wind monster appearing no more than a triviality to him. "There's a hurricane party tonight."

"I know. I haven't forgotten."

"Just that, you know, it isn't very often we have anything remotely interesting going on here. This one just might be the ticket. The Malaprops are under the age limit—no offense Lily."

"None taken. I'm just a boring old bitty. You young folks go and have you a good time."

"You can join us if you want," Kenny said.

"Nooo," Lily mock-shuddered. "I'll stay here and keep an eye on the storm." She rose and walked to the front door to have a peek at the sky.

"Anyway," said Kenny, "I told your brother to let you know I stopped by and ask you to give me a call if he saw you. He didn't ask the same favor in return."

"He's a real…"

Lily glanced over at Barbara and turned up her nose. "Son of a bitch?" she said and they had a good laugh between them.

"And here I was thinking I'm cursed not having any siblings," Kenny said, "but in a way it's a kind of blessing I guess."

"Mine are all dead and gone," Lily shook her head ruefully.

"Were you very close?" Barbara asked.

"Oh heavens yes." Lily replied. "We went on cruises together, me and Dorothy. My sister Teresa could be difficult, really. More the complaining type. But we were always there for one another. Same with my brothers, although I wasn't very familiar with my oldest brother Bo. Oh well, I guess I'm lucky."

Barbara rose to put another pot of coffee on.

"I'm supposed to be drinking decaf," Lily said. "But I guess under the circumstances…" She was giddy. Her table had guests and she was giddy.

"So tell me," Barbara nodded at Kenny, "is Kathy from Connecticut coming this weekend?"

Kenny shook his head. "Change in strategy."

"You make it sound like a game."

"It is a game, isn't it? All of life is, in a sense."

Barbara shrugged. "If that's so, I guess I'd rather not play it with my family."

"But you have to. At least for now."

"The final game."

"Well maybe so."

"I don't want to have to deal with my brother anymore."

Lily, returned to the table, drawing a rumpled Kleenex from the sleeve of her robe and rubbing her nose. "Well," she glanced over at Kenny, "any news on the baby?"

*News on the baby*, thought Barbara. As if they were expecting it any day now.

"Well," Kenny said, running a finger around the rim of his cup, "I'm going to fly up there. I booked a flight."

"Good idea," Lily's face brightened.

Barbara looked incredulous. "You going for just a visit? To stay?"

"I'll go visit and scope things out. Maybe see how we vibe together."

"She'll never move down here you know. To *this* place."

"Maybe I'll move up there."

"Leave your comfortable existence?" Barbara cocked an eyebrow.

"I might. I just might surprise everyone. Including myself."

"What would you do up there?"

"I might sell this place and buy something. Get a job."

"Doing what?"

"I don't know. Whatever."

"Sounds like an amazing plan," Barbara pulled a mock surprise face.

"Well there's always Walmart. Y'know, something just to get started."

"I can just see you," Barbara grinned, "in a Walmart apron. Jeans and a tee shirt. Hello I'm Kenny, welcome to Walmart."

"Okay so maybe I'm too smart for my own good. Overqualified for menial work. Maybe I can sell stuff on eBay or something."

Lily scrunched her eyebrows. "Where's eBay?"

"Well," said Kenny, "I better be going."

"Oh man, I hope I didn't hurt your feelings," said Barbara.

"Not at all," Kenny said as went to fetch the umbrella.

"Maybe you can convince her to move to Asheville. We can all be friends. I can buy my house right next door to yours. Lily can sell this place and buy the old house up the street. Hang out with all the hipsters."

"Hipsters?" Lily scrunched her eyebrows.

"Hey," Kenny said with his hand on the doorknob, "I'll pick you up for the hurricane party at four."

"That early?"

"I hear the Malaprops kick things off early."

"Who doesn't around here?" said Barbara.

*

There were those who fled in the dead of night, gathering belongings willy-nilly and stuffing vehicles. Some of them, like the Hightowers, had friends or family in other retirement communities inland. Others like Ted Cumberbatch, put their stock in hotel vacancies. Those that remained went shopping to stock up and so lines in the supermarket were long, and at the guard gate, long in both directions.

On the golf cart, Marge Cumberbatch trolled along the narrow path in sunglasses, glancing between the traffic jam at the gate and the gloomy sky overhead, when the winds picked up. She knew neither why she took the golf cart nor what she intended to do. Just a compulsion to get away from the house, and it was not the North Club nor the South Club but the supermarket beyond the gate that lured her, just like all the others to stock the refrigerator and cabinets. She tried calling Peggy right after that frantic argument in the street she was sure all the neighbors saw and heard. Ted apologetically trying to coax her into the car, she standing her ground and saying no I'm not getting in the car, until at last he said suit yourself I've got no responsibility here. Teddy, not one for making scenes in public, no matter the gravity of the circumstances, kept waving his hand and miming the words, *come on* and *Mom please.*

But Peggy's line was busy. When she replaced the cordless to its base, she brought her head to her hand, dancing it side-to-side, shuddering and weeping, then erupting into a full-blown cry from the depths. Her nose had become full with snot but she couldn't bring herself to get up to fetch a Kleenex. Instead, she sprawled out on the floor, the dreaded carpet, and faced the ceiling, and that blank white surface became the canvas for all of her racing thoughts. The rain came and went on the other side of it. When she'd emptied herself of tears, she propped herself up on elbows and glanced around the room as if for the first time, the rain had let up and she pushed herself to her feet. She tried once again to reach Peggy and got her answering machine. She fetched the keys to the golf cart, now her only means of transportation. There were taillights glowing all along Pebble Beach Boulevard when she drove along its diminutive annex, the golf cart path. They were blurred and she realized she was still crying.

At the Winn Dixie she was in one of the long lines, double checking her cart for candles and batteries, when she felt a tap on her shoulder. She turned around and there was Kenny Fitzroy, hitching his thumbs in a small backpack, nudging a small shopping basket at his feet.

"I'm sorry, I've forgotten your name," he said matter-of-factly.

"Marge," she said.

"I'm Kenny."

"Well, looks like we're going to get the storm after all."

"The storm yes, but I doubt we'll see the hurricane."

"I won't be disappointed."

"You going to the hurricane party at the Malaprops' tonight?"

"Wouldn't miss it for the world," she said with a blank stare.

When they got outside it had begun to drizzle. Kenny said, "I knew I should have taken the car. Do you mind giving me a lift back to my place? I'm just inside the gate."

He helped her roll down the canvas flaps and they clambered inside.

"I just came to pick up a dessert for the party and a few things for my trip. I'm flying up to Connecticut next week."

"That'll be a nice break from the weather."

"Maybe," he replied, tugging distractedly at the vinyl roof where one of the buttons had come undone.

"My husband and my son just left me stranded."

It was out of her mouth before she knew it and it fell as strange upon her ears as his.

"Left you? Stranded?"

"I'm sorry, I don't..." She sighed. "They tried hard enough. To talk me into leaving. But I didn't want to."

"I don't think we're likely to meet the eye of the storm. I hope not. But people sure are panicking."

"That's what it was," she said, as if it had only now dawned on her. "He was panicking."

"I've talked to a few people who've been through this before," said Kenny. "The locals. Like the maintenance guy at the South Club. They all laugh at the panic. They grew up here. It's different."

"I see."

Marge shook her head at the line of cars at the gate. One lady in a big Buick had her window rolled down in the rain and kept honking her horn. They watched her lips moving on a crimson face.

"Oh here, I should have told you where to turn off the golf cart path. Turn around, then you don't have to go through the guard gate."

"Isn't that antithetical to the security of a guard gate?"

"Yeah. But there are a million ways to get in here on foot."

"Oh. Anyway, Peggy's supposed to pick me up at six for the party."

"If you get a hold of her," said Kenny, "tell her to come earlier if she wants. I think they're kicking things off around four."

When she rolled up to his unit in the Andover neighborhood the golf cart was whipped about in sudden gusts of wind. Kenny stepped off of the cart and gripped the windshield. She went to lower her sunglasses and bid him goodbye and checked herself.

“I’m sorry about your family,” he said. “Abandoning you like that and everything.”

“Oh,” she waved at him, “it’s nothing, really.”

And as she waved him goodbye and took off along the slick blacktop roads, she tried for a moment to convince herself that it *was* nothing. She’d heard that whatever one’s character defects, negative attributes—these only worsened with age. Was Ted’s temper only going to worsen with age, was he in the throes of early onset dementia, had he not demonstrated that this morning? Was there only worse to follow? On the ride home, the golf cart getting whipped around the streets like a feather in the wind, her mind kept racing with anxious thoughts. And not so much about what was happening now, to her and to those who had fled, but rather with what would happen when the storm blew over. She had the sense that everything would appear different, and not just the landscape.

*

At the first sign of the rain letting up, Mike Beamish, who was feeling cooped up, left the house. On the way to Isabel’s place, he ran into Gerry Hagoden. His old hot tub foil glanced up at the sky and shook his head. Cabin fever, he said. You and me both said Mike. An emergency paramedic vehicle crawled along at a pace under the paltry speed limit. Mike waved at the EMT, one of the guys he occasionally played volleyball with, the Sunnyville rescue squad mostly staffed by volunteers like him. He paused before he turned the last corner to her house on Hammersmith Drive.

Last night, he’d gotten antsy and strolled over to her house. Where he didn’t expect it, there was another car parked in her driveway. He paused at the foot of the driveway in the darkness. He stood there like that a good while before turning to walk back in the direction he came. Halfway home, he turned around again and retraced his steps to the same spot in front of her house. The extra car was still parked there, an affront to his confidence. Against his better judgment, he walked around the house with a great deal of stealth and even peeked in the windows. He went from one to another, crawling on hands and knees and then craning his neck to peer over the sill, praying no one would notice. Praying she wouldn’t leave the house and catch him skulking about like a teenager. Her curtains were drawn and so there was nothing to see.

Today the unidentified vehicle was gone. He rubbed at his neck and brought a hand with its scent of expensive cologne to his nose. He seldom wore cologne, hardly ever in the light of day. He’d slapped it upon his face regularly throughout his career in sales. In retirement, he’d left it for special occasions, like this. Even absent the mystery guest, he dilly-dallied there at the foot of her driveway. Then he whisked himself away on the sidewalk to the end of the street and thought about returning home to try her by phone instead. He walked around the block, glancing up at the deep dark gray blanket making its way across the sky. Then he approached her house and after much deliberation brought a finger to the doorbell. She opened the door a crack and looked at him. She did not invite him in. She said, "Were you just here? A few minutes ago?"

He started to shake his head but thought better of it, knowing she'd not have asked if she hadn't spied him. "Yeah," he shrugged, "just thought I forgot something. At home. But I didn't. I got it."

"Oh."

She looked unconvinced. He prayed she wouldn't ask him if he were here last night because that wouldn't be so easy to explain away. But Isabel just stood, supporting herself with a hand on the doorknob.

"Can I come in," he asked. "Just for a little minute."

She cracked the door open, bearing him past the threshold with a roll of her eyes and an exaggerated sweeping gesture.

Mike sat down gingerly on the edge of the sofa, elbows to knees, every movement uneasy and awkward. "You do anything last night?"

"Oh, just the usual trouble."

An open-ended answer to an open-ended question. Words cloaked in ambiguity. He nodded and smiled at her.

"Can I get you something to drink," she asked.

"No thanks."

"So are you skipping town or what," she asked while fixing herself a combination of juices in a tall glass. "I just got back from the gym."

"Oh," he said, "haven't they closed the facilities yet?"

"They just did. That's why I'm back early. I feel guilty."

*What else might be driving this feeling guilty* Mike thought, at the same time feeling his spirits lift. "On second thought, how about two gin and tonics, one for me and one for you?"

"Nah I'm good. What are you gonna do with yourself today?"

He said he had plans although he didn't. His mind wandered back to her question about him skipping town, weighing its implicit uncommitted status against some fantasy about he and Isabella skipping town together. His afternoon was an open book.

"Well," she said. "I'm going to catch up on some work."

"Plans later? Besides duck the hurricane?"

"Maybe a hurricane party. This real cool couple that I met over at the pool? They're hosting one. Sounds pretty fun."

Mike waited for an invitation and when one didn't present he said, "I have no such plans. Maybe we're taking this much too lightly."

"We *are*. It's only death. I'm not afraid of death." She drew a glass of juice to her lips and emptied it, having offered him nothing in place of the gin and tonics.

So now, Mike thought, the possibility of an afternoon swimming in the deep water of philosophy while the winds roared and the rain pounded on the roof. Was it possible that Isabel Amador was letting her guard down for an intimate if sobering discussion, absent the augmentation of spirits? She put some music on and asked if he knew about some up-and-coming artist, and of course he'd never heard of them, he didn't follow these things. The music sounded strange to him. He could have left things at that and just told her to enjoy the party. He should have, later he knew it and it would keep him kicking himself for many days. Instead he asked, "What do you want to do? About us?"

She looked startled and blushed. "What do you mean?"

"I mean, I- I'm not sure where I stand. I really like you."

"I like you too. But we hardly know each other. And last I knew you were married. For like, fifty years." Her face bore a mixture of amusement and indignation.

"Don't you feel anything? Between us. The other night you said you liked being around me. That you don't say that to just anyone. I make you laugh. We- we kissed…"

"Mike we were drunk."

"So you don't say what you mean when you've had a few drinks?"

She shrugged. "I think you're reading more into this than there is."

"Well," he gripped his knees, his eyes welling up. He leaned over to kiss her and, while she didn't pull away, got shortchanged with a mere peck on the mouth. She fetched her empty glass from the table, clutching it to her breast. They locked eyes in silence, then she broke the spell and Mike won the staring contest. He'd let the cat out of the bag and he should have just left it in. It was premature, very much getting ahead of himself. He let himself out and he could hear her lock the deadbolt behind the door as he walked along the path to the street. He'd not gone fifty yards when the sky broke, unleashing a torrent. He was soaked within seconds. It was a long walk home and he sure as hell wasn't going to the North Club to lurk about in his underwear today. Instead, he would appear before his wife of fifty years, soaked to the skin, and she would shake her head, supporting her somewhat stout frame with a hand on the doorknob and say, well for goodness sakes look what the cat dragged in.

*

When Lily reached the supermarket the parking lot was full, and she drove around several times trying to find a spot. At last she found one, quite a distance from the entrance to the Winn Dixie and it had begun to rain. She opened her umbrella and skirted around puddles all the way to the automatic doors. In the store she met panic shoppers and long lines. Overcome by divergent emotions—a measure of relief that there wasn't a mass exodus to make Sunnyville a ghost town, at the same time a dose of the mass anxiety she'd stepped into. The milk had run out, along with the toilet paper. After an interminable wait she checked out at the register and by then the sky had greatly darkened. It was as if the night had decided not to wait. She drew her umbrella from her shopping cart. The automatic doors swung open and she met the torrential downpour. The wind tugged violently at her umbrella. The puddles in the parking lot had turned to lakes with no means to negotiate around, her tennis shoes immediately sopped. A gust of wind ripped the umbrella right out of her hands and she looked on as it danced across the blacktop, over and around cars, and disappeared. She was soaked and so were the groceries, the cart difficult to push and to keep straight. By the time she reached her car she was out of breath and shaking. She opened the trunk and it began to filling up with rainwater as she flung the bags one by one in it. The wind howled as with all her might she pushed at the trunk and leaned against it to force it shut.

Closing the door on the elements, she started the car and sat waiting for the windshield to defrost. While beads of water dripped onto the seat, she wished there was a towel to dry what to her felt like the wettest head she'd ever had on her shoulders. Tentatively she put the car in gear and began backing out, still shaking. She drove at a snail's pace to the exit and onto Pebble Beach Boulevard, hoping and praying there wasn't a phantom car undetectable to her failing eyes. Beyond the frantic windshield wipers, the red blur of taillights. Her bony fingers gripped the steering wheel as if she hung from a tall cliff. The car in front of her slowed to a stop for a red light. She released her iron grip on the wheel and brought her hands to her face, shuddering. The wailing and the stream of tears broke with the same fury as the storm on the other side of the glass.

*

The houses that lined Masterpiece Drive in the Legacy neighborhood in Sunny Glen Palms were the most recent, boasting the largest floor plans. These new builds were finished in the most contemporary style—kitchens fitted out with granite countertops and tile, living room ceilings with ornate crown molding, and double-paned windows throughout. The roughly two-thousand square-foot homes a little on the excessive side for a retirement community, as were some of the occupants—most notably those Canadian snowbird Gastons, whose parties and pool attire begged mention, and not always honorable mention.

Another of these homes belonged to new arrivals Wayne and Marjorie Malaprop, another exception to the minimum age rule by Windmere Properties during a downturn in the housing market, and they were giving the Gastons a run for their money by hosting a full-blown hurricane party. It was as if they'd taken the reins from their free-wheeling Canadien snowbird nearby neighbors in their absence. The serving table behind the enormous cushion couch in the Malaprops' living room was laid out with an array of snack food—family-sized bags of Lays potato chips stacked around a serving bowl filled with same, a jar of sweet pickles, a meat tray, a cheese tray, a cheddar and cracker tray, deli rolls, a loaf of rye bread, a loaf of Italian bread. In the kitchen, on the marble serving countertop, libations somewhat on the economical side—Miller Lite and Bud cans chilling in an ice bucket, boxed wine with pouring spout, an assortment of vodkas, gin and whiskey in plastic bottles, juices, Bloody Mary and Margarita mix, a blender. On their large screen TV, the Weather Channel. A gathering much in the spirit of a Super Bowl Party, only the game on the screen today was Category 5 hurricane Charley. More bottles of liquor stacked in the garage, more food chilling in the enormous freezer compartment of their large capacity refrigerator, because there might be another party on for tomorrow.

Kenny and Barbara were early arrivals. Wayne greeted them, hunched as they were just outside the front door under the eaves, shielded from the driving rain. Not far behind them a golf cart came whirring up onto the grass. Two older ladies on either side of a young guy proceeded along the Malaprops' walk. Barbara introduced Peggy and Marge, and let Teddy Jr introduce himself. They clustered in the Malaprops' foyer, brushing at the damp beads of rain on their coats, the ladies removing their headscarves.

"We're just up the road," Peggy told their host. "In Lancaster."

Wayne nodded with great enthusiasm, already several drinks ahead of his guests, roaring a kind of salute to those who'd not fled in desperation, hadn't abandoned ship, refused to panic in the face of terror.

"To the victors go the spoils," he said while waving them to the living room area, with enough animation to make Barbara wonder if there wasn't some theater acting in his background.

"I was almost one of the deserters," Teddy said.

Wayne clasped a hand to Teddy's shoulder, wiggling a can of Bud out in front of him like a divining rod. "Well thanks for turning up for duty."

Kenny trailed them, muttering almost to himself, I'm in a good mood today and I have no idea why.

When Peggy had turned into Marge's driveway she found her standing beside her son. They filled her in while she followed Kenny's Dodge Dart on the drive to the Malaprops. There'd been a disagreement between father and son from the time they'd left the driveway and he begged his father to pull off to the shoulder. There on the black tarmac under the entrance sign to I-75, he appealed to his father to turn around and go back. But his father was resolute. So the son jumped ship. By the time he got home in the rain, he was soaked to the skin and so was his baggage, one of the wheels bashed beyond function.

He didn't look any worse for the wear to Barbara. In fact, she thought he was kind of cute, if somewhat beset by excess weight and poor posture. He struck up a conversation with her by the serving table, munching on a handful of Fritos and glancing every now and again to the large-screen TV and the weather channel, the sound muted by the Malaprops so as not to impede on their socializing. Meanwhile, the meteorologist announced high winds and a flash flood alert for central Florida, and that Hurricane Charley was now projected to arrive upon the Gulf Coast earlier than expected, overnight and in the early hours of Friday.

"What I'd really like to do," Teddy said between mouthfuls, "is work for myself. Y'know have my own business. Worked for the man my whole life, maybe it's time I struck out on my own."

"It's not as easy as it sounds," Barbara said tentatively.

"Oh, money isn't everything," Teddy said. "What do you do?"

"I work for myself."

"Cool. Doing what?"

"I fabricate. I make things. Sell them at crafts shows. Things like that."

"That sounds pretty cool. Must be fun."

"A meager living. It's okay when you sell something."

"But you're getting to do what you really love."

"Well, love is a strong word. Making them is the fun part I guess, most of the time. But I can tell you I hardly make a fortune. Many days I get a few bites and nothing else. I have to do other things."

"Like what?"

"Waitress. Odd jobs. Caretaking."

"Uh-huh."

"Not a very glamorous life," she added while watching Wayne fix the ladies drinks.

"Well, at least you're your own person. Not pretending to be someone you're not, like some character in a movie about as interesting as watching paint dry."

"Hey that's pretty good. Are you always so prolific?"

"I've been thinking about things, making up things, a lot lately. With all this free time I guess."

"Don't have a girlfriend?"

"Um… yeah I do."

"You don't sound too excited."

"It's complicated."

"Hmm."

"Long story."

"Well," she said, patting his arm and pulling a face, "keep it to yourself for now. Let's have some fun. It's a party after all."

And a party it was. A flood of guests arrived on their heels and the house was starting to fill up. She sauntered over to the bar with him in tow, pouring a concoction of juices—cranberry, orange, grapefruit, a lemon and a lime squeezed over it. She eyed the vodka and decided to leave it alone.

Marjorie Malaprop held court out back on the patio, a joint making the rounds between herself and five others, including Kenny Fitzroy. They were giggling and Kenny didn't catch all the jokes, smiling at them from time to time, untypically short on words.

When he excused himself and rose to go back inside, he was a little light-headed, self-conscious with every step to the door. He found Peggy Beamish squeezed next to Marge on the sofa, chattering away. Underneath her dark sunglasses, which she hadn't removed, Marge's face glazed over like a shock victim while Peggy poked her from time to time to emphasize a point. Kenny sat down across from them, one of the younger set at Sunny Glen Palms—face cast in a worrisome frown, drumming the fingers of both hands at a whiskey and ginger ale (the beer a little pedestrian for his discerning tastes), his eyes darting around a room filling up with strangers. Kenny Fitzroy, an unlikely hero, a boy-like man who'd recently answered the call of duty, the summoning to paternal responsibility. That matter was shoved aside in the worry bank inside that marijuana-befouled noggin of his, it was as if things were settled with that one click of the mouse to book a flight to Hartford next weekend.

So that matter was set aside to make room for another slice of worry. His eyes fell from time to time on Peggy Beamish, sitting across from him, her casual attire in stark contrast to cohort Marge Cumberbatch—who in her enthusiasm at this rare invitation to a party inside the gates, had dressed herself to the nines in a floral print dress, heels, and bracelets of various gemstones decorating her meaty wrists and pearls adorning her bare neck. And the large sunglasses from the beach bag that covered most of her face.

Peggy, in contrast, wore blue jean shorts with a tropical print blouse, hair tied up neatly in a bun, and she had more lipstick and makeup on than usual, her fair-complexioned face of chiseled features and high cheekbones bordering on glamorous tonight, at least to Kenny Fitzroy. But it wasn't her subtle and understated beauty that had him fidgeting, it was rather that dilemma of conscience her husband had foisted upon him—with that bold, if inebriated, airing of his dirty laundry. He wished he hadn't chanced upon Mike Beamish in that moment of weakness in which his confessionary words passed like a secret cargo between ships in the deep sea in the dead of night. And Kenny carried that cargo in the hold of his ship while Peggy Beamish's ship sat tied up to mast awaiting delivery. Was it his solemn duty to declare the cargo? Why on earth did Mike Beamish have to unload it on *him* of all people?

Peggy jiggled her cocktail glass, glancing at the parade of people of all ages, her eyes settling on him from time to time with a wink while Marge had her ear. He went to refresh his glass and seek out Barbara, but merely removing himself from Peggy Beamish's sightline could not quell the flurry of worry in his racing mind. In his haste he nearly collided with Marjorie Malaprop, ceremoniously whisking a tray loaded with a variety of finger food—crackers and cheese, shrimp rolls, baby carrots and sundry others.

Teddy had Barbara cornered by the bookcase at the foot of the stairs, lodging his drink on one of the oak shelves without a coaster, so as to make better use of his hands in embellishing the story. A pang of jealousy pierced Kenny Fitzroy's worrisome fog as he more-than-casually observed a one-sided conversation, Teddy doing all the talking. Talking was Kenny's field of expertise, and handing the reins over to a mere visitor was certainly inadmissible. He marched up to them and offered to refill Barbara's drink.

"Oh I'll get it," she said. "It's a very particular concoction of juices."

Teddy cocked his head. "No booze?"

"No booze," said Barbara.

A rumble of thunder caused all three of them to glance at the picture window on the wall opposite the big-screen TV. They gaped at palm trees baying in the wind and the neighbor's garbage bins rolling around the yard.

Their host appeared with a display of virility, this was his show and he was charged, making broad sweeping gestures, an authority imbued in his New York accent as he regaled them with tales of moneymaking on and off Wall Street. Kenny and Teddy nodded their response as if his voice carried a charge that electrified, while Barbara folded her arms in front of her, regarding the early retiree in the manner a chemist might a specimen.

"I wouldn't go back to that in a million years, you couldn't pay me enough," he was saying, "Marjorie and I are lucky, religious people would say blessed." He cocked an eye, regarding their faces one by one to see if he may have offended anyone—they shrugged and looked down at their glasses. "We like to relax and enjoy ourselves," he tilted his drink at the room and the guests. "After all, money isn't everything."

"Well," said Barbara, "that sure seems to be the consensus among those gathered here today."

Wayne raised his glass and tilted it to those gathered, Barbara clinking hers against those of the others in turn, although she hadn't intended nor expected a toast to her remark.

"Hey," Wayne said, putting an arm around her. "Ya seem cool. C'mon and let me show you something." He nodded at the loft. Barbara followed him up the steps with trepidation. After an inkling of a dubious and private moment crafted by her host, what she found at the top of the stairs was a handful of fringe guests off the main floor, assembled on furniture around a glass-topped table in the center of the room. A television, another large-screen, was switched off. She made the round of introductions and forgot each name in turn. The room was adorned with sports posters, all of them New York teams. Her host boasted to the room of autographed items—a Derek Jeter jersey and a Phil Simms poster, both of them framed and displayed prominently on the wall beside him.

Barbara took in her surroundings while her host stood beside her and addressed the room. People stood around engaged in conversation, most notably a cluster of them hunched over the glass table. At Wayne's speech, they paused from what they were doing to glance over their shoulders. On the surface of the glass table between them was a considerable amount of white powder, what in fact could be defined as a *pile*. A razor blade. Rolled dollar bills. Wayne's speech was wrapping up and she approached the table. He followed her, taking her elbow and bringing his voice down to a more confidential level. "Genuine Peruvian."

Those around the table regarded her. Two of them stood so as not to monopolize the snow feast. In all her illicit drug travels, she'd never come across what aficionados regarded as the finest cocaine on the planet.

They had music playing, something familiar. Barbara wondered was it Lynrd Skynrd or The Outlaws? Her tastes ran far more contemporary and eclectic. She puzzled at these northerners' fascination with southern rock. Perhaps, she thought, it was the exotic aspect of a people so unfamiliar to them, with instincts and interests foreign to them—a sort of fantasy, a culture and lifestyle they knew nothing about, for which they could carve out their own version. A woman in tight jeans and heels was saying how fitting it was that the hurricane was supposed to make landfall tomorrow, Friday 13th. I'm not superstitious or anything, she said, tossing her head back and laughing, but that shit's just too weird.

Barbara thought to herself, *how egocentric is such a remark*. What about the people on the barrier islands who were in its path and ravaged by it all week? Did they give any thought to Friday 13th?

A heavyset guy in a New York Giants tee shirt winked and cocked his head in invitation at the table. "Come on," he urged. "You really gotta try this stuff. Grade A."

Barbara started to lower herself into a cushioned seat and hesitated. The guy snorted a line to each nostril and said, your turn. There were a lot of people sniffling around her. Barbara felt a hand squeeze her shoulder and she turned to meet a young lady who wiped at her nose and said man I never felt better in my life. Against the music and the din of conversation, the sound of heavy rain pelting the roof above her head. She straightened herself, gazing down upon the glass table, then she turned to the woman who'd addressed her and said, tell me your name again?

Downstairs, another round of appetizers were being served. Cute little quiche squares arrived with a disclaimer. "If it's your first time," Marjorie winked, "you may wanna try just a couple of these."

Peggy squinted. "They loaded with calories or what?"

"Oh no," said Marjorie. "They're loaded with shrooms."

"Like, mushrooms?"

"Uh huh," Marjorie beamed. "Psilocybin. The hallucinogenic variety."

"Oh," Peggy tilted her head and puckered her lips in mock curiosity before scooping two of the squares onto her appetizer plate. Marge waved them away and then rose to use the restroom while Kenny took a handful, leaning in when Peggy beckoned with a finger.

"Her *husband*," she rolled her eyes.

"So he just up and left?"

"What a schmuck," she made a face, "I knew it the minute I met him."

"That's horrible," said Kenny.

"Yeah," said Peggy. "I think there's more to it."

"Did he offer to take her with him?"

"Oh yeah," Peggy said with a dismissive wave of the hand. "But she's too smart to panic and drive halfway across the state."

"It's not all *that* far."

"I know that, wise ass. Anyway, am I to understand you're leaving us too? For more noble reasons?"

"Yeah," said Kenny, the old worry tugging at him. "I just want to do the right thing."

"Well," she said, "you're doing the right thing anyway. Getting out of here. This isn't the place for you."

"I guess I could sell my place. I could—"

"Damn right you could," Peggy said, leaning in and placing a hand on his and squeezing it. "Look, I haven't known you very long. I can't say I particularly like you."

"Oh?"

"Don't take that the wrong way. Let's just say I wouldn't ordinarily seek out and befriend someone with your… I don't know… background? I mean, you're not a schmuck or anything."

"Well thanks," Kenny scrunched his eyebrows. "I guess."

"But you, my friend, somehow hit a soft spot in Peggy Beamish. *You*," she said, "are a true heart after all. You're making this old gal real proud."

While Kenny wondered if such high regard was mistakenly attributed to him, she paused to glance furtively about the room to insure no one was within earshot. She gave his hand another squeeze and said, "*I mean that.*"

"Thanks," he said. "I don't think anybody's ever said anything as nice as that to me."

"Well maybe this is your moment," she said. "Maybe this moment has found you. A test of wits."

"You think?"

"I think you'll be a better person for it." She reached for a shrimp and waved it at him, shrugged before dipping it in the cocktail sauce.

"Let's stay friends Peggy."

"Not important. If nothing else, I'm here to deliver a message. Life is full of messengers," she said, pointing the dipped shrimp at him. "You just have to pay attention."

Kenny nodded his head ruminatively.

"Sorry," said Peggy. "I'm beginning to sound like one of those touchy feely woo-woo people."

"No," Kenny shook his head. "Not at all. On the contrary I think—"

Marge clumped her hand on the back of his shoulder and took her place next to Peggy.

"So tell me," said Peggy. "What are we gonna do with that husband of yours?"

Marge straightened her back and jutted her chin resolutely. Then she whispered with the utmost articulation, D-I-V-O-R-C-E.

Peggy laughed, poking Marge playfully in the arm and making a face at Kenny.

"You think I'm kidding," said Marge.

Just above their heads, in the loft. Barbara took a deep breath and tapped at the back of the leather chair, sensing the expectant gazes of those hunched over the exquisitely arranged glass table and its fancy Peruvian snowdrift. Teddy had by now found his way to the conclave.

"Maybe later," she said before charting a course through the throng between her and the stairs, passing Teddy without a word. She was glad to discover that her friends downstairs hadn't budged. She began to weave her way through what was now a crowd to Kenny, Peggy and Marge, eying the large-screen TV in the background and the weather alert band at the bottom announcing flash flooding and an earlier-than-expected landfall for Hurricane Charley.

Marge, out of sight from her son who was occupied one floor above, had taken a few puffs from the funny cigarette they were passing around alongside a few cocktails on the back patio. She'd experimented with it in front of her husband at a cookout years ago in the suburbs. Ted had shaken his head when the joint was proffered him. Later, on the walk home, he chastised her for giving in to peer pressure. *Peer pressure*, she laughed. I think we're a little too old for peer pressure. Ted continued shaking his head and she asked him if he'd never once tried it, even behind her back, when she wasn't looking. Absolutely not, he shook his head. I don't need that stuff. Only clogs your arteries *and* thinking from what I've heard. Obviously, he said, you've taken leave of your senses. The next day, when he broached the subject once again and pushed her far enough, she shook her head. 'Maybe you just don't have the intellectual capacity to enjoy the effect,' she said. 'Just go with it and not be afraid of what you might learn from it.' Marge seldom if ever waxed philosophical, at least not out loud.

When Barbara at last wound her way over to her friends, Kenny rose to offer his seat.

"Wow, will ya look at *him* being a gentleman," Peggy beamed.

Kenny made a face and patted the seat in invitation.

"Thanks," said Barbara affecting a Greta Garbo accent. "but I think I go home now."

"So soon?" Peggy squinted at her. "We just got here."

"I know. I'm just getting a little… claustrophobic. I'm not always one for crowds."

Kenny shot her a sideways glance. "But we were among the throngs in Ybor City. Last week, when we—"

"I know," Barbara winked at him, "But I was so much younger then."

"Actually," Marge puckered her lips, nodding to herself then Barbara, the sunglasses lending her an air of mystery. "I'm with you."

"Well," said Peggy, jiggling the few ice cubes in her glass, "I'm going to fix me another stiff one. You party poopers can take my cart," she said, glancing over at Kenny. "You don't mind giving me a ride home do you, tall dark and handsome?"

"Not at all," he said, "No trouble at all."

"Actually," said Barbara, "I could use the walk."

"Me too," said Marge.

A familiar face appeared from the throng and Kenny shook hands and introduced Ron Shutmeyer to the group, then inquired about his wife.

"Melissa? She's up North."

"Well *my* goodness," Peggy sidled up next to him. "Did she desert you and the hurricane?"

Shutmeyer laughed. "No, she had to go there anyway. Family stuff."

"Oh I see," said Peggy. "You live *here*?"

"Yep."

"What is it with all these young people?" she asked with a wink. "You look awful young to be stuck in this kinda place."

"Hey," he shrugged, smiling and shuffling his feet, "it was my wife's idea." He waved his can of beer at the room. "But with parties like this it kinda works out okay."

"Maybe I just haven't been looking in the right places," Peggy purred. "Would you mind getting an old lady a drink, you strapping young man?"

"No problemo," said Shutmeyer with a wink at Kenny. "What's your poison?"

"Gin and tonic," Peggy said. "And don't be stingy, baby."

Kenny was glad of the distraction his old pal Shutmeyer brought and at the same time anxious to speak to Peggy alone. Outside there was a fresh cloudburst and an angry wind whipped a hard rain against the large picture window. He turned and stared with a fixed intensity as heavy drops of rain pounded the glass panes with a fury. Peggy sauntered over to the window to survey the damage, watching the wind toss the neighbors' trash cans about the yard, palm fronds stripped from trees and thrown to the ground. Ron brought her the gin and tonic and they stood side by side exchanging remarks about the chaos on the other side of the glass.

Barbara and Marge opened the front door only to meet a wind with enough force to make them think twice about the walk home. There was another guest, a woman named Judy with a sharp Midwest accent who'd also gotten antsy and offered to give them a lift with the first little break in the weather.

"You just hop in with me," she said with a wink and a good-natured cheek cluck. "No place is too far in Sunnyville."

Kenny Fitzroy joined his two friends at the picture window, hardly his usual talkative self—Shutmeyer sensed his distraction right away. Indeed, as Kenny uttered his obligatory responses to Ron's running monologue, his mind was busy whipping up a frenzy of thoughts in the same manner as the scene outside the picture window. The question mark of Kathy in Connecticut and the baby, the secret cargo he was considering unloading on Peggy Beamish, and the real and present danger that nature posed—all mingled for a worry cocktail that was making him drunk with anxiety. That dreadful drink also serving to squash the marijuana high. Ron Shutmeyer was just being himself, bouncing from one foot to the other and making animated gestures in that way he always did at social gatherings. There weren't enough parties for him in Sunny Glen Palms, he attended what few there were more often by himself—his wife had lost interest, pursuing a path more aligned with meditation, yoga, homeopathic techniques, books on finding your true self. She studying ways to defy the aging process while Ron did his best to speed it along, and to that end he excused himself from his perch at the picture window and made a beeline for the loft. That left Kenny in the exclusive company of Peggy Beamish. He coughed, returning her smile. There was a lump in his throat, his mouth as dry and barren of words as the High Sierra. Maybe it wasn't such a good idea, what with the stress of the storm and all. Imparting information that was vital to her interests, but if in fact she was intending to file for divorce anyway, what difference could this news possibly make? Yet another indiscretion in what appeared to be a long list of indiscretions. Better left unsaid? The party had expanded and it would pose a challenge to have an awkward conversation at conversational level. The party had spilled into every corner, even the foyer, where a few were gathered with drinks in hand. Barbara and Marge, he noticed with some chagrin, had made good on their promise and left the party early. From the expensive stereo system, party music pumped all the louder around the house.

"Peggy, I um, I think, well I don't know—"

"What is it? You look like a man with something on his mind to spill. C'mon Kenny. You can tell ole Peggy."

"It's just that... I wanted to tell you, or maybe *didn't* want to tell you."

He was off and running, and he could not stop, his mouth was moving and it was like the return of a long-lost friend, he'd wondered how long he might remain mute amidst the company and alcohol, and the pot—yes the pot—he wished there was less gravity in that busy mind of his. He was just warming up to the part about her husband and Isabel and she clearly wasn't catching on. He wanted to excuse himself and fix another drink and slug it down, to dull the senses, bolster the courage—at the same time loathe to leave Peggy alone because it was more than likely he'd find her ear engaged with another member of the party by the time he got back.

"Go and get yourself a drink there little buddy," she said as if reading his mind. "Looks like your nerves are all on edge."

"Aren't yours?"

"Riding out the storm," Peggy shrugged. "Story of my life. Now go and get your poison."

"Wait here," said Kenny, raising a finger. "I'll be right back."

At first Peggy had felt nothing. Then little by little, like a ball of dough changing its form and beginning to rise, the room and its occupants took on larger meaning as everything seemed to slow and normality gave way and left her with a strong compulsion to get up and move her feet and do something. The room was now too small for her and she found herself abandoning social convention, leaving a man who's name she'd forgotten even as he spoke, maneuvering through the crowd to the back door and the patio. The carpet she trod on in her deck shoes textured in the pliability and softness of marshmallow, but all the same she felt out of control in a nice way. She badly wanted to remove her shoes. For a moment she paused before a segment of their wall art, three colorful landscapes that were obviously part of a series. The landscapes riddled with minute gnome-like figures, she had to practically put her nose to the canvas to discern them. She marveled at the delicacy in the brushwork to achieve such level of detail. The colors of the rhododendron, honeysuckle and azalea vibrant and glowing in such a manner as to suggest a pulse. She could stand there and absorb for hours while at the same time a wave of self-consciousness coursed through her in that crowded room. At the sliding screen to the patio she met a humidity so palpable she sensed she might cut it with her hand. A deluge of rain and gusts of wind overwhelmed a canvas table umbrella as those gathered rose, shielding their eyes and scooping up paper plates and cups. If the room had caused her to feel claustrophobic, the rain made her feel hemmed in all the more. She felt as if she could use a walk and perhaps an adventure. There wasn't much adventure in Sunny Glen Palms, but the way she was feeling, she thought she might perhaps manifest one. Guests brushed past her, standing there in the doorframe, the natural white noise of a hard rain drowning out the voices behind her in the room. Music, some kind of jazz or blues with an odd twist. It rang to her ears like a foreign language, exotic and mysterious. The palette of instruments threw an array of sound paint on the canvas beyond her ears. Peggy decided she would leave the party as soon as the rain let up and tour the desolate streets of Sunny Glen Palms. A flood of thoughts washed over her, they felt like a ship untethered and cast upon some sea of an unknown language. She would set out on an adventure. Of course, they'd taken the golf cart, as they usually did inside the gate. She was certain she could drive it joyously and with reckless abandon. She formulated a plan—she would hit the golf links. No one would be watching and she could tool around under the cypresses through the tinsel glow of the headlamps.

Just as Kenny was returning from the kitchen with his poison in hand, the front door opened and there *they* stood, as if they'd read his mind, the very two people who were on his mind, which had begun to bloom into a more heightened awareness of his environment, and now it was his turn to be claustrophobic. He froze as Isabel Amador appeared in the doorway, then right on her heels, Mike Beamish. Both of them soaked to the extent you could see their scalps. And now Peggy Beamish was right up on him, so close he could feel her breath on his neck, could hear the little gasp that escaped from her mouth. "Well," she said, maybe to him maybe to no one in particular, after the newcomers had shaken their umbrellas and made their way over to her, "Just look at what the cat dragged in."

*

Marge had taken Judy up on the offer of a lift home with mixed feelings. On the one hand she felt she was leaving an unusual and vibrant party prematurely, but at the same time she didn't know if she could keep up with her racing mind amidst all those people. Through the windshield there in the front seat of the car it was like watching a movie. The fury of the wind and rain played out in the dimly lit streets. The hefty car was being shoved about by the gales. She wondered if perhaps it wasn't such a good idea to take a few puffs off of the funny cigarette on the patio. Maybe, she thought, it was *her* that didn't have the intellectual capacity to just relax and enjoy the high. Or maybe given the circumstances, this just wasn't the right time. Because when they reached her street it all came flooding back, what happened there. With Ted. She directed Judy to her house.

"Oh my God," she said to Barbara in the back seat, casually pointing toward the house. "The wind got our signpost. I just stuck that back in."

They pulled into her driveway and she bade them both goodnight and clambered out of the car. Barbara waved from the backseat as Judy slowly backed out of the driveway.

Marge, in no hurry getting into the house, stood in the middle of the driveway, raising her arms and lifting her head to the pelting rain. Judy had her eyes glued to the road in front of her and didn't see any of it. From the backseat, squinting through the blur of raindrops, Barbara looked on while Marge lifted the signpost from the ground, paused a moment, then dragged it alongside her like a piece of rubbish to the curb.

In Lily's driveway, the wind came full force and Barbara fought against it until it changed direction and pushed her to the side. She found some shelter and less impediment at the side of the house and when she pushed on the door it opened.

Inside the lights flickered, restored. Lily had the Weather Channel on, pacing in the living room, her face flushed and her eyes wet.

"We're getting it," she said. "Looks like we're gonna be hit."

"Well then," said Barbara, "let's get out of here. Start packing a bag."

"I already have."

No sooner had she spoke, the TV screen fizzled and the house went dark and dead silent, not even the hum of the refrigerator.

*

"I found this poor wayward fellow wandering the streets in this mess," was what Isabel Amador said by way of explanation, and it did have a grain of truth to it. She hadn't intended on inviting Mike Beamish to the party, actually would have preferred to arrive alone, and now all the more so at the sight of his wife, who had a peculiar look on her face.

For his part, Mike Beamish had in fact just been out walking when the weather turned ugly. He had no intention other than to check on whether there were any strange cars in Isabel Amador's driveway. She'd mentioned the party and maybe he just wanted to see if she'd settled on a night at home, what with the weather and all. But no sooner had the skies broken and unleashed a torrential downpour and he'd turned to retrace his steps, make a beeline for home, than the very lady he sought to spy on came up from behind in her sporty jeep and said hop in. A welcome kiss on the lips, a far cry from that spurning at their last meeting. And just like that he was on his way to the very party his wife was almost certainly attending, a mere day before the big gala they'd been forced to cancel. He bore a sheepish look greatly exaggerated with the utterly drenched thinning hair, beads of rain on his chin and the end of his nose.

Peggy studied her husband with his new countenance, drained of the usual swagger. It was as if she beheld a different person entirely. Her eyes brought this image to an unfamiliar consciousness and it overwhelmed her, left her mute amid the din all around her, immobile before the background of the movement of a party in full swing.

After Isabel had slinked around her and made her way into the throng, Mike cleared his throat and announced to his wife that he didn't intend to stay very long.

"Suit yourself," Peggy heard herself say, the words sounding as if she'd conjured them up from a bank of go-tos, an arsenal of protective words. "I'll walk home when I feel like it."

She left her husband standing dripping wet in the Malaprops' foyer. In the living room Teddy Cumberbatch attempted to hold court, trying to compete with the din of conversation by raising his voice to shout level in order to deliver a barrage of verbal gunfire.

"I'm a gonna move down here man," he was gushing at an old couple clutching their drinks with polite smiles, "Make me a fresh start. The ocean has the most powerful energy and I can't wait to see it, it's been years! Sometimes all you gotta do is get out of your present situation, you know? Get out and see everything from a fresh perspective."

She made a detour left to the less-cramped kitchen to refresh her gin and tonic, Kenny in tow. They refilled their glasses by the marble island countertop and watched Teddy navigate his way to the patio to seek out another audience. Their seats were quickly taken, the party had blossomed into a full house, standing room only. The kitchen was getting busy and Kenny spied a couple vacating the hardback chairs in the foyer. He glanced at Peggy and nodded to it. Soon the two were situated side-by-side and could hear one another a little better, out of range of the stereo system.

Kenny puffed his cheeks with a heavy sigh, the difficult and grandiose speech he'd prepared having been diminished to almost nothing upon the arrival of Mike and Isabel. The blandness of the foyer with its coat rack, umbrella stand, lack of wall art and a pile of footwear at the door began to put a serious damper on a burgeoning sense of expansion and adventure, as the mushrooms began to settle themselves in a mind already occupied with troubles. He didn't want to get into this with her. Maybe their arrival in person at the door was part of the mushroom trip, a sort of revelatory gift from the universe that spoke for itself and he ought to just keep his mouth shut.

"Well tell me," Peggy, rapped on his knee, "What is it? Is it about the baby? Aw," she pursed her lips, a giddiness spreading over her face. "of course it is. You're a wreck about having to be a responsible human being."

"You'll never know how much you've done for me. Just listening—"

"Now don't go getting all mushy on me. My mind's working in ways I'm not accustomed to." She squinted at the throng in the living room. "I gotta get out of here," she said determinedly, turning her gaze to the door, smiling. "I wish there were a great big ocean just on the other side of that door. I'd throw myself into it and swim with the dolphins."

*

They were heading inland on Interstate 4, Disney World loosely their destination. Neither of them had ever been and they figured between them that now was as good a time as any to visit, inland being the safest course, in their shared opinion.

Barbara clutched the steering wheel and leaned forward, the windshield now a blur even with the wipers on full speed, the defrost fan cranked to maximum. She wiped repeatedly at the inside of the windshield with paper towels, amid the sound of driving rain on the roof of the car, keeping her eyes fixed to the blurry red taillights of the car in front of her, reflexively applying the brakes when those taillights brightened. Without turning her head she'd told Lily to put her seat back and sleep, but Lily remained bolt upright next to her, the radio mostly static while she scanned the dial for news between FM and AM bands. When they'd got just beyond Lakeland they caught a weather report from an anxious broadcaster. It seemed the storm had touched down south of Tampa and Sunnyville in Punta Gorda and was now heading towards Orlando. Hurricane Charley had a twenty-mile girth. Now the initial sense of initiative was replaced by panic to discover they were driving along in the very path of the hurricane. Barbara squinted at the windshield, slowing down and trying to read the road signs for anything south, or maybe north, she knew not which direction might be the path to safety. Lily fumbled in the glove box for a Florida map, tugging and tugging only to extract a North Carolina map, clearly of no use. Bad luck they didn't take her car, she said to Barbara. Bad luck *period*, Barbara replied without breaking her gaze at the windshield, slamming the brakes with the red blurry taillights going suddenly bright in front of her and fishtailing across the left lane onto the shoulder, the car careening and then the scraping of metal along the cement divider.

*

Words were beginning to fail Kenny Fitzroy and he realized he wasn't going to open up the proverbial can of worms tonight, sitting there on the wooden bench in the Malaprops' foyer. Mike Beamish's confession would remain a secret, at least until the storm blew over. Until the mushrooms and the pot and the alcohol ran their course.

"I better get going," said Peggy. "It's not just the booze starting to go to my head. I kinda like this, but this old gal needs to go on a mission." She raised her voice to match a spurt of enthusiasm. "I'm gonna check on everybody in Sunnyville! Fear not Sunnyville, here I come!"

"Let me drive you home," said Kenny, recoiling a little and scanning the foyer and then the living room to see if anybody was taking notice. "I think I'm ready to go too."

"No," said Peggy resolutely. "You stay. Finish your drink. I've got the golf cart."

"But you might get blown away."

"Nonsense."

Kenny flinched. "I'm not going to have you drive a cart home in this mess. I'll tell Marge's son we're leaving. Wait here and I'll be right back."

He stood and prepared to wind his way through the human obstacle course. When he glanced over his shoulder, he saw that Peggy had already retrieved her raincoat and bonnet. She gave him a little wave with an odd wistful smile before opening the door and throwing herself into the storm.

*

Barbara hadn't even attempted to get out of the car to assess the damage along the driver's side. All she knew was that it was probably all cosmetic and the car was drivable. In a brief remission from the downpour, she spotted a sign for County Road 27 North to that main artery 75 North and she slowed the car, deciding that north was the safest route because north suggested greater land mass, less land basins and less flooding, away from the tip of this insane peninsula that attracted potentially lethal storms like bees to honey—north was the direction *out* of Florida.

They proceeded under the cloak of darkness and heavy rain, a mighty wind whipping across the roads, causing the car to pitch and roll as if with a mind of its own. Highway 4 had been clogged with traffic and when she exited onto the county road she found another long line of blurry brake lights. Not long after merging onto the county road and wistfully passing a Cracker Barrel with empty stomachs, both of them took some measure of relief at the sight of the traffic density thinning enough to afford a safer distance between cars. Barbara thanked her lucky stars she'd topped up on fuel in a light drizzle at the station just before the onramp to the interstate back in Sunnyville. She drove on mutely with brief glances at Lily, who had by now dropped her head back to the headrest and closed her eyes, perhaps resigned to the fact that she was dog-tired and that keeping a vigilant eye on the blurry windshield in front of her would have no effect on events. Further north, the lakes were beginning to swell and appear nearer to the county road where they didn't belong. While the wind played rough with the car, she could only hope they were outracing the hurricane. Out of the darkness and desolation in the windshield, signs of civilization appeared. Gas stations, convenience stores, motels, all sharply illuminated.

Soon they came across a county road with signs for a Hampton Inn, for Orlando. Barbara drove on. As much as she may have been tempted to pull off into one of the motel chains and collapse onto a bed, she passed each one with a single motivation. North. Carefully, so as not to take her eyes off the road for long, she switched the radio on and tapped the scan button. There was static and silence and then as if to affirm her inclination to stay north, a news channel broadcasted a weather update asserting that Hurricane Charley had touched down in Punta Gorda, moving slowly on a trajectory towards Orlando, although now with a diminished category 3 strength since landfall. Just as the station began to disappear in a wave of static the car was blown, it felt to Barbara as if it were lifted from the road, and veered over to the oncoming lane. Lily stirred awake. Barbara eased the brakes, no car was approaching from the other direction, and no one was behind her. She pulled onto the opposite shoulder to gather herself.

*

A break in the storm. It felt to Peggy as if she were in a peaceful oasis far away from the eye of the hurricane, out there on the golf greens become golden greens. It was as if she had driven into a whole new world that displaced that gloom she felt back there in the Malaprops' driveway, jetting the golf cart away from the party. It was as if her husband's dalliances and flirtations were that much more distant as she drifted into new territories of nonchalance, as one having severed the bonds of romance might find themselves at last able to sit through a breakup song or a heartbreaker movie without falling apart, crumbling to pieces.

Peggy parked the golf cart just off the concrete path, fetching a folded beach towel from the basket at the back and placing it on the wet grass to sit upon Indian-style. A sacredness to her leave-taking, the air around her charged with energy she'd been walking in daily while completely oblivious to it. It was as if electrons and protons danced in the fine mist, as if the abatement of heavy wind had left a magnificent desolation, rendering the manicured golf course a meadow, a playground for spirits. A branch caught in the wind danced and before her eyes it became a Seminole brave in full regalia, thumping barefoot in the wet grass, feathered headband over his grease-painted face. The flagstick on the putting green flapped in the wind, summoning the spirit of a squaw—she wore a black hat with a red band above an expressionless face, her neck covered by two scarves, one blue one gold. A loose-fitting blouse with sleeves cut just below the elbow, and under that an ankle-length gown embroidered in multi-colored stripes. The flagstick became a pestle in the squaw woman's calloused hands as she pounded out corn in a hollowed-out tree trunk.

Peggy shut her eyes and where she expected the usual dark void there were rays of light shot through crystalline stones and then explosions of color. She opened her eyes and for all intents and purposes it wasn't 2004, there were no fixed points in time, the grass she ran her fingers through sprung from an earth that was ancient, she sat in a time long before the emergence of the Seminole nation or way after the conquest of those people and establishment of these United States. None of that mattered. The palmettos that lined the fairway and the grass around her glowed silver and emerald, their vibrancy all-the-more powerful in the silence. She stared a long time at the palmettos and after their glow was stolen she glanced up to the sky and saw darkness and no moon. When the clouds moved out of the way and the moon appeared in its fullness, Peggy spread out the towel to lay on her back and in that moment she understood what prayer is. She may have remained like that for an eternity if not for the rainclouds that stamped out the moon like a portent of evil after a feast of good.

She had no idea how long she stayed in that posture of consciousness. She remained in it as the heavens unleashed another torrent, the raindrops pelting her face and arms and legs and she maintaining the lotus posture, relishing nature's shower. She returned soaking wet to the golf cart and sat on the seat staring off into space, clutching the steering wheel as if her life depended on it.

When she turned from the golf cart path and onto the road, the rain picked up significantly, but the wind began tossing the heavy rain about, spraying her about the face and body. The streetlights had gone to black, along with all else—a moon kept disappearing and reappearing behind rain clouds, casting an eerie glow, rendering familiar streets oddly alien. She tugged at the scarf under her chin, lowered her head and gripped the wheel, propelling the golf cart to Sunset Boulevard. From there it was a right turn and not very far to Lancaster and their house was only a few twists and turns away. The calm after the storm seemed to have given way to another round of wind and rain and this matched a return of a rage that she and the mushrooms had quelled. She didn't want to speak to anyone right now, least of all her husband. Nothing mattered other than these visions of herself setting out unencumbered in an RV to a wide-open western landscape and a world where no one was a stranger and she could have all the hallucinogenic experiences her bad old self wished. At the same time, she wanted to sock him a good one in the jaw and lay him out on the floor.

But when at last she reached their house on Lancaster Drive, she discovered her husband already laid out on the floor.

She bumped her knee on the couch getting to him in the darkness, kneeling on the carpet beside him there in the living room, water dripping from a drenched windbreaker. Raising his lifeless arm to check for a pulse, bringing her cheek up against his to check for breathing. She was uncertain about either of these examinations. She brought her fingers to his face to try and pry open his eyes. The darkness seemed to dull every sense. In darkness the invisible hand of instinct summoning her to an emergency response technique. Mouth to mouth. What was once was an act of love a labor of love, an emergency procedure. Pressing her lips firmly to his and leaving them there, something she had lately avoided with the resolve of a committed nun. As with that first kiss fifty years ago, she didn't quite know what she was doing.

She slapped at his face and when he didn't respond she ran to the kitchen, fumbling for a light switch, finding it and failing to summon light despite jiggling it repeatedly. The dialing pad on the cordless cast an eerie green glow, she picked it up and there was a dial tone and in her panic she kept jabbing all the wrong buttons with her finger until at last she managed to punch nine-one-one.

Dripping wet, the cordless slippery in her hands, she frantically gave the details to the operator. She scurried over to his side, again pressing her lips to his to push air from her lungs into his. With some relief in knowing help was on the way she leaned in and pressed her ear to his nostrils and she could hear and feel the faintest intake and release of breath. He began to stir. Peggy fixed her eyes on his pallid face.

"Mike? Honey?"

He was mumbling and she asked what happened, pressing an ear to his mouth.

"Can't move… my legs… arms."

"It's okay. The ambulance is on the way."

She reached over to the end table and groped about the drawer for a flashlight, praying the batteries hadn't run dry. She swung a dim beam of light upon her husband's face, the right side drooped as if the skin were ready to peel from the bone. His eyes opened and closed.

The EMTs arrived within minutes. Adherence to the twenty-five mile-per-hour speed limit always yielded to a reverence for the sanctity of life. There were two of them, one a white-haired athletic looking man she guessed was a volunteer and the other younger than him, a middle-aged woman with her hair tied back in a ponytail. The woman plunked a high beam lantern down onto the kitchen counter and to Peggy's eyes it was stage lighting—illuminating a scene in a play, because this surely wasn't real, not here in her living room in the middle of a Category Five hurricane. She brought a hand to her cheek, squeezed her bottom lip, watching their swift, methodical and coordinated movements in moving him onto the stretcher. He struggled to speak.

"What is it," Peggy asked. "What happened?"

"All the signs of a stroke mam," the woman paramedic said, not losing a beat securing the straps and then wheeling the stretcher to the front door while shadows danced about the walls in the play of their flashlights.

"When did this happen," the woman asked.

"I-I don't know. I was out. I-I just got home."

The woman looked incredulously at the strange woman in before her, soaked to the skin in the middle of the night in her own living room.

"Come along with us," said the man, hurrying the stretcher across the floor and out the kitchen door.

"What about the lantern," Peggy called after them, glancing at the beacon on her counter.

"Leave it."

She trailed along behind the stretcher and climbed into the cab beside the woman, while the man attended to her husband in the back. On the ride out of Lancaster, the EMT vehicle shot around the corners at a rate of speed she never witnessed on those streets. On Sunny Glen Boulevard all the way to the gate, at ten o'clock on wet slick streets laden with fallen palm fronds, bits of them flitting about the wind like butterflies, the driver gunned the vehicle with sirens blaring and a devil-may-care attitude for the momentarily-returned serenity of late-night Sunny Glen Palms, with a life hanging in the balance.

*

The traffic had by now thinned to the point there were no taillights in front of her to keep a safe distance from. The clock on the dashboard now showed 2am. They'd passed a few motor inns before they encountered a barren wilderness, mile after mile of pine forest without so much as a single billboard. Every now and again an intermission in the deluge of rain on the windshield afforded Barbara a view of signs for untenanted destinations. Cypress Ridge Hunting Reserve. Hilochee Wildlife Management Area. She sped along in spite of the wind, or maybe because of it. North, north, north was all she could think. Get as far North as soon as possible. A sign she could barely discern for the Florida Turnpike and 75 North and while fetching a paper towel to wipe at the windshield once again, she felt the car hydroplane. They were in the land of lakes and some of them were overflowing enough to spill out onto Highway 27. She instinctively threw on the brights but they only served to make the road in front of her all that less discernable. After a few more miles of inky blackness, she realized she'd overshot the onramp for the Florida Turnpike and Interstate 75. She slowed the car enough to shine the brights on a blue sign that indicated they were now on County Road 561.

"Where are we?" Lily rubbed at her eyes like a child waking up from a dream.

"I don't know," Barbara replied, and then to buoy the initial tone of dejection in her voice, she added. "I'll drive on until we find a hotel."

And drive she did, until at last signs appeared for locales. Astatula, and a little further, Tavares. Just before the Tavares intersection was a sign for Holiday Inn. When she slowed the car to a crawl so as not to miss it, she exited, a measure of comfort at the sight of a few cars at the intersection. It was pushing midnight and this would be it. After a few traffic lights, the entrance for the Holiday Inn appeared and she turned into it. The parking lot was filled with cars, jeeps, semis. They clambered out of the car and even underneath the overhang were subjected to the elements.

At the front desk they were greeted with the news that there were no vacancies. The desk clerk shrugged and threw his palms up at their inquiry of any other lodging possibilities nearby. Just as they walked despondently across the tile floor of the lobby, they heard a voice from behind.

"Excuse me," said a middle-aged man in a white staff shirt. "I have a room just vacated. It only has a single queen bed. It will take a little time to ready it."

"Sold," said Barbara and Lily nodded her assent.

*

The back porch of Kenny Fitzroy's humble abode consisted of a few piles of corrugated boxes, a rusty washer and dryer, and a folding metal chair—also rusting—upon which he idled, watching the rain fall, a revolver in his lap. A family heirloom, one of the many things he had inherited from his mother. He'd rummaged around the boxes until at last his fingers met chiseled metal, cold to the touch even in Florida summer heat. Wind gusts swirled in every direction and like the rain his thoughts fell every which way. Lightning flashed in the sky between the mighty cracks of thunder—past, present and future all intertwined in the torment that raged behind his eyes. A past riddled with false starts—not just the non-compensatory band efforts but stalled careers. Teaching—primary school, English second language, substitute teaching, teacher's assistant. Then nursing. Pediatric ward. That was tough physical work. He would come home at the end of his shift in the pediatric ward and think, *thank goodness I didn't have to spend a good chunk of my childhood in hospital beds.*

At an early age his sister was struck by a car and killed and then his house would never be the same. His father began drinking and so no more trips downtown for baseball or anything else. His mother grew despondent and everything altered for the worse.

Occasionally he caught glimpses into other people's happiness. He couldn't decide whether it was something they created for themselves or whether it was bestowed upon them merely by luck and happenstance. Maybe it was a little of each. He knew a few musicians in Austin whose music careers brought them a decent enough measure of notoriety. They got to live a life on their terms. There were those musicians and artists he'd fallen in with on the backpack rail pass tour of Europe that his mom had given him as a college graduation present. He'd assumed those foreigners were better able to thrive in the cradle of socialist democracies. Conversely, over the years he'd watched those who'd achieved a kind of contentment in more conventional lifestyles that bred career consistency, job stability and tall mortgages. The latter was something he'd shied away from, even sabotaged a few times, the former was something that for him seemed both troubling and elusive.

The present was an empty void. He had no family, and the friendships he'd cultivated in his many moves inevitably faded with time and distance. Letters no longer arrived in the mailbox or email. The phone never rang. Now when it did, he knew who it was, and there was no laughter to elicit and none to be compelled, only guardedness and tension, summoning him to a shared responsibility with someone he barely knew.

His thoughts about the future were greatly dampened by that part-time job he'd taken until the summer heat had overwhelmed his capacities. The valet parking job at Memorial Hospital. He'd applied for and taken it when both his Mom's tax guy and financial advisor saw shortfalls in cash flow. His sacking by Frank Alsatian from the regular golf foursome opened up even more discretionary time and he enlisted to park cars at Memorial Hospital. For minimum wage plus a tip pool shared between he and his colleagues. He worked primarily at the hospital entrance, opening doors and greeting mostly older folks with a smile, collecting the keys and parking their car inside a five-story parking garage. The middle-age guy who stuck out like a sore thumb among the college kids in their early twenties earning pin money or retirees over sixty-five earning pin money. He'd had always let that old adage *you can't buy health or happiness* go in one ear and out the other until the valet parking—where he regularly witnessed the elderly stay put in the passenger seat of vehicles as loved ones like daughters and sons or siblings, but sometimes scrubs-clad caregivers, helped him extract walkers from the backseat or maybe he ran inside to fetch a wheelchair, before they clambered out of vehicles with great difficulty. The old saying never take your health for granted went quickly from cliche to reality.

Who would be the one pulling on the door handle and then waiting patiently behind the wheelchair when things got to a point where he was a regular visitor to doctors' offices? Who would administer his medications? Who would prepare his oatmeal in the morning? Who would care for him when he became incapable of performing the most rudimentary bodily functions like getting up in the middle of the night to take a piss?

He fixed his gaze on the revolver in his lap. Perhaps his mother had bequeathed it for the purpose of sparing him the vagaries of old age. He'd certainly failed her in hers—she'd had to enlist a home health aide and was going the route of an assisted living facility when the stroke came and killed her. He was spared both the burden of care and the annihilation of the wealth that he was able to inherit. As he was once spared any caregiving in death and dying, he was summoned for caregiving for the business of life, a new life born into the world. What good would he do? He questioned his abilities, his suitability for even an exclusive role of house-husband. He *did* have to change diapers as a nurse, but maybe that didn't count. He was a lousy cook, he was lousy at ironing and laundry.

He lifted the gun from his lap and studied it. The mechanics, how such a tiny piece of metal could be sprung with such stunning velocity. How that tiny bit of metal might so swiftly bring such an immense encumbrance of worrisome thoughts to a grinding halt.

# 8

Under a charcoal-black sky, ill-tempered mother nature unleashed a deluge of rain throughout the night with raging winds—the custom address plaque that Marge had kicked to the curb the previous night blown about, laying face-down in the road. The Cumberbatch household mirrored the tempest beyond its walls—Marge having been up most of the night tossing and turning, Teddy having stumbled back in the pre-dawn hours during a lull in the storm along streets that lent to an otherwise placid no-nonsense over 55 retirement community the desolate appearance of a village ravaged by war—garbage cans, palm fronds, all manner of debris strewn about like the remnants of a major shelling. The party he walked away from also seemed to him—at that odd hour, coming down from the effects of barbiturates, cocaine, marijuana and alcohol—a devastation of his own corporeal mass, much in line with the ravages of nature. A strange deviation from the usual goings-on in his parents' neck of the woods. His mother had courteously left the door unlocked and he'd let himself in and collapsed, fully-clothed, onto one of the twin beds in the guest room.

The phone rang around seven thirty, the extension in the guest room a sonic icepick piercing Teddy's slumbers, then his mother shuffling about intermittently—in the kitchen, the living room, the garage—serving to jab further at his beleaguered mind. Begrudgingly stirred to consciousness, one cell at a time. He tried to prop himself up on an elbow and collapsed onto his back, his mother's voice coming through the door in hushed tones.

*I'll get myself ready and come over there now… Oh, I'm so sorry Peggy… Are visitors allowed?... Right, wait a second, I'll get a pen and jot it down… Kenny Fitzroy… Eight one three… Two seven two… Five six nine three… right, can I bring you anything from the house besides your car?... Oh God I'm so sorry… Yes, I sure hope that's the worst of it, because that damn storm had me on pins and needles all night, everything seems upside-down right now… Okay, I'll call Kenny. I'm on my way.*

The sounds of somebody up-and-at-em—the opening of drawers, the closing of cabinets. What the sleep-deprived mind misread as passive-aggressive or depending on how you looked at it, *active*-aggressive behavior. A wave of distasteful and unbidden nostalgia—those Saturday mornings of teen-hood in the aftermath of the previous night's raging high school party, the breaking out of her punishment toolkit, that old standby, the vacuum cleaner. At seven o'clock in the morning. Outside his door. He closed his eyes, dozing in and out of a half-sleep interrupted by the commotion of the automatic garage door rumbling along the ceiling rails through the wall.

He struggled to his feet—dizzy, almost falling back on the bed, staggering to the door, rubbing at his eyes before pushing it open.

His mother stood before him, hiding her eyes behind sunglasses. They regarded one another silently, as if there were so many things to ask one another that neither could tell quite where to begin. Teddy cleared his throat. "Power still out?"

"Yes," said Marge. "The phone's still working."

"Yeah," he said, "I *heard.*" A gust of wind flung a heavy gush of rain against the window behind him.

"You were out late."

"Yeah," he yawned, stretching his arms and following her into the kitchen. The phone rang and Marge checked the caller ID.

"Aren't you going to answer it?" he asked.

"Oh no." She made a dismissive glance at the caller ID box.

"Who is it?"

"Your father again," she shrugged, her face a blank canvas.

"Why don't you answer it?"

"I'm sure," she said nonchalantly, "that's what he's thinking."

"Mom, I know you're pissed at him," Teddy said, while the cordless phone sounded its persistent shrill ring. "But you know how he gets."

Marge shrugged and made a face.

"He probably feels bad," Teddy yawned. "He'll come back."

"Yes, he will," she said, shaking the phone as if it were somehow an appendage of her husband. "And he'll find that ole Marge isn't going to stand for any of this shit anymore."

Her voice carried a tone odd even to her own ears, as if the expletive was unleashed without her consent—her son, she thought, had probably never heard his mother so deliberately profane.

"Cmon Mom," he shook his head, a man half-awake in the clothes he went to bed in, half-shaven and pale-faced, his eyes completely bloodshot, "Be reasonable."

Behind the dark sunglasses, Marge scrunched her eyebrows. "What were you doing over there last night anyway?"

"Drinking," he shrugged. "Same as you."

"I mean so late. I heard you coming back. Around four."

"Mom. Call Dad."

She removed her sunglasses and pointed to the bruising under her eye. "Maybe this might help to explain things," she said before turning to fetch the keys to the golf cart from the hook near the door to the garage. With a tiny wave she called over her shoulder, "I have other fish to fry."

*

They hadn't even bothered setting the alarm clock. Barbara woke in semidarkness to the sound of Lily's light snoring, purposely averting her eyes from the digital clock on the bedside table, turning on her side in case there was any more sleep to be had. There wasn't and she pushed back the covers, planted her feet on the carpet and switched on the TV, muting the sound on the Weather Channel before tiptoeing to the bathroom to run the shower.

When she stepped out of the bathroom, one towel wrapped around her torso and the other tied on her head like a turban, she found Lily on her feet pacing the carpet in front of the TV.

"I have to pee real bad."

"Oh Lily, I'm sorry, you should have knocked," Barbara said, waving her into the steamy cell. "A full bladder always takes priority."

She dressed hurriedly, self-conscious about the vulnerability imbued in nakedness. Even given their shared adventures, Barbara balanced a spirit of comradeship against the fact they were still strangers up until a few days ago. Lily returned and said she'd slept well.

"You were out like a light," Barbara said, retrieving the hair dryer from the bathroom.

"Was I snoring? I hope I didn't keep you up."

"Nothing could keep me up last night after that insane drive."

Lily sighed, shook her head. "More excitement than I bargained for."

That, thought Barbara, could pretty much be said for the whole week for Lily Westfall. I for sure posed more excitement than she bargained for.

While Lily went about her morning ablutions, Barbara finished drying her hair and fetched Kenny's number from her purse. She sat on the bed and picked up the phone on the table beside it.

He sounded more nervous than usual. "Where are you?"

"I don't know. Somewhere inland. Near Mount Dora, I think?"

"Where's that?"

"Somewhere north of Orlando."

"Oh. I called Lily's place. Thought you might be shopping for supplies or something."

"Supplies?"

"Sure. Like for the storm. They're all out of milk and toilet paper."

"Oh."

"How's the weather there," he wanted to know.

"Miserable. Windy and rainy. What about Sunnyville?"

"Pretty fierce wind and everything. The hurricane is supposed to touch down south of here any minute."

"I thought it already did last night."

"That was just a warmup. We're still in the thick of it."

"Maybe you should get out of there," Barbara said.

"Why? We're all still in a party mood."

"You're a strange bird. You really are."

"But seriously, I can't just run off on friends in their hour of need."

"Huh?"

"Peggy's husband had a stroke. Mike. Mike Beamish. Last night."

"Oh my God. How bad?"

"He's in critical condition. I'm going over there. To the hospital."

"How's Peggy taking this?"

"She's... well, she's pretty tore up."

"Guess that kind of puts the kibosh on her big announcement. About leaving and everything."

"I can't say what she'll do."

"*God.*"

"Yeah."

"Give me her number."

She could hear him rummaging about and he came back on the line and read it out and she tore off a piece of the phone book and scrawled it down. "What about *you* Kenny," she said. "What are you gonna do?"

"I'm gonna fly up there and see what's what I guess. Sort things out."

"I'm proud of you."

"Huh?"

"I'm proud of you. Doing the right thing by her. By the kid."

"You're the second person to say that."

"Say what?"

"That you're proud of me. I've been waiting all my life, in a way. And now twice in one day. Don't know if I'm dreaming or what."

Barbara played abstractedly with the tangled phone cord, Kenny was silent a good while before he sighed and said, "I think Marge is leaving her husband. That's what she says anyway."

"*Jesus,*" said Barbara. "Is that all everyone does these days? Retire to Florida and get divorced?"

*

Marge pulled up to the entrance at Memorial Hospital, stepped out of Peggy's Lincoln and handed the keys to the valet, stuffing the claim ticket into her bag. The day was gray, a mighty wind whipping a light rain to and fro, some of it spraying her despite the overhang at the entrance.

"Some storm," she said to the attendant at the reception desk, a skinny kid with pimples, by way of greeting. "Very busy here?"

"Not much. I just started my shift, but they said last night was pretty dead. We were going to move everyone to the basement, still on alert. But the landfall was south of us. North of Fort Myers."

In the ICU, the nurse in charge led her to a room with a half dozen beds partitioned with blue sliding curtains, medical equipment lining the walls. The Beamishes were on the end near the window, but a view of rain pounding a man made lake that overflowed onto the parking lot was lost on Mike Beamish. His eyes were closed, tubes and wires attached to every part of his body. Peggy sat beside a bed raised so that he was almost sat up, holding his hand. She gave it a few pats before rising to greet her friend.

Marge gave Peggy a brief hug before grasping her elbows and looking her straight in the eye through the sunglasses. "How's he doing?"

"Very touch and go until a few hours ago."

"Oh Peggy I'm so sorry."

"He's going to be okay, I think. They're guessing a lot of time passed. From the time he had the stroke," she wiped at her eyes with a sleeve, "until I found him."

"Oh my goodness."

"They moved us down to the basement just before the crack of dawn. But now they say we're out of the path of it. If that changes, they'll do it again. But they can't move patients, obviously."

A nurse with a clipboard knocked on the doorframe and entered the room, standing at the foot of the bed with a smile Marge surmised to be an essential coping mechanism that came with the territory. "I'm going to have to take his vitals, and administer some medications Mrs. Beamish."

Peggy turned to address her husband. "Mike, I'm gonna step outside a minute, okay?"

Marge watched Mike Beamish's pale unshaven face and thought she could detect the slightest nod in response. The two stepped into the hall.

"Thanks for coming," said Peggy.

"Well," said Marge, "I'll stay as long as you need. We can run your car back together."

"Okay, said Peggy. There's a lounge downstairs."

In the hospital cafeteria, they ferried their coffee and pastries to an empty booth and slid themselves on either side of the Formica table.

"Have you heard anything else about the storm?" Peggy asked.

"It seems to have died down," said Marge. "but the hurricane made landfall south of us. Early morning hours... It's slow moving. The power's still out. I don't know what's going on."

"What about that wayward husband of yours?"

Marge shrugged and pulled a face. "Strange weekend this is shaping up to be."

Peggy took a bite of her donut and shook her head. "Strange life this is turning out to be."

Marge tilted her head inquisitively.

"He's gonna need a lot of care." Peggy said, drumming her fingers on the table and staring at some middle distance.

"Of course," Marge bowed her head and placed a hand over Peggy's.

Peggy shrugged, wiping at fresh tears with a sleeve. Marge wondered whether the tears weren't being shed for the snuffing of her flame of hope, the escape plan she'd hatched with the RV. Heading out west under starry skies, wide-open spaces, beauteous mountains. How far-flung all that must feel to her right now in this institutional and sterile environment.

Peggy toyed abstractedly with her wedding ring—sniffling, glancing up at Marge. "I have my duty."

Marge nodded her head. "How long will he be in the ICU?"

"I don't know."

"Is there anything I can do?"

"Thanks. Cindy is going to bring some dinner by later."

Marge didn't know Cindy from Adam, she realized Peggy had to have fostered friendships long before she showed up. It wasn't something she'd given any thought to, and the mere mention of another friendship caused a covetousness that surprised her. It suddenly seemed strange they'd only known each other for roughly a week. "Well," she said. "You just say the word and ole Marge here will see to it."

Peggy gave her a wan smile. "The doctor told me he'll be convalescing at home for months. Months of physical therapy, speech therapy."

"Oh dear."

"He'll never be the same."

"I'm so sorry."

"You never see these things coming."

They sat wordlessly amid the din of conversation around them.

"Oh Peggy," Marge said at last, "he's not such a bad a guy after all, is he? I mean, I know you guys have your history, the other women, all that... but he's not abusive, doesn't have an awful temper—"

"Our marriage is a farce," Peggy shook her head ruminatively. "Maybe it always has been. He's gentle as a lamb. We don't argue because we don't talk. He's a charmer. Just not with me. And the indiscretions aren't ancient history anymore. So I find out last night."

Marge cocked her head to one side.

"Oh yeah," said Peggy, spreading her fingers and lifting her hand. "That Isabel or whatever her name is."

"Oh my God Peggy."

Peggy pounded the table, her voice a knife-edged whisper. "I wonder if *she'll* turn up anytime soon to visit him. I wonder if *she'll* volunteer to nurse his ass back to health."

"Jesus, I'm so sorry Peggy."

"Don't feel sorry for old Peggy. I'll be on the make for a boyfriend from now on. That'll be part of this deal, the deal I'm gonna strike up with God. I'm gonna get mine on the side, and it won't be on the sly either."

Marge brought a hand to her mouth to stifle a laugh. Peggy gave a wry smile and cocked an eyebrow at Marge. "And how about you," she said. "What's with the sunglasses anyway?"

Marge shrugged noncommittally.

"Come on. I don't see any sun, and unless these fluorescent hospital lights are bothering you..."

Marge removed the sunglasses to reveal a bruising under one of her eyes and Peggy gasped.

"Aw, no... *did he do that?*"

Marge squeezed her eyes shut and nodded solemnly.

"Oh Jesus."

"He just lost control," Marge's voice cracked. "He just..." her voice trailed off and her shoulders heaved.

Peggy squeezed her shoulder. "What are you gonna do?"

"I'm leaving. I mean, he's leaving. I'm staying here. I want the house."

"Good. Good for you."

"He's intolerable," Marge unburied her head from her arms, gathering herself. "We grate on each other's nerves. He spoils every chance we have to make friendships. Relationships. He needs to be by himself. He can take the house up in Michigan. He wants to live with his son, great. He wants to kick him out, that's none of my business."

"Jesus," said Peggy. "You're beginning to sound like me. Anyway, I'd stay as far away from him as you can after this."

"Oh Peggy I don't want to burden you with my problems right now," Marge sighed. "You've got enough of your own."

"Nonsense," Peggy waved her hand.

Marge gave her a half-hearted smile, glancing up at newcomer Kenny Fitzroy, who leaned in to offer an awkward hug to Peggy. Peggy shook his elbow and looked him over. "Thanks for stopping by kiddo."

"How's he doing?"

"Not so good," Peggy said, watching Marge replace her sunglasses.

Kenny stuffed his hands in his pockets, pursed his lips and glanced around shiftily. "Let me get us a round of fresh coffee."

"That's okay," Peggy said. "Save your money for the little bambino."

Kenny winced and went to fetch the coffees and returned with a tray.

"C'mere and sit," Marge patted the bench beside her.

"How's he doing," Kenny settled himself on the vinyl-upholstered bench. "How's he coming along?"

"He's stable," Peggy shrugged. "Stroke. A real doozy. It nearly killed him." Her eyes welled up at her words and she drew the back of her sleeve to wipe at the tears. They watched her shiver as if to shake off something before heaving her shoulders and dropping her face to her hands. Marge reached a hand over to squeeze Peggy's shoulder while Kenny rose from the booth and placed a hand on the other.

*

Barbara left the motel room, the heavy door closing with a loud thunk, light spilling from the tall window at the end of the floor onto the corridor with its stained carpet of earth tones badly in need of replacement, the dull gray maid's cart camped outside a door on the way to the elevator. She waited an eternity, at last opting for the stairs two flights to the lobby. She fetched a tourist guide to Disney World from the brochure rack before approaching the desk clerk, a short middle-aged man with a crew-cut and a good-sized gut.

"I'd call before you head there," he had a wide face with an apologetic look that she guessed was a kind of fixture. "Make sure they're not closing. The governor declared a state of emergency and they usually do when that happens. Anyway," he tilted his head with a sad wince, "it made landfall sometime after midnight. Around Punta Gorda. Slow moving. After that, Orlando's right in the path."

*Great*, thought Barbara, *so the storm is chasing us.*

Back in the room, with the sound on the weather channel muted, she dialed the number. She was placed on hold, sitting down on the bed with the phone cradled in her neck while Lily glanced over from time to time in the way a child might with a holiday trip spoiled. Barbara toyed with the curly phone cord, mock-wincing to let Lily know the news wasn't good. "I see," she said, rolling her eyes at the ceiling then lowering her gaze to the floor. "Well, thank you anyway."

When she replaced the phone. "They're closing the park at one."

"Aw," Lily sighed, tracing a finger on the bedspread.

"Maybe we ought to wait another day before we head back to the ranch," said Barbara.

"You mean book another night in the motel?"

Barbara shrugged. "I really don't know. From what the desk clerk says, Orlando was in the path. Maybe we should head a little further north."

"I just hope they have rooms."

"I think we'll be okay as long as we get a jump on it. If it's that bad, we can just drive on up to Georgia."

"Well," said Lily, squinting at the ominous picture painted by the meteorologist on the TV, "better to be safe than sorry."

*

When Marge returned to the house, power had been restored. Teddy lay fast asleep on the couch by the television—on the screen a weatherman stood in front of a map of Florida with red arrows pointing at different locations along the Gulf Coast. She fetched a blanket from the linen closet and gently drew it over him, silencing the TV, pausing to study a face completely in repose, it was the first time she'd happened upon it since he was a child and she beheld that face in its calmness and blankness—through the wrinkles and beard stubble he was there—Teddy, Junior. How we age, she thought, listening to a downpour on the roof, how timeless everything is in the end, when all is said and done.

Breaking into that peaceful and strange stillness came the roar of the car in the driveway, then the familiar rumble-tumble of the garage door opening. The doorknob turning seemed a direct translation of an anxiety come to visit. He entered through the door through the kitchen from the garage and took his time, wiping his feet on the mat and removing his shoes. In the living room he began once again criticizing the carpet. Who's Lincoln is that in the driveway, he wanted to know.

"Well," said Marge, "you may as well know you're not going to have to worry about the goddamned carpet anymore."

"Just what's that supposed to mean?"

Marge pointed to the couch. "When he leaves, you're going with him."

"Says who?"

"Says me. You can stay here the rest of the week. I'll be at Peggy's."

"*That* woman?"

Marge stiffened, her breathing suddenly stifled, words trapped in her throat.

"She's a bad influence," he pressed.

"You're upset because I managed to make a friend all on my own," Marge shrugged, her outward nonchalance merely a guard for the tensing of every muscle, every nerve in her fiber. "And I'm going to make plenty more without you around to screw things up."

"Now you listen to me. We're gonna get in that car and go inland until we're sure the hurricane is far away from us."

Marge pursed her lips and shook her head resolutely. She brought a hand to her bruised cheek wordlessly, her face going soft as if to ask him what else did he expect, what other outcome for his violence, what other choice did he leave her with?

"I said I was sorry."

Marge merely shook her head slowly in response.

"Look," he said. "It's already made landfall. Now get your things and come with me."

"It won't come near us," some of the confidence in Marge's voice had dissipated, she felt shaky, bringing her shoulders up to her ears, feeling her eyes well up.

"Yes it will godammit!"

The familiarity that intimacy brings, with opposite potentials—one for comfort, the other discomfort. Her stomach churning, lungs fighting for breath. "I'm taking… Peggy's things to the hospital."

"Hospital?"

"Her husband Mike had a severe stroke last night."

Ted lunged at her, poking a finger at the soft hollow of her shoulder. "You're gonna give *me* a stroke!"

Marge stiffened, recoiling and pressing her back against the kitchen counter. "I am *not*. You're going to do that all by yourself mister. *That* and whatever else you want to. Up in Michigan or wherever you go."

Ted went red of face*, Am not! Am not!* he howled, delivering his rage by slapping on the countertop, Marge's own rage dribbling out in tears.

The man child on the sofa was now on his feet, wide-eyed. "Dad!" he bellowed. "Leave her alone already!"

The man-child in front of her continued stomping at his nemesis the carpet. "Come on! Both of you!"

Marge swiped Peggy Beamish's car keys from the counter and it felt to her that her body was in charge now, not her mind, and it told her legs to move as quickly as possible across the freshly-mopped linoleum kitchen floor and out the front door. Praying fervently not to hear footsteps close on her heels. She sprinted to the car and it dawned on her—maybe acute fear kicked worries into overdrive—that she didn't have her pocketbook to clutch to her chest and with it her driver's license, money, means to money.

In the driveway, in his socks, he gripped the sill of the driver's side door as she stuck the gear in reverse.

"Dammit," he shouted, thumping the door, "if you stay for this storm we'll be living apart for all eternity!"

"Fine by me," she muttered, tapping the window switch—he retracted his fingers from the window as it closed shut. She threw the car into reverse and it bolted, as luck would have it, into an empty street. She put it in gear and gunned it, without so much as a glance in the rear-view mirror.

*

They drove another couple of hours north, just to be on the safe side. What would have been a scenic drive through the Indian Lake State Forest and the Lochloosa Wildlife Conservation Area blurred by a steady rain and the windshield wipers. They drank coffee and talked. The roads in some parts were so badly flooded that Barbara had to slow the car and navigate through immense puddles, sometimes off the road. At last she pulled off at Keystone Heights. The proprietor at the Inn at Palmetto said it was their lucky day. Someone had cancelled another night and fled to Georgia, much to the amusement of the heavyset mustached man behind the solid oak counter in a very quaint and cozy lobby. It reminded Barbara of one of the motels she'd stayed in out west, in New Mexico, when she did the craft shows and music performances at coffee houses. The lobby walls were all knotty pine, as were the restaurant and bar and finally, the room to which he led them upstairs.

"I'm tellin ya," he repeated, "it's your lucky day. Hotels getting mighty booked up right now. Hurricane Charley and all."

They settled their bags into a very cozy room with a queen bed they'd have to share. A Victorian oak bed frame to match antique furniture about the room. Fine china trinkets laid out in built-ins, crush velvet drapes on the windows lined with lace, a finely embroidered quilt atop the bed.

"I feel like I'm on vacation," Lily said. "I haven't felt like this in years."

"I have to tell you," said Barbara, the accommodations a stark contrast to what she was accustomed to as an itinerant musician and craftsperson, "I haven't felt this good in years." Much if not all of the frugality embedded in that lifestyle was not fitted out to such luxury as that which she found herself ensconced in now. Not sleeping in noisy tin can motel chains, not sleeping on couches, not those cold nights sleeping in the van.

There were so many years alone. On the heels of a few scattered long-term relationships, the sting of loneliness in their wake. Empty of the tender care and consideration for the well-being of someone other than herself. Empty of obsessing on a relationship, Empty of anxiety about a stressful future, empty of promises for a bright future. *Empty also of a distraction from existential loneliness*, she thought, *which is maybe a good definition of a relationship*.

They lunched downstairs in the dining room, swapping evacuation stories with a young couple dining next to them from St. Petersburg. We have no family down here, the young lady said. We just moved here from New York. We're not used to hurricanes.

I'm not sure, said the proprietor, anyone ever gets used to hurricanes.

*

Mike Beamish's condition had not improved. His speech was still gibberish and his face still drooped. He had changed irrevocably, his wife thought, sitting beside him, along with everything else. In that room in the ICU, staring blankly at the rain being wind-whipped against the window, the hurricane was the furthest thing from her mind. She had looked upon the same Mike Beamish for fifty years and had come to feel that when you age together, you never really appear much different to each other than the day you met. That's what Peggy had always figured, until now.

It wasn't until Marge brought a hand to her shoulder that she realized she wasn't alone.

"How long have you been here," said Peggy, her voice tinged with a sadness greatly at odds with her usual moxie. Marge shrugged, taking in all the equipment involved in stabilizing Mike Beamish.

"I just got here now," she said, wondering what she would do if she received a call with the news that Ted had been in a car accident and was in critical condition. "I brought your things," she placed the cloth shopping bag on the chair across from the hospital bed. "I stopped by the North Club to try and fetch something from the library, for you to, I don't know, take your mind off things, but they're in lockdown. I laid my best charm on the lone security guard—"

"Son of a bitch," she sighed, "Guess he's just doing his job."

"Actually," Marge scooped the bag and extracted a handful of books, "he let down his guard and gave me a few minutes to secure a few items for storm survival. But you didn't hear that from me."

"Well look at you go girl," Peggy's eyes brightened.

Marge returned the books to the bag. "Have you talked to any of your friends? Family?"

"Ah," said Peggy, shaking her head slowly. "People come for events. Parties. Not so much for the sick and the dying. I called Cindy. She's kind of high-strung to begin with so I kinda had to cut it short. My son's coming down, but it won't be until next week with all this weather. Flights are getting cancelled left and right."

"I can imagine."

"Everything's up in the air," said Peggy, puffing her cheeks.

No sooner had she spoke than a nurse appeared in the doorway, an urgency in her tone. "Sorry ladies," she said. "We just received an order to evacuate visitors and non-essential personnel to the basement."

Peggy glanced at her husband and the nurse winced. "I'm sorry Mrs. Beamish," she said. "Just hospital protocol for a storm warning." Peggy and Marge exchanged glances, then looked over at the window beside Mike's bed and the ominous clouds in a darkening sky as the nurse beat a hasty retreat to cover the floor, "I'm sure everything will be just fine," she called over her shoulder.

Marge patted Peggy's hand and rose to gather up belongings. "We can play checkers or chess or I don't know, just gab."

Peggy scrunched her eyebrows. "Chess? I play games like Yahtzee and Scrabble. At least I used to. Years ago."

"Well, I picked up a little combination checkers and chess board. I can teach you."

"Thanks honey. I don't think I want to learn anything right now."

"Maybe we can just play checkers. Just something to, I don't know, take your mind off things."

"Thanks, Marge. You're—"

Marge raised a hand. "Let's leave gratitude unspoken between us," she gave Peggy's hand a good squeeze. "Like old friends."

In the basement they were met with a small crowd with the long faces of the bereaved, the comforters, those in shock. There were a few folding tables with metal chairs and they were early enough to snatch one.

The room began to fill up, more of the long faces now joined by the lively faces and voices of the panicked. A line began to form at the narrow doorway to what was essentially a large storage room, dimly lit but freshly painted. Several metal carts were stacked against the walls with bed linens from the nearby laundry. A couple of visitors helped an orderly navigate a wheelchair with an elderly woman in a hospital gown. More tables arrived, visitors and staff hurriedly setting them up, snapping metal folding chairs open in a focused and deliberate manner. The storage room was soon filled with human cargo and the din of noise. The ladies hovered over the board, their mutual exhaustion seemingly affording an exclusive immunity to the restlessness all around them, as if a protective beam of white light shone on them at that table at the center of that chaotic room. As Marge imparted the fundamentals of checkers to her opponent, it was clear to her that chess would have proved too tall an order for Peggy right now—the dark circles under her eyes all-the-more noticeable upon a pale face absent of even a little rouge. Peggy Beamish suddenly looked old to Marge Cumberbatch, all the humor drawn out of her face. It was as if she were beholding another version of Peggy. With each play her opponent became more listless, eyes heavier, hands slower to make a move.

"Did you manage to get *any* sleep?" Marge asked, trying to imagine how Peggy might have slept other than upright in a chair.

Peggy shook her head.

"Look," said Marge. "Why don't you pack it in when they let us out of here? Go home Peggy. You need to get some rest."

Peggy smiled wanly. "If our house is still standing."

"You need to get some rest," Marge frowned. "I can stay."

"Oh but…" Peggy's voice trailed off.

"It's not like you're miles away. You're just around the corner."

"Listen," Peggy tapped Marge's hand. "Will you stay with me? At the house, I mean."

"I was… going to kind of invite myself anyway."

Peggy tilted her head at Marge. Marge frowned. *How unsanctimonious*, Marge thought, *how vulgar*, how completely self-absorbed would it be for me to go ahead and further belabor the ears of a woman whose husband of fifty years lay upstairs by a window, in critical condition, possibly in the path of a hurricane. "Ted's back," she said to Peggy.

Peggy nodded wanly with a half-smile, a sort of resignation.

*

They had their supper in the dining room of the Inn at Palmetto. An Orlando folk musician was booked as dinner entertainment but cancelled. An elderly couple joined them at their table, due to the full capacity dinner crowd. The couple had evacuated their rental south of Orlando with their kids and grandkids, who they pointed out at a nearby table. Lily asked about Disney World. The man shrugged and said maybe they could hope for a late opening tomorrow. The dinner crowd began to thin out—some having gone to their rooms, confident of a good night's rest clear of the path of the hurricane. Barbara wondered whether she and the refugees she sat among were the brave ones, or conversely those who held the fort despite the hurricane warnings.

They were playing 500 gin rummy at one of the large round oak tables in sturdy oak chairs with arm rails, bantering from time to time with the few evacuees who'd lingered. In the glow of the baseball game on the big screen TV with the sound muted, the room had taken on a murky darkness after the flurry of dinner activity. Barbara drew a winning card and plunked it down on her mail with a flourish. *I'm out*, she announced. Lily shook her head, scrawling with a dull pencil on the scorepad, begrudgingly deducting points from her score and adding to Barbara's.

A handful of guests nearby rose and tucked in their vintage oak chairs and Barbara and Lily bade them goodnight. It left only the two of them.

"Well," said Lily, "If they don't open Disneyland tomorrow—"

"—Disney *World*."

"—we can always come back another time. Make another trip of it."

"Who's deal is it?" Barbara asked, gathering up the cards.

"I believe it's mine," said Lily and Barbara handed her the deck.

"I have to tell you I'm still stunned," Barbara said as Lily shuffled the cards, "about the will."

"Well," Lily stopped shuffling and cleared her throat. "I'm just happy we're going to be neighbors. They're making exceptions to the age rule."

Barbara slumped back in her chair and drew a finger to her mouth.

"You can always change the house," said Lily, "Make it how you like it. I'd be happy to help."

Barbara shook her head slowly. "I'm not real sure how I feel about all this right now. My brother's gonna be awful pissed off."

"Well I don't see how that makes any difference," Lily huffed, batting a hand at the air. "What that old meanie thinks."

"Do you mind," Barbara nodded abstractedly, "if we call it quits for tonight. I just don't think I can keep my mind on cards right now."

"Sure," said Lily. "I'll hold on to the scratch sheet. You're beating me pretty good anyway, maybe we'll just start fresh when we get back. Lord knows we'll have plenty of time for card games."

Lily rose from her chair and replaced the deck of cards to their spot on a bookcase full of books and boardgames. *Plenty of time for card games.* Barbara toyed with her hair and tried to imagine a life in Sunny Glen Palms. Would she not end up like Kenny Fitzroy—comfortably ensconced among the elders, unmotivated, resigned to a life of loafing, battling boredom, turning a deaf ear to the exigencies of her higher self?

"You okay?" Lily asked, tapping the table.

"Yeah. I think so."

*

Back at Peggy's house, they flipped switches to no avail—the power was out once again. Peggy rummaged around kitchen drawers and cabinets for candles before going off to draw a hot bath from what remained in the water heater. Marge folded herself in the recliner along with the book she'd wrangled from the library. While the security guard shuffled from one foot to the other in the doorway, she hurriedly settled on a book with a cover that invited her into an ominous forest she thought she might get lost in. *The Broken Promised Land*, the book jacket stating the story centered around a family insnared in a legal crisis and a marriage in peril. Something to really take her mind off things. She dropped it to her lap and stared at the ceiling. Would Ted come looking for her? They'd parked the car in the garage, along with Marge's golf cart. There was the Sunny Glen Palms directory to look up names and addresses. Ted was awful with names and she doubted he'd remember Peggy's surname after one introduction.

"Marge?" Peggy called from the bathroom. "Come in here a minute."

Candles glowed and gave a faint light to the bathroom. Peggy had her cosmetics splayed about the double sink. She lit a few more votives and then they could see their images in the large wall mirror at the sink. They began talking to the images in the same way they did the night they met at the Club with the spilled drink.

"Come let me show you how to cover that bruise up with a little rouge and such," said Peggy.

"Oh now *really*. It's not necessary."

Peggy handed a facecloth over to Marge. "Wash your face first."

Marge started the tap and dipped the facecloth. "I put ice on it. When it happened. That morning."

"Yeah yeah, but you still got that little shiner and some bruising on your cheek. Ole Peggy'll fix you up."

Marge dried her exposed and wrinkled face while Peggy looked on in the mirror, assembling her makeup kit.

"Now," said Peggy, waving the makeup pad playfully in front of her. "Close your eyes."

Peggy went about the business of applying the foundation, correcting herself, telling Marge to turn her head this way, no this way, just a little bit. Then Marge could open her eyes and she met Peggy's eyes in the mirror, said, you have experience with these things?

"No, thank God." Peggy paused before dabbing Marge's cheek with the makeup pad. "Guess I can thank my lucky stars that's one transgression my Mike hasn't ever been guilty of." She fetched the concealer stick from the sink. "Between the kids' high school theater and my own know-how, we'll figure out how to do this without making you look like a clown."

Peggy was about to apply the concealer when a sharp knock sounded on the door. She left Marge in the bathroom and stood before the door a good while in her white terrycloth robe and a towel wrapped around her head—a knot in her stomach, standing on her toes to peer through the three tiny windows at the top of the door. It was Kenny Fitzroy.

She flung the door open with a somewhat exaggerated flourish—to this he nodded and muttered hey. Peggy ushered him into the living room.

"Wait here, Cassanova." She patted him on the shoulder. "The ladies are prettying themselves up in order to properly stand in your presence."

Peggy finished with Marge's face and they returned to the living room and their guest. Peggy settled next to him on the sofa while Marge tumbled back into the recliner, pulling her feet up under her, setting the book aside.

"The hurricane made landfall just after midnight. It's wide and moving slow," Kenny said. "Heard it just now on the radio driving over. Not far south of here, actually. So I guess we're off the hook."

"We knew that," Peggy waved a hand at him. "They stuffed us in the basement at the hospital."

"A little more north and you'd still be down in that basement," Kenny shook his head gravely.

"Well I'm not religious," Peggy gazed heavenward, "but *hallelujah*."

"I hope they don't call off the hurricane party tonight," Marge said, her face clouding over.

"No hurricane parties for this old gal," said Peggy. "I'm gonna get some serious shut eye tonight."

"How's Mike?" asked Kenny.

Peggy waved her hand at him. "Son of a bitch. Not like he's ever had the best timing, but this time he's really outdone himself."

Kenny pursed his lips, fingers interlocked—a sort of reverential pose.

Marge said, "Not that it's any of my business, but Peggy mentioned last night… on the way over to the party… that you might be leaving us?"

Kenny drew himself upright, folding his arms in front of him.

"You're among friends," said Peggy, nodding over at Marge. "She'll not utter a word to a living soul. Speak openly, if you're so inclined."

Kenny gulped, drumming his fingers on his knees. "Kind of a wait and see I guess. There's this woman up in Connecticut. A kid on the way. Takes getting used to I guess."

The story had been run and rerun in his own head so many times, he had already spilled the particulars to Peggy, and so starting at the beginning and embellishing with details was not in the cards right now. At the same time, his condensing of a major story to a few sentences left him with an unfamiliar taste outside the bounds of his accustomed sense of self.

"You know this girl well?" Marge tilted her head. "I'm sorry, I don't mean to pry."

"That's okay. We, kind of… hooked up several months back and—"

"I get the gist of it."

"But I'm trying to be responsible," he said as if acting responsibly might be entirely new territory for him.

"She close to you in age?"

"She's forty-six," he shrugged and looked over at Peggy. "I finally got around to asking."

"Does she have kids?" Marge asked.

"Come to think of it, yeah."

"*Come to think of it?*" Peggy rolled her eyes and shook her head.

"Wo," said Marge. "Isn't that a real doozy. I mean, to have foisted on you. At your age."

Peggy danced her feet and raised her glass of wine. "Ain't life grand," she said with a smirk. "Full of surprises. Some good, some not so good." She patted Kenny's knee. "You'll do just fine kiddo."

"Thanks for the vote of confidence. I can get pretty down sometimes. Man, I can go to a pretty dark place."

"I kinda guessed that," said Peggy. "Don't stay there. Man up. You've got a big busy brain, my friend. Your heart will grow in leaps and bounds with a kid. Trust me. It may seem like the end of the world right now—"

"But it will get better, trust me." Marge was on her feet to refill her wineglass and on the way, behind the sofa, she touched Kenny's shoulder and mussed his hair. "You'll get what it takes if you don't have it already."

"I had a real bad night last night. Sort of a dark night of the soul."

Marge felt inclined to weigh in with something, if for no other reason than to push back on the darkness being established by the words of those two sat side by side on the couch. "Sometimes," she said, walking her wine back to the living room, "you just have to ride out the storm." *There I go speaking in platitudes*, she thought as she spilled the words. "One day can make all the difference. Sometimes all it takes is just one more day to see things in a new light."

"Yeah," said Kenny.

"Have you got any family?"

"Well there's my aunt and cousins up there in Connecticut—"

"But you don't have any family nearby," Peggy interjected.

"Another aunt, just south of here, in Punta Gorda. Near Fort Myers."

"Oh my, what about the hurricane?" Marge sat bolt upright. "Is she alright? Have you checked in with her?"

"It's alright, she's up near Philly until next month. A true snow bird."

"Beat the heat," said Peggy.

"Yeah," said Kenny. "She skips out for hurricane season."

"Not a bad idea," said Marge, wringing her hands and toying with her wedding band.

"I'll drive down and check on her place when this all blows over."

"So," Marge brought her hands to her lap. "What's next? How far along is she?"

"Not very," Kenny scrunched his eyebrows. "A few months I think."

"He's not one for details," Peggy rolled her eyes.

"We talked about her… terminating the pregnancy," Kenny fidgeted, wringing his hands in his lap.

Marge almost spit out her wine. The three of them remained silent a good while, bearing the gravity of the remark.

"Well," said Peggy. "That's one option."

"What do *you* want?" asked Marge.

"I don't know," Kenny voice was cracking. He cleared his throat as if to summon back composure. "From an objective standpoint, say a broad-view opinion… I support a woman's right to choose. But personally, by my own moral compass, I think I would be inclined to not, not…"

"Terminate the pregnancy," Marge completed his thought, perched on the edge of her seat and staring intently at the floor.

"Was she serious?" Peggy asked.

"She has concerns about her age. Complications. That's what she says. But I wonder if she just sees a deadbeat father and someone who can't be relied upon."

"But you're flying up there for godsakes," Peggy jiggled her wineglass. "You've really stepped up on this Kenny. I'm proud of you."

Kenny dropped his head to his hands, his shoulders heaving up and down. Marge rose and sat beside him, putting an arm around him and letting him sob in the soft crook of her shoulder.

"Awww," Peggy hadn't uttered this maternal tone since she'd held her granddaughter in her arms. She patted Kenny's back. "Everything will be fine. Trust me. Trust ole Peggy."

"You've got so much on *your* plate," Kenny's voice was garbled with his face dropped to his hands.

Marge said, "You can count on us anytime. Your friends will *always* be here for you."

*

The room upstairs at the Inn of Palmetto was old-fashioned cozy, in stark contrast to the more spartan décor of the Holiday Inn. The pillows were feather down and Lily fluffed one and then the other. She rubbed her hands together and nodded. "A real slumber party. She carried her pajamas and a tiny bag of toiletries to the bathroom, humming to herself. Framed embroidered art on floral wallpaper, woven baskets with homemade lye soap sat on the window sill and an accent table. Rain lashed against a small window that illuminated a clawfoot tub beneath it with the muted tones of gray daylight.

While Lily drew the taps for a bath, Barbara collapsed on the quilted queen bed they'd be sharing. Staring at the ceiling, making mental images of the house transformed from her mother's traditional furnishings to that of her own hippy-leaning tastes—colorful bohemian afghans and throws covering up plain upholstery, contemporary cutting-edge wall art replacing peaceful but ordinary landscapes. Mostly she thought of how wonderful it would be to have a *home*, a place that was hers to make of it as she wanted. Not the landlord's loan of space, not the boyfriend's tenuous offering contingent on the whims of lovers, incidental to the relationship. Hers and hers alone. She toyed with the idea alongside the sense of trappings imbued in the idea of doing something she'd sworn never to do in her life—reside in a gated community. It bothered her, as it always did, to be compelled to provide identification and be subject to interrogation simply to gain access to the home of the member of one's own family. But on the other hand, she thought she might get used to all the amenities—the pool, the gym, the pub. She couldn't refute the fact there lay a certain charm in the carefree manner of those with decent retirement portfolios who watered their gardens, joined Bridge clubs, made homemade ice cream, took their time getting out the door in the morning. There was plenty of opportunity to secure income for the expenses of everyday life, even if it were a part-time job at the supermarket. And hadn't Ybor City suggested a bohemian playground nearby? Wasn't nearby Tampa and across the Bay Bridge St. Pete accessible, ready to serve as an antidote to the humdrum inside the gate that Peggy Beamish so regularly railed against?

The loftiness, the playfulness of these thoughts balanced out by the dark side of the equation. What about the home-owners association fees that went along with those amenities? Was she not giving up her restless artistic spirit, resigning herself to a cleverly-cloaked sort of complacency? But had that artistic urge not amounted to anything more than half-fulfilled pipe dreams? An unguided missile that sunk her spirit in the end? Perhaps, she thought, she'd sunk herself. Because she'd sensed, from the minute she found her mother laying there stone dead on the floor, that she didn't know the first thing about herself, as if the Barbara that entered that gate so judgmentally a few days before just evaporated right there onto the floor and away somewhere in the ether with the woman who'd brought her into this world and attached all of her expectations to. And so the habit she'd established early on to rebuff those expectations—there was no breaking it. Was that not a significant component of her inability to focus on one endeavor and stick to it, could it all have been for nothing other than to spite her mother? The music came and went, never became a skill on which to focus on daily, the crafts-making and drawing came in fits and spurts, never quite became force of habit. But the spiting of her mother, was that not a regular habit?

And now her mother had bequeathed her a home. Would it not feel unsettling to dwell in a place where her mother had once walked, slept, ate, along with the other bits of daily life? Were expectations attached to the enormous hand-me-down when her mother drafted her will? Would those expectations not seep through the very walls to find her alone, foregoing creativity and merely going through the motions—reading books, watching TV, biding her time until her shift at the Winn-Dixie or some such place?

From the other side of the bathroom's oak door came the sounds of the bathtub draining and then Lily shuffling about and at last the clunk of the doorknob. In the doorframe Lily appeared gaunt and frail, bedecked in pajamas that looked a size too big. "I guess if they're closed tomorrow over at Disneyland, we can always come back another time."

"Disney *World*, Barbara corrected, returning her gaze to the ceiling. "I'm still thinking about the will," Her voice had a texture that was warm in its coarseness. Lily went about replacing her toiletries in carry-on luggage she'd hadn't occasioned to use since she'd arrived in Florida, until now.

"Did you ever try smoking pot Lily?"

"Huh?"

"Pot. You know, marijuana."

Lily paused in her re-arranging of clothing. "Oh heavens no."

"It's not like, the dangerous narcotic you might be thinking of it as."

"I know that."

"Really," Barbara pressed. "Lots of people do it. Not that it matters."

"My grandfather farmed south of Nashville. Grew hemp during the war. Said he used to put it in his corncob pipe and sit on the porch to watch the sun go down after a day's toiling in the fields."

Barbara propped her head up on an elbow. "Like a glass of wine."

Lily nodded. "I know my sons tried it. Billy more than once I'm sure."

"But not you."

Lily shook her head and turned off the ceiling light before climbing under the covers on her side of the bed. They lay in silence side by side a good in the dim glow of the bedside table lamp.

"Tell you what," Lily said at last. "I'm eighty-four years old. If I don't try it now I suppose I never will. What have I got to lose?"

Barbara brought a hand to her mouth, her eyes lit up with mirth. "I wasn't suggesting you try it now. Or at all for that matter."

"Well."

"Silly."

"Do you have any with you?"

"Any what?"

"Pot. Marijuana."

"A little."

"Well, maybe we can try a little of it tomorrow. At *Disneyland*."

It was clear from Lily's tone the error in nomenclature was intentional and they broke into fits of laughter, Barbara clutching her sides and gasping for air, unable to recall when she'd laughed so hard.

The room returned to silence, but for the hum of the air conditioner, and Lily's thoughts went to the contents of the will. She shut her eyes and imagined many nights of gin rummy and dinners with her new neighbor. She foresaw trips to the beach she wouldn't otherwise have undertaken. Unearthing that one-piece bathing suit from the depths of her wardrobe and the two of them sitting poolside in their sunhats, passing the suntan lotion between them. Barbara coaxing her along to Bingo evenings when she didn't have her addiction meetings. She helping Barbara get settled at the house up the road. She hadn't had a real neighbor in years. Barbara stretched herself across the bed to switch off the light, leaving the room in near-darkness. They bade one another goodnight but soon after, in the darkness, talked about Disney World, causing Lily to feel like a little girl at a slumber party. She began slurring her words and succumbing to sleep. Barbara lay awake and listened to her light snoring.

*Plenty of time for card games.* Barbara turned on her side, facing away from a friend whose hopes and expectations she might betray. Lily must have it all planned out, she thought, in her world it was crystal clear. One inherited a house and didn't even consider putting it up for sale. How would their conversations about the matter go tomorrow? Not long after, she rolled onto her back, crossed her arms over her chest and slowed her breathing. A sliver of light cut through the heavy curtains, piercing the darkness and casting its glow on the face in calm repose just inches from her. It came to Barbara that this trip was compelled by all the elements of practicality, one evacuated a place when danger loomed, after all. And yet it seemed to her, like that sliver of light in the darkness, that alongside that practicality lay a small beam of light into loneliness. Where Lily's loneliness stemmed from physical isolation, Barbara's had evolved from an abundance of people all around her. Lily may have been couped up in a house for several years, but Barbara was moving around—a flood of humanity with whom she engaged at crafts fairs, music shows. Her eyes would sometimes fall wistfully upon families assembling themselves, and she would imagine herself the mother gathering a small child in her arms while on the lookout to insure her other kids didn't stray out of sight. She'd make friends and then move and they would stay in touch for a while and then fade with time and space. Moving around like a ship lost at sea, it seemed as if there was an empty sea all the way to the horizon. Serving the public at the coffeehouse, joining different groups, yoga classes, attending open mic nights—in a constant conscious effort to *meet people*—as an antidote to loneliness. She sank into the sea of sleep carrying the last thought before dropping below the waterline of wakefulness. Would that the kind and gentle bonds of friendship might be secured forever. Side by side lay a couple of kids at heart—their hopeful minds set on Disneyland, Disney World, call it what you will.

# 9

In the gray light of dawn they trolled along Sunset Drive in Peggy's Lincoln, Marge at the wheel, surveying the damage, gazing mutely upon residents clearing yards of debris. Leaves stripped from shrubs and strewn about like confetti on lawns, flowerbeds, streets. Palm fronds ripped from trees. Heavy limbs come crashing down upon the roofs of a few unlucky Sunny Glen Palmers who'd be busy on the phones with their insurance companies. At the side of one house an elderly man in his pajamas stood barefoot in the wet grass, fixing heavy plastic trash bags with duct tape to a window frame where the glass had caved in to the wind. At another house the wind had wrenched a garage door clear from its hinges. At the rear of another, a back porch riddled with shards of glass from a sliding door overcome by wind. If anybody had told Marge a week ago she'd be driving someone else's car in someone else's clothes amid an apocalyptic mess she'd have said they were bonkers. She could see that some color had been restored to Peggy's face, along with it some of her usual high-spiritedness.

"The son of a bitch," Peggy muttered, shaking her head slowly. "Just when I thought I was gonna be cut loose." She squeezed her eyes shut and said tersely, her voice barely above a whisper, "Foot loose and fancy free."

Marge nodded vacantly and pulled over to the curb to make room for an emergency paramedic vehicle. She'd woken up in a familiar room with her strange new convictions intact, resolved that no amount of time and space would sort things out. Maybe they were best apart, it had been that way all along, and the shakeup around a move and now the hurricane only served to draw it out into the light of day. All those years enduring what had seemed perfect sense suddenly made no sense at all. Had she ever truly loved him, had he ever really loved her?

"I'm sorry," said Peggy, removing her leopard print sunglasses, wiping distractedly at them with a tissue. "You've got your own cross to bear—"

"Peggy I—"

"Listen to me Marge. You're doing the right thing. Get out while you can. While he can still take care of himself."

"But we haven't been over the finances. I don't know if we can afford to live apart. What to do about that house up there."

"Well maybe that son of yours can start pitching in. Maybe you just gotta bite the bullet and sell it. It's a little early yet to talk about the money angle. But you're only asking for trouble being around that jerk," she shook her head. "He'll only take years off your life. He'd have me hitting the cocktails first thing in the morning."

"I know what you're saying is right."

"Not to mention physical abuse. The biggest red line you can draw."

"He hit me. Years ago. I packed my things. I was gonna leave. He said he'd never do it again. And he didn't. But I always had that fear. It always kept me in check."

"And now he goes and does it again. And here we are," said Peggy.

"I feel like I should have seen this coming. Like maybe I should have left before it happened. It would have at least left a better memory of him. Of us."

"Or maybe you'd just be scratching your head wondering if you did the right thing. Getting nostalgic. Maybe it's a blessing in disguise after all," Peggy touched Marge's cheek. "The bruise will heal. And so will you.

Marge shrugged. "I just want to be happy. Like everybody else."

They turned onto Sunset Boulevard toward the older developments. Garbage and various objects were strewn about the wide street. A woman was going about her yard with a laundry basket fetching soggy clothes from muddy grass under the clothesline. Peggy made a face. "Now why the hell did she not gather her clothes off the line *before* the goddamned hurricane?"

"Probably just too late," said Marge. "She probably forgot."

"Well, do ya think you might just hold off hanging laundry to dry with heavy rains and a category five hurricane on the way? Jesus. Some of these people are just plain crackers." Peggy bit her nails, her eyes darting about. "Godammit, I'm gonna be stuck here." She squeezed her eyes shut and puffed her cheeks. "I'm gonna be stuck in this place."

They reached the hospital and after Marge parked the car they lingered awhile, staring at the windshield as they addressed one another.

"Do you think every relationship just has a life span?" Marge frowned.

Peggy shrugged. "The younger generation seems to think so, by the look of things. I mean with a divorce rate of over fifty percent and all."

"You don't see that so much here," Marge shook her head. "In Sunny Glen Palms I mean."

"Honey, we're in a retirement community. An exclusively white retirement community I might add. Chock full of an idealistic generation holding on to some old dream of love at first sight. The last lot of company pension beneficiaries. A sort of graveyard of the middle-class."

When they reached his room, clutching their pocketbooks and peering in the doorway blocked by a cart, Mike was sitting up having breakfast. A nurse brought forkfuls of eggs and bits of toast to his mouth. His eyes darted about with an alertness absent yesterday. Taking in the scene, Peggy imagined herself performing these chores in just a few days' time.

*

They were closer to Disney World than they'd thought. A few phone calls had established that not only had the worst of the storm front passed overnight, but that the resorts had long been established as safe spots in hurricanes and some still had rooms available. On the radio, the news that Hurricane Charley had ripped south of Orlando after touching down in Punta Gorda, with some impact on the Tampa area and Sunnyville.

Lily had insisted they stop first in Celebration, a fabricated master-planned community, an elaborate contrivance of the old American Dream synched with the Disney brand, a generous serving of nostalgia. The rain had tapered off to a drizzle as they pulled into the town center. Streets without even the teeniest scrap of litter for yesterday's high winds to scatter. Underneath Lily's one umbrella they strolled over unblemished sidewalks, not a single stray cigarette butt or chewing gum wrapper. The downtown streets were lined with squeaky-clean business storefronts and they took shelter in a combined ice cream parlor and coffee house. She ordered two lattes from the barista, a perky blond teenaged girl with a smile plastered on a face as clear of defects as the sidewalk outside. Everyone inside smiling and joking with one another despite the foul weather—the very antithesis to Sunnyville and the panic that ensued under menacing clouds. If Barbara thought there was a good measure of middle-class naiveté back there in Sunny Glen Palms, this place was a whole other ball of wax. You wouldn't imagine, she thought, that a Category 4 hurricane had reigned down terror on dense populations just a few hundred miles to the east any more than the homelessness, drug addiction, and unendurable poverty it met along its path. These people had their finances in order way ahead of time and from all appearances had no pressing issues. But their carefree demeanors weren't grating on Barbara's nerves in the way they ordinarily may have. Sat across from Lily at a table for two, she felt herself unburdened, away from her troubles in Sunnyville. Lily was smiling, her eyes darting about to take in a quintessential Norman Rockwell 1920s-themed decor—a soda fountain bar with chair rails, War Bond posters on the walls, a checkered tile floor. A warmth of spirit washed over Barbara like a drug and she had a hunch it was much the same for Lily. Maybe the town of Celebration was sprinkled with painkiller dust, or perhaps the water was laced with trace amounts of opium or heroine, just enough to take the edge off without any danger of addiction, if people didn't know they were ingesting the painkillers, they weren't addicted in a purely psychological sense. Or maybe it was just all that feel-good Disney.

"How's your latte?"

"Is this what you call fancy coffee? Never tasted coffee this good."

They huddled under the umbrella and returned to the car, leaving the by-all-appearances problem-free folk of Celebration to their pastimes.

They settled on a resort just a few miles from the theme park entrance. Barbara balked at the price but Lily insisted, saying it's my turn anyway and it's been a long time since I had a chance to stay at a fancy place. The rain was picking up again as Barbara turned into a long drive lined with azalea bushes, pagodas dotting a landscape of neatly-trimmed greens. The banks of a lake were shaded by live oaks, what moss had been spared by the wind draping the branches like silk shawls on the shoulders of elegant ladies.

Barbara parked near the entrance and the they climbed the two steps onto a clapboard porch with wooden rocking chairs and porticos all freshly painted white. The storm hadn't served to cool things off and the air was thick and moist, hot enough to create a vapor on the neatly-clipped grass. Inside at the reception desk, Lily inquired about a senior discount and that, along with a weekend promotion rate, made her face brighten. She waved Barbara's purse away, drawing a credit card from her own.

Their room was on the top floor at the back of the resort, its windows affording an expansive view of the lake and the grounds. It was the most luxurious room that either of them had ever beheld as a guest. Lacquered wooden floors almost mirrors underfoot, walls lined with tasteful original oil paintings, canopy beds decked out with fancy floral print comforters, lacy sheets and pillows. The bellman hefted their bags from the luggage cart and Barbara crushed a few bucks into his hand.

"Lily," she said as they arranged their bags on the mammoth beds, "I think our respective lodging contributions are seriously out of balance."

"Oh now really," said Lily, extracting her bag of toiletries and starting for a bath suite that began with a powder room.

"I'm serious. Let me split the bill with you."

Lily paused in the doorway and turned around to face Barbara. "Will you quit keeping score young lady? This is my treat."

"I-I don't expect you to pay for everything. You've already done so much for me and I- I just don't want—"

"Oh for goodness sakes, won't you let somebody do something for you for once?"

Barbara had slumped down on the bed, playing abstractedly with its fine embroidery. Lily sat beside her and patted her knee.

"This means the world to me," she said. "It's something me and Dan never got around to. I raised my kids on Disney."

Barbara nodded, a smile spreading across her face.

Lily fetched her cosmetic bag and shuffled with hand on hip to the bathroom suite. From beyond the cracked door she called, "I never did imagine we'd make it to Disney Land."

"Disney *World*," Barbara corrected once again.

"Disney *World*. Anyway we're here and we're going to spend all day taking in the sights while this old bird still has eyes to see."

*

Marge was puttering around on Peggy's golf cart in a pair of Peggy's khaki shorts, one of Peggy's flowery blouses and Peggy's straw beach hat. I'm borrowing everything of yours lately, she said to Peggy at the hospital. It's nothing, Peggy had replied. Go and check on things over at your house. But go in disguise.

And so here she was trolling along Tammany Drive and here was Gerry Hagoden out for a walk. She waved to him instinctively, forgetting about the Peggy Beamish costume. He waved back. She wondered if he distinguished her from anyone else along his walks. She'd heard the rumors and wondered how his marriage was going. He appeared at his usual ease among the remnants of the hurricane, stepping around puddles and fallen palm fronds in a devil-may-care manner. An emergency paramedic vehicle lumbered along, and he waved at it as he might a neighbor.

When Marge came upon her house, she saw his car already parked in the driveway, and the signpost returned to its place. Ted and Marjorie Cumberbatch. She stopped the cart.

The door to the house opened and her foot went to the pedal, the golf cart lurched and she found herself trundling along Tammany drive to entrance to the golf course path.

*

Kenny Fitzroy had woken up with a sense of calm greatly at odds with the terror-stricken state which he'd expected to, as if the conscious world were greeting him with a cotton candy cloud on which to drift into his affairs, however bleak they may be. No measure of driving rain, gusts of wind, or rumble of thunder could snare him out of heavy slumbers. After emptying his bladder, he planted bare feet on the faux wood floor and made his way with unfamiliar buoyancy to the linoleum of the kitchen and his familiar morning routine—putting the coffee on, setting a breakfast table for one, popping a Bob Marley and the Wailers disc in the CD player.

The pep-talk from his lady friends replayed itself and he thought perhaps he might actually be seeing things in a new light.

He hadn't been to a hospital since his brief stint at nursing years ago. Walking through its corridors and sitting across from a friend in the middle of a very real and present health crisis served as a sober reminder to him that life is tenuous and people have all kinds of valid reasons to fear and dread it. But as Peggy Beamish said, and had demonstrated unequivocally, the worst things to fear are more often overcome. Her and Marge's words must have followed him home from the hospital and right to bed, it was as if those very words had tucked him in. He might have been carried off to sleep with those comforting words.

He was scooping oatmeal and banana from a bowl while perusing the alternative weekly *Creative Loafing*, and his thoughts kept returning to the answering machine he'd passed with an unfeigned nonchalance contrary to the sense of dread that plagued him the entire week. He had a strange impulse to call her. The previous evening, before bed, winding down with the not uncommon mix of Miles Davis and marijuana, he began to feel the sense of something akin to guilt, but not guilt. It was something he guessed he'd been out of practice with, or maybe had never even been in the game of—that of putting oneself in the shoes of another. Why hadn't he inquired more about her kids—like had she told them and what did they think about it? Why didn't he convey more concern for her? Hadn't the mere mention of an abortion compelled a much deeper discussion he'd failed to initiate? An empathy had insinuated itself into his lightly stoned mind—he had mental images of Kathy from Connecticut facing one of life's most serious and sacred events by herself and if it hadn't been so late he'd have called her right then and there. He promised to himself with an unprecedented calm that he would do so first thing in the morning. Perhaps that was what propelled him into deep slumbers, maybe it was the simple fact that he'd made a decision to act based on the feelings of another, or perhaps it was simply the fact that he'd made a firm decision.

He was still feeling light on his feet when he poured the gratifying first cup of coffee, with generous portions of cream and sugar, and walked it over to the living room. A big zero on the digital display of the answering machine. He fetched a crumpled piece of notebook paper with her number scrawled on it, retreating to the back porch with the cordless in hand. An emergency paramedic vehicle negotiated a path through debris scattered along Sunset Boulevard. Settling himself in the metal chair, he dialed her number.

After a few rings she picked up. The din of noises in the background that accompanied her hello took him off guard—he'd come to expect that she, like him, would be speaking from the quiet comfort of home, the dead silence once again punctuating those awkward pauses. He'd forgotten that the number scrawled on the scrap of notebook paper belonged to a work-issued phone, the Blackberry she toted along with all the other pocketbook items on their one and only sort-of-date weeks ago.

Her voice sounded rounder to him, as if something had opened up inside her to allow for a wider variety of feelings to issue from of her mouth. She was saying it was good to hear from him alongside a tone oddly tinged with sadness. He asked where she was and when she said she was in the hospital the background noise suddenly made sense.

"What happened, what are you doing in the hospital?"

The voices diminished, and he imagined her palming the phone, motioning at those milling about a shared room that this was a personal call and might they grant her a few minutes? Her voice, her breath heaving, preparing herself to impart to him something of the utmost gravity. He knew it. The whole great dome of sky a monotone gray. He shuffled his feet in front of him, sat on the folding chair, and waited. *Kenny, are you still there? Wait a minute… Hold on…* And on it went until the background noise evaporated and made way for the news.

Life, always so tenuous—in the womb, out of the womb. So many components, so many working parts—essential to breathing, to digestion and elimination, to the cognition and instinct requisite to survival. When life is snuffed in the womb, it has its own brand of tragedy, the soul that never had a chance. The expulsion of potential, the termination of what might have been, having developed enough to find itself somewhere along the scale of the most beauteous or ugliest of human beings brought into the world. Your stay on planet earth indeterminate. Might it be the unborn child had held less of the father's deficiencies and more of his virtuous attributes?

Anyway, the mother. Driving yourself to the hospital, your belly on fire with the sharpest of pains, loathe to summon family or friends because you hadn't yet mustered the courage to impart news of the pregnancy to a single one of them. Arriving and waiting in a room with people and charts and muzak and magazines on tables—waiting to be sequestered in your own antiseptically clean quarters, your own hovel of loneliness and despair. Walking through the pain, exhausted as you are. When Kathy had finished the story, had run out of air after coming up for air several times during the telling, he had sparse and solemn words to offer by way of response. What could be considered appropriate, the soft words of condolence. He wasn't sure he was any good at comforting. *I'm sorry*, from someone who was conflicted about the pregnancy and the whole prospect of fatherhood,

*I'll pray* from someone who never prayed and had in fact made a mockery of religion both privately and publicly for much of his adult life. He spoke these words because they were appropriate under the circumstances. The words *I love you* weren't ushered from his mouth before he clicked the off button and dropped the phone to his lap, because those words would have been grossly disingenuous, even inappropriate under the circumstances.

It is here that Marge Cumberbatch marched in and broke the solemn spell cast on Kenny, appearing as she did on the tiny strip of lawn just outside the shabby screened-in porch—in Peggy Beamish's flowery blouse, pink polyester shorts and a woven beach hat. Waving a newspaper at him.

"I saw your car in the driveway," she said. "I knocked on the door several times. Thought I'd have a look before I gave up."

Kenny had been hunched over contemplatively with his lips pressed to interlocked fingers. He glanced up and nodded at her with a wan smile.

"I'm just killing time before I head back to the hospital, thought I'd pop by and say hello, you know, maybe we can drag Peggy away for dinner you know, something to help take her mind off of stuff, maybe shoot some billiards or something. I'm not sure if the North Club has re-opened yet but..." She tilted her head, squinting, her voice rising in pitch. "You okay?"

The screen door was slightly ajar and creaked when she pushed on it, its hinges screaming out mournfully for of a shot of oil.

Kenny looked up sharply. "She's had a miscarriage."

"Oh honey. I'm so sorry."

"Or so she tells me."

"What do you mean?" There wasn't another chair, so Marge found herself squatting down beside him so as to put them at eye-level.

He frowned. "Well. It's not like I pushed her or anything. It's just I had mentioned a few times. About the option of—"

"Oh Kenny, don't think like that. You have to take her at her word."

"I don't know," he shrugged.

"Maybe it's not for you to know."

He pursed his lips and nodded gravely.

"Oh, Kenny." Marge squeezed his shoulder.

He rose to fetch a chair for her, Marge was company he very badly needed. A brief and somewhat awkward hug ensued in which she patted him on the back. He shuddered. Alone in the world as he was, here was someone who for some strange reason actually cared that he was in a world of confusion and pain, someone who was not much more than a complete stranger insuring his not having to bear this moment alone. He allowed himself to cry, he wiped at the tears and went hastily to fetch a chair lest she object on the pretext of some errand, or some personal crisis of her own—which she in fact, ironically enough, was addressing by hiding here at Kenny Fitzroy's modest home in the more ramshackle part of town.

He returned with a folding metal chair. They sat side-by-side watching a neighbor a few yards away clear their yard of fallen branches and debris. Marge did most of the talking, pouring forth a litany of words meant to soothe and lend comfort as Kenny sat in the posture of the penitent—head bowed, elbows on knees, giving sparse acknowledgements, mm-hmms and yeah-I-knows and what all else the comforted might feel obliged to utter while the comforter bears *their* heart as means to soothe and comfort. As it happens, Marge herself had had a miscarriage—it was in fact the product of their wedding night, and as she reflected on it in the telling, it brought her to tears. Kenny raised his head imploringly, signaling her to go on. He needed these words as one might need salve on a wound, it was music to his ears more so than any serving from his extravagant collection of music. Marge Cumberbatch was the singer—her voice commonplace, neither beauteous nor grating—just a regular old gal sat next to a young man whose voyage had left in its wake a life very different from that of her own in the great sea of life. She'd had a miscarriage and could understand something of what he was feeling. And it was indeed only *something* of what he was feeling, because mingled with the sense of loss in the soup of his gut-level emotions, the far greater ingredient, the one he dared not utter out loud, was an enormous sense of relief at—after dragging himself kicking and screaming to a place of acceptance, on the heels of forbearing any selfish impulse, arriving at last to a place of stoic resolve—being let off the hook.

*

To the innocent bystander Disney had the appearance of hopelessness and desolation. At the gates of the Magic Kingdom, maintenance crews went about clearing up debris. Where normally a mass of humanity would be swarming like bees around a busy hive, the lean crowd of visitors stepped gingerly around downed branches. Barbara stood in line while Lily took a seat on a bench nearby. Save my legs, she said. She shuffled over when Barbara got to the ticket window.

"I don't want to go on any rides," she said to the young man behind the glass.

"That's okay ma'am. They're not mandatory."

"Well, just take it out of the price of the ticket. I get nauseous."

"Well, there's one price for admission to the park. I'm happy to let you know we're giving half off the regular price today. You may enjoy any of the park's other amenities."

"I'm just pleased as punch to be here."

Inside the kingdom they joined the paltry crowd. The flowerbeds had remained mostly intact and glowed intermittently as the sun hid and then shone behind puffy clouds. The characters strolled leisurely along colorful walkways in their colorful costumes. Lily gaped at the scene, squinting so as to discern the majestic structures, the Cinderella castle with its sky-blue pointed spires and stained-glass windows set against ornately carved stone. She turned to Barbara. "Isn't it just wonderful?"

"I have to say, it is pretty amazing."

"Snow White was always my favorite," said Lily, tugging at Barbara's elbow. "We've just got to see her. And all them little elves."

"Well," said Barbara. "Let's go find the princess and wake her up."

"Well surely you want to go on the rides."

"I can do without the rides, Barbara shrugged, "I'm a bit old for that."

"Well now, surely you can't come here and not do Space Mountain."

"Okay," Barbara gave a wan smile. "I'll do Space Mountain. Maybe you can do parts of it."

There were trolleys to ferry them around and they took them to save wear and tear on Lily's legs. At the Germany Pavilion at Epcot they met Snow White—a fresh-faced teenager displaying pearly whites with a broad smile, neatly curled jet-black hair with a red bow in front. An Elizabethan stand up collar back of her skinny neck, the tight blue bodice with rumpled red trim, the billowy gown of bright yellow, puffy sleeves of light blue and red. She sat in front of a garden, at the base of a faux water well, gathering children all around her and smiling at parents as they videotaped.

"It's too bad we don't have a camera," Lily said. "I'd love to have my picture taken. With Snow White."

"Dammit," said Barbara. "We don't have a camera."

"We didn't have time to think of everything," Lily frowned.

"Tell you what. Wait here. They might have one of those disposable cameras in that shop over there."

Barbara stepped lively across what looked like a movie set to that relic of retail commerce that pre-dated corporate chain and franchise mania—the General Store. There was a wire basket stocked with Kodak disposable cameras and she fetched a couple of them. Outside, a new batch of kids gathered around Snow White for a photo. Lily sat on a bench nearby and shrugged her shoulders.

"Hey," said Barbara. "Why don't we round up a bunch of these kids to take a picture with you?"

"Me and a bunch of kids around Snow White."

"You'll fit right in."

A few mothers were busy corralling a fresh group of kids in front of Snow White, between turns. Barbara insinuated herself into the fracas with some trepidation, *excuse me* was what she led with. *Excuse me, but would you mind if…* executing a plan that was her own idea, awkward despite years of engaging with parents and kids at the fairs, suddenly as if had her legs not been moving, she may have been immobilized by self-consciousness. She assembled a smattering of kids from obliging parents waiting their turn, and they crowded around Snow White waiting for Lily to enter the picture, some of them sat at the base of the faux well, a little boy and a girl scooped up into Snow White's arms. Lily approached and the kids parted a path to allow her by to lean against the well. A little blond girl crushed against her and she gathered up the child in front of her, dropping her arms over the girl's shoulders in a protective fashion. Barbara snapped a few photos. The kids had gotten restless and scattered, leaving Lily by herself chatting with Snow White. One of the young mothers approached Barbara, beckoning for the camera, nodding at her to sit beside Snow White. One, two, three, she called out and captured in the lens Snow White—costumed in pleated yellow gown with a velvet blue tunic with puffed sleeves, a pink cape, displaying her pearly whites with the broadest smile. Flanked by an elderly lady in a floral print blouse over polyester pants and a young lady in the casual attire of jeans and a tee shirt. A fresh photograph to augment Lily's antique living room collection. The obliging mother returned the camera to Barbara and said with a nod to Lily, your mom will treasure this. Neither Barbara nor Lily felt obliged to correct the woman's assumption. The way Lily felt, the young lady on the other side of Snow White may as well have been her daughter, mirroring Barbara's sentiments.

*

There were a bunch of calls to return and it was one reason Peggy cut her visit to the hospital short. She was between calls when the phone rang, the caller ID displaying an unfamiliar number. She took the call just in case. An unfamiliar voice crackled over the line. It took her a moment to identify a voice imbued with a carefree quality she'd not ascribed to the awkward and self-conscious young lady she'd glanced over her RV catalogue on the pool deck just a little over a week ago.

"You're not gonna believe this," Barbara said.

"Okay, try me." Peggy said, retreating to the back porch—the cordless in one hand, a glass of chardonnay in the other.

"We're at Disney World."

"*We*?" Peggy settled herself on the cushioned wicker chair, setting her feet upon the ottoman.

"Lily. Lily Westfall?"

"Well doesn't that beat the band. Dust already settled in Orlando?"

"Much better today."

"Well we're collecting ourselves here. Watcha up to?

"I'm doing some rides. We got to meet Snow White."

"You did right to get outta dodge."

"Everybody okay?"

"Almost."

"I'm sorry Peggy. Kenny told me the news. About your husband."

"Thanks honey," she sipped at her Chardonnay.

"How is he?"

"He's stable. Better today."

"Oh, that's good."

"Anyway, I'll take care of him. Ole Peggy will take care of him."

"Mighty good of you."

"I don't see any other way. Not now at least." Peggy shrugged, took another sip of her wine.

"I heard you all dodged a bullet. With the storm I mean."

"I look at a storm as like, a problem. Right in front of you. And you don't run away from your problems. You have to face them head on."

"Oh." The playful buoyancy had left Barbara's voice and Peggy could tell she'd inadvertently insulted her.

"Now listen," she said, "don't think I'm calling you yellow. It probably took more courage to take off and try to outrun it."

"Maybe. Anyway, the drive was insane. I could hardly see anything."

"I'll bet."

"Lily was freaked out when I got back to the house Thursday night."

"Wow."

"She's been my guardian angel."

"Well, if I were in my right mind I guess I might've taken a powder too. If I hadn't walked in on Mike like that."

"That must have been a shock."

"I wonder if our friends had another hurricane party. They're crazy enough to have. Anyway, we're all still above sea level and breathing."

"I'm sure glad to hear it."

"So when are you coming back to Sunnyville? When's the funeral?"

"Next week," said Barbara. "I'm not sure I'll attend. My brother," she said. "Bad blood between us."

"Listen to me kid," Peggy said. "I'm going to say this once, and only once. Listen to me. Listen to Peggy. You gotta show up at your mother's funeral. No matter what happened in the past, it's just—"

"I know, but you don't understand—"

"If you show up," Peggy said, "there's a small chance you'll regret it. If you don't show up, there's a bigger chance you'll come to regret it later. Which would you rather?"

"Hmm."

"Look I'm no shrink. But they say that whatever happened in the past, good or bad, you need the burial for closure. Don't let some son of a bitch brother rob you of that."

"I see what you're saying—"

"And that goes for the will too. Don't be naïve. I know your type. Trusting everyone's *inherent* good nature."

"Okay," Barbara sighed.

"Didn't Kenny tell me you came back to try and make amends with your mother?"

"That's right. I did."

"So then, what the hell? You show up at her doorstep and then don't stick around for her funeral?"

"I may be sticking around for a while. Looks like she left the house to me. In the will."

"Wow."

"I'm not sure what I'm going to do yet."

"Well I'll talk to you about sticking around in Sunnyville when you get back. I'd think twice before you accept a sentence to boredom."

"Uh-huh."

"Now don't take that the wrong way kiddo. Selfishly I'd love for you to stick around."

"So would Lily. I could stick around for her friendship alone. Without her help, I don't think I'd ever have made it through all this. The funeral preparations, phone calls to family. But mainly just being there."

"Well, you all just stay safe," said Peggy, studying her nails, "and make it back to us in one piece. Two pieces. You know what I mean."

Peggy clicked the phone off, draining her wine, gazing out the window a while before returning to the call-backs. A mist hung over the golf greens, the sun a glowing ball of gold behind it. She shivered although it was warm inside the house.

*

There were no golfers out on the course. It would be quite some time before the greens dried up sufficiently for play. Marge got to a clearing and headed for the ninth hole. The sun hung low, obscured by cotton candy storm clouds, as colorful a picture she'd ever seen. She drew towels from the back of the cart, spread them out on the artificial turf of the ninth hole putting green and sat Indian-style, craning her neck to take in the painting ingrained into the sky. Her back began going stiff and she pushed herself up, gathered the towels and moved over to a nearby sand trap. The hollow ground afforded enough space for her to sit against the bunker with feet spread in front of her, resting her head against the shelf of turf to take in nature's painting, dashes of pastel strokes against a canvas of sky, the quietude surrounding her as complete as any she'd ever found herself in, broken only by the occasional caw of a bird.

All by herself there in the sand trap, she tried to imagine what it might be like to have a husband less prone to outbursts of temper and more inclined to displays of affection. He would sit beside her and hold her hand and there would be no sermons about the awful state of society, how the country was going down the tubes. There wouldn't be an adult son living at home in a toxic relationship. There would just be the two of them sharing what little was left of their lives in the best way possible under less difficult circumstances. What did Ted have to worry about after all? Did they not have themselves covered financially for the rest of their days? Shouldn't they be more grateful? Maybe she need only show him people their age in far less fortunate circumstances—having to work well into their seventies at menial jobs just to survive. His only response would be that's their own damn fault and why should I be forced to pay for their lifetime accumulation of bad decisions and laziness? This is a country, he would remind her, where anything is possible if you just work hard and save your money. At least until the goddamned institutionalized handouts that hard-working folks like him had to pay for. And so on and so on. If he were sitting here now in the sand trap with her, that's the kind of talk she'd be subjected to, it would only serve to pollute the moment. She'd attempt to steer the conversation elsewhere, she'd deny him even the slightest grunt of acknowledgment. But he would never shut up.

She tried to tamp down these hypothetical thoughts and attach herself to the silence, feeling less alone than she would have if he were there beside her. That's the way it felt all the time lately. She straightened her neck and slowly pushed herself up from a towel now dampened by the wet fake turf. The sun began to dip over the horizon, darkness was imminent. The golf cart was almost a silhouette up there on the mound. She noticed with some measure of remorse, grass stains on the khaki pants she'd borrowed from Peggy Beamish.

*I have to go back*, she thought. *There's no point in waiting.*

The golf cart trundled along empty streets with debris strewn every which way like a kid's messy room and then there was Ted in the driveway, fussing at something in the backseat of the car.

"Well," he said. "You coming in or what?"

Marge cocked her head to one side, regarding him.

The air was thick, the ground dewy, the scent of the freshly-cut grass mingled the scent of wet blacktop covered in a mist of humidity. Sunnyville had never looked like this to Ted and he glanced around him as if he were in another country altogether. He looked upon his wife in much the same manner—dressed in clothes as unrecognizable to him as the curious look on her face, it was as if it were a stranger he encountered in his driveway.

"Honey," he said. "I've thought everything over. I can't tell you how sorry I am for what I did."

"That's water under the bridge."

"No, it isn't. It was wrong. I'll tell you what. I'm going to go back on the meds. I don't want anything like that to happen again. I don't want to hurt you."

"I told you yesterday," she said without taking her eyes from him. "I haven't changed my mind. In fact I'm more convinced that this is the right thing. You can go up north. Sell the house, whatever. We can work out the details later. When the dust settles."

The brooding expression on his face changed to one of consternation.

"Why do *you* get to stay here?"

"Alright," she said. "I'll go up North. You stay here."

He merely shook his head.

"But you better get used to the heat," she said. "Cause there's more to come. Right up until November I'm told. And I know how much you hate it."

Alongside the strange confidence in her tone came a twinge of guilt. She imagined him driving in the rain this morning after a dismal night in a noisy motel in some shitty town inland who's name he'd already forgotten, thinking he could at least take comfort in the belief that Marge had her time to stew and that would be that. It was a brief moment where their past—imperfect, rife with problems as it was—might have overcome this newfound awareness that shook an old stability to its core. Were he to have reached out with any genuine tenderness, some acknowledgement of his shortcomings, they might have entered the house together. But his all-too-familiar scowl sent Marge backpedaling to climb back aboard the golf cart.

"Tell you what," he said. "I'll drive back, with my son to keep me company. Cause that's just the kind of guy I am. I have far too much self-respect to stand here and try to beg you back. You stay here and enjoy yourself. Don't let old Ted rain on your parade."

He started back to the house. When he got to the door he turned around. She was already backing the tiny vehicle from the driveway onto the blacktop, as if unmooring a great vessel out onto a mighty sea.

*

Exhausted from the thick heat, the walking and the excitement, they returned to a luxurious room at the resort. Lily drew a hot bath. Barbara fetched the remote and flopped onto one of the giant beds, clicking on the Weather Channel. Hurricane Charley had wreaked havoc and devastation north of Fort Myers, while largely forgoing Pinellas County and Sunnyville. A young family at Disney with friends in St. Petersburg had imparted the news while they had their ice creams. The news confirmed by a grandmother with a son in Clearwater who stood behind them in the line for Space Mountain.

Barbara dialed the volume down on the television, the better to listen to the sound of Lily splashing in the enormous tub just beyond the door. She sauntered over to the tall windows, drawing the heavy curtains to gaze upon a well-tended garden and greenway. Wondering if this might prove to be both the first and last time she'd spend the night in such luxury. With someone who truly felt like a friend, despite their brief acquaintance. The trajectory of her life didn't indicate a path to riches and she wasn't getting any younger.

Lily dipped herself up to her neckline in the hot water. She'd poured first bath oils and then bubble bath under a fancy and delicate gold tap, so the surface of the water was topped with bounteous white hills. Thoughts very much like Barbara's ran through her mind—an aging mind that began to have trouble retaining things, that sent the same words over and over again to her mouth, struggled to decipher the murky vision of failing eyes. Would she have another opportunity like this? Because her sons certainly weren't visiting with the frequency she would have hoped. She'd been told over and over by everyone after Dorothy died to try and live in the present. But this had not proven easy. Her thoughts too easily strayed to the future, and too often to the past. Now a troubled woman interrupted a predictable and static present by some odd twist of fate, a timing seemingly configured with precision by the universe itself.

When the water had turned lukewarm, Lily turned sideways and, with slow and deliberate motions, pushed herself from the side of the tub to get herself first to her knees and then a standing position. She bent down to open the drain, then stepped from the tub with the trepidation of someone a thousand feet up and stepping from one building to another.

She stood naked in front of the giant mirror, dripping wet, caressing her toes in the plush bath rug and glancing at her full body, every inch of it all at once. Turned around and glanced over her shoulder. The reflection in the mirror blurry without glasses, but clear enough to study a wrinkled body riddled with age spots, what little fat she had sagging in all the wrong places. She cupped a hand over her privates, though no one was watching. After Dan died, she'd become less self-conscious about her body, treating herself more often to sugary things—and yet she still had trouble keeping weight on. She draped an oversized terrycloth towel over bony shoulders and began patting herself dry. Fetched the complimentary bath accessories, examining them one at a time with the curiosity a little girl might her doll and doll things. Dabbed talcum powder with a puffy ball, making a mess. Applied moisturizing skin cream to her nose and cheeks. A sinking feeling blended into the sweet sensations throughout her ablutions, a premonition that this would prove to be the last time. Not so much the luxury, the sense of pampering oneself—there were plenty of ways to pamper herself back home—but rather the sense of adventure, a diversion from the mundane and ordinary with someone near and dear enough to feel as if they were synced in spirit. What she had with Dan, with Dorothy—kinship, goodwill. Like some puzzle piece long gone missing, caring and being cared about. She'd been able to find comfort in herself occasionally, but it wasn't until Barbara turned up that she'd found comfort in another. What irony that comfort had come to be found, given one crisis after another with Barbara. A giggle escaped her, she couldn't remember the last time she'd laughed privately at something sprung from her own thoughts.

She'd forgotten to bring her pajamas into the bathroom. Two white terrycloth robes hung beside the shower and she gathered one around her. When she entered the room, Barbara was at the desk poring over a small bound book with her reading glasses, scribbling into it. She glanced over the rim of her glasses. "It's my journal. I'm starting to write in it again."

"A travel journal?"

"No," Barbara said. "Just an everyday kind of… life journal."

"Oh, I see."

Lily gathered her pajamas and returned to the bathroom, leaving the door ajar. "What sort of things do you write about," she hollered, then her head appeared in the crack of the door. "Sorry, it's none of my business."

"No, that's okay. Barbara furrowed her brow. "I guess I just write about what's going on. What's happening and how I feel about things."

Barbara couldn't help but wonder if she were addressing the wrong generational audience, whether her words did not convey a tinge of self-absorption. She glanced up, tapping her pen on the pad, silently regarding the frail old lady before her who carried the scent of talcum powder, who tugged at a pair of compression socks before slipping her stockinged feet into a pair of bunny slippers. "Well anyway," Lily said to the floor. "I'm just happy you found yourself a home. I *know* you've been looking to nest."

"You're right. I've been looking to nest all my life, in a way," Barbara sighed sauntering over to sit beside Lily on the bed, placing a hand upon frail, bony shoulder. "But I'm afraid it may not be Sunnyville."

"Why not?" Lily pulled a face. "It's as good a place as any."

"Maybe down the road. Just not right now."

"Well I know you're below the minimum age, but they do make exceptions. There's this Canadian couple—"

"Lily, I… not now. I'm not ready to just stop living yet."

Lily's face clouded over and Barbara patted her hand.

"I'm sorry. I didn't mean it like that. It's just… Look, I know it's a nice place. All the amenities. Peace and quiet. All that. But I still want to do something. For myself. Somewhere else."

"Well I was looking forward to having you stick around a while," Lily mock-pouted.

"I have to stick around for the funeral at least."

"Well I'm just glad you're gonna go to your momma's funeral."

"Never said I wouldn't."

"Well. After your brother showed up, I wasn't exactly sure you would." Lily sighed and covered Barbara's hand with her own—bony, bulbous veins under such a thin coat of skin as to make Barbara wonder at her own road ahead and how long would it take until age overtook her own skin-and-bone vessel of mortality.

"Wherever I get settled, you know my door's always open."

"Well."

"You've helped me so much."

"Well now I don't see as how I've done much, really."

"You'll never know," Barbara said, giving Lily's skeletal hand a brief squeeze, "just how much you have."

The phone rang out loud from the desk. It was the front desk putting a call through from Kenny.

"Barbara, I'm glad I caught you in," his voice was laced with concern.

"What's up?"

"I just ran into one of your mom's Bridge friends. One of *our* Bridge friends, Louisa."

"Right."

"She told me the funeral is tomorrow."

"Tomorrow?"

"Seems the priest made an exception to the no funeral masses on Sunday rule."

"At the request of Roger, no doubt," Barbara made a face. "No doubt so he can clear out and be back in time for corporate America on Monday."

"I suspect you're not far off the mark."

Her shoulders slumped. A luxury bed with a top-line mattress all at once just another bed trafficked by the public. The framed art on the walls she'd admired suddenly cheap imitations. The freshly painted walls had cracks and imperfections, the fancy lye soap melted to mud, the kindly old travelling companion became a pathetically naïve woman who knew very little of the world.

"That son of a bitch," Barbara squeezed her eyes shut, "always seems to know just how to spoil a good time."

*

The ladies sat opposite each other in the living room, Peggy's gin and tonic and Marge's glass of Merlot on the coffee table between them.

"I wonder if I've just been miserable for years," Marge stared off into space with a furrowed brow.

"Never too late to wake up."

"Life is short and I want at least a stab at happiness."

"Well now you're talking my language." Peggy took a slug of her drink. "I might have my own day in the sun. Just not anytime soon."

"God bless you for what you're doing Peggy Beamish."

"Don't think I have much choice in the matter."

"At least," said Marge, "he won't be fooling around with any ladies."

"Oh, don't underestimate him." Peggy rolled her eyes.

A rapping knock at the door—they looked perplexedly at one another. Peggy got up and stood sideways in front of the door, her hand resting on the doorknob, though it was unlocked. Who is it, she said to the door.

"It's me, Kenny. Kenny *Fitzroy*."

"Speaking of having responsibilities foisted on you," Peggy pulled the door open wide. "It's our friend Kenny. Kenny *Fitzroy*," she echoed. "As if I know any other guy who calls himself Kenny around here." She made a grand sweeping gesture. "C'mon in, ya big galoot."

Kenny tamped his feet on the mat and Marge patted the seat cushion next to her on the couch. Peggy went to fetch a wine glass, calling out over the sound of cabinets opening and shutting. "Ya got about half an hour, cause these two old ladies are getting ready to wind down and go to bed. Kind of a long day."

Peggy brought a glass and Marge poured from the open bottle.

"Right," said Kenny, situating himself next to Marge on the sofa and looking across at Peggy. "How are you coming along?"

"Me? I'm a work in progress honey. Now this one…" Peggy jerked a thumb at Marge. "Better watch out Sunnyville. Gonna be a real maneater. Marge the maneater."

"Oh please," Marge waved a hand dismissively, heaving a sigh. "I just want some time to myself."

"When's he getting out of Dodge?" Kenny asked.

"I want to give him time to pack. It'd only be fair."

"You can stay at my place," Kenny said. "I'm going to drive down to my aunt's place in Punta Gorda next week. Survey the damage. You can stay at my place while I'm gone."

Peggy rolled her eyes and glanced over at Marge. "You'll have to clean it first. It's a mess."

"*Uh-uh*," Kenny said with a measure of indignation.

"A goddammed mess." Peggy looked from him over to Marge, tapped the arm of her cushioned chair. "You're good here til Wednesday anyway. My daughter and both my sons are coming down with their kids. Hopefully your Ted'll be gone by then."

"Well," said Kenny, "anyone's always welcome to stay at my house." He cleared his throat and shot Peggy a look of mock disdain. "If they don't mind the clutter, that is."

"That's awfully kind of you Kenny," Marge said as Peggy jiggled her glass and gazed at some medium distance. The three of them sat wordlessly a good while.

"Why are you flying south anyway, silly bird?" said Peggy. "I thought you were going north to take care of business."

Kenny took a sip of wine and glanced surreptitiously at Marge.

"I haven't told her yet," Marge said.

Peggy's eyes darted between her two guests. "Told me *what*?"

Marge cocked an eyebrow at Kenny and he cleared his throat.

"It seems," he said. "It seems there's been a miscarriage."

"Oh dear," said Peggy.

Kenny started to speak, but couldn't find the words.

“Well I can’t say I’m real surprised,” said Peggy, “After all, she’s like what, late forties?”

Her nonchalance, in contrast to Marge’s emotional and sympathetic response, was not lost on Kenny. He glanced over at Peggy as if to register his shock. But she did not meet his eyes, staring at some middle distance. Only the hum of the central air, there seemed to be no words appropriate for any of them to break the silence with.

“Hey everybody.” Peggy said at last, tipping her glass at the others, “As bad as things might go, ain’t life a little easier when you have friends?”

“Sure can make a world of difference,” said Kenny, raising his glass.

Marge excused herself. In the guest bathroom, she sat upon the edge of the tub wringing her hands while taking in a space not much bigger than a closet—the embroidered decorative towels, the matching rug, the framed print of a playful beach scene on the wall next to the sink, the seashell soap dispenser. Everything so run-of-the-mill and yet so suddenly so alien, as if her lens had shifted and she saw the simple things in a completely different manner, like a whole different person occupied her body. In just one week. She lowered her head to her hands with a heavy sigh and shuddered. There were no tears to summon and, try as she might, none could be forced.

# 10

The stroke of midnight, ushering in Sunday August 15th 2004. The day's place in many cultures as a day of worship has its origins in the first god ever to be worshipped, the Sun itself. The name of Sunday is derived from Old English *Sunnandæg* and Middle English *Sunnenday*, originally a translation of Latin *diēs sōlis* "Sun's day". A number of popular songs in Western culture feature Sunday, sometimes as a gloomy day for hangovers and melancholy, *Sunday Morning Coming Down*—sometimes a more peaceful respite, *Pleasant Valley Sunday*. The name of Monday is derived from the Old English *Mōnandæg* and Middle English *Monenday*, originally a translation of Latin *dies lunae* "day of the Moon". Soon the cosmos ushers in a New Moon and above the heads of those who lay asleep in Sunnyville, a cloudless sky dotted with stars for them to dream under.

In the Andover section of Sunny Glen Palms, in the darkness of a moonless sky, night owl Kenny Fitzroy is ensconced in peaceful slumbers. The dream folded into his nocturnal downtime runs beneath hair thinning with the onset of old age. There, in the dream, a hairless babe. It speaks to him, strangely, in the manner an adult would. What is the little tike saying? Something about the Stones? He strains to listen. His son—or daughter, he cannot distinguish—is speaking at great length and with the rapid pace of enthusiasm about the influence of country music on the Stones in that very drug-heavy era of the seventies. The proud father looks on. Somewhere in the middle of this oratory, he is tugged from this otherworld. His bedroom is pitch black. His eyes cannot sufficiently accustom themselves to the dark to discern the long black curtains in front of the lone single-pane window. He coughs up phlegm. Exhaustion overtakes him and he melts into the black canvas of his bedroom. He dreams again. He's mowing the grass in the yard of one of those new builds on Masterpiece Drive. Only it isn't Sunnyville. He isn't sure where it is but it really doesn't matter. He cuts the mower. Barbara is at his side with a glass of lemonade, or is it Kool Aid? He downs it in one gulp. He's anxious to finish cutting the enormous yard, because there's something else to attend to or is it… yes, there it is the blue van, no commercial logo, no identifying mark of any kind. Just a plain blue van loaded with workers in plain blue jumpsuits. They are there to pick him up for distasteful work he detests. He hasn't yet finished the front yard and knee-high grass looms in the backyard. When he wakes up this time, he throws his legs over the side of the bed, sits up and carefully treads a memorized path to the bedroom door, groping about for the doorknob. He opens it to a living room lit with the bluish gray hues of predawn. He opens the fridge, and draws a glass of filtered water from the pitcher. From the back porch he gazes out upon a Sunny Glen Boulevard undisturbed by traffic, its streetlights beginning to dim with the dawning of a new day, in the new Moon.

Miles away under a new Moon, Barbara Thunderclap lays curled up in a ball in cozy cotton luxury sheets. Her dream carries her into uncharted territory. She pulls into the familiar driveway of her mother's house on Fairway Drive. Only this time her knock on the door is answered. The door cracks open and there is her mother, beaming down at her from one step above. Her mouth moves and Barbara can't hear a word through the glass, but her invisible eyes of dream world can read her mother's lips. The door opens and her mother makes a broad sweeping gesture of invitation. When she steps up and over the threshold, she is in the living room of her youth, that of knotty pine, a wooden frame television with legs, a ships wheel magazine holder with a table top on which sits dad's pipe holder, walls lined with shelves of fine china trinkets. Her and her mother pass through the room as if it were a replica in a museum, they leave that room for the den on Fairway Drive in Sunnyville. Her mother is alive this time. She begins drawing away from a deeper dream state and into that waking state of semi-consciousness. Her mother gathers her up into her arms and she begins to weep through imaginary eyes. Barbara realizes she is directing the end of the dream, guiding it along to her desired ending. I'm so happy, her mother says. So happy you're here. When she fully awakens, her body her eyes are wet with tears and she wipes at them. Not far away from her, in the dark, Lily snores. Comforted by the fact that someone is nearby, she drifts back to sleep. She dreams again, this time of mountains.

Across from her on the other queen bed, Lily Westfall lays her head on a fluffy feather-down pillow, sunk in a sumptuous sleep. The blurriness of her waking sight does not present in the world that lay under a full head of white hair. She can see with the utmost clarity from her back porch in Sunnyville the scene of children playing. That little patch of grass that bordered a golf course now a great big backyard overrun by youth. Children run about everywhere, exuberant, licking at ice creams, flying kites, kicking rubber balls back and forth. Some of them stop by her screened in back porch for a glass of lemonade and take their turn at cards. She is playing a hand now, on a perfect summer day with a breeze. If it were up to her, she would never wake up from the dream.

On one of the two single beds in the Beamish's guestroom, Marge Cumberbatch lays sound asleep under the spell of Peggy Beamish's valium, her dreams uninterrupted by anxious thoughts for the first time in a good while. Beneath brown hair gathered in an updo, between those diminutive ears, she sees without the use of her eyes. She is sat behind the driver of one of those yellow and black school buses with green linoleum-upholstered seats, some torn by wear or vandalism, stringy white threads draped along like strands of hair. She sees the driver, a man she knows but does not know, a sense of recognition with an inability to attach a name to the face. She has no idea where they are going, but it is somehow of no consequence. From behind her, the sound of kids' chatter. A man taps her on the shoulder and she recognizes him at once, Bobby Whitmarsh. Her first love, her high school sweetheart. He's an older version of himself but by the peculiar and distinctive baby blue eyes she knows it's him. He says he's been on the bus for a long time and when is their stop? When is she getting off, he wants to know. While gazing deeply into those familiar eyes, she stirs from her sleep and the dream, rolls onto her back, the digital clock on the nightstand between the beds is a blur without her glasses but the room has gone from darkness to dimness and she guesses dawn. She dismisses the clock and the time, closing her eyes and rolling again onto her side and into another dream. She is standing inside their house on Tammany Drive. It is daytime, but the house is dark and there is the distant rumble of thunder. Everything is in disarray. She's stepping along the exposed floor joists in the kitchen area with the deliberation of an acrobat on a high wire. The floor has been taken up down to the joists in every corner of the house. From beyond the door, in the garage, she can hear her husband weeping like a child.

Under the same roof, Peggy Beamish lays on her back lightly snoring. Underneath blond-going-to-gray hair rolled up in curlers, the curtains of consciousness drawn closed, a deep sleep. She snaps awake. In her mind she creates a bright blue sky over red rock mountains on the other side of an enormous windshield. The easy glide of the enormous RV, the ease with which it takes the bumps in the road, as if riding waves. She is alone. There is no driver, somehow the enormous vehicle drives itself. She knows her destination, has never felt so entirely unbounded. She has left Sunnyville, enroute to a desert too exotic and enchanting to be attached to a particular state. She glances over her shoulder at the interior of her home on wheels. A cute little kitchen area with a seventies country motif, trinkets and an old-fashioned percolator. Beyond that, a living room area with an art deco boomerang coffee table, a queen-sized bed. She will park where there are no nearby neighbors or neighborhood associations. Call it Peggy's Palace. She enters a dream state and spots an outpost that is her destination from the two-lane highway. She points it out. But to who? The self-driven bus? She wakes up pondering, sweating. Wipes her brow, removes the curlers, turns onto her side. And just like that she is swept into another dream.

*

They were on the road at the crack of dawn, after having hustled their luggage as quietly as possible across the plush carpet in the resort's lobby, where not a soul had yet stirred. They stopped for coffee and gasoline. The roads were clear of traffic until Lakeland, where a massive oak had fallen and blocked the Interstate, forcing them to a lengthy detour through the swampy backwater Florida of old. Houses on stilts with paint peeling, fields of wild reeds and rushes with no purpose other than to bay in the wind, weathered shacks gone to ruin. Their stomachs grumbled and they pined after a full breakfast at Denny's in Sunnyville, if they could hold out that long. When they returned to the highway, Barbara gunned the car and Lily flung her hands onto the dashboard and braced herself against the seat with a bit of exaggeration. They spoke little, having attained that level of friendship where mutual silence is not awkward.

The highway sign for Sunnyville on I-75 had been toppled by the wind and Barbara almost missed the exit, executing a hairpin turn that had Lily bracing herself more determinedly against her seat. The tires squealed and Barbara eased the brakes a little, a rush of fear coming over her. The car stabilized and they rolled to a stoplight with collective sighs of relief.

The parking lot at Denny's was full. Inside they were put on a waiting list. A steady clientele coming and going from church, or forgoing church on the heels of a hurricane. Storm survivors with the same idea, thought Barbara, let's treat ourselves to something after all that stress, a respite for some before tackling clean-up, insurance claims adjustors, cancelled plans. She and Lily wondered aloud about their own houses. The aroma of fresh-brewed coffee mingled with the savory scent of sizzling bacon from the kitchen, where the short order cooks worked feverishly to keep up with growing demand. They were guided over to a booth. With much eagerness they took laminated tri-fold menus from a pimply teenager who left to fetch their coffees. Among the throng of fresh arrivals, Barbara spied none other than Kenny Fitzroy—jittery, eyes darting about a dining room already filled to capacity, not even an empty stool over at the counter. His face brightened when she motioned him over and slid over the bench to make room for him.

Kenny was not long out of bed, he'd woken much in the spirit of the clientele at Denny's in Sunnyville. The usual spartan oatmeal and fruit routine just wouldn't do today and so off he went in Mom's Dodge Dart outside the gate. The Sunnyville Café had a long wait and he was crestfallen to discover the same scene at Denny's—a franchise restaurant he assumed had an operations model to avoid long waits and foregone sales. Delighted all-the-more at the sight of one of the few people he knew in Sunnyville, someone he'd recently spoken to over the telephone, someone nearer his age and ideology. Barbara and Lily made room for him while he basked in his good fortune. Smiles and condolences. Two deaths, one with a more practical and immediate urgency.

"So glad I found you," Kenny said, accepting the menu from Lily. "I have news about Alice's funeral." He cleared his throat. "Seems your brother got a hold of the monsignor and changed the arrangements. They moved the time up on the funeral Mass at Our Lady of Lourdes. Now two o'clock."

The waiter returned and took their orders, scooping up their menus. After he shuffled off, Barbara replaced her polite smile with a frown. "It will be such a small gathering. I don't know if I can stand it. With him."

"Well," said Lily, reaching a hand across the booth to pat Barbara's. "That's where we come in."

"Damn straight." Kenny nodded with affected bravado. "I've faced your brother down once. Not afraid to do it again."

When their orders came they ate in silence a good while, and now it was Kenny's turn to reflect on the comfort of silence among friends who had overcome the formality of obligatory pleasantries, feeling compelled to speak at every turn. A calm sea bereft of word-storms. Uncharted waters for Kenny Fitzroy. They finished and Lily picked up the tab amid Barbara's protestations.

"It's your mother's funeral day and let's just leave it at that," she tsked. "Goodness sakes."

No sooner had Kenny bade them goodbye out in the parking lot than Frank Alsatian rolled up in his Ford Explorer. Kenny watched him park and then dart to the passenger side to guide his wife Libby safely down to the blacktop. Kenny guessed Frank had picked up his breakfast date from the assisted living place he'd admitted her into months ago when dementia had her wandering away on a regular basis from their house on Tammany Drive.

Kenny felt compelled to assist Frank, to at least announce himself to a former golf partner who'd sent him packing after a blowup over politics, fucking politics, in the heat of passion arguing over that goddamn war in the Middle East. He wanted to assure Frank there were no hard feelings on his part, wanted to tell Frank that his cushy life in his Mom's inherited home and auto had been penetrated with the gravest and most sacred responsibility that could be thrust on a man and may have propelled him a little closer to the world Frank inhabited—one of parental and spousal obligations. He wanted to tell Frank. He wanted to tell Frank that he might make himself available to help out with Libby, because he'd been sprung from duties of his own he'd come to accept only to find himself relieved of those duties. He wanted to tell Frank that he was in fact a changed man but that would not necessarily mean his fundamental principles and ideals had changed along with these more primal and essential attributes. He'd quelled this compulsion until Frank and Libby started up the steps for the door. Just like that, Kenny sprinted and arrived in time to open the door for them. Frank's attention went from navigating the steps to the sight of the young man he'd run off with his unique brand of belligerence. Kenny smiled and said I hope you guys didn't have any damage, from the storm. Frank said they were just fine, thanks. Kenny held the door for Libby and then nodded at her back. Let me know if you need anything, he said to Frank. Frank gave a nod with a wan smile and returned his attention to a wife with irregular and unpredictable behavioral responses joining a throng of people. Kenny sensed no more goodwill than bad from his former golf partner, it somehow didn't matter one way or the other. He was leaving Denny's after a sumptuous meal with new friends and he was on this way to the hospital to meet more new friends. He climbed back into the Dodge Dart and drove like an old lady, staying in the right lane, a leisurely cruising speed of thirty-five miles per hour.

At the hospital the parking lot was fuller than he'd expected. The walk, he thought, would do him good. He reached Mike Beamish's room in the ICU and did a double take, rechecking the room number lest his own eyes betray him. The room was empty of all but furniture and equipment, the bed made up neatly, curtain drawn. He turned on his heels and approached the nurse's station.

"Beamish?" he said and a young man behind the tall desk looked up from his paperwork.

"He's been moved to the regular ward. Let me see. Room 777. Take the elevator in the West Wing to the top floor."

Kenny formally saluted the nurse and started down the hallway, nearly colliding with Gerry Hagoden.

"Hey old pal," said Gerry. "Watcha doin?"

"Here to see Mike Beamish. You too?"

Gerry looked perplexed. "I didn't know he was in here. He goes to Our Lady of Lourdes, doesn't he?"

Kenny nodded.

"Well," said Gerry, "I'll follow you and say hello. Nah, it's Shirley's sister Alma. Some kind of lady thing."

"Lady thing?"

"Need-to-know basis. I just show up with flowers."

"Why are they keeping it a secret?"

Gerry shrugged and dropped his jaw, dubious. "Who knows. I just do what I'm told."

Kenny started for the West Wing and the elevator with Gerry in tow.

"Too hot for golf," said Gerry. "But let's hit the links when it starts to cool down a little, waddya say?"

"Sure."

"How's that lady friend of yours?"

"She's *Mrs.* Beamish."

"Ooooh," Gerry scratched his chin. "She might want to join us, once Mike is up and at em. He's a golfer too."

"Any good?"

"I dunno. I had him queued up to play. Like I said, too hot hot hot."

"Well anyway," said Kenny, pushing the button at the elevator, "I don't think we can count him in. Pretty bad stroke."

"Dear Jesus," Gerry frowned.

Kenny punched the button again, and then once more. "Happened the night of the storm. She just walked in and there he was. On the floor."

"Oh God."

In Room 777, they found Peggy and Marge arranging things—Peggy stuffing clothes in a two-drawer bureau, Marge fussing with a Styrofoam cup and an assortment of other items on the bedside swivel tray.

Gerry was uncomfortable from the moment he entered the room—he immediately began checking his watch. He introduced himself to the ladies as one of Mike's fellow parishioners at Our Lady of Lourdes. Then he spoke to his fellow parishioner, whose adjustable bed had him upright with the bed linens drawn up to his belly and a blue-checkered hospital gown. His churchmate had only vague utterances, slurred whisper words by way of response. The eager and cherubic face he'd encountered in the hot tub just a few days ago suddenly devoid of expression, as if his face had frozen.

Kenny walked out into the hospital corridor with Gerry, flanked him all the way to the elevator. Gerry hurried his steps and said it was time for him to get to church.

"Hey Gerry," Kenny said when they reached the elevator, "there's a funeral at your church this afternoon. "If you don't mind hanging around. Kind of last minute, crazy week with the storm and all—"

"Who?" Gerry winced, as if priming his face for bad news.

"Alice Thunderclap?"

Recognition shone on Gerry's face. "Alice?"

Kenny nodded solemnly.

"Shirley's bridge partner?"

"Yep, that's right."

"She was a peach," Gerry stared off into some near distance. "Shirley couldn't say enough good things about her. And that's… highly unusual."

The elevator dinged. Gerry gave Kenny's rib a playful jab, squeezed his elbow. "I'll tell Shirley. Thanks for the heads-up kiddo."

Kenny walked a slower pace back to Room 777, unable to shake from his mind the image of shell-shocked Gerry Hagoden. Was it just too much at once? Libby lost to dementia, Mike Beamish lost to something as random as a stroke, Alice Thunderclap just lost *period*? Was it just too much death at once? Would anyone ever get used to the sting of losing somebody on a regular basis? Was it something that was beginning to catch up with Gerry Hagoden? Was it something he could just walk off? Bumping a kneecap, or stubbing a toe was one thing, but what about the bruising of loss? Was it something you could just walk off?

Marge and Peggy were speaking in low tones outside Mikes room. A newly-arrived nurse was inside checking his vitals. Kenny approached and matched their solemn voices, announcing Alice Thunderclap's expedited funeral.

"That's just a few hours from now," Marge gasped.

Kenny pursed his lips and nodded. "They made it back in time. I just had breakfast with them at Denny's."

"Well," Marge jiggled her keys. "I'm gonna be there. I need to run by the house and get ready." In the wake of speaking her words, the prospect of fetching any of her belongings from the house made her face cloud over, the thought mirrored by the dubious expressions of her confidantes. She brought a hand to her forehead, squeezing her eyes shut.

"Why don't you just doll up at my place?" Peggy said. "Makeup and wardrobe. Nobody around to bother you. You don't want him finding out about the funeral anyway."

Marge puffed her lips. "I'll just say I'm collecting a few of my things."

"I have a lot of dresses to choose from. You know, lose weight gain weight, all over the place. I've been meaning to drop by Goodwill and keep forgetting. Or procrastinating, I don't know which."

"That's alright Peggy. I've already borrowed enough of your clothes." She hugged at Peggy, then gave Kenny a sideways hug and called over her back to them. "See you at two."

Trundling along in the golf cart, approaching Our Lady of Lourdes in the designated lane, she glanced at the traffic entering the church parking lot and prayed her husband wouldn't spot her because she was sure he'd be bound and determined to make morning Mass. At the thought of it, she made a hard left, bringing the golf cart into a thicket of bougainvillea so as to provide her a hidden vantage point from which to screen the incoming cars. When at last their car turned up and her husband and son clambered out, she determined to make it home pronto, now that the coast was clear.

At the house she went into a frenzy, rifling through her wardrobe closet for, among everything else, a good funeral outfit. At the sink in the master bathroom, gathering up and shoveling toiletries into a suitcase. In the driveway, stacking a suitcase and an assortment of dresses and blouses at the back of the golf cart. An emergency paramedic vehicle ambled down Tammany Drive, sirens off. She drew the cart out of the driveway with less of the finality she'd felt to her core yesterday, it was as if she were returning to the scene of the crime. She steered the cart to Lily Westfall's.

"Well," she shrugged when Barbara appeared at the door. "Looks like we're both refugees. For a little while anyway."

"Lily's been so nice, letting me stay here."

"Peggy's opened her door to me."

"Strange to be talking about people," Barbara shook her head, "along with you and Kenny, I-I never even met until just about a week ago."

"Well, we sure have *that* in common. Anyway," a wan smile came over Marge's face, "I'm going to your mother's funeral. Peggy told me to tell you that you better be there."

"I'm going over to the hospital to visit. Before the funeral."

"Come sit down," Lily's called from the kitchen. "Have lunch with us. I'm afraid it's just cold cuts and chips." She filled their glasses with purified water from a pitcher. "Barbara's told me all about poor Kenny."

"Yeah," Marge puffed out her cheeks. "I guess when it rains it pours. It's probably for the best anyway. I mean, he hardly knew her."

"Now why would he go ahead and do a thing like that?" Lily frowned.

"Huh?" Barbara and Marge said in unison, Marge thinking how could Lily puzzle over the oldest primal urge in all the animal world and Barbara thinking just how generationally separated she and Lily were after all. They finished their sandwiches and chips. Barbara passed on dessert, leaving Lily and Marge to tea and grocery-store key lime pie.

In the driveway, her car wouldn't turn over. She gave it a few seconds and still nothing. She brought her head to her hands. When she'd collected herself, she withdrew the keys from the ignition and returned to the house through the garage.

"Never happened before," she said to the ladies when she entered the kitchen. "Guess there's a first time for everything, and it may as well be now on top of everything else. Like Marge said, when it rains it pours."

Lily shrugged. "Thank goodness we didn't try and drive it all the way to Disneyland."

"Disney *World*," Barbara corrected.

"Let's try and give you a jump," Marge said, rising from her chair.

"I have cables in the garage," said Lily, "but I wouldn't know the first thing about how to connect them."

"Let's see if I can remember," said Barbara.

Lily backed her car out of the garage and drew it up next to Barbara's. With both hoods raised, they began to tinker. Marge had the jumper cables, positive claw in one hand, negative in the other.

"I'm afraid we'll just blow everything to smithereens," she said. "Does anyone even have the faintest idea…" her voice trailed off as both Lily and Barbara turned their attention over her shoulder to Ed Wackbender, the wayward next-door neighbor, standing behind her in the wet grass in a pair of orthopedic shoes, compression socks, a stained polo shirt, khaki shorts.

"Oh shit," Lily murmured, covering her mouth as if to avoid another expletive escaping. "Hi Ed!"

In all the excitement she'd forgotten to check on him. Now here he was checking on her, shuffling towards them. *Watcha tryin to do*, he wanted to know.

Barbara forced a smile. "Car won't start."

"Here, let me see those," he said and Marge handed over the reins to a man who's mind, Lily knew, was slipping—who's cylinders weren't firing in the right order, who's pistons were rusty.

"Oh shit," she murmured.

Ed apparently didn't hear or at least wasn't paying attention. He was bent over Lily's car attaching the cable clamps to the battery terminals, instinctively running the clamps at the other end to the other car. As he attached the last clamp his face clouded over.

"I think you start the car that… works first," said Barbara said without much conviction to Marge, nodding at Lily's car.

Marge hopped in and cranked the ignition.

Ed held up his hand to Barbara. "Give it a few minutes."

Everyone watched Ed to give the sign, and here he placed a free hand in his shorts unselfconsciously to scratch at his balls. His lady company all averted their gazes—Lily and Marge coughing politely, Barbara bringing a hand to her mouth to suppress a laugh.

Barbara cranked the ignition, the engine whinnied, didn't catch. She tried again and again but each time the car failed to come alive.

"Oh for heaven's sake, take my car," said Lily.

"That's right," Marge said. "Lily can come with me in the golf cart."

"Where's everybody going," Ed asked with a boyish innocence that gave Barbara cause to stifle a laugh again, thinking to herself they may as well have been a bunch of neighborhood kids out playing in the yard.

"Funeral," Marge said matter-of-factly.

"Oh," Ed rubbed ruminatively at a whiskered chin. "Nobody I know, I hope."

The ladies exchanged glances. Marge said, "I don't think so," nodded over at Barbara. "This young lady's mother. Alice Thunderclap."

Ed's face was blank.

"She lives up the street," Marge continued. "Well, she *used to* anyway. Meet your new neighbor." She nodded once again at Barbara.

Barbara went to offer a hand in greeting, then withdrew it immediately upon recalling where the odd man had just removed his own from.

"Well, did you make it through the hurricane alright Ed?" Lily asked, wondering how her neighbor made it through life, from the daily routines like paying bills and feeding himself to the major decisions that present on a regular basis. He was her neighbor from the get-go and she'd hardly seen anyone coming or going next door.

"No leaks," Ed's face suddenly brightened.

Marge and Lily responded simultaneously and while Marge said *That's nice*, Lily said *Let me know if you need anything,* words that she'd never spoken to her neighbor in any of their infrequent encounters outside in their yards.

Barbara said, "I must be on my way if I'm going to make my mother's funeral. I think I still have time to stop by the hospital and see Peggy. I somehow want to beat my brother to the church."

Marge squeezed Barbara's elbow. "Don't walk into that church alone. Peggy'll go with you. We'll gather in the parking lot. Half an hour before."

Barbara folded into Marge's arms and Marge clapped her on the back. "See you there."

At the hospital, Barbara parked Lily's car and walked hastily through the double doors and over to the receptionist's counter. The elevator took what seemed an eternity and when it came to a stop on the seventh floor, she charged out of it, nearly colliding with a maid's cart. She gave a polite grimace in apology and sprinted down the polished floor. Peggy threw her arms wide open in greeting. She'd just stepped outside of Mike's room while just beyond the door the nurse went about protocol.

Peggy pulled from the embrace and squeezed Barbara's elbows. "You wanna get a cup of coffee?"

"I don't know if I have time."

"Oh nonsense. We'll get you to the church on time. Let me get my bag. We can take my car. Sunnyville Café is in our sights."

The Café was bustling, immediately upon opening the door the aroma of breakfast wafted from the kitchen. There was a table near the wall and Peggy rushed to claim it while a waitress was wiping it down and gathering dirty dishes.

"I'm eating light," said Barbara.

"I heard you already had your recommended daily allowance of greasy spoon," Peggy smirked, grabbing the tri-fold menu, perusing it. "Guess I'll do all the eating for us."

After they'd placed their orders and handed over the menus to a chummy and playfully sarcastic waitress, Barbara leaned in.

"So tell me. How are you holding up?"

"Oh you know," Peggy puffed her cheeks. "One day at a time I guess. Like the last fifty years."

"Well," Barbara shrugged. "Guess there won't be a fiftieth wedding anniversary bash after all."

"Not anytime soon."

"And your other plans?"

"The great escape?" Peggy shrugged, unfolding a paper napkin and arranging it in her lap. "I wouldn't last a day without remorse eating me alive."

"I understand."

"You never had kids, did you?"

"No. At least not yet."

"Let me tell ya, every time I think about getting outta dodge I think of the kids."

"Even though they're grown?"

"I know, it's weird, isn't it? Having children is," she sighed, "a kind of trap. But a delightful trap at that."

"The older I get, the more I realize it's all about duality. Everything in life is duality."

"Now you're waxing philosophical," Peggy pointed a fork at Barbara. "Don't go blowing my mind."

"Seriously. I mean everything has two sides. I was thinking about it while we were trying to bring my car to life this morning. Electricity."

"Positive and negative, you mean?"

"Light and dark. Good and evil. Black and white. Male and female. Every single thought, argument, opinion in imbued with duality."

"You young people have entirely too much time on your hands."

"Seriously though. My brother may appear to be superior in a certain context. But put us in a different context and he's suddenly inferior."

"Explain," said Peggy, staring at her plate, taking a bite of sausage.

"Let's say the monetary system crashed tomorrow and money became meaningless. Just think of the people who couldn't deal with it, who would have a meltdown." Barbara said. "I always think of Roger. He would be a basket case."

"So let me get this straight," said Peggy. "You're a basket case so long as there's a functioning monetary system, he's a basket case if there isn't."

"Like I said," Barbara shrugged, waved her toast at Peggy. "Duality."

After the waitress dropped their tab on the table, Peggy started fishing around her pocketbook for her purse. Barbara tapped the table in protest, thinking how stubborn in their generosity this generation ahead of her can be. But she didn't let Peggy off the hook, leaving a twenty and a few singles, while telling Peggy to put her card away.

Dark clouds loomed when they returned to the parking lot but no rain fell from the sky. They clambered into Lily's car for the short drive to the church, just a few blocks away. Kenny had arrived ahead of them in his mother's Dodge Dart and Barbara pulled up in the spot next to him. The driver's side door was flung open and they could see only his feet. He was rummaging around in the glove box, under floormats, the passenger seat.

"Whatcha looking for?" asked Peggy.

"I bought a card," he said evenly.

"What kind of card?" she asked, sauntering over.

"A card for Barbara. A condolence card."

"You mean a sympathy card."

"Alright. A sympathy card." He was getting annoyed. It was hot and humid and the old car's air conditioning system was problematic. He'd made a point to stop by the dollar store on his way back from breakfast. He hadn't had occasion to buy a greeting card for anyone for as long as he could remember. He had deliberated over a wide selection of cards. He'd invested time and thought into the words he'd scrawled neatly in the inside left panel, hemmed and hawed over signing the card with the salutation *My dear friend Barbara*, and the word *Love* preceding his name in the signature.

"Hey," Peggy lowered her voice, hunching over hands on knees like a home-plate umpire, gently placing a hand on his shoulder, "Why don't you go fishing for it later?" She cocked an eyebrow over toward Barbara. "She needs all the moral support she can get right now. Strength in numbers."

At the sound Peggy's voice, accompanied by a gentle and reassuring touch, his foul mood dissipated. There was serious business at hand and he was being summoned by a member of the team.

The rest of the team had assembled themselves on the granite church steps. There was Lily and Marge. Beside Gerry Hagoden stood his wife Shirley, fussing with his necktie, patting the collar of his starch white short-sleeve dress shirt. They must have told Tommy and Debbie D'Antonio, who both loomed in the background with an old crone leaning on a cane. Kenny did a doubletake at the sight of Flora Wheeler, at one-hundred years of age Sunnyville's oldest resident. He knew this because he'd attended her big bash last winter at the North Club. He was happy to see she'd survived the hurricane. Probably wasn't a single act of nature could bring her down, he thought. He was glad to see they'd all survived the hurricane. It was as if the mighty heavens had erased the tablet of his life and left him with a new parchment on which to write. He felt all at once light and untethered, and immediately recriminated himself at such a feeling of folly at a funeral.

Barbara Thunderclap, on the other hand, was feeling anything but cheerful at the prospect of bringing her new team to flaunt in front of her brother, no matter how much of a jerk he'd developed into over the years. Try as she might, she couldn't allow resentment at his having packed his rude, condescending and soulless behavior to take along to sunny Florida. It was, in fact, not the sunny Florida she'd stumbled into just a little over a week ago. She tried to conjure up the resentment she'd felt at the news that he had streamlined the funeral so as not to allow her and other family members to attend. She wondered what he knew about the contents of the will, a copy of which was retained by her mother's attorney in Tampa.

They huddled in the vestibule, like a pregame. To honor the passing of a devoutly religious Catholic, Barbara's friends gathered around her, a small congregation of the mostly non-religious. The D'Antonios were the venerable Flora Wheeler's ride today and soon they introduced themselves, Tommy's usual lighthearted and jovial demeanor usurped by one more grave and solemn. Flora motioned Barbara over to a bench beside the wall of the vestibule. Setting her old hickory cane against the bench, waving off an attempt to assist her, she took Barbara's hand in hers and gazed directly into her eyes.

"I met your mother years ago, in the crafts room. Sweet lady. Had lunch with her more than once. Dinner. At her house, at my house. Hung around the pool together when I was still hanging around the pool. Before I looked so silly in bathing suit. Before I had to take the sun in doses."

Barbara gave a start.

"Anyway," Flora batted a hand at the air, "she talked a lot. About her family. Mentioned mine a time or two. We'd get to being like two hens. She mentioned you."

"I guess you've formed a pretty dismal opinion."

"Quite the contrary." Flora gave a wistful smile. "Fancy expression I learned from my great-great-grandchild. *Quite the contrary*. Lord, just listen to fancy Flora." She rolled her eyes and her face brightened, she seemed to lose her wrinkles by half. "Anyway, your mother was very fond of you."

"I should have called her more often."

"Yes, you should have."

Barbara's glance dropped to the tiled floor. Lily squeezed her elbow.

"Now don't take that the wrong way child. I only mean your mother had a hard upbringing, her folks drank too much and loved too little."

"She never talked much about her childhood."

"For good reason."

"I wanted to make amends. That's why I came here."

"I know. She told me you were coming. She wanted so badly to clear the air with you."

Barbara sniffled, wiping at her eyes with the sleeve of her blouse. Flora patted her knee, said, "We hadn't spoken much lately. Probably not since my birthday bash in January. And then only a few words, you know, like you do at such things."

"She was never really one for parties." Barbara smiled faintly.

"Well, she sure turned up for mine. Anyway, she rang me last week," Flora continued. "Asked if she could stop by. Of course, I said. Come whenever you want I said to her, I'm not goin anywhere anytime soon."

The team was shuffling their feet, glancing at watches, an unspoken concurrence not to breach the double doors to the church's innards until they might accompany Barbara. It was getting close to two o'clock.

"She said she had been cleaning the house to a sparkle, said she had changed her will. She said you told her you were going to those meetings, you know the ones for—"

"Addicts. Alcoholics."

"Anyway, she wanted to make amends with you too. She was cleaning the place, readying it for your visit. I know how much it meant to her. To have you here. And now Lily tells me you might be staying on for good."

"You know Lily?"

"Not too good. I met her and her sister at the pool a few times after she moved here."

"Wow, it's such a large community. You seem to know everybody."

Flora wiggled her head. "I don't get out much anymore. Lily told me she doesn't get out as much as she ought to. But listen to me. Your mother had faith that this time your turnaround would stick. She wanted to offer you whatever you needed to help."

"She had before. My brother and her resented—"

Flora waved a hand dismissively. "All that's in the past, child." She patted Barbara's hand. "I think this place… Sunnyville. I think it's the right place for you to keep away from the temptations." A smile broke out on Flora's wizened face. "If you steer clear of Pub Night, at any rate."

Barbara heaved a sigh.

"Look honey, what've you got to lose? Place worked a charm on my great-great-granddaughter. Her momma, the schools I guess, had her on all these darned mood pills. She was here just a week and stopped them completely. A month down here was all she needed to start feeling better."

"But—"

"Listen, what have you got to lose?"

"I just… thank you…"

"Flora," said Flora, patting Barbara's hand, then squeezing it in her bony fingers, repeating for emphasis. "*What have you got to lose*?"

"You're right," Barbara nodded.

"Anyway, it'll add years to your life. You'll be good for Lily. You ran across her for a reason. If there's one thing I've learned in all my years it's that folks need each other, even if just for a little time."

"Can I ask you something?"

"Sure."

"How do you get your eyes to sparkle like that?"

"Genes, young lady. It's all in the genes."

"Thank you. For talking to me. I mean it, I needed to hear this."

"I'm just an old messenger."

Barbara glanced around the vestibule at the small group assembled on short notice in her mother's honor. Marge whispering earnestly at Peggy, Peggy nodding along with a patent self-assurance, Kenny fidgeting and cracking his knuckles, the D'Antonios standing stiffly as if at attention, Shirley Hagoden snapping her gum and punching Gerry playfully on the arm. Perhaps, she thought, she was right where she needed to be.

She put her arm in the crook of Flora's. Flora retrieved the cane and they shuffled over to join the others. Tommy D'Antonio leaned his stocky frame into an immense oak door and so began the procession up the center aisle, to the unmasked dismay of Roger Thunderclap, the lone occupant of the entire line of pews on the left side. The enormous nave with its vaulted ceiling, colossal columns and arches silent, echoey. They seated themselves on the right in the arrangement of groom side and bride side at a wedding. The marble altar beneath high and mighty ceilings was adorned with white poinsettias. A marble lectern flanking this. In the wings, alcoves housing statues—to the left the Virgin Mary cradling the baby Jesus in her arms, on the other side St Francis of Assisi cradling a birdseed bowl. Under both statues, votive candles held flame on a stand with an offering box, the scent of incense lingering. Ornate heavy brass light fixtures hung by chain from a high ceiling. On the side walls, stained-glass windows marked the stations of the cross, gray clouds muting the sun's rays and robbing them of their full glory.

Barbara glanced at her brother, absent his wife Natalie and the kids, presuming that the hurricane had precluded their jumping a plane to be at his side. Oddly she felt no contempt but rather the stirrings of sympathy—it was after all *his* mother's funeral as well as hers. And hadn't Peggy told her at lunch about how hate can only eat you up and give power to the object of your hate? Her sister-in-law, after all, was not a vile person prone to take every opportunity to vilify her husband's wayward sister, never indicated an unfavorable opinion of Barbara, nor openly displayed any disdain or condescension. Any ill regard she may have held was never conveyed. How better, Barbara thought, if Natalie had been able to make this hurried and makeshift funeral. At least her presence might have served to mitigate this inclination towards sympathy that ran counter to the rage and resentment. Natalie might have served as a mediator, as she'd done many times before, as Roger loomed gloomily over his wife's shoulder, while the two women engaged in the pleasantries and civilities families were obliged to honor.

The priest appeared from the sacristy to meet a sparse congregation. He was a young priest—his face fair of skin, bordered by dark curly hair with a receding hairline. Roger, with great ceremony, presented the urn and Father Patrick O'Leary placed it on the altar before him amid a silence so absolute that its tiniest thud echoed along with Roger's footsteps, Peggy's cough. While Christ gazed down from the cross, high on the wall behind the altar, Father Patrick gazed benevolently at the audience of strangers before him, one face at a time. Barbara wondered if her mother might also be looking down, her sins all forgiven, at the small ceremony in her honor, absent of fanfare. She doubted it. Rather she imagined it was overtime for the young priest, he may be missing the golf links, or a baseball game on television. She caught her thoughts going in this direction and chastised herself. Why, she thought, am I so pre-disposed to be condemnatory of organized religion? Why not just believe that Father Patrick is genuinely attached to humanity with compassion and empathy? That he believes that the souls who have passed on are indeed looking down at funerals from a higher consciousness called heaven? That he is always rooting for the bride and groom at weddings, even given a divorce rate of over fifty percent? Because as much as she doubted, even refuted the idea of an afterlife where all sins were forgiven, where angels hovered about 24/7, where there was even the possibility of a perpetual happy hour, she still felt a compulsion to seek answers from Father Patrick. As did the skinny fellow beside her who'd shelved the beat-up Converse high tops, jeans and scrubby golf shirt for a white-collar shirt, khaki pants and penny loafers. He still carried his big questions, Kenny the Coin.

"Were I able to have given the last rites to our dearly departed Alice," Father Patrick spoke soft and gentle into the lapel microphone clipped to his vestments, "I'd have implored Christ who was crucified to bring her freedom and peace. I offer that prayer on behalf of the congregants before me today."

Freedom and peace. In the pew Barbara mulled over these words. Was it possible that her mother, who had allowed conformity and fear to be her guide through her earthly existence, might suddenly be released from those bonds and truly achieve freedom and peace? She again mentally checked herself—who's to say she herself, her mother's daughter, isn't so bound by conformity and fear? Even when she might flatter herself to believe otherwise? What fear in remaining immobilized in old belief systems of my own? What conformity in medicating myself to avoid fundamental change?

"Her death was as sudden and swift as the hurricanes Mother Nature brings," Father Patrick was saying. What a poor analogy, Barbara thought and checked herself. *Here I am reflexively critiquing the sermon at her own mother's funeral*—but really what a poor analogy—it may have been appropriate in biblical times but hurricanes and storms were anticipated and forecasted with remarkable accuracy in the modern age. Conversely, she could not have imagined she'd have found her mother struck down dead on the floor before her upon arrival for a visit that both had anticipated with the mixed feelings of the estranged. She shuddered. She was robbed the chance to make amends, bury the hatchet, clear the air. It hit her as sudden and swift as might the immense steel crucifix tumbling from way up high to the granite floor with the thunderclap boom of a two-thousand-pound bomb. Her shoulders heaved. Kenny somewhat tentatively placed an arm around her as she brought her head to her hands. The rest of her team glanced furtively over to her and then back to Father O'Leary, who was now raising the Holy Eucharist with both hands in front of him. The body of Christ, he said, the blood of Christ—shed for humankind that we may be free of our sins, untethered from this mortal coil we are bound to during our all-too-brief time on earth.

The funeral mass was brief. As many years had passed since she'd set foot inside a church, Barbara reflexively conjured up most of the liturgical responses, thinking to herself how repetition is learning and that learning is ingrained in memory and almost impossible to unlearn. She waited in dread for the sign of peace and the awkwardness it would bring between her and her brother. When that time came, when the congregants were compelled to display with one another some sign of *peace*, she hugged her friends one by one and averted her gaze. Father O'Leary's sermon laid out the case for Alice Thunderclap, a fine lady of the old school—a dedicated parishioner, passionate volunteer, loving mother, a force for good in a world where evil persisted. He knew the right words from years of practice. Barbara was glued to them nonetheless, in both mind and spirit. Her take was that this young fellow had a profound and sacred reverence for the dead and a genuine compassion for the bereaved. Her friends appeared to be a captivated audience as well, even Kenny Fitzroy seemed as engrossed in the spoken words as he might be in a great novel. Lily clutched Alice Thunderclap's journal against her bosom. None of those gathered around her exhibited any daydreaming or restlessness. Except Roger, shifting his weight from one foot to the other, gazing around the church distractedly, checking his watch repeatedly. All the same, after Father Patrick spoke the final words, go in *peace*, Roger beat the band to meet and greet the priest at the edge of the altar, where he proceeded to monopolize the celebrant of their mother's funeral under the auspices, thought Barbara, that he was a practicing and devout Catholic—his sister a mere heathen, a dropout from the club who hadn't paid her dues and so lost all membership privileges. And she was, anyway, a person of lesser value than he—in fact she may as well have been invisible. The team gathered around her had little effect on her brother, they may as well have also been invisible and not members of a receiving line that people who honored social convention politely moved along in, didn't prolong a conversation with the one receiving. Instead, he kept on with the young priest, exhibiting a keen interest in his background, where he was born and raised in the old country across the pond. Mother's maiden name was Ahearn after all, he told Father Patrick. The priest's eyes began to dart at short intervals over Roger's shoulder to the expectant faces of the congregants, but Roger kept his back to them. At last Peggy Beamish took the bull by the horns and stepped up, bumping against Roger's elbow as she sidled up to the communion rail to extend a hand to the priest. She took his hand in hers and squeezed his elbow, claiming hers and Barbara's territory.

"Hey stranger," Father Patrick winked good-naturedly. "Haven't seen you around much lately."

"Yeah well, you know," she winked. "Crisis of faith. Existential angst, that kinda thing." She gave his arm a playful jab.

"It is only through doubt that we come to faith," he replied.

While Roger held his ground, Peggy turned to snare Barbara by the elbow and present her as one might a reticent young girl upon her first communion.

“This young lady,” she announced to the priest, “is Alice’s daughter Barbara. She takes after her mother, she’s as nice as people come. And all of us here are like family.” She turned to face the others. “And we’re all going to be there for her in her time of grief, aren’t we?”

At this, Roger turned on his heels. But he would have to face his sister and her assembled team at the gravesite for the burial of his mother’s remains, which he clutched to his breast as if it were his rightful birthright, evidence that he and he alone was his mother’s pride and joy.

*

*Cohasset, Cohasset, a distant memory. What lessons unfolded before my eyes, a mere girl should not have to witness the downfall and demise of an adult. But there before my own eyes Father downgraded the family name as liquor the liquid devil claimed his soul. How all his forebears must have rolled over in their graves nearby. How it seemed the very wind off the Atlantic drove us from our home.*

*

They all gathered at Alice Thunderclap’s final resting place. Serenity Meadows cemetery, in the town of Riverview, just outside of Sunnyville. No husband to be laid beside in death. Flora Wheeler stood among them, supporting herself with both hands on the hickory cane. The young priest’s eager face gone soft and solemn. A light drizzle. Underneath her raincoat, Lily Westfall clasped Alice Thunderclap’s epistolary journal to her breast, lest she present it to Barbara in a condition less than immaculately dry after the burial. Kenny Fitzroy fetched an immense umbrella, a relic from under the passenger seat of the Dodge Dart, and held it over Barbara’s head, affording her grief a privacy.

*

*Cohasset, Cohasset. Seems far off and long ago most days, but there are days when it may as well have been yesterday for all that I learned. Maybe writer learned nothing. Was writer any better with progeny than own flawed forebears? Swore off alcohol. Occasional glass of wine for social graces and taste. How many more entries left for this vessel for inner thoughts? Consulted attorney, keep amending as mind changes with age, bequeathed this roof and all underneath it to daughter who seemed lost from birth. Along with precious metals obtained during market crisis in 2000. Feared return to poverty all my born days and still do. Death nearer at hand and heart is heavy and mind on the Fates. Let Clotho (the Spinner) unfold daughter’s thread as she chooses, no matter writer's dogged attempts at interference. Let Lachesis (the Allotter) be at least as generous with threaded earthly days for writer's daughter as has been for writer. Let Atrapos (the Inevitable) not cut the thread on writer until writer has laid eyes and words on daughter. Awaiting arrival of daughter with great anxiety and trepidation. What will I do but fill the air with platitudes? Why not 'I love you' instead? Afraid to speak such elementary sentiments out loud in her presence. Mind bungled with thoughts seeking emancipation, please God I might not take them to the grave. I have spilled them out of their privacy and onto a blank page, in a ramshackle diary anyone might happen upon.*

*

Later on, at Peggy Beamish's patio, in the early evening, under a roof of bougainvillea, they convene. The exotic blend of pink and orange hues in the evening sky lends to the patio the genteel mystique of a European villa. Her flower garden remains intact, although debris lays scattered about the golf greens. The palm fronds stripped from faraway trees appear to Marge like oversized models, laying there so close on the ground. She glances over at Kenny—scratching at his neck, biting his nails. He looks as if he has something on his mind, always has that look she thinks, but tonight more so than ever. Across from him, sat beside one another at the wrought iron table set, Barbara and Lily's faces appear to have carried with them the cherubic merriment of Disney World to the devastation they met in Hillsborough County and right on through the gates of Sunny Glen Palms. Peggy snaps her cigarette at an ashtray, takes a puff, blows a deep sigh of smoke. An old habit she's revisiting for a spell, so she tells Marge. She sits enthroned on a large-backed wicker chair as if presiding regally over the subjects of her patio domain. There are a few open seats for Kenny but he remains standing, pacing from time to time along the perimeter of the golf greens.

"Whatever's on your mind young man," Peggy says while fussing at her fingernails, "you may as well spill it. No secrets here. Among us."

Kenny purses his lips, nods sagely, playing footsie with a downed palm branch. "Just, you know. What everybody already knows. Flying up there."

"That's very sweet of you," says Marge, "You'll get to see your family anyway."

"You know what they say," Kenny shrugs. "You can pick your friends but not your family."

"I think you're the fastest friends I've ever made," Barbara says to the pastel sky.

"Well, we sure hope you'll be a good friend and stick around a while," Peggy raises her cocktail to Barbara. "What are your plans?"

"Oh," says Barbara, tipping her glass of ice water back at Peggy. "I'm going to stick around a while and have a warm winter."

Lily's face brightens. Marge beams, raising her glass, "Neato torpedo. Another gal pal."

"Gonna have to find us some *guy* pals," says Peggy Beamish, peering over her sunglasses at Marge. Everyone laughs and they carry on like this, a collective unburdening, a sigh of relief if only for a spell, because all those gathered know that even in the presumably calm environs of Sunny Glen Palms and retirement, one must battle and conquer unforeseeable burdens right up to the time they are lowered into the shallow Florida ground.

When the colorful sky has given way to black and is dotted with stars, Peggy's guests one-by-one excuse themselves and take their leave, driving home on un-trafficked streets. After nine o'clock most streets are empty. Tonight the dead streets have the look of a war zone, wayward fronds from the few palms that decorate tiny islands in the blacktop of cul-de-sacs or along Sunset Boulevard. Broken glass, stray roof shingles, splintered wood, garbage bins and other debris are strewn about neatly-trimmed lawns and sidewalks. A figure appears—wending his way along Meadowbrook Lane, carefully sidestepping the artifacts of Hurricane Charley, surveying the damage. Gerry Hagoden has just had yet another bout of marital discord, a disagreement with his wife Shirley over what she deems to be the unequal division of the household chores. He likens the disarray and disruption to the effect of these spousal spats, more frequent now with their closer-than-ever proximity, on his peace of mind. He finds his mind wandering to such creative and insightful imaginings with increasing focus and vitality. He thinks perhaps he will bring these walkabout musings to the written page, over at the computer lab, do what most people only dream of but never actually set themselves to accomplish—write the great American novel in the golden years of retirement.

## ABOUT THE AUTHOR

Ricko Donovan is an award-winning singer-songwriter and multi-instrumentalist who has performed his own brand of music, Americeltic, in Europe and the USA. He is the author of two novels—*Sunnyville* (2014) and *The Broken Promised Land* (2015). He resides in Hot Springs Arkansas.
www.rickodonovan.net

Made in the USA
Columbia, SC
17 November 2024